"This book takes stock of journalism in contemporary global societies, taking theory seriously without resorting to idealistic notions about journalism's democratic potential or assuming the universal relevance of Western experience. Presented in an accessible format and taking its examples from topical events and movements such as Extinction Rebellion and Black Lives Matter, the book will inspire students of journalism to reflect critically on the diversity and complexity of journalism as it is practiced around the world today."

— **Herman Wasserman**, *Professor of Media Studies, University of Cape Town*

"Journalism Studies can no longer proceed from an uncritical belief in the good of journalism for democracy. This book is a welcome intervention and a must-read for anyone who wishes to better understand how power, profit and culture shape and are shaped by journalism."

— **Nikki Usher**, *author of News for the Rich, White, and Blue: How Place and Power Distort American Journalism*

"*Journalism, Culture and Society* is literally the book that has been 'missing' from studies about journalism in liberal democracies. It not only explores the role that journalism plays in society but also places journalism in the wider context of being a product of liberal democracies, as opposed to being separate from it. Its analysis of modern journalism is piercing and beautifully marries theory and practice as informing and shaping one another."

— **Marcus Ryder**, *Head of Consultancies, Lenny Henry Centre for Media Diversity, Birmingham City University*

"*Journalism, Culture and Society* offers excellent, very accessible discussions connecting social and cultural theories with journalism studies and examining the key concepts and latest developments in journalism from theoretical perspectives and with examples from around the world."

— **Dr Jingrong Tong**, *Senior Lecturer in Digital News Cultures, Department of Journalism Studies, University of Sheffield*

JOURNALISM, CULTURE AND SOCIETY

Drawing upon a range of theoretical perspectives, including cultural studies, postcolonial theory, critical race studies, political economy and sociology, *Journalism, Culture and Society* examines journalism as a democratic necessity that often fails to live up to its promise.

This text takes a step back from prevailing idealistic approaches in which theory is often seen as a threat rather than a service to the better understanding of practice, and mainstream journalism in western democracies is seen as unproblematic. Instead, using international examples, the authors provide a critique for those who seek to improve journalistic practice, whilst not losing sight of the profound practical dilemmas that journalists around the world experience in their working lives – from the resources available to them, to the institutions and political contexts in which they work. Readers are encouraged to consider why journalists choose (or are expected to choose) particular subjects or tropes in their work, and the implications of these choices.

Journalism, Culture and Society is a valuable resource for students, academics and practitioners in the areas of media, journalism and communication.

Omega Douglas is a Lecturer at Goldsmiths, University of London.

Angela Phillips is Emeritus Professor at Goldsmiths, University of London.

Communication and Society
Series Editor: James Curran

This series encompasses the broad field of media and cultural studies. Its main concerns are the media and the public sphere: on whether the media empower or fail to empower popular forces in society; media organisations and public policy; the political and social consequences of media campaigns; and the role of media entertainment, ranging from potboilers and the human-interest story to rock music and TV sport.

For a complete list of titles in this series, please see: https://www.routledge.com/Communication-and-Society/book-series/SE0130.

An Introduction to Political Communication
Sixth edition
Brian McNair

Misunderstanding News Audiences
Seven Myths of the Social Media Era
Eiri Elvestad and Angela Phillips

Culture Wars, Second edition
The Media and the British Left
James Curran, Julian Petley and Ivor Gaber

Journalism and Celebrity
Bethany Usher

Gender and Media second edition
Representing, Producing, Consuming
Tonny Krijnen and Sofie Van Bauwel

Journalism, Culture and Society
A Critical Theoretical Approach to Global Journalistic Practice
Omega Douglas and Angela Phillips

JOURNALISM, CULTURE AND SOCIETY

A Critical Theoretical Approach to Global Journalistic Practice

Omega Douglas and Angela Phillips

LONDON AND NEW YORK

Cover image: Courtesy of Mark Jean-Marie

First published 2023
by Routledge
4 Park Square, Milton Park, Abingdon, Oxon OX14 4RN

and by Routledge
605 Third Avenue, New York, NY 10158

Routledge is an imprint of the Taylor & Francis Group, an informa business

© 2023 Omega Douglas and Angela Phillips

The right of Omega Douglas and Angela Phillips to be identified as author[/s] of this work has been asserted in accordance with sections 77 and 78 of the Copyright, Designs and Patents Act 1988.

All rights reserved. No part of this book may be reprinted or reproduced or utilised in any form or by any electronic, mechanical, or other means, now known or hereafter invented, including photocopying and recording, or in any information storage or retrieval system, without permission in writing from the publishers.

Trademark notice: Product or corporate names may be trademarks or registered trademarks, and are used only for identification and explanation without intent to infringe.

British Library Cataloguing-in-Publication Data
A catalogue record for this book is available from the British Library

ISBN: 978-0-367-48024-0 (hbk)
ISBN: 978-0-367-48021-9 (pbk)
ISBN: 978-1-003-03765-1 (ebk)

DOI: 10.4324/9781003037651

Typeset in Bembo
by codeMantra

CONTENTS

Acknowledgements   *ix*

   Introduction: Why Journalism Matters   1

1 Public Spheres and National Media Systems   6

2 News Production in Democracies   25

3 Choosing News   45

4 Ideology in Practice   68

5 Representing "Others"   92

6 Sources Matter   119

7 Audiences, Algorithms and Optimisation   140

8 Advertising, The Devil's Pact?   160

9 The Role of Public Service Media   180

10 Press Freedom, Regulation and the Law   202

11	Ethics in Practice	223
12	Global Flows	244
Index		*269*

ACKNOWLEDGEMENTS

We would like to offer our huge thanks for help and encouragement to Clea Bourne, Luciana Coelho, James Curran, Aeron Davis, Eiri Elvestad, Des Freedman, Rizwana Hamid, Gholam Khiabany, Elenora Mazzolli, Anamik Saha and Jingrong Tong. Your comments on drafts were invaluable.

INTRODUCTION

Why Journalism Matters

What can you see out of your window? Perhaps a block of apartments, or the backs of other houses. The homes you visit are probably a lot like your own, and the people you talk to will have interests that you share. From your daily movement around the streets and shops, you can deduce a little about the wider community by the way people dress and behave. The worlds beyond your streets, your families and friendship groups are mediated via other people, using a variety of platforms: social media, television, radio, printed magazines and newspapers and their online presence.

These mediators, from individuals to news organisations, extend our knowledge and allow us to learn about new ideas in every arena of life, from books and music, to fashion and sport; help us reassess our identities and understand how to adapt to (or resist) cultural shifts and participate in political and cultural exchange. As Raymond Williams put it, media are: "talking together about the processes of our common life" (Williams in Curran, 1991, p. 33).

Given our dependence on various forms of media to tell us what is happening, the quality of the information supplied is critical to our understanding of the world and our ability to act within it. As individuals we learn early on how to judge trustworthiness. We are not always correct in our judgement and we often lean too heavily on characteristics that tell us if our informant is "like us" (therefore trustworthy) or "unlike us" (untrustworthy), but at a social level, the integrity of information provided is our most critical defence against what Hannah Arendt describes as "organised lying."

> The historian knows how vulnerable is the whole texture of facts in which we spend our daily lives; it is always in danger of being perforated by single lies or torn to shreds by the organized lying of groups, nations, or classes,

> or denied and distorted, often carefully covered up by reams of falsehoods or simply allowed to fall into oblivion. Facts need testimony to be remembered and trustworthy witnesses to be established in order to find a secure dwelling place in the domain of human affairs.
>
> *(Arendt, 1971)*

For Arendt, media, free and un-corrupt, are the best means we have to call the bluff of the organised liars. It is also the best means we have to engage with the political realm and to ensure that a participatory democracy enjoys the participation of the people. The capacity to influence government requires a space outside the state, in which people can engage, find common cause and bring their concerns to the attention of the wider public in order to effect change (see **Chapter 1**).

In a democracy, the right to freedom of debate and assembly is theoretically protected by law, and enshrined in conventions and constitutions, but a rise in anti-press rhetoric and limits to press freedom, linked to growing authoritarianism, is a matter of concern, particularly in transitional democracies (Bajomi-Lazar, 2014; Dobek-Ostrowska and Glowacki, 2016; Lohner, Neverla and Banjac, 2019). In Poland, for example, a law passed in 2021 levies advertising tax in a way that discriminates against independent media (Kość, 2021). In Hungary most media are owned by the Government or its allies and the last independent broadcaster lost its license to broadcast in 2021 (Kisbenedek, 2021).

> Ownership bias consists in creating such configurations of ownership which produces fake pluralism and ensures the leading state role. Such production at the top–down level of practices consists in limiting access of foreign capital in the field of the media (mainly in television) and in distributing the most influential parts of the media to loyal elite groups.
>
> *(Kiriya, 2019, p. 12)*

More subtle threats in the form of ownership structures that privilege particular groups, and editorial policies that marginalise minority voices, also risk distorting debate. Journalists in democracies are not free agents. They work for organisations that, in spite of apparent plurality, tend to institutionalise pre-existing elite structures because of the way they are controlled (Benson and Neveu, 2005). In order to function as agents of democracy, rather than agents of the elite, journalists need to understand how power structures society and shapes the way we understand facts.

But it is not enough to understand the limits within which we work, we also need to understand that the freedom to publish is itself a form of power which must be used thoughtfully. Careless journalism can have real-world repercussions. Deliberate lies, or selective facts, are often weaponised to suit a particular political agenda. They are dangerous, whatever the intention of the writer, because misinformation destroys the structure of trust upon which democracy rests.

Journalism, Culture and Society takes a critical cultural studies approach to consider these, and other pressing issues, in the fast-changing world of contemporary global journalism. Our aim is to enable students who are studying journalism, media and communications around the world to think critically about practice, both their own and that produced by others, in order to develop their understanding of the relationship between power and all genres of journalism, be it text based or broadcast, focused on news, arts, sport and so on.

In the tradition of critical cultural studies, we are concerned with illuminating how journalism reflects and reinforces problematic power structures but is also a means of resisting oppressive structures. We connect discussions from cultural studies and related critical conceptions from postcolonial theory, critical race studies, political economy and sociology, to consider journalism from a range of theoretical perspectives relevant to the contemporary condition and the global nature of journalism.

We review the major scholarly debates on issues such as representation and ideology using examples from around the world. This book approaches journalism as a democratic necessity that often fails to live up to its promise. In taking a critical cultural studies approach, which calls for being politically engaged and applying research and theory in real world situations, we set out to provide a critique for those who seek to improve journalistic practice, whilst not losing sight of the profound practical dilemmas that journalists experience in their working lives – from the resources available to them, to the institutions and political contexts in which they work.

Structure of the book

The book begins with the recognition that content, thus representation, is always subject to cultural and geo-political framing, and cannot be meaningfully considered without accounting for the context in which it is produced. A focus on one or the other in isolation, for example, the representation of women, without consideration of their position, experiences, or opportunities within newsrooms, is not conducive to sustainable change and will not address recurring patterns of inequality. As such, the latter half of the book addresses media structures and institutions within a global comparative context and critically addresses the politics of representation. By this we mean the production dynamics, the position different actors occupy within the journalistic field and institutional structures, the treatment of socially constructed markers of identity, such as race and sexuality, and related representational outcomes.

Chapter 1 addresses the purpose of news in democracies and other political systems. Using public sphere theory and its critiques, we argue for the importance of a shared space in which public opinion can be formed. Such spaces are particularly vital at a time of increasing polarisation. In **Chapter 2**, we consider field and institutional theory to map the ways in which media organisations are made and the ways individuals are both constrained by and yet also influence their creation. We move on, in **Chapter 3**, to consideration of how decisions regarding news selection have changed and the role of the editor, the audience and journalists in making news choices, as well as the issue of diversity and whether journalistic subjectivity matters in news production. In **Chapter 4**, we take a step back from individual choices to explore theories of framing and agenda-setting, and consider how agenda-setting is used to establish normative accounts of the world. Leading on from this, **Chapter 5** considers how journalists represent "others." We discuss theories of representation and how concepts of race, in particular, are reproduced and intersect with other socially constructed categories like religion. Using examples across recent history (and geography), we address the role that journalism plays in amplifying notions of "otherness" as well as contesting stereotypical frames. **Chapter 6** addresses source theory and whether the use of social media has changed the power balance between sources and journalists.

We move to broader consideration of production contexts, addressing the role of audiences, algorithms, advertising, public service media, regulation and ethics in the context of journalism today. In **Chapter 7**, we explore how the platforms and data intermediaries make use of the affordances of the internet to give audiences what they want to buy, rather than what they need to know, and how journalists ride the waves of algorithmic selection in order to make editorial decisions. **Chapter 8** dives into the history of advertising and the press, how advertising opened the doors to a commercial and popular press, and goes on to question whether advertising has democratised media or merely popularised the news agenda. The central question considered in **Chapter 9** is: when and under what conditions is public service media a force for public understanding and social cohesion? This chapter also considers the structures in place to ensure that public money provides public representation. **Chapter 10** explores media regulation: how it is used to uphold democracy and maintain the media field and how it is also misused to limit what audiences can access. We then move to consideration of what ethical journalism is in **Chapter 11**, how individuals can uphold ethical values when they are under pressure from many directions, and we explore ethical approaches to the protection of journalism and journalists around the world. We end by questioning, in **Chapter 12**, whether, in the global media era, western news values continue to dominate information flows, or if shifts in geo-political power relations are significantly altering these flows and the way journalism is constructed.

References

Arendt, H. (1971) 'Lying in Politics: Reflections on The Pentagon Papers', *New York Review of Books*, 18 November. Available at: https://www.nybooks.com/articles/1971/11/18/lying-in-politics-reflections-on-the-pentagon-pape/.

Bajomi-Lazar, P. (2014) *Party Colonisation of the Media in Central and Eastern Europe: Modern Business Decision Making in Central and Eastern Europe*. Central European University Press. Available at: https://muse.jhu.edu/book/36150 (Accessed: 20 July 2020).

Benson, R.D. and Neveu, E. (2005) *Bourdieu and the Journalistic Field*. Cambridge; Malden, MA: Polity.
Curran, J. (1991) *Rethinking the Media as Public Sphere. Communication and Citizenship. P. Dahlgren, Sparks, Colin*. London: Routledge.
Daniszewski, J. (2020) *AP Definitive Source | The Decision to Capitalize Black*. Available at: https://blog.ap.org/announcements/the-decision-to-capitalize-black (Accessed: 21 February 2022).
Dobek-Ostrowska, B. and Glowacki, M. (2016) *Democracy and Media in Central and Eastern Europe 25 Years On*. Peter Lang. doi:10.3726/978-3-653-04452-2.
Kiriya, I. (2019) 'New and Old Institutions within the Russian Media System', *Russian Journal of Communication*, 11(1), pp. 6–21. doi:10.1080/19409419.2019.1569551.
Kisbenedek, A. (2021) *Hungary's Leading Independent Radio Station Loses Broadcast Licence, France 24*. Available at: https://www.france24.com/en/europe/20210210-hungary-s-leading-independent-radio-station-loses-broadcast-license (Accessed: 28 February 2022).
Kość, W. (2021) *Polish Media Suspend Reporting to Protest a Planned Tax on Advertising, POLITICO*. Available at: https://www.politico.eu/article/polish-media-suspend-reporting-to-protest-a-planned-tax-on-advertising/ (Accessed: 10 February 2021).
Lohner, J., Neverla, I. and Banjac, S. (2019) 'Conflict-Sensitive Journalism? Journalistic Role Perceptions and Practices in Democratization Conflicts', in Voltmer, K. et al. (eds) *Media, Communication and the Struggle for Democratic Change: Case Studies on Contested Transitions*. Cham: Springer International Publishing, pp. 59–81. doi:10.1007/978-3-030-16748-6_3.

1
PUBLIC SPHERES AND NATIONAL MEDIA SYSTEMS

We open this book with a discussion of *public sphere* theory, and how it can be applied in differing national media systems, because it provides us with a place from which we can start thinking analytically about the news media. Sociologist, Jurgen Habermas, used the term *public sphere* to describe an idealised arena between the institutions of the state and the privacy of the home, in which open debate takes place that is capable of translating common concerns into public campaigns and finally into social change. In an ideal democracy, the media both enable and extend debate so that all citizens can participate.

The concept of a public sphere is useful because it provides a standard against which media systems can be judged and compared. No two countries have the same media system; each has its own characteristics which impact on the way in which news is gathered, distributed, regulated and received. Even in nations in which the news media are a direct instrument of the state, there needs to be some sense in which it undertakes to inform citizens so that they can make sense of their world. However, it is the degree of independence afforded to public debate that characterises a truly *public* sphere. In this chapter we will discuss the ideas behind public sphere theory, consider the ways in which they have been criticised or refined and look very broadly at the way different classifications of national media systems help us compare media across borders.

The public sphere

According to Habermas: "Citizens behave as a public body when they confer in an unrestricted fashion – that is, with the guarantee of freedom of assembly and association and the freedom to express and publish their opinions-about matters of general interest." (Habermas, Lennox and Lennox, 1974, p. 49)

The right to freedom of expression, and its corollary freedom of the press, springs from the writing of enlightenment philosophers such as John Stuart Mill and politicians like Thomas Jefferson[1], who saw in them the bricks upon which democracy could be built. These early thinkers of the liberal tradition saw freedom of expression as an *individual* right. Habermas took this understanding and extended it in his critique of late eighteenth- and nineteenth-century England, when the newly emerging bourgeoisie made common cause in asserting rights to freedom of expression, against the authority of the church and the monarchy.

> ### John Stuart Mill (1859):
>
> First, if any opinion is compelled to silence, that opinion may, for aught we can certainly know, be true. To deny this is to assume our own infallibility. Secondly, though the silenced opinion be an error, it may, and very commonly does, contain a portion of truth; and since the general or prevailing opinion on any subject is rarely or never the whole truth, it is only by the collision of adverse opinions, that the remainder of the truth has any chance of being supplied. Thirdly, even if the received opinion be not only true, but the whole truth; unless it is suffered to be, and actually is, vigorously and earnestly contested, it will, by most of those who receive it, be held in the manner of a prejudice, with little comprehension or feeling of its rational grounds. And not only this, but, fourthly, the meaning of the doctrine itself will be in danger of being lost, or enfeebled, and deprived of its vital effect on the character and conduct: the dogma becoming a mere formal profession, inefficacious for good, but cumbering the ground, and preventing the growth of any real and heartfelt conviction, from reason or personal experience.
>
> (Mill, 1859, p. 98)

Habermas moved beyond liberal theory to consider the role of economic power. He argued that, in the early stages of the rise of the bourgeoisie, citizens used the tools of rational debate, rather than force or social status, to create a new sense of a public with rights that had developed outside the existing power structures. For such a public sphere to exist, he argued, participation had to disregard status, cover matters of common concern and be inclusive so that all interests could be represented and discussed. He saw this brief flowering of unfettered debate, freed from state coercion and not yet subject to lobbying by powerful interest groups, as a model (though flawed) of how a democracy should work.

The public sphere must, in addition, to amplify the pressure of problems, that is, not only detect and identify problems, but also convincingly and influentially thematize them, furnish them with possible solutions, and dramatize them in such a way that they are taken up and dealt with by parliamentary complexes.

(Habermas, 1997, p. 91)

He went on to describe how those who accrue economic power, through the development of trade and industry, extend that power into the political realm, by using the influence of public opinion to change laws. They did this through the emerging news media. The commercial model of press was welcomed by liberal thinkers as the beginning of a market in ideas. However, for Habermas and other *critical theorists*, the liberal concept of a democratic sphere, based on individual liberties, was consumed by its own success, as the fight for a free press culminated in the establishment of the commercial media we see today, in which the profit motive transformed the "public" into an audience, less concerned with debate, than with entertainment (Habermas, Lennox and Lennox, 1974, p. 53).

Habermas described how, as the media became concentrated in the hands of a small group of people with money and political influence, the unitary public sphere of the enlightenment, which had (he argued) put aside sectional interests to argue for a common good, had been transposed into a number of fragmented and competing interest groups. Debate, which had, Habermas believed, been open and inclusive, turned inwards and arguments took place behind closed doors. He described this process as the *re-feudalisation* of the public sphere in which the exercise of power and influence had become more important than freedom of debate and inclusivity. Once lobbying had replaced direct discussion, powerful interest groups soon controlled the outflow of ideas and the interface with policymakers.

This concern about the commercialisation of the media underpins *critical political economy* (Hardy, 2014) approaches to journalism which argue that a commercial press is only really free to those with the economic capital required to build a media empire capable of reaching into the homes and consciousness of ordinary voters. It is also the starting point for *radical democratic* theory which argues for regulatory intervention to extend democratic engagement in the media: "the free market can never be an adequate basis for organizing the media because it results in a system skewed in favour of dominant class interests." (Curran, 1991, p. 34).

Critical responses

Habermas's description of the rise and fall of the bourgeois public sphere has been influential in providing a model of how democracy could work as well as a means of highlighting its flaws, but it has also been subject to criticism both from critical theorists and from radical democrats. Critical theorist Nancy Fraser contends that Habermas's description of a single public sphere is a flawed concept. Far from being inclusive, she contends, it would have been: "the arena, the training ground, and eventually the power base of a stratum of bourgeois men, who were coming to see themselves as a 'universal class' and preparing to assert their fitness to govern" (Fraser, 1990, p. 60). Such a public sphere would, she argued, have excluded those who could not read, people of colour and most women (Landes, 1988).

Fraser (1990) also argued that a formulation which idealised an almost exclusively unitary, male public, ignored the importance of organisation taking place beyond or apart from this unitary space. She suggested that there could never have been, and should never be, a single, public sphere because of the way dominant groups maintain "hegemony"[2] through processes of exclusion, becoming exclusive by default.

She was describing the ways in which we all form groups around what we see as taste and preference. These groups of friends, colleagues, co-religionists or other communities identify like-minded people to include and tend to ignore, or generate hostility towards, those who are unlike them. These processes happen at all levels of society but, when the "in group" is composed of people with power, upon whom out-group members are in some way dependent, such processes of "distinction" (Bourdieu, 1984) establish, "ways in which social inequalities can infect deliberation [and participation], even in the absence of any formal exclusions." (Charles and Fuentes-Rohwer, 2015, p. 18).

Fraser saw the fragmentation that Habermas was concerned about as seedbeds of radical change where, she argued, *subaltern counter publics* provide "parallel discursive arenas where members of subordinated social groups invent and circulate counter discourses which in turn permit them to formulate oppositional interpretations of their identities, interests, and needs" (Fraser, 1990, p. 67). Fraser re-habilitates the idea of a public sphere by re-formulating it. Far from being a corruption of the ideal, she argued that this fragmented public was a more complete model because it allowed for parallel debates to take place in which under-represented groups could formulate ideas amongst themselves. Free from domination by elites, under-represented groups could then carry their ideas forward without the prior compromises that would inevitably occur in a single forum.

She used as an example, the women's movements of the 1970s, which organised separately in order to develop political ideas and strategies and established its own media to disseminate those ideas, many of which were quite quickly taken up by the mainstream media, ushering in a period of political reform in which equality laws were introduced and changes made to women's reproductive rights. Indeed, it is hard to imagine how liberation struggles would ever have come into being without the capacity to debate and organise outside the mainstream.

Fraser's re-formulation of Habermas has been taken up by others, including Habermas himself (Habermas, 1997), as a way of considering how marginalised groups are able to influence the mainstream and in turn have an impact on public policy. Charles and Fuentes-Rohwer (2015) discuss the formation of just such a *subaltern public* in the organisation of Black students at the University of Michigan Law School in the mid-nineteen nineties. Their exclusion from the elite white group chosen to work on the University Law Review suggested a lack of equality on the grounds of race, which could have long-term consequences on the career

Using journalism as a revolutionary tool outside the dominant public sphere

Sonwalkar writes of India:

> By as early as 1835, print journalism had emerged as a site where the first impulses of Indian nationalism were being expressed. Journalism had also become an effective tool for social and religious reform. It had become a key aspect of what was then a new form of political protest—constitutional agitation—which included petitions to EIC officials, town hall meetings in Calcutta, seeking legal alternatives and raising issues through the press. Later, Mahatma Gandhi, Jawaharlal Nehru and other leaders of India's freedom struggle followed the example set by the first leader-journalists such as Rammohun Roy, H. L. V. Derozio and Bhabani Charan Bandopadhyay, and used journalism to powerful effect.
>
> (2015, p. 625)

progression of possible candidates for the courts and academia. Given the critical role of lawmakers in the US constitution, this act of social exclusion would be expected to have profound long-term consequences on the future make-up of the US public sphere, embedding inequality into decision-making processes in the long term.

> [T]hese students were disturbed by their perceived lack of voice at the law school. They were concerned by the fact that the law school administration was less responsive to the needs of students of color than they were to white students. They came together to create a journal and in the process to discuss issues of concern to them at the law school and in the larger society.
>
> *(Charles and Fuentes-Rohwer, 2015, p. 17)*

By organising separately and publishing their own journal, *The Michigan Journal of Race and Law*, they were able to create a discourse on issues of race and, collectively, pressurise the academic establishment to acknowledge them as equals. This fits well into Fraser's conception of the role of a counter-public in which, "a certain parity of the educated" (Habermas, 1992, p. 32) fails to be achieved because of the exclusionary tactics of white bourgeois society.

However, Fraser's critique still depends heavily on the liberal assumption, that speech between educated people, acting as equals and without coercion will, by itself, be enough to change the status-quo. Arguably, a *subaltern counter-public* is not so much concerned with changing power relations as in changing the make-up of the power elite so that it is more representative of the nation and, therefore, more responsive to a diversity of needs and opinions.

> **Exercise: Tactics of Exclusion**
>
> Consider a moment in your life when you have felt excluded. What were the tactics of exclusion? Were they overt or covert? Were they deliberate or unconscious? How did you feel? How did you react to that feeling?
>
> If you cannot remember any such moment think about what that might mean about your own position in your social circles? Do you think you might have been responsible for the exclusion of others? If so, how did you feel? How did you react to that feeling?

Radical democratic approaches to the public sphere

Chantal Mouffe is critical of the suggestion that rational speech is the only legitimate means of creating a public. She suggests that this formulation of the "correct" way to create public opinion leaves out the role of emotion and anger in animating opposition and that this limits participation to an elite minority who have learned the rules of a particular form of debate. The public sphere, she argues, cannot function adequately unless there is an acknowledgement of *antagonism* because change often comes from a place of rage rather than calm deliberation.

Indeed, by the time a calm and rational debate can take place, most of the change has often already happened. The end of slavery in America, the end of apartheid in South Africa, the end of colonialism in Kenya, the end of the Troubles in Northern Ireland all came about against a background of conflict. For Mouffe, public debate should be able to contain antagonism rather than smothering it under the banner of rational consensus-building. In such an "agonistic" approach to democracy, the media would reflect the value of difference rather than taking refuge behind a pre-existing hegemony which simply reflects the power of the existing elite – or those who seek to join it (Mouffe, 2016).

Mouffe clearly sees a role for anger and emotion but argues that, in a democracy, each side should respect the right of others to feel similar anger and that compromise is more likely to be the end point of democratic debate than rational choice. This more radical conception of democracy is one that can contain anger and emotion, and provide space for social movements that deploy tactics other than speech – such as the roadblocks employed by Extinction Rebellion or the statue toppling of Black Lives Matter.

These movements are concerned with wider change which goes beyond elite representation, harnessing symbolic and sometimes aggressive action to their cause. Such media spectacles are an important part of democratic debate and come from genuine and justifiable feelings of anger or exclusion, which may result in spontaneous public action. As Martin Luther King said: "riots are the language of the unheard" (Kocurek, 2019). Alternatively, action may be designed precisely because it is able to capture media attention. Often, however, such action is treated by journalists, not as a legitimate contribution, but as an outrage or public nuisance which undermines democracy (Di Cicco, 2010). Note, for example, the way in which the *cause* of anger is not emphasised in a news report in May 2020 following George Floyd's murder by a police officer.

> **A day of widespread protests devolved into a night of fire and fury across the nation as tensions boiled over in dozens of American cities. Police cars and government buildings were set aflame, windows were shattered, stores were ransacked, monuments were vandalized and authorities in riot gear fired pepper pellets, tear gas and rubber bullets at demonstrators who had amassed to protest.**
> *Washington Post 31 May 2020. (Flynn, 2020)*

A headline in the online publication *Slate* suggested how the same, largely peaceful events, following the killing of George Floyd, could be covered: "Police erupt in violence nationwide." *Slate*, 31 May 2020 (Dessem, 2020)

And what of those who do not have the means or contacts to present their arguments to the listening media? Gayatri Spivak is concerned that, without access to the kinds of speech that is identified with the dominant elite, people are effectively rendered speechless. Provocatively she asks us to consider: "Can the Subaltern Speak" (Spivak, 1988)? She is not suggesting that these are people without voices but that they are never allowed to speak for themselves, they are always represented by others who speak for them, and perhaps more importantly, those that presume to represent them are, in fact, adding to their subordination by speaking in place of them (see **Chapter 5**).

An example of this was the press coverage of what became known as the Muhammed cartoons affair. A Danish mass-market newspaper organised a competition to produce a cartoon image of the Prophet Muhammad. Producing images of the prophet is forbidden among most strands of Islam and this led to weeks of demonstrations by Muslims across the world and weeks of commentary in newspapers. One of the features of this debate was the lack of Muslim voices in the western press.

In Norway, some attempt was made to improve the balance: an editorial in the newspaper *Aftenposten* asked for Muslims to come forward and contribute to the discussion. In Sweden, 28 percent of the commentators were Muslim, but in the United Kingdom, a mere 7 percent of comment writers were identifiably Muslim and three of the newspapers studied had not a single Muslim contributor (Eide, Kunelius and Phillips, 2008, p. 109). Even where voices were heard it was Muslim intellectuals who spoke. The people demonstrating were spoken for by others who used forms of speech deemed acceptable by the elite, and many of the "speakers" disapproved of the demonstrations.

> The subaltern is never engaged qua the subaltern, and the Western subject is never addressed vis-à-vis the subaltern. In other words, the subaltern can speak as long as they speak in a "language" that is already recognized by the dominant culture of the West. Reason and rational communication, mediated via the market or the academy, prevail as the meta-language, and the subaltern are forced to compete in a bazaar of ideas where the deck is stacked against them by years of colonial rule.
> *(Maggio, 2007, p. 431)*

An alternative and perhaps more flexible analytical framework, which rests on the possibility of communication beyond the merely rational debate recognised by Habermas, is suggested by Roger Silverstone. Silverstone's *mediapolis* is a concept of an idealised communicative space which recognises that any responsible act of communication involves an effort of understanding and an act of de-coding:

> There is no rationality in an image, and no singular reason in a narrative… The political, civic space of mediated representation, globally, nationally, locally, depends on both the capacity to encode and to decipher more complex sets of communications than mere reason enables.
> *(Silverstone, 2007, p. 34)*

Silverstone argues that the active process of communication requires that all those who participate should accept responsibility for engaging *truthfully*, with *hospitality* and with *proper distance*. These terms suggest that a genuinely open public sphere cannot spring into being simply by existing. It requires that participants act with sincerity, listen carefully and recognise that there is a validity in difference.

This conception of responsible communication has much in common with the concept of *conviviality*, an alternative conception which is based more on African understandings of reciprocity and belonging than on the individualism of the European enlightenment:

> Conviviality allows for the empowerment of the individual and group alike, not the marginalisation of one by or for the other. It implies a sense of accommodating togetherness beyond mere tolerance where the individual can express themselves in a hospitable space but may also have to exercise restraint to maintain the comforts of being part of the full.
> *(Nyamnjoh, 2017, p. 262)*

These ideas go beyond a discussion of the structures that might allow for a useable public sphere and start to engage with the question of individual human agency.

A public sphere, in which individuals have speech rights, does not demand that people act responsibly, merely that they participate. If we are to demand a hospitable public space which encourages and encompasses difference, we then need to consider how such a space could arise and whether it needs to be protected from people or organisations that are explicitly anti-democratic or see no obligation to use communication rights responsibly (see also **Chapter 10**).

Anti-publics

For Fraser, *subaltern counter-publics* would include those organisations that may use antagonistic methods and may even have anti-democratic and anti-egalitarian intentions. Mark Davis (2019) argues that anti-democratic organisations cannot be contained within any concept of a public sphere because they "have little respect for the ethical principles of democracy or traditional 'public sphere' commitments to deliberation, mutuality, reciprocity" (Davis, 2019, p. 129). Nor can they be contained within Mouffe's characterisation of an "agonistic" public sphere because they show no inclination to respect difference. Davis refers to these groups, mostly on the far right, but encompassing conspiracy theorists such as anti-Vaxxers, and interventions by authoritarian regimes (at home and abroad), as *anti-publics* whose object is not to engender public debate but to impose their own order.

While a definition of an *anti-public* is useful conceptually, it doesn't much help us to consider what should be done about material that is damaging to democracy. Should anti-democratic news sources be suppressed? For liberal democrats, such as Mill, this approach would be anathema. In this conception of speech rights, it is only through airing 'wrong' ideas that they can be countered and overcome. This approach assumes that there is always a rational end point to any argument and that everyone is equally concerned about discovering it. It also brackets out the vital role of power in establishing a common narrative and downplays the damaging impact of hate speech.

Most democracies now accept that there is a limit to absolute freedom of speech (see **Chapter 10**) and that harmful speech can be legally suppressed in certain circumstances (see **Chapter 10**), but the concept of what is harmful speech changes with public attitudes and any limitation of speech rights, based on the censorship of harmful ideas, cedes enormous power to the censors. In mid-twentieth-century Britain, the National Viewers and Listeners Association was sufficiently powerful to limit media expressions of gay sexuality (Barker, 2001). In China, journalism advocating democracy is considered harmful to the maintenance of order, as we have seen in the crack-down against the democracy movement in Hong Kong (see **Chapter 4**). In Sweden and Norway, right-wing websites are considered "ideologically deviant" and thus beyond the boundaries of legitimate debate (Nygaard, 2020, p. 779).

Journalists operate on the front line of democracy because it is their job to look for the people who will provide the evidence with which to piece together the story to be told. If there are groups whose object is to damage and limit the rights of others, it is editors and journalists who make the primary decisions about whether we owe them the right of representation within the public sphere. Does responsible journalism require journalists to reflect on the consequences of what they choose to publicise or is their role to uncritically reflect what is said? As mediators, journalists have a choice about whose voices they amplify. The act of selection is discussed further in **Chapter 6**.

In every interpretation of public sphere theory, one thing is a constant: the news media have an important role. Whether writing about music, sport, fashion or politics, journalists are engaging in acts which help to construct society – as well as representing it. The choices journalists make can create an environment that is either hostile or hospitable to those on the margins. It is, therefore, vital that journalists engage with these ideas and enter the debate as knowledgeable participants rather than merely as cogs in the wheels of commercial enterprise.

The material discussed in this chapter provides a framework for such discussions because as Fraser explains:

> Something like Habermas's idea of the public sphere is indispensable to critical social theory and to democratic political practice. I assume that no attempt to understand the limits of actually existing late capitalist democracy can succeed without in some way or another making use of it.
>
> *(Fraser, 1990, p. 57)*

Exercise: Anti-publics

Consider the concept of an anti-public. How could this concept be used in the regulation of information and in what ways can it be abused? Use specific examples to illustrate your ideas.

Media systems and comparative journalism studies

There are a multitude of different media systems across the world, some of which are designed and supported to facilitate open debate and some of which are designed so that the state sets the agenda, and the news media are merely the pipes through which information flows. In between we find the bulk of the world's journalism: some politically aligned; some commercially run but owned and controlled by individuals or organisations with a political agenda, and others subject to laws that make genuine investigation an imprisonable offence.

In other words, journalism is shaped by its unique political, economic and cultural circumstances, and every country (or group of countries) has charted its own distinctive means of creating a mediatised space in which debate can (or perhaps cannot) take place. To understand the way in which a specific media system functions, it helps to compare it with other countries.

The public sphere concept provides a useful starting place against which a variety of scholars, from a myriad of different disciplines, have attempted to measure these differences.

As a starting point for comparison, *normative media theorists* attempted to establish distinct typologies of journalism based on the presumed relationships between political and media systems. The Four Theories of the Press (Siebert, Peterson and Schramm, 1963) divided the world into Authoritarian, Libertarian, Social Responsibility and Communist. Critics point out that it fails to do justice even to the complexity of European media systems with public service media and entirely fails to empirically analyse systems beyond the Global North.

Hallin and Mancini (2004) argued for an empirical approach, developing ideal types for the purpose of comparison. They decided on four qualities by which, in their judgement, the structure and disposition of a media system could be judged:

1 Whether the majority of people are engaged with debate via a mass market press.
2 The degree to which media are reflective of political parties, rather than independent of them.
3 The development of journalistic professionalism (which is perhaps a proxy for autonomy).
4 The degree and nature of state intervention.

They then measured western media systems on the basis of these categories and divided them into three distinct groups:

- *Polarised Pluralist*, which encompassed most of the Mediterranean countries where newspapers follow political divisions and are mainly consumed by the elite.
- *Democratic Corporatist*, which is exemplified by the Nordic countries where there is high newspaper readership, state intervention to underpin some degree of plurality and independence and high levels of professionalism (as measured by independent journalism organisations and training).
- *North Atlantic or Liberal* which is exemplified by the United States. This is a highly commercial model with mass readership of newspapers, little political parallelism and high expectations of professionalism.

This model has been criticised for assuming a normative position for the US system rather than recognising it as an outlier (Hardy, 2008). Brüggemann and colleagues (Brüggemann *et al.*, 2014) found that Hallin and Mancini had only been able to categorise the Liberal model as the dominant model by under-estimating the enabling role of the state in supporting, rather than undermining, independence and professionalism in Europe. They suggest that the role of the state should be teased out to examine three different dimensions: public broadcasting, regulation and subsidy. Taking these dimensions into account, they suggest a slightly different typology: a Southern cluster (similar to the *Polarised Pluralist*), a Northern cluster (which corresponds with the *Democratic Corporatist* model) and a Central cluster which would include countries with strong public service broadcasters but an economically liberal press. These would include the United Kingdom, Germany and Austria. That leaves the United States as an outlier in a western cluster which is oddly grouped with Ireland (which has a strong public service broadcaster), Portugal and the Netherlands.

At the time of this research, the western cluster would have fitted with the United States quite well but, in the interim, the United States has climbed to the very top of most scales of media polarisation while Ireland, Portugal and the Netherlands (all of which have public service broadcasters) remain among the least polarised (Fletcher and Jenkins, 2019, p. 29; Boxell, Gentzkow and Shapiro, 2020). Of all the countries analysed by Hallin and Mancini and Brüggemann, the United States is the most dependent on the private sector for news production, the least regulated and the most dependent on "professional norms" to maintain trust. This renders the system fragile. A frailty which has become clearer in the internet era. Without the anchor of an established, and trusted, publicly funded broadcaster, the US media have become increasingly polarised undermining the capacity for mediation between groups.

The question of polarisation has become an increasingly important issue for researchers as it has become clearer that the original typologies, in which polarisation was tied to overt connections with political parties, need to be re-visited. This covert manipulation of audiences is not easily accounted for in these broad media typologies although it might well have a powerful influence on what audiences are accessing, particularly in those countries where there is no countervailing normative voice in the shape of public service media (see **Chapter 7**).

While, as the earlier part of this chapter made clear, there is no perfect system, a growing body of comparative research points towards the *democratic corporatist model* or *Northern model* as the one which, under current circumstances, comes closest to providing citizens with the requirements of a public sphere. It allows for a range of opinions as well as protecting journalists so that they are able hold the powerful to account. This is the model of the news media found in the Nordic countries, in which public service broadcasting and public subsidy take centre stage. In these countries, the public and private sectors work alongside each other (see **Chapter 9**) to the benefit of each (Barwise and Picard, 2014; Nielsen *et al.*, 2016; Sehl, Fletcher and Picard, 2020). While the public sector learns from the private sector in its delivery, it, in turn, puts pressure on the private sector to maintain higher professional standards. In these countries, where the independence of public sector broadcasting is safe-guarded, it tends to be the most trusted form of media (Newman *et al.*, 2018).

This may be because public service media (PSM) is under scrutiny from all sides and is, therefore, under pressure to adhere to rules of greater fairness in representation. While the sphere of legitimate debate may be circumscribed (see **Chapter 6**), PSM does at least provide a space in which debates can be heard by the vast majority of the population, rather than a small elite or a polarised group (Aalberg, van Aelst and Curran, 2010; Esser et al., 2012; Aalberg et al., 2013). If pluralism requires that people should be able to listen to one another, even if they disagree, then it is necessary for the project of democracy that they should, at the very least, be able to hear each other speak.

Herrero et al. (2017) went on to consider the post-Soviet countries of Eastern Europe. This is where it becomes important to think more critically about the meaning of state intervention. In Germany, Scandinavia and the United Kingdom, state intervention (in particular via the establishment of public service broadcasting) has broadly supported plurality, independence and professionalism. In some of the post-Soviet countries, the intervention of the state through cronyism and political interference (often through covert indirect subsidies) has more often reduced plurality (Balčytienė et al., 2015), whereas private foreign ownership, at least initially, appeared to offer some (sometimes fragile) protection for journalistic autonomy:

> A northern cluster (Estonia, Latvia, Lithuania, and Slovakia) showed the highest levels of press freedom, the highest levels of foreign ownership, and the lowest levels of political parallelism. Estonia ... showed the highest rates of online news use, inclusiveness of the press market, and press subsidies, with substantial similarities to the Scandinavian countries.
>
> *(Herrero et al., 2017, p. 4811).*

Studies of other regions found a number of different factors coming into play. Guerrero and Márquez-Ramírez (2014) describe Latin American media as a *captured liberal* model. By this, they refer to the characteristics of a highly commercialised media along the same lines as the United States which is neither subsidised nor regulated. This model deviates from Hallin and Mancini's (2004) *liberal model* because of the lower level of journalistic independence, which means that there has been nothing to stand in the way of capture by business and political interests. In a number of Latin American countries, broadcast licenses are handed out as a form of political patronage and government advertising is used as a means of control. Without either journalistic standards that are capable of being upheld, or statutory intervention to protect their autonomy, it is particularly hard for journalists to play the normative role of mediating between groups and redressing power imbalances.

The *captured liberal* concept is useful because it focuses attention on what is meant by the term liberal. In its original conception, it applied to individual freedom of thought and expression. In the captured model, it refers only to the freedom to publish and that freedom lies in the hands of those who have economic power, usually closely aligned with political power. The term might equally be applied to some East European countries as well as some in the Global South. In a study of Kenya, Wasserman and Maweu found that: "corporate control is mainly exercised either through the corporate sponsorship of news and programmes or through advertising revenue" (2014, p. 625). In a comparative study of Kenya, Egypt and Serbia, similar characteristics were observed:

> Among the most influential means of exerting influence, journalists particularly in Egypt and Kenya mention *political ownership and advertising*, referring to the massive influence of politically active businessmen as owners or advertisers of private media and the direct influence of the state, and thus the current government, in public service or state media.
> *(Lohner, Neverla and Banjac, 2019, p. 9)*

However, as Hallin points out, it is important to be specific when describing media systems. For example, while the category of a *captured liberal* system might apply in some Latin American countries, it does not apply across the board. Chile and Uruguay have highly concentrated private media ownership, but the media are relatively independent. In Argentina and Venezuela, populist leaders have (with varying success) used state power to undermine the private media sector, whereas in Mexico and Honduras, "violence against journalists is a central force shaping the media systems. This represents a different mechanism of control from those involved in capture: If the actors involved had captured media, they would not need to exercise violence." (Hallin, 2016, p. 11)

In several Latin America countries, researchers reported, "an 'ideological hegemony' that privileges the points of view of wealthier social groups, who are the target audiences of media, and the social groups from which journalists and media mangers are recruited" (Hallin, 2016, p. 11). While the gap between the ruling elite and the people is particularly stark in Latin America so that arguably the privileging of an elite point of view is more visible, ideological hegemony, the process by which the ruling class maintains its influence, and therefore its dominance, is common in every kind of society in which the consent of the people needs to be won, rather than being enforced through force of arms (see **Chapter 4**). Even in countries where journalists are relatively independent, news organisations tend to uphold the status quo (Croteau, Hoynes and Hoynes, 2006), and the use of the media by vested interests is a common feature of news media everywhere.

Given the entanglement between media and politics, the media will always be at least partly a creation of the social forces in ascendency at the time. This is why, for some critical scholars, concern about the protection of press freedom is seen merely as a strategic game played by the western press; a form of "paradigm repair" (Koliska and Assmann, 2021) used to fend off criticism. While it is certainly the case that an appeal to philosophers like Mill and Locke is often wheeled out in defence of egregious intrusions into privacy, and as a bulwark against regulation, that doesn't in any way diminish the need to defend press freedom. Critical scholarship allows us to see the holes in the fabric of democracy, but the object of such scholarship must be to encourage repair, not to engender despair. If the media are to be the site of democratic debate (however flawed), rather than the creature of the ruling elite, then protecting their freedom from the state and from corruption is always worthwhile.

The important lesson to be taken from discussions about differing media systems is that the political public sphere is created by the interplay of political and economic forces, it is responsive to the state, and to civil society and its part in democracy is not fixed but must be maintained by constant vigilance. When journalism is shackled by powerful interest groups, it loses trust and its power is eroded. When journalists operate in a system which allows them to hold power to account then democracy can be enabled. Media respond to political shifts in often unexpected ways, but largely within the particular context of national states and the characteristics of the *journalism field* (see **Chapter 2**) in that country.

Exercise: Evaluate your Own Media System

Criteria used to evaluate different media systems include:

- Inclusiveness of the press market – whether the press reaches out to a broad audience or is aimed at the elite.
- Political parallelism – the extent to which the media are politically aligned and serve partisan interests.
- Journalistic professionalism – the extent to which journalists are autonomous, follow distinctive ethical principles and are protected in exercising their ethical judgement.
- An enabling state, providing public broadcasting (complementing private media), press subsidies for private media.
- A disabling state which licenses media and regulates media content.
- The degree to which Government subsidies are provided, or withheld, on political grounds.
- The degree of polarisation: are citizens easily able to access the same material or are they only likely to access points of view they agree with?

How free is your media system? Use publicly available resources for your evaluation such as: Reporters Without Borders Press Freedom Index.

Summary

- *Habermas* defines the *ideal public sphere* as a space between the private realm and the state where people debate without coercion with a view to changing society for the better.

- He was concerned that the commercialisation of the press had led to the *re-feudalisation* of society, as free debate between individuals was replaced by a competition for voice and power amongst interest groups.
- Critics of Habermas argue that this idealised, *unitary* public sphere was, in fact, the arena in which an emerging merchant class, overwhelmingly white and male, prepared to govern in place of the monarchy.
- Critics, such as *Nancy Fraser*, posit an alternative reading in which *subaltern publics* organise and argue for a hearing, using the media as an arena for their struggle to be heard.
- Others, such as *Chantal Mouffe*, suggest that the notion of a public sphere as a space for rational debate between equals is itself flawed. She argues that opposition is not only expressed through rational debate, but can be incoherent or angry and that democracy requires that these voices should also be heard and responded to. For Mouffe, often a conclusion is a compromise between irreconcilable needs.
- For *Mark Davis*, the space of the public sphere should be reserved only for those who recognise a shared responsibility for maintaining democracy and should exclude those whose intentions are to destroy democracy. He refers to the spaces where this debate takes place as "*anti-publics.*"
- Media Systems vary across nation states according to political systems, the degree of state intervention (positive and negative), and the degree of autonomy of journalists and media owners from economic and political power.

Notes

1 It's important to note, as Khiabany and Williamson (Khiabany and Williamson, 2015) do, that freedom of speech and freedom of the press are universalizing concepts that have always been delimited by race. Liberal democracy, they assert, is built upon a "historic entanglement of emancipation and de-emancipation" (2015, p. 571), with the emancipation of some equating to the de-emancipation of "others". They note (2015, p. 576) how celebrated liberal western thinkers advocated the repressive and inhumane treatment of the working class at home, and colonial "others" abroad, and that "even for the most radical of liberal thinkers, John Stuart Mill, democracy was only fit for 'civilised' community." (Khiabany & Williamson, 2015, p. 577). Similarly Jefferson was a slave owner, so advocated freedom for some but not others.
2 Gramsci used this term to describe the ways in which the elite continue to maintain power (see **Chapter 4**).

References

Aalberg, T. *et al.* (2013) 'International Tv News, Foreign Affairs Interest and Public Knowledge', *Journalism Studies*, 14(3), pp. 387–406. doi:10.1080/1461670X.2013.765636.

Aalberg, T., van Aelst, P. and Curran, J. (2010) 'Media Systems and the Political Information Environment: A Cross-National Comparison', *The International Journal of Press/Politics*, 15(3), pp. 255–271. doi:10.1177/1940161210367422.

Balčytienė, A. *et al.* (2015) 'Oligarchization, De-westernization and Vulnerability: Media between Democracy and Authoritarianism in Central and Eastern Europe: A Roundtable Discussion'. Available at: https://www.vdu.lt/cris/handle/20.500.12259/31396 (Accessed: 9 September 2021).

Barker, D. (2001) 'Mary Whitehouse', *The Guardian*, 24 November. Available at: https://www.theguardian.com/media/2001/nov/24/guardianobituaries.obituaries (Accessed: 13 December 2021).

Barwise, P. and Picard, R. (2014) *What If There Were No BBC Television? The Net Impact on UK Viewers*. SSRN Scholarly Paper ID 2755460. Rochester, NY: Social Science Research Network. doi:10.2139/ssrn.2755460.

Bourdieu, P. (1984) *Distinction: A Social Critique of the Judgement of Taste*. Boston, MA: Harvard University Press.

Boxell, L., Gentzkow, M. and Shapiro, J.M. (2020) *Cross-Country Trends in Affective Polarization*. Working Paper 26669. National Bureau of Economic Research. doi:10.3386/w26669.

Brüggemann, M. *et al.* (2014) 'Hallin and Mancini Revisited: Four Empirical Types of Western Media Systems', *Journal of Communication*, 64(6), pp. 1037–1065. doi:10.1111/jcom.12127.

Charles, G.-U. and Fuentes-Rohwer, L. (2015) 'Habermas, the Public Sphere, and the Creation of a Racial Counterpublic', *Michigan Journal of Race & Law*, 21, p. 1. Available at: https://heinonline.org/HOL/Page?handle=hein.journals/mjrl21&id=7&div=&collection=.

Croteau, D., Hoynes, W. and Hoynes, W.D. (2006) *The Business of Media: Corporate Media and the Public Interest*. Thousand Oaks, CA: Pine Forge Press.

Curran, J. (1991) *Rethinking the Media as Public Sphere. Communication and Citizenship*. P. Dahlgren, Sparks, Colin. London: Routledge.

Davis, M. (2019) 'Transnationalising the Anti-public Sphere: Australian Anti-publics and Reactionary Online Media', in Peucker, M. and Smith, D. (eds) *The Far-Right in Contemporary Australia*. Singapore: Springer, pp. 127–149. doi:10.1007/978-981-13-8351-9_6.

Dessem, M. (2020) 'Police Erupt in Violence Nationwide', *Slate*, 31 May. Available at: https://slate.com/news-and-politics/2020/05/george-floyd-protests-police-violence.html (Accessed: 2 March 2022).

Di Cicco, D.T. (2010) 'The Public Nuisance Paradigm: Changes in Mass Media Coverage of Political Protest since the 1960s', *Journalism & Mass Communication Quarterly*, 87(1), pp. 135–153. doi:10.1177/107769901008700108.

Eide, E., Kunelius, R. and Phillips, A. (2008) *Transnational Media Events: The Mohammed Cartoons and the Imagined Clash of Civilizations*. Gotenburg: Nordiskt Informationscenter. Available at: http://research.gold.ac.uk/id/eprint/14606/ (Accessed: 23 June 2021).

Esser, F. *et al.* (2012) 'Political Information Opportunities in Europe A Longitudinal and Comparative Study of Thirteen Television Systems', *The International Journal of Press/Politics*, 17(3), pp. 247–274. doi:10.1177/1940161212442956.

Fletcher, R. and Jenkins, J. (2019) *Polarisation and the News Media in Europe*. European Parliamentary Research Service. Available at: https://reutersinstitute.politics.ox.ac.uk/our-research/polarisation-and-news-media-europe (Accessed: 8 February 2022).

Flynn, M. (2020) *Mass Protests and Mayhem Continue into a Sixth Night; Thousands Nationwide Are Arrested during Weekend, Washington Post*. Available at: https://www.

washingtonpost.com/nation/2020/05/31/george-floyd-protests-live-updates/ (Accessed: 2 March 2022).

Fraser, N. (1990) 'Rethinking the Public Sphere: A Contribution to the Critique of Actually Existing Democracy', *Social Text*, 25/26, pp. 56–80. doi:10.2307/466240.

Guerrero, M.A., and Márquez-Ramírez, M. (2014) The "Capture" of Media Systems, Policies, and Industries in Latin America: Concluding Remarks. In *Media Systems and Communication Policies in Latin America*, edited by Guerrero, M.A. and Márquez-Ramírez, M., pp. 293–304. London: Palgrave Macmillan UK, 2014. https://doi.org/10.1057/9781137409058_17.

Habermas, J. (1992) *The Structural Transformation of the Public Sphere: Inquiry into a Category of Bourgeois Society*. New Ed edition. Cambridge: Polity Press.

Habermas, J. (1997) *Between Facts and Norms: Contributions to a Discourse Theory of Law and Democracy*. Cambridge: Polity Press.

Habermas, J., Lennox, S. and Lennox, F. (1974) 'The Public Sphere: An Encyclopedia Article (1964)', *New German Critique*, (3), pp. 49–55. doi:10.2307/487737.

Hallin, D.C. (2016) 'Typology of Media Systems', in Hallin, D. C. (ed) *Oxford Research Encyclopedia of Politics*. Oxford University Press. doi:10.1093/acrefore/9780190228637.013.205.

Hallin, D.C. and Mancini, P. (2004) *Comparing Media Systems: Three Models of Media and Politics*. Cambridge; New York: Cambridge University Press.

Hardy, J. (2008) *Western Media Systems, Routledge & CRC Press*. Available at: https://www.routledge.com/Western-Media-Systems/Hardy/p/book/9780415396929 (Accessed: 24 May 2021).

Hardy, J. (2014) *Critical Political Economy of the Media: An Introduction*. London: Routledge. doi:10.4324/9780203136225.

Herrero, L.C. et al. (2017) 'Rethinking Hallin and Mancini Beyond the West: An Analysis of Media Systems in Central and Eastern Europe', *International Journal of Communication*, 11(0), p. 27. Available at: https://ijoc.org/index.php/ijoc/article/view/6035 (Accessed: 26 January 2021).

Kocurek, C.A. (2019) 'Who We Were When the World Was Watching', *American Quarterly*, 71(1), pp. 295–300.

Koliska, M. and Assmann, K. (2021) 'Lügenpresse: The Lying Press and German Journalists' Responses to a Stigma', *Journalism*, 22(11), pp. 2729–2746. doi:10.1177/1464884919894088.

Landes, J.B. (1988) *Women and the Public Sphere in the Age of the French Revolution*. Ithaca, NY: Cornell University Press.

Lohner, J., Neverla, I. and Banjac, S. (2019) 'Conflict-Sensitive Journalism? Journalistic Role Perceptions and Practices in Democratization Conflicts', in Voltmer, K. et al. (eds) *Media, Communication and the Struggle for Democratic Change: Case Studies on Contested Transitions*. Cham: Springer International Publishing, pp. 59–81. doi:10.1007/978-3-030-16748-6_3.

Maggio, J. (2007) '"Can the Subaltern Be Heard?": Political Theory, Translation, Representation, and Gayatri Chakravorty Spivak', *Alternatives*, 32(4), pp. 419–443. doi:10.1177/030437540703200403.

Mill, J., Stuart (1859) *On Liberty* (Batoche Books, Kitchener vol). Available at: https://socialsciences.mcmaster.ca/econ/ugcm/3ll3/mill/liberty.pdf.

Mouffe, C. (2016) 'Democratic Politics and the Dynamics of Passion', in Pulkkinen, T., Palonen, K., and Rosales, J.M. (eds) *The Ashgate Research Companion to the Politics if Democratisation in Europe*. London: Routledge, pp. 89–100.

Newman, N., Richard, F., Antonis, K., David, L., and Rasmus, K.N. (2018) 'Digital News Report 2018', *Reuters Institute Digital News Reports*, 144.

Nielsen, R.K. et al. (2016) *Analysis of the Relation Between and Impact of Public Service Media and Private Media*. SSRN Scholarly Paper ID 2868065. Rochester, NY: Social Science Research Network. doi:10.2139/ssrn.2868065.

Nyamnjoh, F.B. (2017) 'Incompleteness: Frontier Africa and the Currency of Conviviality', *Journal of Asian and African Studies*, 52(3), pp. 253–270. doi:10.1177/0021909615580867.

Nygaard, S. (2020) 'Boundary Work: Intermedia Agenda-Setting Between Right-Wing Alternative Media and Professional Journalism', *Journalism Studies*, 21(6), pp. 766–782. doi:10.1080/1461670X.2020.1722731.

Sehl, A., Fletcher, R. and Picard, R.G. (2020) 'Crowding Out: Is There Evidence That Public Service Media Harm Markets? A Cross-National Comparative Analysis of Commercial Television and Online News Providers', *European Journal of Communication*, p. 0267323120903688. doi:10.1177/0267323120903688.

Siebert, F., Peterson, T. and Schramm, W. (1963) *Four Theories of the Press*. Champaign, Illinois: University of Illinois Press.

Silverstone, R. (2007) *Media and Morality on the Rise of the Mediapolis*. Cambridge; Malden, MA: Polity Press.

Sonwalkar, P. (2015) 'Indian Journalism in the Colonial Crucible', *Journalism Studies*, 16(5), pp. 624–636. doi:10.1080/1461670X.2015.1054159.

Spivak, G., Chakravorty (1988) 'Can the Subaltern Speak?', in Nelson, C. and Grossberg, L. (eds) *Marxism and the Interpretation of Culture*. London: MacMillan, pp. 24–28.

Wasserman, H. and Maweu, J.M. (2014) 'The Freedom to Be Silent? Market Pressures on Journalistic Normative Ideals at the Nation Media Group in Kenya', *Review of African Political Economy*, 41(142), pp. 623–633. doi:10.1080/03056244.2014.928277.

2
NEWS PRODUCTION IN DEMOCRACIES

In **Chapter 1**, we looked at the way in which national news systems differ. In this chapter, we will shift focus and ask why it is that, within national news systems, the news considered important is so similar. In order to understand both the similarities and the differences, we turn to institutional, or "field theory" (Cook, 1998; Sparrow, 1999; Bourdieu, 2005). The term "field" is used by scholars of new institutionalism (Cook, 1998; Sparrow, 1999) as well as by French sociologist, Pierre Bourdieu (2005), to describe a sphere of action, such as politics, education or religion, which is sufficiently specialised to create its own rules of engagement (see **Chapter 4** for more on Bourdieu). The education field, for example, consists of schools, colleges and universities and the bureaucracies that support them, which have developed together over time. Every new educational institution will develop in relation to others and in line with the tacit rules that already exist in that field. They may be innovative, or mainstream, but they will be judged in relation to one another. This process of competition and assimilation means that a field has a coherence even if the individual parts of it may appear to be independent.

The journalism field

The journalism field also develops "relationally" through a process of conflict, absorption and domination and establishes its own legitimacy, or "rules of the game" (Bourdieu, 2005). For New Institutionalists, this process creates "path dependency" in which each organisation assimilates the lessons of the past and becomes more and more like every other institution in the field. Bourdieu also suggests that: "all fields of cultural production today are subject to structural pressure from the journalistic field [as a whole], and not from any one journalist or network executive, who are themselves subject to control by the field" (Bourdieu, 1998, p. 56). Cook and Sparrow see the pressures of the field as a largely homogenising force. Bourdieu sees this too, but he is more interested in the production of difference: he is interested in thinking about why and how fields change.

> The ongoing production of difference is the fundamental dynamic of cultural fields. Given that all meaning is produced relationally, any moving of the media's musical chairs will produce some discursive change. The key word is: some.
>
> *(Benson, 2006, p. 192)*

The central forces in Bourdieu's concept of the field are economic capital on the one hand and cultural capital on the other. He refers to these as the "poles" of the field. On one side journalism organisations are pulled towards economic success, measured in advertising revenue and sales. This Bourdieu refers to as the *heteronomous* (or commercial) pole. Bourdieu suggests that the power of the state is on the side of commercial power, an assumption which is contested by Benson (Benson, 2006) and will be discussed in more detail in **Chapter 9**. On the other side of the field lies the cultural acceptance which is unique to that field. In the journalism field, cultural success (or what Bourdieu terms: *cultural capital*) is measured in terms of "scoops," awards, recognition by one's peers and political and cultural influence. This Bourdieu designates the *autonomous* pole of the field. Of course, "scoops", awards and recognition occur across both poles, but the *autonomous* pole is less constrained by commercial factors, and tends to be richer in cultural, rather than economic, capital.

The publications or TV channels at the heteronomous end of the field make the most money and will have the biggest budgets; they will be able to pay higher wages and hire more staff. This gives them a built-in advantage when every organisation is competing for audiences and for advertising revenue. However, in Bourdieu's conception, *cultural capital* also has a value because it confers *legitimacy* on an enterprise or institution:

> Economic capital, on the whole, is more powerful, but cultural capital is always needed to transform good fortune into "legitimate" fortune. Fields are arenas of struggle in which individuals and organizations compete, unconsciously and consciously, to valorize those forms of capital which they possess.
>
> *(Benson, 2006, p. 190)*

Bourdieu recognises that this need for *legitimacy* creates a tension. It ensures that economic capital doesn't have the field to itself and that news organisations compete with one another for both economic and *cultural* success because, as Bourdieu explains: "Cultural capital remains on the side of the 'purest' journalists"

(Bourdieu, 2005, p. 41). This dynamic means that journalists, provided they can find an employer whose world view more or less accords with their own, may have a degree of autonomy in pursuing investigations, unearthing unusual stories and interpreting events in ways which contribute to their organisations' cultural capital. However, the desire for legitimacy is also a desire to influence public opinion and participate in the public sphere (see **Chapter 1**). It is this that draws journalism into the *field of power*,[1] where different factions compete for the right to determine how the "rules of the game" are set for everyone.

Whereas Habermas saw the public sphere as an arena that should be based on reasoned debate, in which ideas are thrashed out between equal citizens, Bourdieu sees this more as a competition for *symbolic power* in which the dominant organisation is able to impose: "the legitimate vision of the social world" (Bourdieu, 2005, p. 29). It is this close connection with the *field of power* that ensures that commercial success, though important, is not the only factor in shaping the contest within the field. The role of journalism in shaping *symbolic power* inevitably creates opportunities for news organisations to influence Governments and electorates – and not always in the public interest (see **Chapter 10**).

Exercise: Mapping the Field

Considering the media in your own country, draw a map with the news organisations arranged in relation to the *field of power* at the top, their degree of cultural autonomy to the left and heteronomy (tied to advertising and audience ratings) to the right. Consider also whether your conception of the field is affected by your own political and cultural positioning (see *habitus*, below). Would someone with a different political position place these organisations differently?

Disrupting the field

As we said earlier, one of the chief differences between Bourdieu and the New Institutionalists is that Bourdieu is interested not only in how fields are constructed and maintained but also in how and why fields change. He argues that, in their struggle for domination of the field, new entrants (agents) can act as forces of transformation or of conservation. In a very competitive market, new entrants (organisations and individuals) are forced to compete for opportunities and are likely to conform to the existing rules to ensure advancement (this is discussed further in the section on *habitus* below), but every now and again a new agent arrives that changes the rules: "the more energy a body has the more it distorts the space around it. And a very powerful agent can distort the whole space, cause the whole space to be organized in relation to itself" (Benson and Neveu, 2005, p. 43).

The online news company BuzzFeed provides a good example of how an agent of transformation can work to alter the field. In this case, Jonah Peretti, the founder of BuzzFeed, made use of emerging technologies to fundamentally change the way in which news production was funded.

The case of BuzzFeed

The company started in the United States in 2006 using computer automation for finding and then sharing popular, and often very silly, content with the intention of increasing readership and advertising revenue. It was initially an experiment in finding out how to make money from riding the waves of search engine algorithms. By 2014, its revenue had passed 100 million dollars (Weprin, 2014), but, like the New York Sun in 1883 (see **Chapter 8**), it didn't just make money, it changed the dynamics of the journalism field, moving it further towards the commercial pole, as other news organisations found themselves forced to compete for advertising income with a company that specialised in joke stories, or what became known as "click bait" (see **Chapter 7**).

As mainstream news organisations scrambled to find shareable stories which would bring in more adverting to fund their operations, BuzzFeed decided to use its deeper coffers to buy journalistic "legitimacy." It started a serious news division and, in 2013, hired Mark Schoofs, a Pulitzer prize-winning journalist, as head of investigative reporting and, following the same "rules of the game" as any other American news organisation, garnered awards for break-through investigations. To underwrite this new direction, it produced a publicly available style-guide which states that: "BuzzFeed editorial must follow the lead of our editors and reporters who come out of a tradition of rigorous, neutral journalism that puts facts and news first. If we don't, it makes it harder for those reporters to do their jobs" (Hilton, 2015). BuzzFeed founder, Jonah Peretti, explained what he thinks rigorous journalism should do:

> Does it result in a law being changed? Does it result in wrongdoing being exposed or the public being informed? Looking at that as the metric is more powerful. Otherwise, the only kind of news people would do is the kind of quick aggregation, viral news sort of stories. Those are the stories that get the most traffic.
>
> (Martinson, 2015)

Like many other advertising-funded online news organisations, BuzzFeed was soon badly affected by changes to social media algorithms which downgraded news companies in their news feed (see **Chapter 7**). Just as the company had started to expand internationally, its income started to spiral downwards. By 2017, BuzzFeed news started to shed staff, and with them, its investigative news sections. Perhaps ironically, BuzzFeed news has now been undermined by the very "click-bait" revolution it fostered (see **Chapter 7**).

> **Exercise: Changing the Rules of the Game**
>
> Can you think of other technical changes, or media organisations that have used them, that have distorted the field? When the dust settled, and the news media re-formed, how different did the media landscape appear and how much was it the same?

Political and legal disruption

The force of disruption comes not only from changes in technology and business structures. It can also come from changes in the political sphere which alter the structure of the field. For example, until the late 1980s, in line with most other democracies, television in the United States was bound by rules of fairness, to enable political parties to have an equal chance of media exposure. This produced a form of journalism which tended to reproduce the status quo, allowing the voices of those considered to be legitimate spokespeople (see also **Chapter 6**) for established political parties to comment on issues of public concern. It also marginalised dissenting voices. Where there was dissent, it tended to be amongst the elite (Hallin, 2005).

The "Fairness Doctrine" was lifted in 1987 and news organisations were left free to make their own decisions about how to represent news events. This disruption had little impact on the legacy news organisations but it ushered in the era of right-wing "shock-jocks" on radio. Then, in 1996, the advent of Fox News threw centrist politics to the winds (Brock, 2012) and fundamentally altered the US news media field. Today the audiences of the United States are among the most polarised in the world (Fletcher and Jenkins, 2019; Boxell, Gentzkow and Shapiro, 2020). While most of the mainstream newspapers (and their websites) maintain their stance of professionalism and objectivity in covering events, they have lost their supremacy in determining how the journalism field should be constituted. Indeed, it is reasonable to suggest, as Bourdieu predicted (Benson and Neveu, 2005), that the entire field has been reorganised in relation to Fox News.

Changes of a similar nature took place in India in the 1990s, when a liberalisation of the laws which had constrained the private ownership of television stations, opened the industry up to new, and foreign, investment. From one television news channel in 1998, there were 40 by 2007, and 403 by 2015 (Thussu, 2008; Lakshman, 2015). The intense competition for audiences dramatically shifted the field. Where there had been one low-budget, pro-Government state news channel (*Doordarshan*), there was now a frenzy of competition for dramatic and sensational stories to win audiences and the advertising revenue that comes with them.

So intense was the competition that even one of the most serious Hindi news channels, *Aaj Tak*, began running items on the supernatural to attract audiences

(Thussu, 2008, p. 103). In an over-crowded marketplace, the drive to compete for audience results in "convergence" in which all the agents in the field are drawn closer to the commercial pole. As one would expect in such a competitive market, the plethora of news companies gradually merged as the economically strongest bought up the minnows. By 2019, just four companies owned 76.45 percent of the Hindi language market across the country (Reporters Sans Frontier, 2019). According to an article in Quartz, the owners are increasingly aligned politically with the current Prime Minister Narendra Modi (Inamdar, 2020).

The shift towards the commercial pole in both India and the United States was enabled by a political trend which tends to see individual liberty (in this case, the liberty of individual media proprietors), and the right to make large sums of money, as of greater importance than social responsibility and fairness.

However, this elision of market freedom with the concept of media freedom is contested. In Europe, market regulation and a well-funded public sector in the media dilute the power of individual media companies, and in much of the world, there are regulations to ensure a degree of fairness in broadcasting (see **Chapters 9 and 10**). The first five places on the World Press Freedom Index (RSF, 2021) are all Northern European countries, while the sixth is Jamaica. The United States is 45th and India is 142nd so, by these standards at least, a degree of regulation, which is itself a product of reasoned debate or competition for *symbolic capital*, enables greater press diversity.

The rules of the game

This field structure is not imposed from above like a cookie cutter, nor is it only the outcome of organisations colliding in space and shaping one another from the outside. It is also maintained by the way individuals are collectively drawn to repeat patterns that create and maintain structures from the inside. In some professions, these patterns are maintained through the use of specific training and certification, but journalism tends to be viewed as an occupation, not a profession, like medicine or law. The practitioners of journalism in a democratic society do not usually need licenses to perform and the attainment of qualifications is usually a nice to have rather than a must have (McQuail, 2008). Nevertheless, journalists operate according to a set of tacit rules, and journalism organisations, though they vary from one nation to another (see **Chapter 1**), operate in a way which is internally coherent. If you were to move from one newsroom to another, in the same country, you would understand what Bourdieu describes as the "rules of the game" even if the way in which those rules are used vary considerably.

In the Italian media field (as we explain in **Chapter 1**), the news media are aligned with the major political parties (Hallin and Mancini, 2004) but, in the event that a journalist working on the right-wing Italian newspaper, *Libero*, moved to the left-wing newspaper, *Il Manifesto*, they would share a discursive style and understand that political alignment is an expectation, not an aberration.

> **Exercise: Is Journalism a Profession?**
>
> The chief criteria of a profession, according to McQuail (2008, p. 56), can be set out as follows:
>
> - Having a core skill, requiring a high level of education and training
> - Having an institutional embodiment for control of entry, standards and accountability
> - Having an ethic of service to the client
> - Having an ethic of service to the society
> - Following known codes of ethics and norms of conduct
> - Having a degree of autonomy
> - Having an attitude of detachment and impartiality in performing the role
> - Being potentially a vocation or calling
>
> Consider for each criterion whether journalism aims to achieve this and whether or not it succeeds in doing so.

They would understand who they would need to quote and who they would be expected to shun. The political approach would be diametrically opposed, but the processes would be similar.

In the United Kingdom, a journalist moving from an upmarket news organisation, such as *The Times*, to a popular one such as *The Sun*, would find that the style of writing and the hierarchy of the newsrooms are different. They would probably find the demands of *The Sun* for pithy, pared-down prose a challenge, but would understand what was required and recognise the need to conform to the style and editorial direction of the paper. They would also be aware that the political direction of the newspaper is well established. As Curran and Seaton (1997, p. 49) explain: "What made the press magnates different is that they sought to use their papers, not as levers of power within the political parties, but as instruments of power against political parties." They were describing the evolution of the British press, but the same rules still apply even though the press is now more often owned by public companies. In other words, these newspapers compete for *symbolic power* and thereby strive to establish the *rules of the game*. This will be discussed further in forthcoming chapters.

Journalists in the United States would, traditionally, have even less trouble changing newsrooms because of the adherence to what Gaye Tuchman referred to as a "strategic ritual of objectivity" (Tuchman, 1972, p. 660) in which political preferences are never overtly expressed and opinions are hidden in an attempt to achieve a balanced report-based entirely on the facts of the case. While there have been some changes in the adherence to the maxim of neutrality (see **Chapter 11**), it is still broadly speaking the practice in legacy newsrooms. Tuchman refers to this approach as:

> ... a routine procedure which has relatively little, or only tangential relevance to the end sought. Adherence to the procedure is frequently compulsive. That such a procedure may be the best known means of attaining the sought end does not detract from its characterization as a ritual.
>
> *(Tuchman, 1972, p. 661)*

The ritual of objectivity was even invoked as a *legitimising* strategy when Fox News launched with its slogan: "Fair and Balanced," even though it was clear from the start that it intended to lean to the right of the political spectrum.

Tim Cook, building on Tuchman's theories, saw journalism as the product of *path dependency* in which the institution of journalism reproduces itself and human agency is constrained:

> When reporters make choices on who and what to cover and how to cover it, these choices are governed less by personal values prior to becoming a journalist or by their placement within the social structure as a whole than by a "logic of appropriateness" based on their professional and craft-related roles as journalists.
>
> *(Cook, 1998, p. 61)*

What Cook terms the logic of the structure, Bourdieu would refer to as the *doxa*. These are sets of implicit rules created by institutions. They may be there to improve efficiency or, for example, to establish trust, but over time, they often become detached from their original moorings, becoming habits of behaviour which newcomers are expected to adopt in order to progress in that institution. Some of these rules are perfectly valid and useful. For example, identifying who said what (attributing sources) creates an aura of trust and authenticity, but it also has an intrinsic value because it allows other people to check the facts for themselves. On the other hand, the rule that "authoritative sources" (usually representative of the state) should always come first in a news story often tilts the coverage in favour of authority and against marginalised people (see **Chapter 6**).

Similarly, creating "beats," so that journalists specialise in particular subjects or areas, and giving editorial control to a small group of people at the centre, is useful when an organisation is trying to coordinate and publish rapidly changing information. But, it also creates a line of authority that can give disproportionate power to those editors who assign stories and control content.

In a tight labour market, when journalists have few employment options, the power to assign stories can be used to discipline trainee journalists and ensure they toe the editorial line and learn to do things the "right way." It can also be used to intimidate journalists into writing material that doesn't necessarily conform with their own ethical standards because: "precarity of employment is a loss of liberty through which censorship […] can be more easily expressed." (Bourdieu, 2005, p. 43).

This journalist started his career on a local paper and then got an opportunity to work for a major UK national newspaper. He said of one particular story:

> I thought the story was appalling. I thought all along that it was a ludicrous exercise with no logic whatsoever and I felt very ashamed about it but if I lost my job I wouldn't be able to pay the rent or anything like that which probably isn't an excuse but there was still that thought there.
> *(Phillips, Couldry and Freedman, 2010, p. 56)*

Despite the tendency to path dependency, journalism is not a rigid system in which there is no change; indeed, it acts both an agent of change *and* a means of reproducing the status quo as we discuss below.

Cultural capital

So far, we have talked about organisations in the journalistic field, but organisations are not machines, they are composed of people, each of whom has their own life experience. Bourdieu tends to down-play the power and autonomy of individuals, in favour of a structure in which individual choices are limited by the position of the institution they work for in the field and their individual place in that institution. Nevertheless, he does not see journalists as entirely subject to the pressures of the field. "For a journalist, the degree of autonomy will depend on one's position in the field, which means, for example, one's authority." (Bourdieu, 2005, p. 44).

Senior editors and journalists working for news organisations at the autonomous end of the field will have more freedom of action than their counterparts at the more commercial end of the field, where the need to demonstrate commercial success is always paramount. They will also have more freedom than those working within autocratic regimes where the rules of what can be said are constrained by law and practice. However, where news organisations are owned by individuals interested in political power, proprietors will have built in a degree of compliance, by appointing editors who agree with them politically.

Those with less seniority will have less autonomy, wherever they work, because they are expected to follow the instructions of senior staff (the *doxa*). People will be promoted if they can demonstrate that they embody the cultural capital that is recognised within the organisation as valuable. Bourdieu saw *cultural capital* as:

- an understanding of that which is considered to be culturally valuable;
- the embodiment of culturally appropriate behaviour and
- the educational credentials that provide evidence of these achievements and qualities.

Cultural capital is not fixed. Those things considered valuable in 1950 are in many ways different to those that are valued today, and cultural capital in India, for example, will be in many ways different to that which is recognised in Germany. But, it is through an understanding of cultural capital that people demonstrate their distinction and carve out ways of reproducing what is seen by the organisation as valuable.

Habitus

While cultural capital can be accrued by watching and learning, *habitus* is a product of family, cultural life and socially constructed markers of identity – it is the personal baggage individuals carry with them into fields and institutional spaces:

> *habitus,* as the product of social conditionings, and thus of history ... is endlessly transformed, either in a direction that reinforces it, when embodied structures of expectation encounter structures of objective chances in harmony with these expectations, or in a direction that transforms it and, for instance, raises or lowers the level of expectations and aspirations.
> (Bourdieu, 1990, p. 116).

Thus, we gravitate to people like ourselves, and when *habitus* and work culture fit together, we are inclined to see it as a happy accident. It is when habitus and work culture don't match that habitus comes into focus. We feel edgy and uncomfortable. In most situations, it is incumbent on the face that doesn't quite fit to adjust to the majority culture. The accumulation of cultural capital can help to ease this disjuncture and so does the conscious adjustment of one's behaviour.

The case of Vogue magazine

A look at British *Vogue* suggests how the intersection between *habitus* and *doxa* works in practice. *Vogue* is a style icon which defines and promotes the cultural values of the country of its publication and of the international elite. It is also a commercial product which depends on its cultural status for its economic success. For the company that owns *Vogue* (Conde Nast), the appointment of an editor has to balance the requirements of both cultural capital and economic capital. Vogue must keep pulling in the very expensive advertising that keeps it in business, but it also needs to differentiate itself in the field. So, it appoints an editor who embodies the values the company wishes to project, while also demonstrating the autonomy that is likely to lead to *differentiation* within the bounds of commercial success.

> To exist in a field is to differentiate oneself. It can be said of an intellectual that he or she functions like a phoneme in a language: he or she exists by

virtue of difference from other intellectuals. Falling into undifferentiatedness ...means losing existence.

(Bourdieu, 2005, pp. 40–41)

Alexandra Shulman was editor of British *Vogue* from 1992 to 2017. Brought up in one of London's wealthiest districts, her mother specialised in writing books on etiquette and her father was a well-known theatre critic. Some of her earliest work was for *Tatler* magazine, the bible of the British upper classes. What Shulman had gained from her family was not just economic capital but a wealth of social and cultural capital: a network of influential friends and associates, a deep understanding of British elite culture but also a connection with popular culture through her love of popular music (Aitkenhead, 2017). As a white, upper-class individual Shulman, at least with regard to these two aspects of identity (class and race, which contribute to informing *habitus*), wasn't different from the majority of editors of mainstream British magazines and newspapers (Thurman, Cornia and Kunert, 2016).

But, the *Vogue* brand *is* distinct in the field and Shulman was by all accounts a very successful editor, willing to be controversial within the acceptable bounds of elite culture and managing to steer the magazine through the early years of the online era. Like so many people in positions of power, she recruited people in her own image, with many recruits starting out on unpaid work-experience, relying on their parents for financial support. This employment method tends to limit the field of recruitment to those who can afford to work for free, thereby introducing a structural constraint, but the constraints of *habitus* and "path dependence" can have deeper effects.

In Shulman's final September edition, a picture of the *Vogue* staff revealed that they were all white. Many critiqued the lack of racial diversity, which is starkly unreflective of the British population.[2] Shulman defended the whiteness of her editorial team in an interview in *The Guardian*, saying:

> I have never been somebody who's box-ticked. I'm against quotas. I feel like my Vogue had the people in who I wanted it to. I didn't look at what race they were. I didn't look at what sex they were. I didn't look at what age they were. I included the people I thought interesting.
>
> *(Aitkenhead, 2017)*

However, one of the most prominent critics was the model Naomi Campbell. She is one of just two Black models to have had solo British *Vogue* covers between 2002 (when Campbell featured) and 2014 (when Jourdan Dunn featured) (Cartner-Morley, 2017). Campbell tweeted the *Vogue* staff image and wrote: "Looking forward to an inclusive and diverse staff now that @edward_enninful is the editor."

Edward Enninful, who took over from Shulman, is British-Ghanaian and the first Black (and male) editor of *Vogue* since the magazine launched over 100 years ago. His mother was a dressmaker, and he was exposed to Ghanaian fashion from an early age. As a 16-year-old, he was approached by a fashion scout and became a model, mixing with some of the most influential people on the cultural scene and beginning to develop his own ideas about style. He too had a unique mix of social capital, garnered through the friendships he developed via the world of fashion, and cultural capital, developed through his ability to blend African and European styles in a way which caught the zeitgeist. He was already fashion editor of *i-D* magazine before completing his degree.

The appointment of Enninful as editor allowed *Vogue* once more to sustain and accumulate cultural capital. He had an excellent track-record in the industry. He also embodied differentiation from his predecessor as well as from other editors of dominant British magazines and newspapers. On taking over the magazine, he has clearly affected much needed change at the level of representation, featuring more Black and brown cover stars, including Laverne Cox who is also British *Vogue's* first trans cover star. He has changed the staff as well as the style to something that accords better with his sense of the world. He said:

> I think with my appointment people who were maybe intimidated before felt that they could now apply for that job. That's what I hear. I've been very lucky that there was no pushback. It was like, yes, we need to change.
>
> *(Indvik, 2019)*

Under Enninful's editorship,[3] British *Vogue* has also contributed to Conde Nast's growth in economic capital (Tobitt, 2019). On the one hand, this is a very welcome rebuke to those in many quarters of the mainstream western media industry who have long maintained that Black people can't feature prominently in mainstream western narratives, whether at the level of production or representation, because of the entirely baseless, racist claim that Black people "don't sell" (Douglas, 2019). On the other hand, Enninful's contribution to boosting Conde Nast's economic capital also serves as an illustration of how organisations extract "racial capital." This is "the economic and social value, derived from an individual's racial identity" (Leong, 2013, p. 2190) which tends to benefit institutional whiteness without necessarily addressing structural racism within the organisation.

Despite the change of editor and Enninful's welcome stated wish to champion diversity (Butler, 2018), Conde Nast has attracted criticism too for continuing the practice of unpaid internships that are rife within the journalistic field (Cohen and Peuter, 2019). These "opportunities" allow those in charge to assess whether a young person will be a good fit. They are told that they will: "learn how our workplace operates, test their interest in a possible future career, as well as providing invaluable opportunities to network and improving their skillset in relation to future employment." (Graduate Fog, 2018)

Graduate Fog complains that these internships:

> take advantage of those who do them, entrench privilege and exclude diverse talent. *Vogue's* four-week placements may be short, but unless they pay a wage they are out of reach for most young people, who simply can't survive in London for a month without any money. The fact that these placements can lead to paid jobs at *Vogue* is actually a point against them as it underlines how rotten the entry system is.
>
> *(Graduate Fog, 2018)*

Thus, organisations continue to offer more opportunities to those with shared *habitus*, due to their socio-economic position, reproducing some of the values of the organisation. This process of acculturation is so powerful that, even when an organisation is deliberately setting out to change the kind of personnel it attracts, for example, by instituting diversity policies, it will almost certainly continue to some extent to maintain the status quo.

This demonstrates that change at the top is not necessarily reflected in changes further down, or at the level of organisational *doxa* more broadly. In other words, Enninful's *habitus* may be different to Shulman's on multiple levels (race, class, gender, sexuality – Enninful is gay), and he has drawn on this to shift *Vogue's* look and content in important ways. However, Enninful's vital changes at the level of representation don't seem to have triggered the kind of institutional change necessary to enable young journalists to enter the institution on the basis of merit alone, rather than on their ability to support themselves financially during unpaid internships.

The tensions between *habitus* and *doxa* within media organisations of course play out globally. Habits of thinking and a reflexive return to cultural norms create path-dependency and reproduce approaches to framing and story selection which will be discussed in more detail in the next chapter.

Changing the status quo

With every wave of cultural or technical change, new faces and voices emerge from the fringes. Sometimes, they appear threatening, and attempts will be made by people or organisations within the field to lock them out and chip away at their legitimacy. Sometimes, they are embraced as a form of differentiation and rapidly absorbed. Occasionally change is seismic, and the entire system is shaken. In the field of media, technical changes regularly shake up the journalism field: the printing press, the electric telegraph, radio, television and the internet. In each wave of change, some institutions have been eliminated and others have grown up to take centre stage.

Those who already have power in the field will usually attempt to defend their privilege against newcomers. When legendary Sixty Minute anchor, Mike

Wallace, started in television, most of the big names had come from radio. Wallace had a background in acting and brought a very different style to news and current affairs. According to his biographer Avi Belkin: "he suffered from a little stigma as well. When he came to CBS in '63, the old Murrow boys and Cronkite looked down on him" (Bowen, 2019). Bloggers were also derided as ignorant key-board warriors before many were absorbed into mainstream news organisations, and young people with computer skills were initially kept separate from the newsroom and usually paid less than traditionally trained journalists (Lee-Wright, Phillips and Witschge, 2011).

Cultural change also finds its way into newsrooms. In the 1970s, for example, a wave of university-educated women entered journalism. They found that most jobs were on the features' pages. It took real determination, as well as ability, to break into news and most felt that they had to mirror the characteristics of the dominant male journalists in order to be accepted (Leslie, 2008). The movement of women into positions of greater authority has been painfully slow and they are still under-represented in positions of influence in news organisations (Macharia, 2020).

The same is true of Black and other minority journalists in white majority countries. In the United States, for example, minorities comprise 40 percent of the population but less than 17 percent of newsroom staff and only 13 percent of those in senior positions in newspapers (Arana, 2018). In the United Kingdom, students from Black or minority backgrounds are over-represented among journalism students, but under-represented among those moving into work in the industry: 85 percent of white and 75 percent of ethnic minority leavers move into journalism jobs (Spilsbury, 2017). In Australia, 58 percent of the population has an Anglo-Celtic background, but people from this group make up 75 percent of presenters, reporters and commentators across television news and current affairs programmes (Rodrigues, 2020).

These figures are dispiriting because the need for diversity is about much more than equality of opportunity for journalists. Greater diversity within journalism, in terms of socio-economic positions, sexuality, gender, disability, religion, race, nationality and other markers of identity, has a bearing on journalists' story selection, who they may talk to, and how they frame stories (see **Chapter 4**). These markers of identity inform everyone's lived experiences and, thus, *habitus*. Bourdieu describes *habitus* "as socialised subjectivity" (Bourdieu and Wacquant, 1992). Organisations that employ journalists with a range of socialised subjectivities should generate stories that are more varied as well as more reflective of their audiences' concerns about local, national and international issues.

In a speech in 2019, Dorothy Byrne, former head of news and current affairs at Britain's Channel 4, said:

> If you want a successful newsroom, it has to be representative of the diversity of your population in terms of gender, sexuality, disability and

ethnicity, adding that a failure to achieve this will lead to news organizations getting the news wrong (Byrne, 2019).

What this recognises is that *habitus* matters in the production of content.

There has been an ongoing push for greater diversity and inclusion in journalism so that it better reflects the population, which consists of multiple and overlapping minority groups across lines of class, gender, religion, sexuality, disability and race. Major British broadcasters (BBC, Channel 4, ITV, Channel 5 and Sky) officially monitor and manage diversity and inclusion via formal systems, such as allocating minority staff spaces, in the way of surveys or forums, to express their views. However, if this is to be more than a box-ticking exercise (Douglas, 2019) or a game of "bodies in the room" (Eddo-Lodge, 2017), news organisations need to do more than ensure that people from minority groups are present. They must also be adequately included within the workplace if the organisation is to be able to draw on their experience to inform story selection choices, and not just those related to a singular marker of their identity, like race, rather than expecting minorities to conform to dominant ways of seeing and doing.

Without a reasonable level of representation, at all levels of power, the influence of journalists from socially marginalised groups on decision-making will be limited. A 2011 study found that: "issues and topics traditionally seen to be particularly relevant to women tend to be pushed to the margins of the news where the implicit assumption is that they are less important than those which interest men" (Ross and Carter, 2011). One might have hoped to see significant change since then but, according to a 2020 global report into women and news:

> findings since 1995 have been remarkably stable: Women's severe under-representation has persisted as has their relative invisibility in the news in contrast to men. The outcome of underrepresentation is an imbalanced picture of the world, one in which women are largely absent.
> *(Macharia, 2020)*

For Black journalists working in mainstream western newsrooms, there is a similar pressure to conform to the existing norms of story-making. One senior Black journalist had this to say about how he managed to get non-racially stereotypical stories featuring Black people into a national UK newspaper:

> I try and use the same [...] news criteria. But I try and fit the stories that I want in the paper into those criteria and I try and show them why they fit the criteria. I find it then makes it very difficult for them to argue that they shouldn't be in the paper. Occasionally you have to go to the editor and say: "If these people were white and lived in Cobham would you run this story?"[4]

What this journalist experienced was the way in which organisational *doxa* is reproduced and how journalists are forced to conform to the rules. A 1955 report found: "a process of social control, in which deviations are punished, (usually gently) by reprimand, cutting one's story, the withholding of friendly comment by an executive" (Breed, 1955, p. 332). This "policing" of the field is a reflexive response to challenge. Journalists who do not "fit" will find that their ideas are less likely to be heard or are only noted when repeated by someone who is culturally "acceptable," but culture is a creation, not a set of fixed characteristics. We make culture as well as being made by it. We all have a role to play in re-establishing norms so that they more closely reflect society.

Rules of the game reconsidered

While many of the rules we follow are constricting and limit necessary changes, it would be wrong to suggest that they all do. When journalists and their organisations use the power of institutional norms to insist on adherence to ethical guidelines, or demand that journalism must be evidence based and sourced, they are doing a valuable job in protecting a field which is not only open to positive but also to negative change. While journalistic norms vary from one country to another, it is striking, for example, that when asked what they believe to be the key attribute of a journalist, independence is one of the few that united journalists from almost every country surveyed (excluding Russia). A worthwhile aspiration even when it is hard to achieve (Thussu and Nordenstreng, 2020).

Turkish journalist, Emre Kizilkaya, is a case in point. He resigned from the independent newspaper *Hürriyet* when it was sold to a pro-government conglomerate because he felt unable to continue working for an organisation that was effectively a Government mouth-piece. He instead established a non-profit platform as a means of passing on normative standards of journalism for "next generation journalists." Whether this enterprise survives the increasingly heavy-handed media repression in Erdoğan's Turkey remains to be seen, but Kizilkaya welcomes the fact that:

> Hundreds of young journalists graduate from more than 100 communication faculties in Turkey each year and most of those to whom I talked voice their determination and resilience to serve the public good and provide the citizens a healthy diet of information against all odds.
>
> *(Kizilkaya, 2020)*

Some norms are worth upholding.

Summary

- A field is a sphere of action which is specialised enough to create and defend its own rules.
- Media organisations can be seen as bodies within a field.
- Within a field, organisations act in relation to one another, in line with often un-stated rules.
- These rules tend to ensure that organisations, even though they may compete with each other, work in very similar ways, generating *path dependency,* which keeps new entrants operating along similar lines.
- In Bourdieu's concept of the field, bodies are also held in tension between economic and cultural capital, each of which exerts its own influence.
- *Economic capital* confers status and influence through money, which enables actors and organisations to achieve a degree of dominance in the field.
- *Cultural capital* confers legitimacy, or recognition, this also confers status and influence in the field. Bourdieu suggests that economic capital needs to be transformed into cultural capital to some degree in order to achieve legitimacy. This means that power is not all on the side of money.
- Bourdieu also suggests that debate does not play out through logical debate but through control of the narrative through which *symbolic power* can be exercised. Control of symbolic power is usually the preserve of the *field of power* (the space in society where decisions are made), but the media are typically very close to the field of power.
- Fields can be disrupted by new agents. Some agents are sufficiently powerful to reorganise a field.
- *Habitus* is a term used by Bourdieu to describe the cultural circumstances from which an individual emerges. *Doxa* is the term used to explain how rules are passed on within an organisation.
- Individual *cultural capital* can be accrued either by being born in the "right" circumstances so that your background (*habitus*) "fits" the doxa of the organisations you are moving into, or it can be acquired by watching, learning and creating.
- Those with *cultural capital* may be able to use their knowledge to differentiate themselves within the field and thereby accrue greater cultural and economic capital.
- These structures are embedded within fields, independent of political structures, they explain why change is slow but also why change is possible.

Notes

1 The field of power describes the space in society where decisions are made – e.g. within politics.
2 According to the 2011 Census, 14 percent of the population of England and Wales was from an ethnic minority (GOV.UK, 2018) https://www.ethnicity-facts-figures.service.gov.uk/uk-population-by-ethnicity/national-and-regional-populations/population-of-england-and-wales/latest.
3 Enninful has since been promoted to Editor-in-Chief of British Vogue and European Editorial Director of Vogue.
4 Interview with Angela Phillips 2002.

References

Aitkenhead, D. (2017) 'Former Vogue editor Alexandra Shulman: "I find the idea that there was a posh cabal offensive"', *The Guardian*, 10 November. Available at: https://www.theguardian.com/media/2017/nov/10/former-vogue-editor-alexandra-shulman-find-idea-that-there-was-a-posh-cabal-offensive (Accessed: 11 August 2020).

Arana, G. (2018) *Decades of Failure, Columbia Journalism Review*. Available at: https://www.cjr.org/special_report/race-ethnicity-newsrooms-data.php/ (Accessed: 2 March 2022).

Benson, R. (2006) 'News Media as a "Journalistic Field": What Bourdieu Adds to New Institutionalism, and Vice Versa', *Political Communication* [Preprint]. doi:10.1080/10584600600629802.

Benson, R.D. and Neveu, E. (2005) *Bourdieu and the Journalistic Field*. Cambridge; Malden, MA: Polity.

Bourdieu, P. (1990) *The Logic of Practice*. Stanford, CA: Stanford University Press.

Bourdieu, P. (1998) *On Television*. New York: New Press.

Bourdieu, P. (2005) 'The Political Field, the Social Science Field, and the Journalistic Field', in Benson, R. and Neveu, E. (eds) *Bourdieu and the Journalistic Field*. Cambridge; Malden, MA: Polity Press, pp. 29–47.

Bourdieu, P. and Wacquant, L.J. (1992) *An Invitation to Reflexive Sociology*. Chicago, IL: University of Chicago Press.

Bowen, B. (2019) *A Showman for the Truth | The Argonaut Newsweekly*. Available at: https://argonautnews.com/a-showman-for-the-truth/ (Accessed: 14 January 2021).

Boxell, L., Gentzkow, M. and Shapiro, J.M. (2020) *Cross-Country Trends in Affective Polarization*. Working Paper 26669. National Bureau of Economic Research. doi:10.3386/w26669.

Breed, W. (1955) 'Social Control in Newsroom: A Case Study in the Selection of News', *Social Forces*, 33, pp. 326–335.

Brock, D. (2012) *The Fox Effect: How Roger Ailes Turned a Network Into a Propaganda Machine*. Illustrated Edition. New York: Anchor Books.

Butler, S. (2018) 'Vogue Criticised for Unpaid Internships', *The Guardian*, 8 February. Available at: https://www.theguardian.com/fashion/2018/feb/08/vogue-criticised-for-unpaid-internships (Accessed: 26 February 2022).

Byrne, D. (2019) *If Your Newsroom Is Not Diverse, You Will Get the News Wrong, Reuters Institute for the Study of Journalism*. Available at: https://reutersinstitute.politics.ox.ac.uk/risj-review/if-your-newsroom-not-diverse-you-will-get-news-wrong (Accessed: 29 June 2020).

Cartner-Morley, J. (2017) *Edward Enninful Addresses Diversity Debate with First Cover for British Vogue, the Guardian*. Available at: http://www.theguardian.com/fashion/2017/nov/07/enninful-fronts-up-to-diversity-debate-with-first-british-vogue-cover (Accessed: 4 March 2021).

Cohen, N.S. and Peuter, G. de (2019) 'Interns Talk Back: Disrupting Media Narratives about Unpaid Work', *The Political Economy of Communication*, 6(2). Available at: http://www.polecom.org/index.php/polecom/article/view/96 (Accessed: 26 February 2021).

Cook, T.E. (1998) *Governing with the News: The News Media as a Political Institution*. Chicago, IL: University of Chicago Press.

Curran, J. and Seaton, J. (1997) *Power Without Responsibility: Press, Broadcasting and the Internet in Britain: Press and Broadcasting in Britain*. London; New York: Routledge.

Douglas, O. (2019) *Backstories / Black Stories: Black Journalists, INGOs and the Racial Politics of Representing Sub-Saharan Africa in Mainstream UK News Media*. Doctoral. Goldsmiths, University of London. Available at: http://research.gold.ac.uk/id/eprint/26352/ (Accessed: 4 March 2021).

Eddo-Lodge, R. (2017) *Why I'm No Longer Talking to White People About Race*. London: Bloomsbury.

Fletcher, R. and Jenkins, J. (2019) *Polarisation and the News Media in Europe*. European Parliamentary Research Service. Available at: https://reutersinstitute.politics.ox.ac.uk/our-research/polarisation-and-news-media-europe (Accessed: 8 February 2022).

Graduate Fog (2018) 'Vogue Editor Under Fire Over Unpaid Internships', *Graduate Fog*, 8 February. Available at: https://graduatefog.co.uk/2018/5399/vogue-edward-enninful-unpaid-internship/ (Accessed: 12 August 2020).

Hallin, D. (2005) *We Keep America on Top of the World : Television Journalism and the Public Sphere*. London and New York: Routledge. doi:10.4324/9780203977477.

Hallin, D.C. and Mancini, P. (2004) *Comparing Media Systems: Three Models of Media and Politics*. Cambridge; New York: Cambridge University Press.

Hilton, S.O. (2015) *The BuzzFeed News Standards and Ethics Guide, BuzzFeed News*. Available at: https://www.buzzfeednews.com/article/shani/the-buzzfeed-editorial-standards-and-ethics-guide (Accessed: 6 August 2020).

Inamdar, N. (2020) *How Narendra Modi Has Almost Killed the Indian Media, Quartz India*. Available at: https://qz.com/india/1570899/how-narendra-modi-has-almost-killed-indian-media/ (Accessed: 10 August 2020).

Indvik, L. (2019) *Edward Enninful on Vogue, Gen Z and What Makes a Great Editor, Vogue Business*. Available at: https://www.voguebusiness.com/companies/edward-enninful-interview-editor-in-chief-british-vogue (Accessed: 10 August 2020).

Kizilkaya, E. (2020) *As Erdoğan Cracks Down, Turkey's Independent Journalists Need Digital Skills and Business Acumen, Nieman Reports*. Available at: https://niemanreports.org/articles/as-erdogan-cracks-down-turkeys-independent-journalists-need-digital-skills-and-business-acumen/ (Accessed: 6 August 2020).

Lakshman, R. (2015) 'Six New Channel Licenses Issued, Total Number of Channels in India Has Reached 832', *TelecomTalk*. Available at: https://telecomtalk.info/total-number-tv-channels-india/139844/ (Accessed: 4 August 2020).

Lee-Wright, P., Phillips, A. and Witschge, T. (2011) *Changing Journalism*. 1st edition. Abingdon, Oxon: Routledge.

Leong, N. (2013) *Racial Capitalism*. Available at: https://harvardlawreview.org/2013/06/racial-capitalism/ (Accessed: 4 March 2021).

Leslie, A. (2008) *Killing My Own Snakes: A Memoir*. Main Market edition. London: Macmillan.

Macharia, S. (2020) 'Global Media Monitoring Project (GMMP)', in *The International Encyclopedia of Gender, Media, and Communication*. American Cancer Society, pp. 1–6. doi:10.1002/9781119429128.iegmc074.

Martinson, J. (2015) 'BuzzFeed's Jonah Peretti: How the Great Entertainer Got Serious', *The Guardian*, 15 November. Available at: https://www.theguardian.com/media/2015/nov/15/buzzfeed-jonah-peretti-facebook-ads (Accessed: 10 August 2020).

McQuail, D. (2008) 'Journalism as a Public Occupation: Alternative Images', in Carpentier, N. et al. (eds) *Democracy, Journalism and Technology: New Developments in an Enlarged Europe*. Tartu: Tartu University Press. pp. 47–61.

Phillips, A., Couldry, N. and Freedman, D. (2010) 'An Ethical Deficit? Accountability, Norms, and the Material Conditions of Contemporary Journalism', in Fenton, N. (ed.) *New Media, Old News: Journalism & Democracy in the Digital Age*. Los Angeles, CA: Sage, pp. 52–67.

Reporters Sans Frontier (2019) *Media Ownership Monitor: Who Owns the Media in India? | Reporters without Borders, RSF*. Available at: https://rsf.org/en/news/media-ownership-monitor-who-owns-media-india (Accessed: 24 February 2021).

Rodrigues, U.M. (2020) 'Whitewash on the Box: How a Lack of Diversity on Australian Television Damages Us All', *The Conversation*. Available at: http://theconversation.com/whitewash-on-the-box-how-a-lack-of-diversity-on-australian-television-damages-us-all-143434 (Accessed: 4 March 2021).

Ross, K. and Carter, C. (2011) 'Women and News: A Long and Winding Road', *Media, Culture & Society*, 33(8), pp. 1148–1165. doi:10.1177/0163443711418272.

RSF (2021) *2021 World Press Freedom Index: Journalism, the Vaccine Against Disinformation, Blocked in More Than 130 Countries, RSF*. Available at: https://rsf.org/en/2021-world-press-freedom-index-journalism-vaccine-against-disinformation-blocked-more-130-countries (Accessed: 9 December 2021).

Sparrow, B.H. (1999) *Uncertain Guardians: The News Media as a Political Institution*. Baltimore, MD: JHU Press.

Spilsbury, M. (2017) 'Diversity in Journalism', *National Council for the Training of Journalists*. Available at: https://www.nctj.com/downloadlibrary/DIVERSITY%20JOURNALISM%204WEB.pdf.

Thurman, N., Cornia, A. and Kunert, J. (2016) *Journalists in the UK*. Oxford: Reuters Institute for the Study of Journalism.

Thussu, D. (2008) *News as Entertainment*. London: Sage.

Thussu, D.K. and Nordenstreng, K. (eds) (2020) *BRICS Media: Reshaping the Global Communication Order?* 1st edition. New York: Routledge.

Tobitt, C. (2019) *Vogue and GQ Publisher Conde Nast Swings Back into Black, Press Gazette*. Available at: https://www.pressgazette.co.uk/edward-enninfuls-british-vogue-helps-swing-conde-nast-back-into-profit-in-2018/ (Accessed: 24 February 2021).

Tuchman, G. (1972) 'Objectivity as Strategic Ritual: An Examination of Newsmen's Notions of Objectivity', *American Journal of Sociology*, 77(4), pp. 660–679.

Weprin, A. (2014) *Buzzfeed Passes $100 M. in Revenue for 2014, POLITICO Media*. Available at: http://politi.co/21qgjEd (Accessed: 6 August 2020).

3
CHOOSING NEWS

Wherever we live in the world, there are certain incidents and occasions that we expect our news media to cover: major sporting events like the Olympics, natural disasters such as the 2004 Indian Ocean tsunami, epidemics and pandemics, from the 2014 to 2016 Ebola outbreak to Covid-19, will make national headlines whether you're in Tokyo, Maputo, Madrid or Buenos Aires. In an ideal world, the purpose of news is to inform us about significant occurrences that impact our lives. In order to be able to participate in the *public sphere* described in **Chapter 1**, we need to know about: what our government, military and police are up to, whether there is corruption within our public and private institutions, environmental issues like rivers being polluted and so on.

Issues that we need to know about because they're consequential for a large number of people, such as those related to politics, business or violence, are typically termed *hard news*, and this arena of storytelling is heavily researched. *Soft news*, meanwhile, refers to topics that we enjoy finding out about, like celebrity, arts, culture or sport, but tend to be considered less likely to significantly affect our lives. However, *soft news* is crucial in terms of transmitting cultural values, which are present in *hard news* but usually less overtly than in *soft news*. For instance, *soft news* coverage of Ellen DeGeneres coming out of the closet on her popular US sitcom *Ellen* in 1998 and *RuPaul's Drag Race* several decades later has arguably done as much as, if not more than, *hard news* reporting to shift opinion on LGBTQ+ lives in parts of the world (Curran and Hesmondhalgh, 2019).

Ideally then, we should have a healthy diet of *hard* and *soft* news, and journalists should be free to pursue information that's in the public interest, so everyone can enjoy living freely in societies where powerful people and institutions are held to account by a robust news media.

DOI: 10.4324/9781003037651-4

These ideals mean the decisions that editors and journalists make when deciding what events will and won't be reported matters because the news we receive shapes our understanding of ourselves and others and affects the choices we make and, therefore, how we live. How can we get rid of an incompetent government if the news about their actions isn't available? How can we make decisions about the best way to protect our health if we're not furnished with reliable information?

But, there are impediments to the idealised function of news, the most obvious being national political systems (see **Chapter 1**). Other impediments include the fact that news doesn't simply arrive, unfiltered, via whichever medium you consume it through. A huge amount of information we receive comes from just a few global news agencies (see **Chapter 12**), as well as public relations (PR) material generated by organisations with the resources to run a press office, meaning there is always potential for bias. This potential has been heightened by technological changes, which have sped up how quickly news is produced, made journalists increasingly desk-bound and impacted on the time they have to generate original stories. As a result, organisations outside the *journalistic field* (see **Chapter 2**) have more space to try and insert their agenda into the news production process (Davis, 2002; Cottle, 2003; Davies, 2008; Fenton, 2010; Douglas, 2019).

Choosing which aspects of reality to report is a complex process determined by editors' and journalists' subjectivity (does the event fit their cultural understanding of the world and, thus, what they deem important), as well as economic, cultural, political, technological and organisational factors, as noted in previous chapters. In short, news is a *social construct* informed by multiple variables, and media scholars (e.g. Galtung and Ruge, 1965; Harcup and O'Neill, 2017) have developed a variety of approaches to explain how news is selected.

This chapter will review the literature on news values, a term coined by Lippmann (1922) to describe aspects of an event that determine the likelihood of it becoming news. We address the way decisions have changed during the past few decades, and the role of editors, journalists and algorithms in making news choices (Marris and Thornham, 1996; Boczkowski and Mitchelstein, 2013).

Culture and subjectivity in news choices

In the previous chapter, we considered how the *habitus* of editors may impact on journalistic production contexts and content. We build on that discussion here by addressing subjectivity in news production, the related issue of newsroom diversity and the way this impacts story selection because news values are never culture free. In other words, the cultural background of journalists, as well as social norms, influences the news selection process, as does the ownership structure, working culture and rules of the organisation.

Bourdieu (see **Chapter 2**) used the term *doxa* to describe institutional rules and the way individuals must absorb them and adopt similar behaviour to those who established the rules in order to be accepted. But therein lies a conundrum: what if you don't subscribe to the rules because you find them culturally, ideologically and/or politically jarring? Bourdieu employed the notion of *habitus* (see **Chapter 2**) to explain the relationship between individuals and institutions, and the tensions that arise when someone's understanding of the world doesn't comply with that espoused by the institution where they work. Although *habitus* is subject to change, Bourdieu asserts that early experiences and practices influence those that follow (Benson and Neveu, 2005, p. 3).

Interestingly, Bourdieu's own life experiences clearly shaped key aspects of his scholarly work. Born to a working-class family in France, Bourdieu applied ideas like *habitus* to analyse the social class structure – including the marriage strategies of rural peasants and how marriage rules preserved the inheritance lineage of families, and thus the French class system. As such, he is often seen mostly as a theorist of class. However, this ignores the portability of his methods, which is why they're so useful, the important colonial and postcolonial influences on his work and the way the inequalities he observed within the colonial system informed his thinking (Puwar, 2009).

Bourdieu's first book, *The Algerians*, was based on fieldwork he did whilst teaching in Algeria in the 1950s during the war between France and the Algerian independence movement. Because of his experiences in Algeria, where he also did military service, many of his early ideas, including those on *habitus*, were informed by his thinking on colonialism, which he saw as a "racialised system of domination, backed by force, which restructures social relations and creates hybrid cultures" (Go, 2013, p. 49).

Such ideas correspond with the vital work by the Martinican psychiatrist, philosopher and anti-colonial activist, Frantz Fanon, who also worked in Algeria (in a hospital) during the struggle for independence. Fanon's work on identity and social psychology overlaps with Bourdieu's notion of *habitus*. Before Bourdieu, Fanon wrote about the violence embedded within the colonial apparatus (Fanon, 1991, 1994) and mapped the visceral effects of racism on one's being. As such, Bourdieu, "probably drew much from Fanon regarding the racial character of colonialism, the nature of violence, and colonialisms impact" (Go, 2013, p. 56).

These theories help us understand how decision-making is inevitably inflected by our own experiences and that includes decisions about what news is emphasised and what is ignored.

Fanon asserted that the sense of inferiority imposed on the colonised by the colonial system and its institutions and ideas of superiority constructed about the coloniser are so embedded that they persist in the postcolonial period. This view partly explains why, for example, some journalists working in post-Colonial settings may still take dominant western media as a guide for what is important to report on and/or what style of reporting to adopt. Fanon sees this as a sense of inferiority arising from colonial power which stripped people of their cultural identity by consistently delegitimising it and presenting western ideals as the only legitimate way of seeing and doing. For Fanon, such a strategy leads some to unconsciously identify with the oppressing culture and imitate "whiteness" (see also Allan, 1999). Fanon writes powerfully about the psychological conflict and inner turmoil that arises as a result for individuals mediating between "the colonial past and the postcolonial future" (Go, 2013, p. 62). We discuss how this might operate in practice, towards the end of this chapter.

Hybridity, a widely used concept in postcolonial theory, speaks to this tension too. Critical theorist Homi K. Bhabha describes how the conflict that arose when colonisers attempted to control colonial subjects (in part, by imposing a fixed, constructed identity on them which did not correlate with their sense of themselves or account for the ambivalent, fluid nature of all identities)[1] produce a *third space*. In this *third space*, the coloniser's constructed superiority is disrupted, and colonial and postcolonial power relations and norms are subverted via everyday cultural and political practices. Towards the end of this chapter, we also discuss how engaging in *third space resistance* is desired by some journalists working in some postcolonial settings. However, such resistance is not enacted because it is not institutionalised in those newsrooms via, for example, editorial guidelines regarding news choices, and guidance to avoid sourcing stories from western outlets that perpetuate stereotypical conceptions of the Global South (see Serwornoo, 2019).

What's important to understand here is how these concepts – *doxa*, *habitus*, *Fanonian social psychology*, *Bhabha's work on hybridity* – though distinct, also overlap as they highlight the interplay between individual agency and social structures. Therefore, their ideas can be used as tools to make sense of an array of social situations and institutional practices, and how individuals negotiate them. This includes, as we'll see, the way journalists engage with contemporary news selection practices where such norms may be reproduced.

News values and selection

News values form the basis of the rules, or *doxa*, within journalism because they inform the story selection process. They are a set of organisational routines and normative practices which journalists tend to follow in order to rationalise that what they report is "social fact" (Tuchman, 1978). News values are also the reason why, when events are constantly unfolding, only some will be chosen as news, and once selected, certain stories will be given more prominence than others (once you've read this chapter, do the "them" and "us" exercise in the box at the end of the chapter to consider why this may be).

Despite the existence of practices that inform news selection, when asked why some events are covered and others aren't, many journalists struggle to offer an explanation (Brighton and Foy, 2007; Harcup and O'Neill, 2017), often pointing to their "gut instinct" as a deciding factor.

Scholars have attempted to establish what influences journalists' news selection (Galtung and Ruge, 1965; Tuchman, 1978; Golding and Elliott, 1979; Staab, 1990; Harcup and O'Neill, 2001; Bednarek and Caple, 2014; Harcup and O'Neill, 2017). They have identified economic, social and cultural issues that shape choices, as well as organisational factors and journalistic routines like meeting deadlines and competing for exclusives (Phillips, 2015), PR (Cottle, 2003; Brighton and Foy, 2007), and advertising and ownership (Caple and Bednarek, 2015). News content and the researchers experience of journalism have also been analysed (Golding and Elliott, 1979; Harcup and O'Neill, 2001), and others have conducted ethnographic studies and interviewed journalists about how they select news (Schlesinger, 1978; Schultz, 2007).

One thing we do know is that news is not neutral, or necessarily fair (e.g. Dijk, 1991; Khiabany and Williamson, 2015), news values aren't objective criteria (Donsbach, 2004), and cultural background is a predictor of news value judgement and source selection (Jenkins, 2016; see **Chapter 6**). This is why, for example, stories relating to tragedies affecting white people are treated as more important in some newsrooms than those that affect people of colour.

For instance, on June 7, 2020, two women of colour, sisters Bibaa Henry and Nicole Smallman, were celebrating Bibaa's birthday with friends in a west London park. They were reported missing after calls from their family the following morning went unanswered. Tragically they were found dead, having been stabbed by a young man. Two police officers were also jailed following the horrific finding that they took and shared photos of Nicole and Bibaa's bodies. The sister's case received far less attention from mainstream British news media, the public and politicians, than that of Sarah Everard, a white woman who also went missing in London on March 3, 2021 while walking home. Sarah was tragically found dead, too. A police officer was arrested for her kidnap and murder.

Both are horrendous incidents, equally worthy of news attention, but the comparatively greater coverage UK news organisations dedicated to Sarah's case led Nicole and Bibaa's mother to say her, "daughters' deaths [were] not as urgent because of race" (BBC News, 2021).

This bias in news coverage stems from a range of issues, including systemic racism, as in the cases above, and the news organisation's agenda. The framework in which journalists work is always weighted in a particular direction, and news selection, is usually the product of the dominant culture. If journalists don't sit on the same side of the scales as their colleagues, due to their *habitus*, they are likely to feel conflicted doing their work. Journalists ability to make choices about what they report, and how they report it, depends not only on the event they're covering, where in the world and for what news organisation, but also on their social and/or cultural standing within the organisation.

How events become news

An early, influential European study by Galtung and Ruge set out to answer the question: "how do 'events' become 'news'?" (Galtung and Ruge, 1965, p. 65) by studying the structure of foreign news coverage in the Norwegian press. The scholars devised a list of 12 hypothesised news selection factors, 8 of which they asserted were *culture-free* and 4 *culture-bound*, and concluded that the greater the number of factors that could be applied to a story, the higher the chance of it being covered. The 8 *culture-free* factors are frequency (the time needed for an event to occur and acquire enough meaning to be reported), threshold (the size of the incident), unambiguity, meaningfulness, consonance (predictability), unexpectedness, continuity (the story is ongoing) and composition (good fit with other stories covered). The *culture-bound* factors are negativity, reference to elite nations and people and personalisation (meaning events can be linked to the actions of individuals). The latter two categories help explain why prominent public figures, from celebrities to politicians, often attract news coverage, even in relation to topics like their fashion choices.

The *culture-bound* factors were deemed to apply to the news selection criteria of journalists in the north-western world (western Europe, Canada, north America), and the *culture-free* factors were considered independent of cultural boundaries, thus universal. However, the distinction between *culture-bound* and *culture-free* is, in itself, bound up with cultural assumptions, and a division between the two is problematic because there will always be some cross over. For instance, coverage of a disaster depends not only on the size of the disaster ("threshold"), but also on the location (is it near or far from the country reporting on it), and the geo-political positioning of the place it occurs (reference to "elite" nations and people).

The war in and around the Democratic Republic of Congo, for example, killed 5 million people between 1997 and 2003 (Burke, 2018), making it one of the deadliest conflicts in the last few decades. Yet, western news media were mostly oblivious. During a similar period, large western news organisations devoted 50 times more coverage to conflict in Israel–Palestine, which led to around 7,000 deaths between 1987 and 2007 (Harvey, 2012). The so-called *culture-free* factor of "threshold" intersected with the *culture-bound* factor of "reference to elite nations" and both, coupled with the geo-political positioning of the countries involved, no doubt contributed to informing news coverage of these conflicts in dominant western news institutions.

Viewing news through different cultural lenses

Although Galtung and Ruge categorised "meaningfulness" and "unexpectedness" as *culture-free* news factors, the extent to which something is deemed meaningful is, as Stuart Hall observed, dependent on our "maps of meaning which we learn and unconsciously internalize as we become members of our culture" (Hall, 1997, p. 29). Our maps of meaning, as we discuss above, are shaped by our cultural experiences (*habitus*) but also by more prosaic questions such as our geographical location. For instance, the possibility of a dormant volcano erupting in St Vincent and the Grenadines was covered by local news organisations in the Caribbean, and those serving the diaspora, several months before the volcano erupted in April 2021. Early reporting was done because the possibility of an eruption was obviously meaningful for those from or near the region, and this incremental storytelling meant that when the eruption happened it wasn't unexpected for domestic and diasporic audiences. However, major international news organisations, like *The New York Times*, didn't run the story until the eruption occurred. The absence of prior coverage by dominant global news institutions meant the story fitted the "unexpected" category for these organisations when the volcano erupted.

Volcanic eruptions and other natural disasters, like floods and wildfires, occur all the time, all over the world, but whether or not they'll be covered by local, national and international news media is also dependent on proximity, a factor which Galtung and Ruge didn't account for. This is a surprising omission[2] given that Lippmann (1922) highlighted proximity as a news selection factor decades earlier. Proximity remains important and can be psychological (you feel close to an event because you have a connection with the people or the place affected by it), geographic (it's in the same country) and historical and political (there are close historical ties between the countries and/or political/national interests at stake meaning the event is of interest to domestic press, no matter how distant).

Exercise: Proximity and News Values

List any natural disasters, recent or historic, you recall being covered by the news media in your country. How did these disasters fit the "proximity" factor (psychologically, geographically, historically and politically) in relation to your country? Do you feel these disasters warranted more or less national news attention? If you feel they warranted more attention, how would you convince a news editor?

The framing of news stories is sometimes so culturally bound that the way the story is sold, via headlines, will make little sense to those who don't share "maps of meaning." Take, for example, the following headline from the *Times of India*: "World T20, Ashes loom for Australia after disappointing season" (Times of India, 2021). Anyone not from a cricket-playing nation, like Australia or India, would be forgiven for having no idea what this story is about, or assuming it may be an odd reference to a fire, or perhaps even a volcano. But cricket is a popular sport in India, and in many other former British colonies where, fan of the game or not, most would understand that "ashes" refers to a cricket trophy that Australia and England compete for. The casualness of the headline is dependent on cultural understanding. In this case, that understanding is rooted in colonial culture and the export of a quintessentially British sport throughout much of the Commonwealth, including India, which became so culturally embedded it created a common language.

Galtung and Ruge's binarised allocation of news factors beneath either a *culture-free* or *culture-bound* category is sometimes helpful. News conventions differ in different regions. For instance, both Golding and Elliot (in Marris and Thornham, 1996, p. 405) and Galtung and Ruge (ibid) identify negativity in reporting as a *culture-bound* news factor, rather than a universal news value (Golding and Elliott, 1979, p. 409).

Chinese news media, for example, which is largely owned by the state and used as a propaganda tool by the ruling Communist Party of China, issues "specific guidelines for the media on what to report, how to report, and what to avoid" (Zhang et al., 2006, p. 141). It emphasises "peace and prosperity" (Zhang et al., ibid, p. 141) and avoids "negativity." State control and an emphasis on positive news meant, for example, that the reporting of the death of Doctor Wenliang Li from Covid-19 in February 2020 proved problematic for the Chinese government. Dr Li was censured for trying to warn colleagues about the outbreak and investigated by the police for "spreading rumours" (Tan, 2020). His death sparked demands for freedom of speech on the Chinese social media platform Weibo before the posts were deleted by Chinese authorities.

A study (García-Perdomo et al., 2018) exploring which news values are present in news stories shared on social media by audiences in Brazil, Argentina and the United States also focuses on the question of the extent to which news values are universal, or mostly country specific. The researchers are interested in an issue which has become increasingly urgent for newsrooms around the world: the shareability of content and the role audiences play in that process. The scholars find, at least in relation to the north and south American democracies studied, that human interest, conflict and controversy are the news values most likely to prompt audiences to share stories on Twitter and Facebook. However, whilst there are commonalities vis-à-vis which news values are present in stories audiences share most, the news organisations in each country emphasise different values: timeliness in Argentina, conflict/controversy and impact/prominence in Brazil and US news organisations sit between the two, with the most frequent values there being timeliness and conflict/controversy.

Despite its flaws, the Galtung & Ruge study remains a useful springboard for thinking about which news values are shared and which are nation and/or culture specific. As a result, research has been conducted to see how much of their findings remain today (Harcup and O'Neill, 2017). But journalism is such a complex, fast changing global industry, particularly due to technological changes, that no study can be conclusive or account for approaches to news selection in every country. We now consider how technological tides have swept in over the last few decades and re-shaped the landscape from which news is harvested.

The audience, algorithms and news choices

Digitisation, particularly the personalisation of news (see **Chapter 7**), has triggered a wave of studies on how the internet, social media and algorithms (e.g. Cornia et al., 2018; Elvestad and Phillips, 2018) are reorganising editorial priorities and leading to content decision-making not simply being down to editors.

For example, studies find that Facebook drives the bulk of traffic to news media sites (Newman, 2012; Cornia et al., 2018). Because traffic, or "clicks," generate revenue (see **Chapters 7 and 8**), journalists' news selection choices can be, among other aforementioned factors, influenced by the number of clicks a story generates, or is thought likely to generate. Therefore, both technology and audiences[3] are important in the news selection process: audiences due to their role in sharing news via social media, and technology because of the way it enables journalists to monitor and predict how stories will perform, sometimes using the information generated to make decisions about what to report. Cost-cutting in many newsrooms and the pressure to produce content quickly means the reverse is also true: social media posts, particularly from Twitter, are now part of news stories, or form the stories themselves.

Not only does technology feedback to journalists, so they instantly know which of their stories is being engaged with most, in some instances technology is replacing journalists and being used to curate news. Known as automated, or "robo" journalism, it involves software converting data into stories with little requirement for "human intervention beyond initial programming" (Thurman, 2017). Such software has already been used by the Associated Press to write business stories, and in May 2020, Microsoft sacked many journalists who work on the organisation's MSN website and its Edge browser, and replaced them with artificial intelligence (AI) software designed to select and edit news articles on Microsoft's homepages. Although the journalists who worked on the news homepages on Microsoft's MSN site did not generate original content, instead selecting stories produced by legacy news organisations like *The Guardian*, journalists were responsible for critical aspects of news production, including avoiding stories from untrustworthy sources (Waterson, 2020).

Whilst there are cost-saving benefits to organisations using AI to curate news, the extent to which technology can replicate the skills of journalists, including the judgement required for news selection, is questionable (Thurman, 2017) if not impossible. Furthermore, Elvestad and Phillips (2018) highlight how when news is accessed by audiences online, journalists and editors may have worked hard to select a variety of stories to cover, but problematically algorithms will:

> Cut out information considered less interesting to that particular individual and prioritise (by pushing them higher up the news feed) stories that are likely to be considered important. This has the effect of narrowing news choices for those who are more interested and filtering out news stories for those who are less interested.
>
> *(Elvestad and Phillips, 2018, p. 28)*

As Caple and Bednarek (2015, p. 445) assert, digitisation has also led to news discourse becoming a more visual product. Images have long played a key role in the way stories are told because they can shape how issues are thought about and acted upon by publics and governments. Anyone who has watched the Netflix series, *The Crown*, or is old enough to remember the 1980s AIDS crisis and the stigma surrounding the illness, will be familiar with the moments Princess Diana was photographed visiting HIV/AIDS wards and hugging and shaking hands with patients. The first images of her doing so were taken in London's Middlesex Hospital in 1987. The story made international headlines and the image of her shaking hands, without gloves, with a man who had the illness is credited with contributing to changing attitudes to the virus which, until that point, had received little research or public education.

Despite the power of photography to change hearts and minds, Caple and Bednarek (2013, 2015) highlight a lack of academic research exploring the relationship between news values and press photography[4] which, in conjunction with design, can emphasise certain values such as "negativity" and "personalisation." They map how specific news values, which are usually just associated with choices made when journalists select and/or edit stories, can also be detected *within* the images chosen to illustrate news. In order to analyse news values within images, Caple and Bednarek use a discursive approach, meaning they're interested in every component marshalled to construct a story (language, typography, layout, photography, etc.), but images are their focus because, "little research has specifically addressed the resources and practices that are used for constructing news values discursively, especially those that are non-linguistic" (Caple and Bednarek, 2015, p. 441). For them, the visual aspect of news is as revealing of what stories will and won't be covered, as any other. Image choice is also revealing of who news organisations imagine their audience to be.

> **Exercise: Images and News Values**
>
> Think of one or two divisive events that the news media in your country, or elsewhere, has covered. For example, elections or politicians leaving office are one of the most obvious ways the press tend to differ in terms of how they present topics by, amongst other things, selecting images which flatter the politician or party they feel their audience supports, and belittle politicians they believe their audience oppose. This may be done subtly or overtly. Once you've decided on a divisive event, have a look at the image choices made by different press outlets. How do the images differ and what does this say about who these news organisations imagine their audience to be?

Audiences

A news brand's identity is partly shaped by implicit assumptions about who the audience is (see Chapter 7). These assumptions inform news values and, therefore, the types of stories news organisations cover and, as highlighted above, how they present them (Golding and Elliott, 1979; Caple and Bednarek, 2013, 2015). Magazines and newspapers build audiences through understanding what they want and also what advertisers want (see **Chapter 8**). For example, a magazine that's aimed at mothers of babies is unlikely to carry articles about football matches, and a newspaper that aims for an audience of highly paid professionals is likely to feature more in-depth stories than a tabloid that people read during their tea break. Successful media have to be good at understanding their audience and creating a sense of connection.

The assumptions made about audience often build on a sense of "us" and "them" which is deliberately created to build brand loyalty. However, the assumptions made may also be based on prejudice, and/or a very narrow view of "what works", and may in reality be exclusionary. For example, in a study on how western correspondents reporting on east and southern Africa view their audience, Nothias (2017) found such journalists think of their audience as white, and this perception fuels racially stereotypical reporting. The "relevance"[5] (Harcup and O'Neill, 2017) criteria that contribute to news selection are racialised in such instances, because African stories that feature white people are perceived to be more likely to resonate with a western audience. As one western correspondent said in relation to coverage of the 2013 Westgate attack in Nairobi, when 67 people were killed, including 4 British citizens, and 175 injured:

> The images of the little white girl running alone in the mall had an impact.
> *(Nothias, 2017, p. 75)*

Such perceptions contribute to the racist colonial/imperial rooted view that white western lives are more valuable (see also Mbembe, 2003 and **Chapter 5**), and therefore more deserving of news attention, than Black lives, or the lives of other global majority people who are racially marginalised in certain contexts.[6] The view of audiences as white also points to hypocrisy within some western news organisations that brand themselves global. They are clearly not truly inclusive of international audiences if people of colour are metaphorically erased as being significant to, or a significant part of, the audience. Nor are they truly inclusive of Black and other racially marginalised publics in the Global North who form part of western audiences.

However, Nothias's study also found that social media are making foreign correspondents and news organisations more accountable to people who live in the countries they report on. Local responses to racially stereotypical coverage of African news events, for instance, contribute to sometimes re-shaping the narrative. For example, in 2015, many Kenyans took to Twitter to post under the hashtag #SomeoneTellCNN after the American news network described the country as a "hotbed of terror" in a story ahead of Barack Obama's visit to Kenya during his presidency.

The social media outcry highlighted the fact that, while Kenya has suffered attacks by the Somalia-based al-Shabab militant group, in the same way a number of western countries have suffered terrorist attacks over the years, terrorism is far less likely to occur in Kenya than in many other parts of the world, and Kenya is largely peaceful. This social media-enabled audience response prompted CNN to remove the story and send one of their senior executives to Nairobi to apologise, which in itself was covered as a story by international news organisations.

As well as social media platforms providing a channel for audiences to air their dislike or approval of news choices which, as with #SomeoneTellCNN, can lead to incorrect coverage being amended and/or the subversion of stereotypical reporting, new media tools like analytics should in theory help broaden perceptions of audiences. This is because news organisations that previously relied on vague measures like focus groups or the gut instincts of journalists (Carlson, 2017) are now able to track who is engaging with content. These tools open the possibility of disrupting perceptions that Kenyan audiences,[7] say, are not active and significant viewers and readers of news produced by American organisations like CNN, alongside their national and regional news media.

Such acknowledgement is ethically and economically important given that global audiences for major western news organisations are in the hundreds of millions. For instance, although most people around the world primarily get their news from national outlets, including in Kenya, Nigeria and India, these countries are the BBC's biggest *international* markets (BBC, 2020), and in 2016, the BBC World Service announced the launch of 11 new language services to maintain and expand its reach (BBC, 2016, see **Chapter 12**).

From assumptions to algorithms

Social media are now so important to the news selection process, that news organisations have created jobs like engagement editor and social media editor who mediate between the audience data they gather and journalists in the newsroom, meaning they play an important gatekeeping role as journalists increasingly negotiate between their instincts and metrics to make decisions regarding news selection (Carlson, 2018).

Though potentially constraining for journalists and problematic on other levels (see below and **Chapter 7**), metrics can affect positive change when utilised to push the parameters of who the audience is deemed to be, and thus story selection. For example, when the *Financial Times* (*FT*) hired their first-ever head of audience engagement, Renée Kaplan, several years ago (Hazard Owen, 2018), she worked with a data team and established that 80 percent of the newspapers subscribers were men. This prompted a decision to try and attract more female subscribers by monitoring what content they were engaging with on the newspaper's website and making that information available to the newsroom to encourage editors to commission more on items that performed well with women readers.

This doesn't mean the *FT* suddenly adopted a feminist "standpoint" (Harding, 1998; Hill Collins, 2000) in terms of their news selection practices, but this metrics-informed editorial shift does speak to the intensely competitive nature of news production and the fact that roughly 50 percent of the world's population is women, so producing content they may find appealing makes good business sense. It's also arguably no coincidence that the person who instigated the gendered analysis of the *FT*'s audience is a woman, so conceivably she spotted a gap in content that may not have been visible or compelling to male journalists at the newspaper.

However, as noted, there's a problematic side to journalists and editors using audience analytics to inform editorial decision-making. Whilst it holds the potential to broaden coverage and attract previously marginalised readers, the need to get clicks can lead to an overemphasis on what's popular, rather than what's in the public interest. Consideration of "what works best on Facebook" (Bell 2015 in Harcup and O'Neill, 2017, p.1475; Elvestad and Phillips, 2018) has become important for news organisations in the business of trying to drive traffic to their sites. The "what works best on Facebook" strategy, as Phillips (2012, p. 675) observes, has serious implications regarding content: "Most of the stories that attract large numbers of hits are also the jokey stories that people pass on."

Furthermore, Mare and Moyo (2019), who researched the use of online analytics in Kenyan, Zimbabwean and South African newsrooms, assert that using data to inform news choices can trigger a cascade of misinformation whereby stories are manipulated for business purposes by, for instance, inserting headlines that don't match the content of the story but are purely designed to trigger clicks. Known as *clickbait*, this misleading practice, they assert, contributes to the spread of "fake news, misinformation […], as well as the growth of sensational blogs" (Mare and Moyo, 2019, no page) and is becoming widespread in east and southern Africa, just as it is in many other parts of the world.

Despite commercial pressures that foster click-based journalism, journalists are not simply selecting news to satisfy social media shareability. In their research on what online news sites in seven countries in south and north America and western Europe publish, and what readers click and share, Boczkowski and Mitchelstein (2013) found what they term an "information gap." This speaks to how their findings, which are also shown in other studies (Wendelin, Engelmann and Neubarth, 2017), reveal a gap between the preferences of journalists and audiences, with audiences displaying a preference for news about sport, crime, entertainment and weather and the news sites analysed, like *The Guardian* and *USA Today*, dedicating a significant proportion of top stories to economics, international relations and politics.

The age-old journalism dilemma regarding whether audiences should be given what they want, or what editors and journalists think they need, is central here, and it is a serious concern in the digital age when audiences can simply click "to get the news we want and ignore the rest" (Boczkowski and Mitchelstein, 2013, p. 3). The researchers describe this as a tension between "what is interesting and what is important" (2013), highlighting their normative view of the press in democracies: that the news media have a public service duty to inform citizens, so they are equipped with the knowledge necessary to participate in civic deliberation. However, this duty to act as watchdog in democratic countries and inform publics fairly is complicated by issues of newsroom diversity and inclusivity, which we now address.

Newsroom diversity, journalistic subjectivity and news choices

As previously highlighted, journalists have a responsibility to hold power to account and represent citizens across the democratic spectrum so everyone's involvement in democracies is encouraged and supported by mainstream news. In order for news to be a broad, accurate reflection of society, editors and journalists need to be representative of the wider population. However, liberal democracies have never been fully inclusive and the ability to speak and be heard by those in positions of power has long been tied to one's class, ethnicity, sexuality, religion, gender or whether someone is disabled.

Ongoing socio-political and economic disparities in western democracies, where most major global news organisations are based, are also found in western newsrooms where the majority of journalists are white men (French, 2016; Thurman, Cornia and Kunert, 2016; Women's Media Centre, 2019). As such, news choices, which are often made through a narrow prism of subjective experience, are unreflective of the demographic makeup of the nation(s) covered (Byrne, 2019). Newsrooms will struggle to cover major global social movements, like #MeToo and #BlackLivesMatter, if the majority of those occupying top editorial positions have different experiences to those directly affected by the issues at hand.

As noted in **Chapter 2**, activists have long campaigned for more diverse and inclusive mainstream news media in western societies as well as globally where concern about the dominance of north American and western European news organisations led to the UNESCO New World Information Order (NWIO) 1970s debates (MacBride, 1980, see **Chapter 12**). The literature on diversity within news organisations in democracies spans decades and addresses a range of issues including the vital role of Indigenous people in shaping news coverage in Australia (e.g. Nolan *et al.*, 2020), journalists' gender (e.g. Beam and Di Cicco, 2010), race (e.g. Campbell, 2016; Douglas, 2019), caste in India (e.g. Balasubramaniam, 2011) as well as, crucially, why media diversity initiatives endlessly replicate existing power dynamics rather than diversifying media institutions in meaningful, *sustainable* ways (Gray, 2016; Saha, 2017; Douglas, 2021).

While not all research supports the idea that journalists' subjectivity matters in the production of news, much does. For instance, in their international study looking at women's status in newsrooms and their representation in news content, Byerly and McGraw (2020) find a correlation between the presence of women reporters in news organisations and the inclusion of women as subjects of news stories. Their findings provide:

> Additional evidence that supports the claim that women's numbers in the newsroom matter to news content about women. The former Soviet states

of Bulgaria, Romania, and Estonia are among the nations with both significant numbers of women in senior reporting ranks, as well as the largest amount of news content about women.

(Byerly and McGraw, 2020, p. 218)

Whilst women journalists are employed in significant numbers and also outnumber men in some countries, including Finland and Brazil, more recent research (Robertson, Selva and Nielsen, 2021) on women in news leadership across four continents finds that the majority of top editors are men, with the exception of South Africa where 62 percent of journalists and 60 percent of top editors are women. In contrast, no major news outlet in Japan has a woman as their top editor. The researchers find no link between gender equality in society and women in senior editorial positions, but the findings do show a positive correlation between the number of women editors and the percentage of women working as journalists in some countries.

We cannot assume that content which features more women portrays them in non-stereotypical ways. Content analysis is required to establish whether having more women journalists and editors in these countries not only alters the journalism produced, but the *way* women are represented. However, the greater the range of people free to communicate, the more varied the conversations, perspectives and ideas are likely to be. News choices that adequately and fairly represent society stand a better chance of occurring in newsrooms that aren't dominated by one gender or group, and in which all are empowered to produce content reflective of lives that are marginalised in dominant discourse and institutions (see Saha, 2017; Douglas, 2021).

When it comes to race, Jenkins (Campbell and Jenkins, 2016) discusses coverage of police brutality and murders of unarmed African-Americans to illustrate how racialised subjectivity impacts on the news choices of Black and white journalists. One example was that of the fatal shooting of Trayvon Martin in 2012, who went out to buy sweets and was shot by a neighbourhood watchman. The historical tendency to view whiteness as universal and, thus, invisible means that white journalists often fail to see race as a factor that influences their reporting. In the case of Martin, some reporting by mainstream US news media implied that the teenagers' clothing (he was wearing a hoodie) somehow contributed to his death. The hoodie, a garment associated with racist stereotypes about black criminality in America and other parts of the world, has since been used as a symbol of defiance by racial justice campaigners.[8]

Symbols, like the hoodie, are powerful because they are loaded with meaning which comes from culture, and, as noted earlier, our cultural understanding of the world informs our "maps of meaning" (Hall, 1997), and therefore, how we interpret events. So, if a journalists' "understanding" of Black men, or any racialised group, has been learned in limited ways, via racially stereotypical representations, rather than in nuanced and limitless ways perhaps through familial or friendship ties or because they identify as belonging to that group of people, this may lead that journalist to perpetuate, rather than question and contest, stereotypes.

Likewise, if journalists don't have lived experience of forms of discrimination, such as ableism, homophobia, sexism and Islamophobia, they may miss problematic aspects of coverage that those who do have lived experience may spot. In her research on the racialisation of mainstream UK news coverage of sub-Saharan Africa, Douglas (2019) found that Black journalists frequently sought to contest racially stereotypical reporting that some white colleagues were oblivious to. One commercial television reporter threatened to resign over what they considered to be racist framing of a news story about female genital mutilation in an African country. The reporter explained that it was only *them*, the sole Black journalist in the newsroom, who took issue with insensitive, objectifying footage in the story which showed a Black girl being cut:

> It was, 'let's go in and see what these barbaric people are doing, oh fuck they're cutting a child – zoom in on that'. I had a completely different perspective on it to everyone else. The whole idea of me having African heritage and trying to reclaim the narrative is […] antithetical to my colleague's existence. When I complained about the piece it put me in a really bad place with my boss.
>
> *(Douglas, 2019, p. 102)*

The above examples illustrate the ways in which aspects of journalists' identity, or subjectivity, may inform news choices and framing. Subjectivity is also found to be an influencing factor in the emerging field of data journalism (Tong and Zuo, 2021). However, it's important to remember that our identities are not singular, but complex, fluid and intersectional (Crenshaw, 1989; Shohat and Stam, 1994). So, you may be empowered on one level (say gender) but disempowered on another (say class), and belonging to a marginalised or dominant group does not mean you cannot step outside your experience and do the work necessary to develop understanding of different experiences. Nor is belonging to particular socially constructed categories, along the lines of class, gender, race, nation and so on, any guarantee of outlook and/or story selection, as we now discuss.

Western news values in non-western contexts

We made the point earlier that news values are never culture free. Due to human migration, which has been a feature of our world since time immemorial, as well as histories of colonialism, imperialism and the more recent phenomenon of globalisation, culture does not stop at borders but flows back and forth, especially between countries with deep historical ties. Ideological discourse, which Hall (1973) argues news values are part of, is a major current in this flow and served the relationship of power and domination the west had over its colonies. The legacy of imposition, though vigorously resisted, continues to this day.

In his study of news values influencing representations of Africa in the Ghanaian press, Serwornoo (2019) finds that global news organisations from north America and Europe, particularly the BBC, influence the foreign news selection of Ghanaian journalists. Practical issues, such as access to resources which leads to the dominance of certain news sources, contribute to this. But what's interesting is what Serwornoo's study reveals about the psychology of news choices amongst the journalists interviewed, and the way colonial legacies inform cognitive news values.

Drawing on the work of Fanon and Bhabha, which we highlighted earlier, Serwornoo suggests that some journalists in the Global South may absorb imperialist stereotypes due to the way racism works at the psychic realm to produce internalised oppression within racialised subjects. This, Serwornoo asserts, can, sometimes, lead people to view themselves as inferior and "accept their subjected position as being the natural order of things" (Serwornoo, 2019, p. 1361). Serwornoo argues that these dynamics continue to manifest in Ghana, where western approaches to journalism, such as the news values that inform story selection, are seen by some as the professional gold standard even though journalists interviewed for the study believe that foreign news coverage of Africa often conforms to negative stereotypes.

Serwornoo utilises Bhabha's concept of *hybridity* to illuminate the possibility of resistance to postcolonial power dynamics. But, Serwornoo finds that whilst ideas of resistance are present among Ghanaian journalists, *third space* resistance is not enacted because it is not institutionalised. For example, editorial guidelines do not stipulate journalists must avoid repeating stereotypical tropes found in western news.

What's at play here is the tension between *doxa* and *habitus* (or subjectivity), as described in **Chapter 2** and addressed at the beginning of this chapter. No journalist, no matter where they're from or what their social positioning, stands outside of this tension, some may just feel it less than others. But no matter the degree to which such tension may or may not be felt, it's imperative for all journalists to take a step back, if only for a blurry moment, and consider how their subjectivity impacts on their story selection, which in itself is always contingent upon cultural, psychological, social, political, historical and organisational variables.

Journalists must also reflect on how their subjectivity positions them in relation to the subject(s) of their storytelling. This is vital because a large part of a journalist's job is to represent *"others"* (see **Chapter 5**). In order to do that fairly and accurately, it's important to acknowledge that news value judgements are never neutral; therefore, journalists must question their "gut instincts," make an effort to stand outside their experiences and attempt to disrupt normative news values (or pass a story to another journalist) if doing so will be more productive of fair, accurate reporting.

Exercise: "Them" and "Us"[9] as a News Value?

On November 13, 2015, an Islamic State terrorist attack in Paris left 130 people dead and hundreds wounded. The incident gained more western news coverage than terrorist attacks in Beirut the previous day, when 44 people were killed and many injured, attacks in Turkey a month before on October 10, when Isis attacked a peace march in Ankara, killing 102 people and injuring 400, and the shooting at Garissa University in Kenya when 147 people were killed by al-Shabab militants in April 2015 (Hanusch, 2015).

List the news values you think applied to these stories and consider why one received more western news attention. Which event received the most coverage in your national news media? Do you think journalists should report such atrocities equally, no matter where they occur? Why/why not? What ideas would you draw on from this chapter and elsewhere in the book to support your point?

Summary

- The news choices journalists make matter because information we receive about events helps shape our understanding of ourselves and others, and informs the decisions we make.
- News values are never culture-free and news selection is influenced by a range of factors, from politics and economics, to organisational issues and journalistic subjectivity.
- The internet, social media and algorithms play an important role in news selection, as do audiences.
- A lack of newsroom diversity is likely to lead to narrow news choices and getting the news wrong.
- Problematic norms, such as colonial ideas which constructed the Global North (and whiteness) as superior to the Global South (and Blackness and brownness) and centred the former in relation to the latter, continue to shape story selection in some newsrooms.

Notes

1 It's important to note that Bhabha's analysis of relations between coloniser and colonised emphasise how the identity formation of both is interconnected, ambivalent and fluid and *all* cultural identity emerges from a space of ambivalence and contradiction, not just that of the colonised.
2 However, it's important to note that they never claimed their list was 'complete'.

3 Audience demographics or assumptions about readership/audience have always informed journalists' story selection, but the ability of audiences to respond to stories instantly has altered the journalist-audience dynamic.
4 However, Golding and Elliot (Golding and Elliott, 1979) added visual elements as necessary selection criteria for TV news.
5 Relevance is defined by Harcup and O'Neill (2017) as stories that relate to individuals, nations or groups considered to be influential or culturally or historically familiar to the audience.
6 Assumptions about audiences also leads to gendered and classed news coverage, as well as reporting that is not inclusive of other marginalised groups.
7 The main international news providers in Kenya are CNN, Al-Jazeera and the BBC, but they're mostly consumed by the socio-economic and educational elite (Geniets, 2011).
8 https://www.56blackmen.com/
9 "Us" refers to a perceived common identity in opposition to one viewed as different, "them".

References

Allan, S. (1999) *News Culture*. Reprinted. Buckingham: Open University Press (Issues in cultural and media studies).
Balasubramaniam, J. (2011) 'Dalits and a Lack of Diversity in the Newsroom', *Economic and Political Weekly*, 46(11), pp. 21–23.
BBC (2016) 'BBC World Service Announces Biggest Expansion "since the 1940s"', *BBC News*, 16 November. Available at: https://www.bbc.com/news/entertainment-arts-37990220 (Accessed: 26 April 2021).
BBC (2020) 'BBC News Reaching Highest Ever Global Audience', *BBC News*, 23 July. Available at: https://www.bbc.com/news/world-53517025 (Accessed: 15 April 2021).
BBC (2021) 'My Daughter's Deaths Not As Urgent Because of Race', BBC News, 26 March. Available at: https://www.bbc.co.uk/news/av/uk-56532215 (Accessed: 16 August 2022).
Beam, R.A. and Di Cicco, D.T. (2010) 'When Women Run the Newsroom: Management Change, Gender, and the News', *Journalism & Mass Communication Quarterly*, 87(2), pp. 393–411. doi:10.1177/107769901008700211.
Bednarek, M. and Caple, H. (2014) 'Why Do News Values Matter? Towards a New Methodological Framework for Analysing News Discourse in Critical Discourse Analysis and Beyond', *Discourse & Society*, 25(2), pp. 135–158. doi:10.1177/0957926513516041.
Benson, R.D. and Neveu, E. (eds) (2005) *Bourdieu and the Journalistic Field*. Cambridge; Malden, MA: Polity.
Boczkowski, P.J. and Mitchelstein, E. (2013) *The News Gap: When the Information Preferences of the Media and the Public Diverge*. Cambridge, MA: MIT Press. Available at: https://mitpress.mit.edu/books/news-gap (Accessed: 29 June 2020).
Brighton, P. and Foy, D. (2007) *News Values*. 1st edition. London ; Thousand Oaks, CA: SAGE Publications Ltd.
Burke, J. (2018) 'The Wars Will Never Stop - Millions Flee Bloodshed as Congo Falls Apart', *The Guardian*. Available at: http://www.theguardian.com/world/2018/apr/03/millions-flee-bloodshed-as-congos-army-steps-up-fight-with-rebels-in-east (Accessed: 15 April 2021).
Byerly, C.M. and McGraw, K.A. (2020) *Comparing Gender and Media Equality across the Globe: A Cross-National Study of the Qualities, Causes, and Consequences of Gender*

Equality in and through the News Media. Gothenburg: Nordicom, University of Gothenburg, 191–232. Edited by M. Djerf-Pierre and M. Edström, p. 342.

Byrne, D. (2019) 'If Your Newsroom Is Not Diverse, You Will Get the News Wrong', *Reuters Institute for the Study of Journalism*. Available at: https://reutersinstitute.politics.ox.ac.uk/risj-review/if-your-newsroom-not-diverse-you-will-get-news-wrong (Accessed: 29 June 2020).

Campbell, C. and Jenkins, C.D. (2016) *The Routledge Companion to Media and Race*. 1st edition. London; New York : Routledge, Taylor & Francis Group: Routledge. doi:10.4324/9781315778228.

Caple, H. and Bednarek, M. (2013) 'Delving into the Discourse: Approaches to News Values in Journalism Studies and Beyond', *Reuters Institute for the Study of Journalism, University of Oxford*, p. 29.

Caple, H. and Bednarek, M. (2015) 'Rethinking News Values: What a Discursive Approach Can Tell Us about the Construction of News Discourse and News Photography', *Journalism* [Preprint]. doi:10.1177/1464884914568078.

Carlson, M. (2017) *Journalistic Authority: Legitimating News... - Google Scholar*. Available at: https://scholar.google.com/scholar_lookup?hl=en&publication_year=2017&author=M+Carlson&title=Journalistic+Authority%3A+Legitimating+News+in+the+Digital+Era (Accessed: 17 June 2020).

Carlson, M. (2018) 'Confronting Measurable Journalism', *Digital Journalism*, 6(4), pp. 406–417. doi:10.1080/21670811.2018.1445003.

Cornia, A. *et al.* (2018) 'Private Sector News, Social Media Distribution, and Algorithm Change', Oxford: Reuters Institute for the Study of Journalism. p. 43. https://reutersinstitute.politics.ox.ac.uk/sites/default/files/2018-10/Cornia_Private_Sector_News_FINAL.pdf.

Cottle, S. (2003) *News, Public Relations and Power*. London. doi:10.4135/9781446221594.

Crenshaw, K. (1989) 'Demarginalizing the Intersection of Race and Sex: A Black Feminist Critique of Antidiscrimination Doctrine, Feminist Theory and Antiracist Politics', *The University of Chicago Legal Forum*, 140, pp. 139–167.

Curran, J. and Hesmondhalgh, D. (eds) (2019) *Media and Society*. 6th edition. New York: Bloomsbury Academic USA.

Davies, N. (2008) *Flat Earth News: An Award-Winning Reporter Exposes Falsehood, Distortion and Propaganda in the Global Media*. Paperback – 1 January 2009 edition. London: Vintage.

Davis, A. (2002) *Public Relations Democracy: Public Relations, Politics, and the Mass Media in Britain*. Manchester; New York: Manchester University Press ; Distributed exclusively in the USA by Palgrave.

Dijk, T.A. van (1991) *Racism and the Press*. London; New York: Routledge (Critical studies in racism and migration).

Donsbach, W. (2004) *Psychology of News Decisions: Factors Behind Journalists' Professional Behavior - Wolfgang Donsbach, 2004*. Available at: https://journals.sagepub.com/doi/10.1177/146488490452002 (Accessed: 29 June 2020).

Douglas, O. (2019) *Backstories / Black Stories: Black Journalists, INGOs and the Racial Politics of Representing Sub-Saharan Africa in Mainstream UK News Media*. Doctoral. Goldsmiths, University of London. Available at: http://research.gold.ac.uk/26352/ (Accessed: 29 June 2020).

Douglas, O. (2021) 'The Media Diversity and Inclusion Paradox: Experiences of Black and Brown Journalists in Mainstream British News Institutions', *Journalism*, p. 14648849211001778. doi:10.1177/14648849211001778.

Elvestad, E. and Phillips, A. (2018) *Misunderstanding News Audiences : Seven Myths of the Social Media Era*. Routledge. doi:10.4324/9781315444369.

Fanon, F. (1991) *Black Skin, White Masks*. New Ed edition. London: Pluto Press.

Fanon, F. (1994) *A Dying Colonialism*. Translated by H. Chevalier. New York: Grove Press.

February 21 and Women's Media Centre (2019) *The Status of Women in U.S. Media 2019-Women's Media Center*. Available at: https://womensmediacenter.com/reports/the-status-of-women-in-u-s-media-2019 (Accessed: 1 July 2020).

Fenton, N. (ed.) (2010) *New Media, Old News: Journalism and Democracy in the Digital Age*. London: SAGE.

French, H.W. (2016) 'The Enduring Whiteness of the American media | Howard French', *The Guardian*, 25 May. Available at: https://www.theguardian.com/world/2016/may/25/enduring-whiteness-of-american-journalism (Accessed: 29 June 2020).

Galtung, J. and Ruge, M.H. (1965) 'The Structure of Foreign News: The Presentation of the Congo, Cuba and Cyprus Crises in Four Norwegian Newspapers', *Journal of Peace Research*, 2(1), pp. 64–90. doi:10.1177/002234336500200104.

García-Perdomo, V. et al. (2018) 'To Share or Not to Share', *Journalism Studies*, 19(8), pp. 1180–1201. doi:10.1080/1461670X.2016.1265896.

Geniets, A. (2011) 'Trust In International News Media in Partially Free Media Environments. A Case Study of Five Markets in Africa and South Asia', *Reuters Institute for the Study of Journalism, University of Oxford*, February 2011, p. 92.

Go, J. (2013) 'Decolonizing Bourdieu: Colonial and Postcolonial Theory in Pierre Bourdieu's Early Work', *Sociological Theory*, 31(1), pp. 49–74. doi:10.1177/0735275113477082.

Golding, P. and Elliott, P.R.C. (1979) *Making the News*. 1st edition. London; New York: Longman.

Gray, H. (2016) 'Precarious Diversity: Representation and Demography', in Curtin, M. and Sanson, K. (eds.) *Precarious Creativity: Global Media, Local Labor*. Oakland: University of California Press. pp. 241–253. https://www.ucpress.edu/book/9780520290853/precarious-creativity

Hall, S. (1973) 'The Determinations of News Photographs (1973)', in Greer, C. (ed.) *Crime and Media*. 1st edition. Routledge, pp. 123–134. doi:10.4324/9780367809195-13.

Hall, S. (1997) 'The Work of Representation', in Stuart, H., Jessica, E., and Sean, N. (eds.) *Representation: Cultural Representation and Signifying Practices*. The Open University, p. 47.

Hanusch, F. (2015) 'Disproportionate Coverage of Paris Attacks Is Not Just the Media's Fault', *The Conversation*. Available at: http://theconversation.com/disproportionate-coverage-of-paris-attacks-is-not-just-the-medias-fault-50761 (Accessed: 30 June 2020).

Harcup, T. and O'Neill, D. (2001) 'What Is News? Galtung and Ruge Revisited', *Journalism Studies*, 2(2), pp. 261–280. doi:10.1080/14616700118449.

Harcup, T. and O'Neill, D. (2017) 'What Is News?: News Values Revisited (Again)', *Journalism Studies*, 18(12), pp. 1470–1488. doi:10.1080/1461670X.2016.1150193.

Harding, S.G. (1998) *Is Science Multicultural? Postcolonialisms, Feminisms, and Epistemologies*. Bloomington: Indiana University Press (Race, gender, and science).

Harvey, N. (2012) 'Why Do Some Conflicts Get More Media Coverage Than Others?', *New Internationalist*. Available at: https://newint.org/features/2012/09/01/media-war-coverage (Accessed: 15 April 2021).

Hazard Owen, L. (2018) '"If the Financial Times Were a Person, It Would Be a Man." Here's How the Paper Is Trying to Change That.', *Nieman Lab*. Available at: https://www.niemanlab.org/2018/04/if-the-financial-times-were-a-person-it-would-be-a-man-heres-how-the-paper-is-trying-to-change-that/ (Accessed: 17 June 2020).

Hill Collins, P. (2000) *Black Feminist Thought: Knowledge, Consciousness, and the Politics of Empowerment*. 2nd edition. New York: Routledge (Routledge classics).

Khiabany, G. and Williamson, M. (2015) 'Free Speech and the Market State: Race, Media and Democracy in New Liberal Times', *European Journal of Communication*, 30(5), pp. 571–586. doi:10.1177/0267323115597855.

Lippmann, W. (1922) *Public Opinion*. New York: Harcourt, Brace and Company.

MacBride, S. (1980) *Many Voices, One World*. Kogan Page. Available at: http://digitallibrary.un.org/record/80 (Accessed: 29 June 2020).

Mare, D.A. and Moyo, D. (2019) 'How Metrics Are Changing Editorial Decisions in African Newsrooms', *The Conversation*. Available at: http://theconversation.com/how-metrics-are-changing-editorial-decisions-in-african-newsrooms-111230 (Accessed: 17 June 2020).

Marris, P. and Thornham, S. (eds) (1996) *Media Studies: A Reader*. Edinburgh: Edinburgh University Press.

Mbembe, A. (2003) 'Necropolitics', *Public Culture*, 15(1), pp. 11–40. doi:10.1215/08992363-15-1-11.

Newman, N. (2012) *Digital News Report 2012, Reuters Institute for the Study of Journalism*. Available at: https://reutersinstitute.politics.ox.ac.uk/our-research/digital-news-report-2012 (Accessed: 1 July 2020).

Tan, Y. (2020) 'A Weibo "Wailing Wall" for a Whistleblowing Doctor', *BBC News*. Available at: https://www.bbc.com/news/world-asia-china-53077072 (Accessed: 26 June 2020).

Nolan, D. et al. (2020) 'Analysing the Indigenous News Network in Action: IndigenousX, The Guardian and the Wakul App', in Maddison, S. and Nakata, S. (eds) *Questioning Indigenous-Settler Relations: Interdisciplinary Perspectives*. Singapore: Springer (Indigenous-Settler Relations in Australia and the World), pp. 69–86. doi:10.1007/978-981-13-9205-4_5.

Nothias, T. (2017) 'Mediating the Distant Other for the Distant Audience: How Do Western Correspondents in East and Southern Africa Perceive Their Audience?', *Africa's Media Image in the 21st Century*. Routledge. doi:10.4324/9781315659510-19.

Phillips, A. (2012) 'Sociability, Speed and Quality in the Changing News Environment', *Journalism Practice*, 6(5–6), pp. 669–679. doi:10.1080/17512786.2012.689476.

Phillips, A. (2015) *Journalism in Context: Practice and Theory for the Digital Age*. London; New York: Routledge, Taylor & Francis Group (Communication and society).

Purcell, K. et al. (2010) 'Understanding the Participatory News Consumer', *Pew Research Center: Internet, Science & Tech*, 1 March. Available at: https://www.pewresearch.org/internet/2010/03/01/understanding-the-participatory-news-consumer/ (Accessed: 1 July 2020).

Puwar, N. (2009) 'Sensing a Post-colonial Bourdieu: An Introduction', *The Sociological Review*, 57(3), pp. 371–384. doi:10.1111/j.1467-954X.2009.01856.x.

Robertson, C.T., Selva, M. and Nielsen, R.K. (2021) 'Women and Leadership in the News Media 2021: Evidence from 12 Markets', *Reuters Institute for the Study of Journalism*. Available at: https://reutersinstitute.politics.ox.ac.uk/women-and-leadership-news-media-2021-evidence-12-markets (Accessed: 12 April 2021).

Saha, A. (2017) *Race and the Cultural Industries*. Cambridge: Polity Press.

Schlesinger, P. (1978) *Putting 'Reality' Together: B. B. C. News*. Available at: https://www.abebooks.co.uk/9780094620407/Putting-Reality-Together-News-Communication-0094620407/plp (Accessed: 12 January 2022).

Schultz, I. (2007) 'The Journalistic Gut Feeling', *Journalism Practice*, 1(2), pp. 190–207. doi:10.1080/17512780701275507.

Serwornoo, M.Y.W. (2019) 'Postcolonial Trajectories of Foreign News Selection in the Ghanaian Press', *Journalism Studies*, 20(9), pp. 1357–1375. doi:10.1080/1461670X.2018.1519637.

Shoemaker, P.J. and Cohen, A.A. (2006) *News Around the World: Content, Practitioners, and the Public*. 1st edition. New York: Routledge.

Shohat, E. and Stam, R. (1994) *Unthinking Eurocentrism: Multiculturalism and the Media*. London; New York: Routledge (Sightlines).

Staab, J.F. (1990) 'The Role of News Factors in News Selection: A Theoretical Reconsideration', *European Journal of Communication*, 5(4), pp. 423–443. doi:10.1177/0267323190005004003.

Thurman, N. (2017) 'Robonews – What Journalists Think of Their New Automated Rivals', *The Conversation*. Available at: http://theconversation.com/robonews-what-journalists-think-of-their-new-automated-rivals-73930 (Accessed: 29 June 2020).

Thurman, N., Cornia, A. and Kunert, J. (2016) 'Journalists in the UK', Oxford, Reuters Institute for the Study of Journalism. p. 64. https://reutersinstitute.politics.ox.ac.uk/sites/default/files/research/files/Journalists%2520in%2520the%2520UK.pdf

Times of India (2021) 'World T20, Ashes Loom for Australia after Disappointing Season', *Cricket News - Times of India*. Available at: https://timesofindia.indiatimes.com/sports/cricket/news/world-t20-ashes-loom-for-australia-after-disappointing-season/articleshow/81390326.cms (Accessed: 14 February 2022).

Tong, J. and Zuo, L. (2021) 'The Inapplicability of Objectivity: Understanding the Work of Data Journalism', *Journalism Practice*, 15(2), pp. 153–169. doi:10.1080/17512786.2019.1698974.

Tuchman, G. (1978) *Making News: A Study in the Construction of Reality*. New York: Free Press. Available at: http://books.google.com/books?id=X61iAAAAMAAJ (Accessed: 29 June 2020).

Waterson, J. (2020) 'Microsoft Sacks Journalists to Replace Them with Robots', *The Guardian*. Available at: http://www.theguardian.com/technology/2020/may/30/microsoft-sacks-journalists-to-replace-them-with-robots (Accessed: 29 June 2020).

Wendelin, M., Engelmann, I. and Neubarth, J. (2017) 'User Rankings and Journalistic News Selection', *Journalism Studies*, 18(2), pp. 135–153. doi:10.1080/1461670X.2015.1040892.

Zhang, G.-L. *et al.* (2006) 'What's News in China?', in Shoemaker, P.J. and Cohen, A.A. (eds) *News Around the World*. 1st edition. London: Routledge. pp. 76–95.

4
IDEOLOGY IN PRACTICE

This chapter steps back from a focus on the role of journalists and editors in the process of news selection, to consider the ideological nature of news production and content, and how story selection and presentation influences what audiences think about. We will explore theories of agenda-setting (McCombs and Shaw, 1972) and framing (Entman, 1993) and, making use of examples of national and international events seen from a variety of perspectives, discuss how agenda-setting in news is used to establish normative accounts of the world.

How the media set the agenda

By choosing to cover certain events more than others, and exploring issues from limited perspectives, mainstream news delineates what is *thinkable*. In other words, whilst the media cannot dictate audience attitudes towards topics covered (see **Chapter 7**), the more attention an issue receives, the more salient it will be for the public, thus influencing what we think about and discuss. This is termed agenda-setting.

In their seminal study on the agenda-setting function of the mass media, McCombs and Shaw (1972) investigated the extent to which the way journalists and editors present news contributed to determining which issues Americans perceived to be most important during the 1968 US presidential campaign. Drawing on an observation by American political scientist Bernard Cohen (1963) that the press, "may not be successful much of the time in telling people what to think, but it is stunningly successful in telling its readers what to think about," McCombs and Shaw hypothesised that, "the mass media set the agenda for each political campaign, influencing the salience of attitudes toward the political issues" (1972, p. 177). In other words, McCombs and Shaw had a hunch that by emphasising certain aspects of what candidates say and do during political campaigns, and excluding other aspects, the news media are able to set the parameters of what audiences think about and, therefore, influence voter judgement and shape "political reality" (1972, p. 176).

During the 1968 election, even though the presidential candidates had opposing takes on issues and emphasised them differently, McCombs and Shaw's study revealed that it was what journalists made salient, rather than what politicians emphasised, that influenced how voters viewed campaign issues. More recent studies show media agenda-setting can also influence people's decisions to vote (Vreese, 2003) and how they vote (Jansen *et al.*, 2019) (see **Chapter 7** for a more detailed discussion of audiences).

Agenda-setting theory suggests the news media are likely to be particularly influential when reporting on topics the audience is less familiar with (McCombs, Shaw and Weaver, 2014), or when covering socially important issues that have uncertainty attached to them, like a health crisis (Feezell, 2018). This is because, unless you have superpowers, none of us knows everything or are able to be everywhere, all the time, gaining first-hand knowledge of situations or specialist areas – from politics and medicine to education and law – where decisions are made that affect our lives. Whether you're a politician, zookeeper or surfer, we all look to trusted sources of information to orientate us so we can make sense of and participate in the world.

Orientating (and disorientating) audiences

Our need for orientation was particularly pronounced during the Covid-19 pandemic. However, according to a report by the World Health Organisation (Boseley, 2021), the pandemic was characterised by poor global political leadership, mixed messaging and a lack of consensus. In some countries, like New Zealand (BBC, 2020) and Britain (Stewart, 2020), the government set the news agenda during the height of the pandemic in 2020 by holding regular press briefings alongside trusted *sources* (see **Chapter 6**), such as scientists and doctors, to relay and attempt to reinforce health messaging.

In other parts of the world, governments shunned scientific advice for ideological reasons creating, in the case of Brazil for example, competing agendas. Brazil's populist president, Jair Bolsonaro, took an anti-science stance, denied the seriousness of the pandemic, didn't order national lockdowns, dismissed international scientific advice on social distancing and made scare-mongering remarks about vaccines. According to his ex-health minister, Luiz Henrique Mandetta,[1] he ignored warnings that his anti-scientific approach was putting lives at risk (Phillips, 2021).

Bolsonaro's claims were shared widely on social media, including via his weekly Facebook Lives, and gained traction amongst his supporters (Duarte, 2020). He had, in fact, harnessed social media before the pandemic, using it to by-pass major Brazilian news outlets during his 2018 presidential election campaign. Against a backdrop of political corruption and economic decline in

Brazil (Anderson, 2019), he won the election, demonstrating how certain actors, such as members of the political elite, can use social media platforms to promote their agenda without relying on mainstream news to mediate their message (see Feezell, 2018).

Contesting agendas

However, the fact that Bolsonaro's social media messaging on Covid-19 contrasted with coverage of the pandemic by most major Brazilian news outlets also illustrates how agendas can be contested in democracies with media plurality. This is discussed further below in the section on *framing* and in **Chapter 6**.

Although some major Brazilian news outlets, like *Record TV* and *SBT*, whose target audience belong to lower-income groups,[2] were aligned with Bolsonaro's agenda, other leading Brazilian news organisations (Carro, 2021), such as *Globonews, Folha De Sao Paulo* and *Extra Newspaper*, contested the president's claims (Al-Jazeera, 2021). These outlets promoted a pro-science, pro-vaccine agenda by providing Brazilians with facts they weren't getting from the government. Journalists from these news organisations, which normally compete for stories and audiences, worked together to bypass government misinformation. They did so by gathering data on death rates and hospitalisations from governors and health secretaries in different Brazilian states to build a data base that could be used by any media organisation.

Whilst Bolsonaro's views on Covid-19 became a salient issue in Brazil, the contestation by some major news outlets meant there was ideological ambiguity vis-à-vis Covid-19 in the Brazilian *public sphere*. Contestation was informed by divergent ideological positions, and journalists mediated pandemic-related news via these ideologies. Thus, in addition to accounting for the *sociological* aspects of news when addressing the agenda-setting function of the media, as McCombs and Shaw (1972) did, it's also important to consider the *ideological* nature of news production and content. Revealing this additional layer enables an understanding of how ideology functions within democracies to sustain normative beliefs.

How ideology is reproduced via news media

As highlighted above and in previous chapters, news is never entirely neutral. Indeed, liberal mainstream journalism is itself guided by professional ideologies which, "are defined in terms of typical actions of newsmaking values such as press freedom, objectivity, fairness […], as well as the relations to […] readers, sources, news actors and the state" (van Dijk, 2008, p. 193).

In addition to professional ideologies, which form the basis of journalistic *doxa* (Bourdieu in Benson and Neveu, 2005), dominant ideology from other social spheres (e.g. politics and religion) seeps into journalism. However, the extent to which an ethic of neutrality is upheld, and ideology in news reporting is covert or overt, depends on a range of factors, including media systems (see **Chapter 1**), national political context and attitudes to freedom of expression. In mature democracies, like Britain, agenda-setting is more of a contest between political elites and, if we take public sphere theory into account, the right to define the political norm is generally contested at the periphery and takes time to filter into the mainstream. In authoritarian regimes, like China, open contestation is suppressed and the media agenda is controlled by the state. In polarised pluralist countries, contestation takes place between media backed by different political parties (this is termed *political parallelism*). However, countries don't necessarily neatly slot into singular media systems (see **Chapter 1** for more on media systems).

Whatever media system exists in a country, it's helpful to think of national systems as reflecting diverse forces, and ideology informs the way media systems are structured. Furthermore, ideology is produced discursively (through talk, text and other forms of communication). Thus, the media have long been an important site for theorists interested in the way cultural production facilitates social domination.

Key theory on ideology in the media

Italian Marxist, Antonio Gramsci, developed the concept of hegemony (cultural leadership) by drawing on Karl Marx's assertion that dominant ideology in society reflects the interests of the ruling class. For Marx, because the dominant class own the means of production, they "control the means of producing and circulating a society's ideas" (Hall, Evans and Nixon, 2013, p. 344) via the press and other forms of communication. Marx believed the ruling class is able to gain and retain dominance by "subjecting the masses to ideologies which make social relations of domination and oppression appear natural" (Hall, Evans and Nixon, 2013, p. 344).

Similarly, hegemony describes how the (re)production of ruling class ideologies via soft power mechanisms, like journalism, enables the elite to rule by consent rather than force. For Gramsci, hegemonic ideology is disseminated in the west through institutions like schools, churches and media organisations, which naturalise the beliefs and values of the dominant group so they become "common sense". Thus, they are viewed as legitimate and serving everyone's interests, rather than just the elite.

However, Gramsci saw opportunities for resistance to dominant ideology. Drawing on Engle's analysis of war (Blackledge, 2019), he described a *war of position*, which involves publics utilising culture (and thus forms of representation) to imagine change, resist domination, subvert hegemony and construct a more equitable social order in western democracies (Gramsci and Buttigieg, 1992; Egan, 2014). Gramsci asserted that dominant groups must continually work to earn the consent of those who are dominated in order to curtail dissent. As Hall et al explain:

> Hegemony is won in the to-and-fro of negotiation between competing social, political and ideological forces through which power is contested, shifted, or reformed. *Representation* is a key site in such struggle, since the power of definition is a major source of hegemony.
> *(Hall, Evans and Nixon, 2013, p. 344, their emphasis)*

French philosopher Michel Foucault was also interested in the intersection of ideology and power. Like Gramsci, Foucault did not see power as fixed, but as vulnerable to resistance thus always in flux. However, for Foucault, power does not operate in a top-down fashion, transmitted from the ruling elite to the masses. Instead, we are all (the dominant *and* the dominated) complicit in perpetuating power relations, which Foucault saw as operating in a circular fashion. In other words, like a beating heart, power requires a constant flow of activity to keep it going. A simple example of Foucault's conception of the circulatory nature of power is how dominant ideas in some cultures lead boys to believe that they should build with bricks, play with trucks and never wear pink or play with dolls. If boys (or their parents) adopt this hegemonic view of masculinity, they are complicit in maintaining normative power structures, so the cycle continues.

Bourdieu, whose ideas we discuss in **Chapter 2** and elsewhere, took a similar view regarding our complicity in upholding structures we exist within. For Bourdieu, dominant ideas function as forms of "symbolic violence" (Bourdieu, 1989), whereby symbolic systems, such as the journalistic field, conceal, legitimise and reinforce social hierarchies, containing "people who dominate and people who are dominated" (Bourdieu, 1998, p. 40). *Symbolic violence* operates as a legitimising force due to the way dominant norms are often unconsciously and consciously accepted by the dominant and dominated, who must abide by them to get by. The complicity of the dominated in upholding structures they exist within, but where they tend to possess little power to make lasting change, subjects them to further *symbolic violence* (see also Douglas, 2021). However, like Gramsci and Foucault, Bourdieu saw space for resistance and believed, for instance, that individuals may draw on their *habitus* to contest institutional *doxa*. Attempts to instigate change may be more or less successful depending on the *capital* (power) individuals acquire in fields they exist within.

The truth about truth

When thinking about contests over meaning and the mediation of dominant ideology within journalism, where facts (or truths) and opinions are kicked around 24/7, it's useful to return to Foucault. If we apply Foucault's thinking within the context of agenda-setting, we can see that there is an agenda behind *every* version of the truth. Each version is attached to a knowledge/power axis in as much as, by disseminating knowledge (via news or social media, for instance) individuals and groups seek control (power) over the narrative, so no one agenda (or set of truths) is more innocent than another, because a quest for power of some sort informs it. For Foucault,

> Knowledge linked to power not only assumes the authority of 'the truth', but has the power to *make itself true*. All knowledge, once applied in the real world, has real effects and, in that sense, at least, 'becomes true.'
> *(Hall, Evans and Nixon, 2013, p. 33)*

That's not to say that Foucault dismissed the idea that some things can be true and others false, rather his point was that "truth isn't outside power" (Foucault, 1980, p. 131 in Hall, Evans and Nixon, 2013, p. 34). As such, "truth" must never be viewed in isolation, but always in relation to the context in which it is asserted where it exists as part of, and to sustain, what Foucault described as a *regime of truth*.

If we apply Gramsci's, Bourdieu's and Foucault's ideas within the context of media agenda setting, the conception of dominant ideology being transmitted via culture, always in flux, thus open to resistance, speaks to how groups compete to set the agenda in democracies to make certain views and ideas ("truths") more influential, and common sensical (e.g. boys play with trucks), than others. As van Dijk observes, ideologies, which can either be used to fuel division or foster understanding, are:

> Fundamental [...] beliefs underlying the social representations shared by a group, featuring fundamental norms and values (such as those of freedom, justice, equality, etc.) which may be used or abused by each social group to impose, defend or struggle for its own *interests* (e.g. freedom of the press, freedom of the market, freedom from discrimination, etc.).
> *(van Dijk, 2008, p. 193)*

We can think about this by returning to the example of how coverage of Covid-19 played out in Brazil. Because of his status as president, Bolsonaro had the power to make his anti-science claims and arguments about the economic damage of lockdown measures appear true and transmit them widely via social media and some mainstream Brazilian news platforms which sought to maintain hegemony. For example, *Record TV* ran a bulletin that suggested Covid-19-related restrictions had caused poverty to triple in Brazil (Al-Jazeera, 2021), thereby operationalising *symbolic violence* by legitimising the president's views. Bolsonaro's ideological opposition to lockdown measures, and argument that the economic damage would be worse than the effects of Covid-19 itself, had *real effects*. Brazil, in 2020, recorded the second highest death toll[3] in the world after the United States (Phillips, 2020b).

Bolsonaro's anti-science agenda pitted him against leaders and health experts overseas and in Brazil. Many state governors, in contrast, followed the advice of health officials and implemented lockdown measures locally (Andreoni, 2021). So, a *war of position* (or resistance to *symbolic violence*) was taken by opposition politicians and other powerful actors (e.g. scientists, doctors) who used alternative Brazilian news outlets to set their agenda, and also by ordinary Brazilians, many of whom protested against Bolsonaro's Covid response (Reuters, 2021).

What the Brazilian example demonstrates is that in countries where there is relative press freedom, different versions of the same event are allowed to emerge in the national news media. Furthermore, the circulation of accessible truths from trustworthy sources is vital as it can mean the difference between life and death.

Suppression of internal dissent

In authoritarian regimes, like China, truths are carefully sieved by the state before they reach the public. This occurs offline and online where there's extensive censoring of keywords and URLs. Any facts that don't fit the agenda (or *regime of truth*) of the Chinese Communist Party (CCP) are removed from the sieve, like a lumpy bit of flour, and discarded. Because the state sets the agenda directly, via its control of the media, there will be no, or minimal, internal dissent in terms of the way an event, particularly one where national political interest is at stake, is covered by Chinese media. Indeed, different versions of such an event may only be available in news produced in other countries with opposing ideologies. International coverage of the 2014 Hong Kong protests (known as the Umbrella or Occupy Central Movement) offers a good example of this.

A British colony until 1997, control over Hong Kong was returned to China on the basis of an agreement[4] that it could retain democracy and political autonomy from China. The Umbrella Movement was organised almost two decades later, to protect democracy in Hong Kong, which has a different political and media system to that of mainland China. The movement was triggered by China's decision to restrict candidates for elections to a list approved by the Chinese government.

The protests, which involved thousands occupying Hong Kong's financial centre, drew global media attention. British, US and Chinese news media coverage was markedly different and clearly aligned with each country's opposing political systems (Du, Zhu and Yang, 2018) and dominant ideologies: democratic values, press freedom and the right to protest versus authoritarianism, press control and online restrictions.

Chinese state media framed the Hong Kong protests as illegal, while many elite western news organisations framed the protests as a legitimate demand for democracy. Coverage included accusations by Chinese state media that the West was responsible for fuelling the protests. *People's Daily*, the CCP's official newspaper, ran an article at the height of the demonstrations in October 2014, lambasting international, particularly US, coverage of the protests. Conforming with *People's Daily* ideological alignment with the CCP, the piece read:

> It is hardly likely that the US will admit to manipulating the 'Occupy Central' movement, just as it will not admit to manipulating other anti-China forces. It sees such activities as justified by 'democracy', 'freedom', 'human rights' and other values. [...] The US purports to be promoting the 'universal values' of 'democracy', 'freedom' and 'human rights', but in reality the US is simply defending its own strategic interests and undermining governments it considers to be 'insubordinate'. In US logic, a 'democratic' country is one that conducts its affairs in line with American interests.
> *(Yiwen, 2014)*

The New York Times, a liberal US newspaper, used the headline: "Some Chinese leaders claim U.S. and Britain are behind Hong Kong protests" but still essentially poured cold water on Chinese claims of interference by the strategic placing of the word "claim," which is routinely employed to discredit. It went on:

> There is no dispute that diplomats representing the United States and other Western governments have met on occasion with members of the pro-democracy camp, nor that American-funded non-governmental organizations have invited Hong Kong citizens to conferences extolling the merits of democracy.
>
> But in several dozen interviews with protesters and protest leaders over the last week, all emphatically denied that their movement had been directed or manipulated in any way by any foreign government. The United States has also denied playing any guiding role.
> *(Bradsher, 2014)*

What these snippets of coverage make clear is that *framing*, which we discuss below, exists in different media systems, both those where the state censors the media, and those where press freedom is upheld as a central tenet of democracy. Wherever you are in the world, political systems, interests of the powerful and normative values contribute to the way events are covered.

The limits of democratic dissent

Even in democracies where internal contestation is allowed, the versions of events that emerge tend to only be those that are considered important by elites. As Hallin found in his study of US television news coverage of the Vietnam war, where he explored the suggestion that American news media took an oppositional stance on the war, it was only when officials disagreed on the war and *elite consensus* vis-à-vis US foreign policy broke down that differing agendas were covered by the media (Hallin, 2005). Furthermore, the professional ideologies of objectivity and neutrality that guide US journalists "required the journalist to pass on official information without comment on its accuracy or relevance" (2005, p. 44). Thus, Hallin asserts:

> News content may not mirror the facts, but the media, as institutions, do reflect the prevailing pattern of political debate: when consensus is strong, they tend to stay within the limits of the political discussion it defines; when it begins to break down, coverage becomes increasingly critical and diverse in the viewpoints it represents.
>
> *(2005, p. 49)*

Thus, the agenda may be contested in democracies, but often within a framework provided by the elite. This is in keeping with Marx's theory, highlighted above, and Gramsci's assertion that the media reinforce the hegemony of dominant ideology. Therefore, the version of political debate that filters down to the audience is largely the debate that is established by powerful players.

Shifting agendas

As per Foucault's view of power circulating and being diffused in multiple directions, the media don't merely reflect or reinforce the status quo, it is at times actively involved in changing the status quo. The debate around Brexit in the United Kingdom is a case in point. Opinion polls show that the UK public were not much bothered with the European Union (EU) in the years up to the 2016 referendum to leave. The debate was manufactured by the right-wing UK press partly because of the political agenda of certain editors, but possibly because it was a topic that caused controversy and therefore raised newspaper sales.

As Phillips (2020a) argues, right-wing British newspapers, which dominate the UK newspaper market, set the agenda on Brexit. Crucially, not only did these papers set the agenda amongst their own readership, but also across broadcast news, including the BBC, which is regulated to be impartial, and social media, where the majority of web links shared on Twitter were not from "fake news" sources, but mainstream news outlets. Thus, digital media reinforced rather than diluted the national agenda-setting role of the popular press, demonstrating how dominant agendas flow through all platforms.

The right-wing press attacked the Remain side, which included prominent British politicians, including then Prime Minister David Cameron, and immigration became a dominant theme. This agenda intersected with that offered by the Leave campaign, and even Remain supporting newspapers focussed on immigration.

> There were more leading front pages about immigration during the campaign than about the economy. Six in 10 [...] were published by [...] the

Daily Express, the *Daily Mail*, and the *Daily Telegraph*. According to Leave campaigners and these Leave-supporting news outlets, immigration and immigrants were to blame for many of the UK's political, economic and social problems.

(Moore and Ramsay, 2017, p. 165)

As Moore and Ramsay find, coverage was less focused on giving Britons nuanced information about the implications of Brexit for issues like the environment, education and foreign policy, and instead became so binary that the campaign wound up being framed in divisive *us* (positive) and *them* (negative) terms. Such reductive messaging, where complex information is presented in simplistic terms, has been shown to strengthen issue salience (Yagade and Dozier, 1990). Depicting debate in a polarised manner is also characteristic of ideological structures that serve to reinforce:

> The basis of the (positive) self-image of a group, organized by fundamental categories such as the desired […] identity, actions, norms and values, resources and relations to other groups.
>
> *(van Dijk, 2008, p. 193)*

So-called "immigrants" were positioned as the "other" group against which the right-wing press and the Leave campaign constructed a "positive" self-image of Britishness. This was organised around mythical, emotive notions of British exceptionalism (the imperially rooted idea of Britain's superior position in the world) via headlines like: "Brexit will make Britain great again, insists Trump as he forecasts break-up of the EU and warns that Europe will be 'unrecognisable' without migration curbs" (Linning, 2016).

Reporting on immigration more than tripled during the campaign, making it the most prominent referendum issue, pro-immigration versus anti-immigration was a central *us/them* theme and politicians in the Leave camp, including Britain's current Home Secretary, Priti Patel, and Prime Minister, Boris Johnson, often made negative claims about immigration (Moore and Ramsay, 2017).

Mainstream news media's focus on making certain actors and singular issues more salient, as opposed to conducting balanced coverage of a variety of critical issues, speaks to Shaw and McCombs finding, in relation to media agenda-setting on the US presidential campaign over four decades earlier, that:

> A considerable amount of campaign news was not devoted to discussion of the major political issues but rather to analysis of the campaign itself. This may give pause to those who think of campaign news as being primarily about the issues.
>
> *(McCombs and Shaw, 1972, p. 179)*

The power to determine meaning

Ultimately, agenda-setting is about the power to determine meaning in order to gain or retain power. As Foucault (1978, p. 27) observed, power often plays out in discourse through what is unsaid, rather than what is said. Through exclusion (or silence), discourse sets parameters for the things we can discuss and understand. Therefore, Foucault argues, discourse produces rather than merely reflects what it claims to describe (Foucault, 1972, p. 49 in Tonkiss, 2004, p. 373). Transferred to journalism, exclusions within reporting, via the process of agenda-setting and framing, which we now discuss, *produce* certain realities rather than innocently reflecting them. Thus, in the case of Brexit, the discussion of leaving the EU barely mentioned the impact on business or education schemes like Erasmus+, focussing instead on immigration, therefore *producing* a solution (leaving the EU) to a problem that many were unconcerned about in the years running up to the campaign (Phillips, 2020a).

Detecting agendas in factual stories

Because the media's definition of reality sets agendas and influences what we think, it is helpful to consider *how* the way a story is written encourages audiences to interpret events in particular ways. Framing theory is one tool that enables us to do this. The merger of agenda-setting with framing is termed *second-level agenda-setting*. This additional level moves on from establishing the amount of attention news media gives a topic, thus defining the parameters of *what* we think about (*first-level agenda-setting*), to consider the textual elements within a story that shape *how* we think about issues (Ceron, Curini and Lacus, 2016).

An interdisciplinary approach used in a range of subjects, from psychology and anthropology to media studies, framing theory (Tuchman, 1978; Gitlin, 1980; Entman, 1993) can be used to illuminate how any system of communication works, and the outcomes of the way it works. In media studies, framing theory helps us understand the ways in which presentation and framing influences audience understanding. However, framing theory goes further than agenda-setting by attending to language, images and story composition, to explore how these factors work together to make certain elements more salient. Drawing on work by Erving Goffman (1974), Robert Entman (1993) proposed framing theory as a research paradigm and defines framing thus:

> To frame is to select some aspects of a perceived reality and make them more salient in a communicating text, in such a way as to promote a particular problem definition, causal interpretation, moral evaluation, and/or treatment recommendation for the item described. Typically frames diagnose, evaluate, and prescribe.
>
> *(Entman, 1993, p. 52)*

Furthermore:

> The text contains frames, which are manifested by the presence or absence of certain *key words, stock phrases, stereotyped images*, sources of information and sentences that provide thematically reinforcing clusters of facts or judgements.
>
> *(Entman, 1993, pp. 52–53, emphasis added)*

Applied to journalism, the framing process occurs as soon as journalists identify a *hook* (also known as a *peg* or *angle* in English-speaking newsrooms). This is the reason for covering an event or issue, it is the central point of the story and it will be made prominent in the headline or tweet (if the story is text-based) or opening line (if broadcast), to draw the audience in. Crucially, the *hook* structures the story, helping the audience understand what's going on, and the journalist emphasise what they believe to be the most important aspect of what's happening. The rest of the story content, including imagery, will relate to the *hook*. This means that even if there are divergent opinions conveyed in the story, the point the journalist led with will remain prominent. So, audiences won't come away with an entirely balanced view of events, as an attempt (consciously or not) has been made to guide their thinking.

However, like agenda-setting, frames can *only* guide, rather than fix, audience interpretation of events, and attempts to guide are certainly no guarantee that journalists or editors will be able to lead audiences in a particular direction. This is because audiences aren't passive, they read, watch or listen to information via their own frames (Druckman, 2001; Scheufele, 2004) (see **Chapter 7**). Just like journalists, audiences filter information via their bespoke "maps of meaning" (Hall, 1997), so they may use their map to merrily (or angrily) head in a different direction to the one pointed to in the story. Entman highlights (1993), as Hall (1997) does, that our cultural standpoint influences the way we interpret information. Therefore, along with the communicator, the text and the receiver, culture is a vital variable that helps shape interpretation.

Framing occurs in relation to reporting on all events, be it *hard news* topics like war, or *soft news* on art exhibitions or sports results. A journalist reporting on a football match is likely to emphasise whichever team their audience supports whether they win or lose. For instance, after England lost to Croatia in the 2018 World Cup semi-final, *The Sun*, a British tabloid, still put a positive spin on the story and invoked the myth of British stoicism with the headline: "We'll hold our heads up high" (Parker and Terrell, 2018). In one sentence, the paper sided with the losing national team and England fans by implying that they, and the team, were brave and dignified in the face of defeat. Meanwhile, some Croatian newspapers, not content with just celebrating their home teams win, framed England as sore losers, with photographs and mocking headlines focusing on English players and fans in despair, such as "Look how the English cry after losing to Croatia" (Vecernji List, 2018).

80 Ideology in Practice

> **Exercise: Framing Sport**
>
> Frames tend to be pretty evident when national media report on international sporting events where the home nation is represented. Via an online search, look at how print news media in two different countries cover their team/athletes during the same event, compared to the opposing side. Consider the framing: what key words, phrases, images, sources of information and sentences are used to reinforce positive or negative judgements about the home and opposition side?

Framing is not fixed. It varies not only according to the national frame but also according to the context. For example, social and cultural theorist Paul Gilroy describes how the ambivalence of Britishness plays out in the context of race. When Black Britons "positively" represent the UK overseas (think of athletes wrapped in the Union Jack), their Britishness is emphasised in media frames and they are woven into the national fabric. When they are in Britain, their *'otherness'* is often made salient so that Blackness and Britishness are produced as mutually exclusive categories (Gilroy, 2003 [1987], p. 61). Similarly, disabled athletes during the Paralympics are framed heroically. At other times, they are considered victims or simply ignored (Alexiou, 2020).

Persistent frames

Certain frames persist and these can be particularly influential in changing, confirming or reinforcing audience attitudes (Gavin, 2018). Entman (1993:52) highlights the cold war framing of US foreign affairs for many years as an example of the way frames *define problems* (e.g. civil wars), *diagnose a cause* (communist guerrillas), *make moral judgements* and *suggest remedies* (US support for the opposition). When analysing frames, it's important to be aware that:

> A single sentence may perform more than one of these four framing functions, although many sentences in a text may perform none of them. And a frame in any particular text may not necessarily include all four functions.
> *(Entman, 1993, p. 52)*

Like the cold war frame, news coverage of immigration in many parts of the world persistently frames it as a problem. As discussed earlier, political agendas informed the anti-immigrant debate by Britain's right-wing press in the run up to Brexit. The xenophobic framing, which included stereotypical and alarmist *stock phrases* and *key words*, such as "swamping," "influx" (Greenslade, 2020) and headlines like: "Revealed: Every Syrian refugee *accepted* into Britain will *cost* taxpayers up to £23,420 a year" (McTague, 2015, emphasis added) and "*Illegal migrants flood* in" (Dawar, 2015, emphasis added),[5] performed a key framing and agenda-setting function by influencing audience attitudes about the issue (Gavin, 2018). In a YouGov poll[6] a few weeks before the referendum, when there was a huge amount of anti-migrant press (Greenslade, 2020), 56 percent of participants thought immigration and asylum were the most important issues facing the United Kingdom. After the Brexit vote, 46 percent considered it most salient, and the following year, 35 percent of people believed it was the most important issue, mirroring the decrease in media coverage of immigration.

In South Africa, cross-border migration has been framed as a problem for years (Danso and McDonald, 2001). Most recently, migrants have been framed as negatively contributing to the Covid-19 pandemic. Tabloid, the *Daily Sun*, ran a story in October 2020 that began: "More than 200 people were bust in the Tshwane CBD. They included illegal immigrants [...] who weren't adhering to Covid-19 regulations" (Medupe, 2020). Here, in addition to seemingly making the pandemic worse, immigrants are also *defined* as *a problem* via wording which implies their criminality ("bust," "illegal"). The use of the word "nets" in the headline ("Anti-crime blitz nets 200!"), which instantly conveys the story *hook*, also reduces immigrants to the status of animals that require being hunted and contained. Such language reinforces a dehumanising theme long used to justify the inhumane treatment of certain groups.

In the United States, there are regular heated debates about immigration, and the use of the word "invasion" to demonise certain people arriving in the United States has a long history. In 1873, the *San Francisco Chronicle* ran a notice which read: "The Chinese Invasion! They are coming, 900,000 strong. What are you going to do about it? Nations of the earth take warning." This kind of language has real consequences contributing, in this case, to the US Congress passing the Chinese Exclusion Act of 1882, the first law to ban a national group from a country (Zimmer, 2019).

Research shows that US reporting continues to frequently frame immigrants from certain regions as an enemy force by using similar racist tropes, including using metaphorical language to represent Latinos as "invaders," "parasites" and "animals" (Santa Ana, 2002). This, for example, was the first interviewee[7] quoted in an *LA Times* article (Enriquez, 1994): "People are saying, 'I don't like this Third World takeover'. It is literally an invasion." (Zimmer, 2019). During his presidency, Donald Trump also used "invasion" to describe migrants attempting to cross the border into the United States from Mexico. News media repeated the word in coverage of his speeches (e.g. Reuters, 2019), reinforcing the idea and, intentionally or not, facilitating Trump's xenophobic framing.

Frame building

The process whereby political frames are taken up by the media, via journalists quoting or paraphrasing statements from powerful actors, like politicians, which then influence news frames, is termed "frame building" (Hänggli, 2012; Rodelo and Muñiz, 2019). "Build the Wall" (against immigrants) was a dominant frame built by Trump during his presidential campaign and presidency. This enacted the framing functions identified by Entman: immigration was falsely (Hinojosa Ojeda and Telles, 2021) *defined* as one of the major *problems* which had *caused* white working-class prospects to decline in America. Thus, a *remedy* was to stop so-called illegal immigration by building a wall along the US–Mexico border, which was one of Trump's signature promises during his election campaign.

Immigration was the second most covered issue by the US news media in the early days of the Trump administration (Mitchell *et al.*, 2017), thus supporting the notion of political frame building. Although most US news coverage of the Trump administration was negative at the time, the president or members of his administration were quoted more frequently than other sources, and around 1 in 6 stories contained a tweet from Trump (Mitchell *et al.*, 2017). So, Trump and his administration managed to *build* a media frame which exploited racist attitudes about the supposed "threat" immigrants (particularly Latinos) posed to the white majority, to galvanise his support base.

How frames reveal the origins of media agendas

Persistent news frames, like the agendas informing them, can of course be contested, and contestation is always informed by an agenda of some sort. Fifty years after their study, McComb's and Shaw revisited agenda-setting theory and found it has evolved to include seven distinct facets. One is the *origins* of the media agenda:

> Which range from the prevailing cultural and ideological environment to news sources, the influence of the media on each other, the norms and routines of journalism, and the individual characteristics of journalists.
> *(McCombs, Shaw and Weaver, 2014, p. 782)*

National and international press coverage of the Zimbabwean land reform issue in the early 2000s illustrates how framing of the issue is ideological and how that changes the possible analysis of the problem and the way it ought to be resolved. In Zimbabwe, and many other former colonies, the issue of land reform is a thread which runs through politics. It tends to be seen in a colonial oppression frame or a legal frame, depending on the *origins* of the media agenda, the positioning of the media organisation and the national political system. Depending which frame is used, the *diagnosis* of the problem, *moral judgement* and *suggested remedies* (Entman, 1993) will vary.

Zimbabwe has a mix of state-owned newspapers and broadcasting,[8] which are controlled by the Information Ministry, and non-state-owned press which is constrained by draconian laws. Journalists are often arrested and imprisoned (RSF, 2022), and the country ranks 130 of 180 on the 2021 World Press Freedom

Index (RSF, 2021). The state sponsored media became increasingly unpopular in the 1990s as the country struggled economically and exposure of corruption by the private press made these outlets a target for government, including suing newspapers for civil defamation (Saunders, 1999).

Against a backdrop of economic and social decline, following relatively prosperous post-independence years in the 1980s, a new political party, the Movement for Democratic Change (MDC), was founded in 1999, to stand against ZANU-PF, the party led by Robert Mugabe, who had been in power since independence. Just before the elections in 2000, Mugabe initiated a policy of reclaiming land from white farmers, who had occupied it since colonial times, violently displacing Indigenous peoples and forcing them onto marginal land (see Zambakari, 2017). The issue of land ownership is critical in most ex-colonies where white colonisers and their descendants continued to occupy the most fertile land after independence. In an attempt to redress this unjust imbalance, Robert Mugabe used violent tactics to take the farms back. This led to national and international condemnation.

Nationally, as Willems (2004, p. 1) argues, "media representations of the land question in the run-up to the June 2000 parliamentary elections came to parallel the polarised political environment." In an analysis of the framing of the land issue by *The Herald*, a government controlled daily newspaper, and *The Daily News*, a paper launched in 1999 with foreign and local investment, Willems finds both newspapers had distinct agendas and used imagery and words to either support (*The Herald*) or contest (*The Daily News*) the Government's land reform programme. Binary coverage, Willem's argues, means an opportunity for nuanced debate about land reform was missed by influential segments of the Zimbabwean press.

> The *Daily News* headlines would state that certain actors condemned land "invasions", whereas headlines in *The Herald* would point out that certain actors supported land reform. In this case, headlines served to make clear ideological statements about the attitude of the newspaper.
> *(Willems, 2004, p. 4)*

The selective framing of the land reform issue in national Zimbabwean newspapers also occurred in dominant western press coverage. Although over 190 Black people (mostly supporters of the MDC) were killed in Zimbabwe between 2000 and 2004, and ten white farmers were killed (Willems, 2005), mainstream western press emphasised the violence perpetrated against white farmers. Headlines in both liberal and conservative outlets included: "White farms looted, destroyed in Zimbabwe" (CNN, 2001); "White farmer killed by Zimbabwe war veterans" (McGreal, 2001) and "Zimbabwe mobs widen attacks on white farmers" (Thornycroft and Blair, 2001).

An exclusionary *us* and *them* frame took hold which was politicised and racialised. Zimbabwean media largely focused on internal *political* divisions, whilst western media framed the issue as a Black versus white conflict (Willems, 2005). This framing serves two functions. First, it filters events that predominantly impact Black and brown people via stories that feature white protagonists. This makes content compatible with racialised economic rationalities (Saha, 2018; Douglas, 2021) and a marketable form of western news coverage on the Global South that is premised on the assumption that western news audiences are white (Nothias, 2017) and/or more likely to connect with coverage of white people (see **Chapter 3**).

A second framing function is then enacted in that such correspondents (and/or their editors) racialise *meaningfulness*, a news selection factor (Galtung and Ruge, 1965) which is central to the norms and routines of journalism. At work here is the baseless assumption (see also Douglas, 2019) that in order for audiences to connect with stories, those featured need to be racially alike.

The characteristics of journalists

As discussed in **Chapter 3**, the subjectivity (*habitus* or *characteristics*) of journalists reporting on an issue may shift exclusionary frames, if space is made available for journalists to draw on their *habitus* within the *doxa* of the institutions they work for.

In April 2000, Black British journalist, Gary Younge, flew to Harare to cover the Zimbabwean land reform issue for *The Guardian*. His front-page story, which centred Black, rather than white, victims of the political violence, momentarily changed mainstream British news framing of the events.

Younge attended the funeral of a Black Zimbabwean MDC supporter, Tichaona Chiminya, who was murdered by supporters of Robert Mugabe's Zanu-PF party. Younge's report combines sensitive observation of a family in mourning with quotes from family and MDC members including one, used to headline the — article – "This is not racism, it's politics" (Younge, 2000) – which broadened the framing beyond reductionist Black/white terms and, unlike many other mainstream western news reports, underscored the centrality of politics to the issue. Younge also overtly countered the racial bias in many of those reports, by stating that the deaths of Chiminya and other Black Zimbabweans had been largely ignored, whereas David Stevens, the first white farmer to be killed, "triggered headlines of impending civil war." As Phillips observes (2007), Younge added important context to a story that had, otherwise, been framed simplistically in the UK public sphere. He also conceivably drew on his subjectivity (*characteristics*)[9] as a Black journalist to expand the narrow framing of events and make ordinary Black Zimbabweans, whose stories had been side-lined or erased, visible.

National and international frames

As we've seen, framing influences coverage of domestic and foreign events, and national and international news may frame the same event very differently.

However, Nossek contends that when the national interest is at stake in relation to foreign affairs national news media may also speak with one voice.

> When a foreign news item is defined as "ours", then journalists' professional practices become subordinate to national loyalty; when an item is "theirs", journalistic professionalism comes into its own.
>
> *(Nossek, 2004, p. 343)*

Nossek explored his hypothesis in relation to foreign news coverage of political violence (war and terrorism) by elite newspapers in the United States, Britain and Israel in the aftermath of September 11, 2001, and the subsequent wars in Afghanistan and Iraq. He found that if journalists classify the violence as *ours*, patriotism rises to the fore, reporting will be framed as a national issue, and there will be no attempt at neutral reporting. If the story is deemed *theirs*, journalists and editors will apply "professional" values of apparent impartiality. What's central here is an argument for the ongoing primacy of the nation state.

In addition to the cultural filtering of news discussed elsewhere, "the domestic filter is considered as a professional requirement which it is incumbent on journalists to apply when addressing their particular audience" (Nossek, 2004, p. 347). Furthermore, foreign news coverage is often aligned with the foreign policy of the government where the news organisation is based (Paterson, 1999 in Nossek, 2004, p. 347).

Nossek finds that foreign news is reported via a "national" or "professional" frame, depending on the national connection to the foreign event being covered, which explains differences in the way countries cover the same event.

However, the notion of *ours* and *theirs* is complicated, as we saw in relation to the Zimbabwean land issue, by the fact that frames adopted aren't necessarily split along national lines. In the Zimbabwean case, different frames emerged within the same country, sides were taken nationally and transnationally and the taking of sides didn't just reflect external ideological and politico-cultural pressures on the journalistic field, but also reflected editorial positioning vis-à-vis a political issue.

Overall however, debate mostly occurred amongst the powerful, rather than involving all concerned. Major global media outlets established the salience of the issue, and national media framed the events according to a range of factors, including assumptions about audiences, which were productive of different frames in the same national context.

Summary

- Agenda-setting theory highlights the media's ability to influence the public agenda and *what* audiences think about.
- Framing theory is concerned with the way texts are constructed (language and images), so they influence *how* audiences think about things.

- Frames can *only* guide, not fix, audience interpretation of events, but certain frames persist.
- News is never entirely neutral. But, the extent to which a pretence of neutrality is upheld, and ideology in news reporting is covert or overt, depends on media systems and the national political context it operates in. Therefore, news agenda-setting and framing should be considered within the context of national political and media systems.
- Ultimately, agenda-setting and framing is about power and struggles to determine meaning.

Notes

1 Bolsanaro sacked Mandetta in April 2020 after Mandetta publicly challenged his defiance of social distancing.
2 It's important to note people's characteristics and/or background in the context of the agenda-setting effect the media is able to have because "demographic variables, including level of education, age, and income, can explain the strength of the agenda-setting effect" (Wanta and Alkazemi, 2018, p. 191).
3 A 2021 Senate inquiry into Brazil's handling of Covid-19 found that Bolsonaro should be tried for "crimes against humanity" (The Economist, 2021).
4 This is referred to as "one country, two systems."
5 Note the key words we emphasise in these headlines and consider what they do to audience understanding.
6 YouGov (2019).
7 Guy Weddington McCreary, a North Hollywood Chamber of Commerce member who supported the initiative.
8 Zimbabwe Broadcasting Corporation (ZBC) runs four radio stations and two television networks. There are also two licensed national private radio stations and the internet is relatively free from government interference but is expensive (https://www.bbc.co.uk/news/world-africa-14113511).
9 Another way of interpreting how frames may change depending on the characteristics of the journalist covering the event is via the concept of "journalist frames," which "are located within journalists' thoughts about an issue, person, or event. [...] Functionally, a journalists frame forms a context for understanding, interpreting, and ultimately, expressing the facts of an issue" (Vos, 2018, p. 210).

References

Alexiou, G. (2020) *Disabled Talent 'Shut Out' and 'Invisible' in TV Industry and Hollywood*, Forbes. Available at: https://www.forbes.com/sites/gusalexiou/2020/06/29/disabled-talent-shut-out-and-invisible-in-tv-industry-and-hollywood/ (Accessed: 1 June 2021).

Al-Jazeera (2021) *Brazil: Battling Bolsonaro's COVID Misinformation | Media | Al Jazeera*. Available at: https://www.aljazeera.com/program/the-listening-post/2021/4/17/brazil-battling-bolsonaros-covid-misinformation (Accessed: 14 January 2022).

Anderson, P. (2019) 'Bolsonaro's Brazil', *London Review of Books*, 7 February. Available at: https://www.lrb.co.uk/the-paper/v41/n03/perry-anderson/bolsonaro-s-brazil (Accessed: 13 January 2022).

Andreoni, M. (2021) 'Coronavirus in Brazil: What You Need to Know', *The New York Times*, 2 June. Available at: https://www.nytimes.com/article/brazil-coronavirus-cases.html (Accessed: 12 June 2021).

BBC (2020) 'Coronavirus: How New Zealand Relied on Science and Empathy', *BBC News*, 20 April. Available at: https://www.bbc.com/news/world-asia-52344299 (Accessed: 14 January 2022).

Blackledge, P. (2019) 'War and Revolution: Friedrich Engels as a Military and Political Thinker', *War & Society*, 38(2), pp. 81–97. doi:10.1080/07292473.2019.1566981.

Boseley, S. (2021) 'Covid Pandemic Was Preventable, Says WHO-Commissioned Report', *The Guardian*. Available at: http://www.theguardian.com/world/2021/may/12/covid-pandemic-was-preventable-says-who-commissioned-report (Accessed: 2 July 2021).

Bourdieu, P. (1989) 'Social Space and Symbolic Power', *Sociological Theory*, 7(1), pp. 14–25. doi:10.2307/202060.

Bourdieu, P. (1998) *On Television and Journalism*. London UK: Pluto Press.

Bradsher, K. (2014) 'Some Chinese Leaders Claim U.S. and Britain Are Behind Hong Kong Protests', *The New York Times*, 10 October. Available at: https://www.nytimes.com/2014/10/11/world/asia/some-chinese-leaders-claim-us-and-britain-are-behind-hong-kong-protests-.html (Accessed: 2 July 2021).

Carro, R. (2021) *Brazil. 2021*. Oxford, United Kingdom: Reuters Institute for the Study of Journalism. Available at: https://reutersinstitute.politics.ox.ac.uk/digital-news-report/2021/brazil (Accessed: 26 January 2022).

Ceron, A., Curini, L. and Iacus, S.M. (2016) 'First- and Second-Level Agenda Setting in the Twittersphere: An Application to the Italian Political Debate', *Journal of Information Technology & Politics*, 13(2), pp. 159–174. doi:10.1080/19331681.2016.1160266.

CNN (2001) *CNN.com - White Farms Looted, Destroyed in Zimbabwe - August 13, 2001*. Available at: https://edition.cnn.com/2001/WORLD/africa/08/12/violence.zimbabwe/ (Accessed: 14 January 2022).

Cohen, B.C. (1963) *The Press and Foreign Policy*. Princeton, N.J.: Princeton University Press. Available at: https://doi.org/10.1515/ (Accessed: 22 June 2021).

Danso, R. and McDonald, D.A. (2001) 'Writing Xenophobia: Immigration and the Print Media in Post-Apartheid South Africa', *Africa Today*, 48(3), pp. 115–137.

Dawar, A. (2015) *Illegal Migrants Flood in: 18,000 Are Now Sneaking into UK Every Year*, *Express.co.uk*. Available at: https://www.express.co.uk/news/uk/582609/Illegal-migrants-UK-border-Britain (Accessed: 2 July 2021).

Douglas, O. (2019) *Backstories / Black Stories: Black Journalists, INGOs and the Racial Politics of Representing Sub-Saharan Africa in Mainstream UK News Media*. doctoral. Goldsmiths, University of London. Available at: http://research.gold.ac.uk/26352/ (Accessed: 29 June 2020).

Douglas, O. (2021) 'The Media Diversity and Inclusion Paradox: Experiences of Black and Brown Journalists in Mainstream British News Institutions', *Journalism*, p. 14648849211001778. doi:10.1177/14648849211001778.

Druckman, J.N. (2001) 'The Implications of Framing Effects for Citizen Competence', *Political Behavior*, 23(3), pp. 225–256. doi:10.1023/A:1015006907312.

Du, Y.R., Zhu, L. and Yang, F. (2018) 'A Movement of Varying Faces: How "Occupy Central" Was Framed in the News in Hong Kong, Taiwan, Mainland China, the UK, and the U.S.', p. 22.

Duarte, T.R. (2020) 'Ignoring Scientific Advice during the Covid-19 Pandemic: Bolsonaro's Actions and Discourse', *Tapuya: Latin American Science, Technology and Society*, 3(1), pp. 288–291. doi:10.1080/25729861.2020.1767492.

Egan, D. (2014) 'Rethinking War of Maneuver/War of Position: Gramsci and the Military Metaphor', *Critical Sociology*, 40(4), pp. 521–538. doi:10.1177/0896920513480222.

Enriquez, S. (1994) *Valley Chambers Vote to Support Prop. 187, Los Angeles Times*. Available at: https://www.latimes.com/archives/la-xpm-1994-09-17-mn-39478-story.html (Accessed: 2 July 2021).

Entman, R.M. (1993) 'Framing: Toward Clarification of a Fractured Paradigm', *Journal of Communication*, 43(4), pp. 51–58. doi:10.1111/j.1460-2466.1993.tb01304.x.

Feezell, J.T. (2018) 'Agenda Setting through Social Media: The Importance of Incidental News Exposure and Social Filtering in the Digital Era', *Political Research Quarterly*, 71(2), pp. 482–494. doi:10.1177/1065912917744895.

Foucault, M. (1978) *The History of Sexuality*. 1st American ed. New York: Pantheon Books.

Galtung, J. and Ruge, M.H. (1965) 'The Structure of Foreign News: The Presentation of the Congo, Cuba and Cyprus Crises in Four Norwegian Newspapers', *Journal of Peace Research*, 2(1), pp. 64–90. doi:10.1177/002234336500200104.

Gavin, N.T. (2018) 'Media Definitely Do Matter: Brexit, Immigration, Climate Change and Beyond', *The British Journal of Politics and International Relations*, 20(4), pp. 827–845. doi:10.1177/1369148118799260.

Gilroy, P. (2003) *'The Whisper Wakes, the Shudder Plays': 'Race', Nation and Ethnic Absolutism | Taylor & Francis Group*. Available at: https://www.taylorfrancis.com/chapters/mono/10.4324/9780203995075-9/whisper-wakes-shudder-plays-race-nation-ethnic-absolutism-paul-gilroy (Accessed: 1 June 2021).

Gitlin, T. (1980) *The Whole World Is Watching: Mass Media in the Making and Unmaking of the New Left*. Berkley: University of California Press.

Goffman, E. (1974) *Frame Analysis: An Essay on the Organization of Experience*. Boston, MA.: Northeastern University Press.

Gramsci, A. and Buttigieg, J.A. (1992) *Prison Notebooks*. New York, NY: Columbia University Press (European perspectives).

Greenslade, R. (2020) 'Migrants Are Off the Agenda for the UK Press, But the Damage Is Done', *The Guardian*. Available at: http://www.theguardian.com/media/2020/jan/26/migrants-are-off-the-agenda-for-the-uk-press-but-the-damage-is-done (Accessed: 2 July 2021).

Hall, S. (1997) 'The Work of Representation', *Representation: Cultural Representation and Signifying Practices*, Milton Keynes: Sage; The Open University.

Hall, S., Evans, J. and Nixon, S. (eds) (2013) *Representation*. Second edition. Los Angeles : Milton Keynes, United Kingdom: Sage; The Open University.

Hallin, D. (2005) *We Keep America on Top of the World : Television Journalism and the Public Sphere*. Routledge. doi:10.4324/9780203977477.

Hänggli, R. (2012) 'Key Factors in Frame Building: How Strategic Political Actors Shape News Media Coverage', *American Behavioral Scientist*, 56(3), pp. 300–317. doi:10.1177/0002764211426327.

Hinojosa Ojeda, R. and Telles, E. (2021) 'Trump Paradox: How Immigration and Trade Affected White Voting and Attitudes', *Socius*, 7, p. 23780231211001970. doi:10.1177/23780231211001970.

Jansen, A.S. *et al.* (2019) 'Who Drives the Agenda: Media or Parties? A Seven-Country Comparison in the Run-Up to the 2014 European Parliament Elections', *The International Journal of Press/Politics*, 24(1), pp. 7–26. doi:10.1177/1940161218805143.

Linning, S. (2016) *Brexit Will Make Britain Great Again, Insists Donald Trump*, Mail Online. Available at: https://www.dailymail.co.uk/news/article-3661657/Brexit-make-Britain-great-insists-Trump-forecasts-break-EU-warns-Europe-unrecognisable-without-migration-curbs.html (Accessed: 2 July 2021).

McCombs, M.E. and Shaw, D.L. (1972) 'The Agenda-Setting Function of Mass Media', *The Public Opinion Quarterly*, 36(2), pp. 176–187.

McCombs, M.E., Shaw, D.L. and Weaver, D.H. (2014) 'New Directions in Agenda-Setting Theory and Research', *Mass Communication and Society*, 17(6), pp. 781–802. doi:10.1080/15205436.2014.964871.

McGreal, C. (2001) 'White Farmer Killed by Zimbabwean War Veterans', *The Guardian*. Available at: http://www.theguardian.com/world/2001/aug/08/zimbabwe.chrismcgreal (Accessed: 2 July 2021).

McTague, T. (2015) *Every Syrian refugee will cosy Britain up to £23,420 a year*, Mail Online. Available at: https://www.dailymail.co.uk/news/article-3279493/Every-Syrian-refugee-accepted-Britain-cost-taxpayers-23-420-year.html (Accessed: 2 July 2021).

Medupe, K. (no date) *Anti-crime Blitz Nets 200!*, DailySun. Available at: https://www.dailysun.co.za/News/anti-crime-blitz-nets-200-20201029 (Accessed: 2 July 2021).

Mitchell, A. *et al.* (2017) 'Covering President Trump in a Polarized Media Environment', *Pew Research Center's Journalism Project*, 2 October. Available at: https://www.journalism.org/2017/10/02/covering-president-trump-in-a-polarized-media-environment/ (Accessed: 18 June 2021).

Moore, M. and Ramsay, G. (2017) 'Acrimonious and Divisive: The Role the Media Played in Brexit', *LSE BREXIT*, 16 May. Available at: https://blogs.lse.ac.uk/brexit/2017/05/16/acrimonious-and-divisive-the-role-the-media-played-in-brexit/ (Accessed: 24 May 2021).

Nossek, H. (2004) 'Our News and their News: The Role of National Identity in the Coverage of Foreign News', *Journalism*, 5(3), pp. 343–368. doi:10.1177/1464884904044941.

Nothias, T. (2017) 'Mediating the Distant Other for the Distant Audience: How Do Western Correspondents in East and Southern Africa Perceive Their Audience?', *Africa's Media Image in the 21st Century*. Routledge. doi:10.4324/9781315659510-19.

Parker, N. and Terrell, A. (2018) *Kane Left 'Gutted' as England's Brave Lions Fall Just Short*, The Sun. Available at: https://www.thesun.co.uk/world-cup-2018/6755209/england-croatia-fans-world-cup-semi-final/ (Accessed: 2 July 2021).

Phillips, A. (2007) *Good Writing for Journalists: Narrative, Style, Structure*. London: Sage.

Phillips, A. (2020a) 'The British Right Wing Mainstream and the European Referendum', in Nadler, A. and Bauer, A.J. (eds) *News on the Right, Studying Conservative News Cultures*. Oxford University Press, pp. 141–156.

Phillips, T. (2020b) 'Brazil Overtakes UK with World's Second-Highest Covid-19 Death Toll', *The Guardian*. Available at: http://www.theguardian.com/world/2020/jun/12/brazil-coronavirus-death-toll-second-highest (Accessed: 2 July 2021).

Phillips, T. (2021) *'Bolsonaro Ignored Repeated Warnings About COVID, Ex-health Minister Says'*, The Guardian. Available at: http://www.theguardian.com/world/2021/may/04/brazil-bolsonaro-coronavirus-health-minister-inquiry (Accessed: 8 June 2021).

Reuters (2021) 'Brazilians Stage Nationwide Protests against President Bolsonaro's COVID Response', *Reuters*. Available at: https://www.reuters.com/world/americas/

brazilians-stage-nationwide-protests-against-president-bolsonaros-covid-response-2021-05-29/ (Accessed: 14 January 2022).

Reuters, R. (2019) 'Trump Calls Migrant Caravans 'Invasion' at Campaign Rally,' *Reuters Video*. Available at: https://reut.rs/2YbVuRm (Accessed: 14 January 2022).

Rodelo, F.V. and Muñiz, C. (2019) 'Government Frames and Their Influence on News Framing: An Analysis of Cross-Lagged Correlations in the Mexican Context', *Global Media and Communication*, 15(1), pp. 103–119. doi:10.1177/1742766518818862.

RSF (2021) *World Press Freedom Index | Reporters Without Borders, RSF*. Available at: https://rsf.org/en/ranking (Accessed: 14 January 2022).

RSF (2022) *Zimbabwe*. Reporters Without Borders. Available at: https://rsf.org/en/zimbabwe (Accessed: 4 March 2022).

Saha, A. (2018) *Race and the Cultural Industries*. Malden, MA: Polity Press.

Santa Ana, O. (2002) *Brown Tide Rising Metaphors of Latinos in Contemporary American Public Discourse By Otto Santa Ana*. Austin: University of Texas Press. Available at: https://utpress.utexas.edu/books/sanbro (Accessed: 13 January 2022).

Saunders, R. (1999) *Dancing Out of Tune*. Harare, Zimbabwe: R. Saunders.

Scheufele, B. (2004) 'Framing-Effects Approach: A Theoretical and Methodological Critique', 29(4), pp. 401–428. doi:10.1515/comm.2004.29.4.401.

Stewart, H. (2020) 'No 10 Says Scientific Advisers Will Return to Covid-19 Briefings', *The Guardian*. Available at: http://www.theguardian.com/world/2020/may/27/no-10-says-scientific-advisers-will-return-to-covid-19-briefings (Accessed: 2 July 2021).

The Economist (2021) 'Jair Bolsonaro is accused of crimes against humanity in Brazil', *The Economist*, 23 October. Available at: https://www.economist.com/the-americas/2021/10/23/jair-bolsonaro-is-accused-of-crimes-against-humanity-in-brazil (Accessed: 14 January 2022).

Thornycroft, P. and Blair, D. (2001) *Zimbabwe Mobs Widen Attacks on White Farmers*. Available at: https://www.telegraph.co.uk/news/worldnews/africaandindianocean/zimbabwe/1337554/Zimbabwe-mobs-widen-attacks-on-white-farmers.html (Accessed: 2 July 2021).

Tonkiss, F. (2004) 'Analysing Discourse', in Seale, C. (ed.). London: Sage, pp. 245–260. Available at: http://www.sagepub.co.uk (Accessed: 22 June 2021).

Tuchman, G. (1978) *Making News: A Study in the Construction of Reality*. New York: Free Press. Available at: http://books.google.com/books?id=X61iAAAAMAAJ (Accessed: 29 June 2020).

van Dijk, T.A. (2008) 'News, Discourse, and Ideology', in Wahl-Jorgensen, K. and Hanitzsch, T. (eds) *The Handbook of Journalism Studies*. 1st Edition. New York: Routledge. pp. 191–204.

Vecernji List (2018) *See How the English Cry After Losing to Croatia p. 5 | Večernji.hr*. Available at: https://www.vecernji.hr/sport/pogledajte-kako-bahati-englezi-placu-nakon-sto-su-izgubili-od-hrvatske-1257874?page=5 (Accessed: 14 January 2022).

Vos, T.P. (ed.) (2018) *Journalism*. Boston/Berlin: Walter de Gruyter GmbH & Co KG.

Vreese, C.H. de (2003) *Framing Europe: Television News and European Integration*. Amsterdam: Aksant.

Willems, W. (2004) 'Selection and Silence: Contesting Meanings of Land in Zimbabwean Media', *Ecquid Novi: African Journalism Studies*, 25(1), pp. 4–24. doi:10.1080/02560054.2004.9653275.

Willems, W. (2005) *Remnants of Empire? British Media Reporting on Zimbabwe*. London: University of Westminster (Westminster Papers in Communication and Culture).

Yagade, A. and Dozier, D.M. (1990) 'The Media Agenda-Setting Effect of Concrete versus Abstract Issues', *Journalism Quarterly*, 67(1), pp. 3–10. doi:10.1177/107769909006700102.

Yiwen, H. (2014) *Why Is the US so keen on 'Color Revolutions'? - People's Daily Online*. Available at: http://en.people.cn/n/2014/1011/c98649-8793283.html (Accessed: 2 July 2021).

Younge, G. (2000) 'This Is Not Racism, It's Politics', *The Guardian*. Available at: http://www.theguardian.com/world/2000/apr/20/zimbabwe.garyyounge (Accessed: 2 July 2021).

Zambakari, C. (2017) 'Land Grab and Institutional Legacy of Colonialism: The Case of Sudan', *Consilience*, (18), pp. 193–204.

Zimmer, B. (2019) 'Where Does Trump's 'Invasion' Rhetoric Come From?', *The Atlantic*. Available at: https://www.theatlantic.com/entertainment/archive/2019/08/trump-immigrant-invasion-language-origins/595579/ (Accessed: 31 May 2021).

5
REPRESENTING "OTHERS"

The "other" is anyone who is different to oneself, it is *anyone* you are not. So, in simply telling stories about other people's lives, journalists are always representing the "other." Every representation is an act of power, and journalists need to consider their power whenever they put a story together. Ideally, they should always give subjects of the story space to speak, represent all sides and include adequate context. That way, audiences gain a rounded sense of those represented and can relate to them as fellow human beings, so even though they remain "other", as in separate from oneself, they are not *othered*.

Othering occurs when journalists represent people and places in ways which do not correlate with the experiences of those represented. In the worst cases portraying others as if they are intrinsically different, somehow lesser beings. It is this latter form of representing the "other" that concerns us.

We will consider theories of representation and how concepts of "difference" are developed, reproduced and intersect. Our focus will be primarily on racial "difference," but the theories we discuss can be applied to examine the multiple ways people are othered due, for example, to their sexuality, religion, gender, nationality, class or disability.

Crucially, we are concerned with the role journalists play in highlighting and amplifying "difference" in ways that fuel *othering* and foster divisions, as well as their vital role in addressing "difference" in ways that do not de-humanise, but contribute to cultivating understanding to such an extent that those represented are not othered.

Why representation of the "other" matters

Representation of people who are positioned outside dominant discourse because of socially constructed markers of "difference," such as class, gender and race, has

Representing "Others" 93

been explored by scholars for decades (e.g. Fanon, 1991[1952]; Hall, 1997; hooks, 1999; Chouliaraki, 2006; Kapuściński, 2018). Markers of "difference" used to classify people permeate every mode of representation, from art and literature to film and advertising. But, it is journalistic representation that concerns us. News media are how, as Moeller (1999, p. 320) asserts, we are introduced to our global neighbours and those introductions influence how we perceive others.

Such is the importance of global news media representation of ourselves and others that when the South Korean television network, Munhwa Broadcasting Corporation (MBC), used stereotypical images and captions during the 2020 Tokyo Olympics to describe some of the countries represented by competing athletes, there was a flood of complaints. As athletes entered the stadium for the Parade of Nations during the opening ceremony, images MBC used included Chernobyl for Ukraine, salmon for Norway, pizza for Italy and Dracula for Romania (Vigdor, 2021). The problem lay in the fact that using singular, stereotypical representations to demarcate "difference" between people and places is reductive. It homogenises – ironing out nuance and simplifying and fixing the fluid, complex nature of identity. Following complaints, MBC issued an apology.

Being represented in reductive terms, whoever you are and wherever you're from, is offensive. However, reductive representations that are also rooted in histories of discrimination and oppression are deeply problematic because they contribute to sustaining discriminatory patterns. For example, in western societies, images of women wearing a hijab (or veil) are often used to represent Muslim people, in general. Such images are frequently linked to the Islamophobic trope long perpetuated by western media that Muslim is synonymous with terrorist (Hamid, 2021) and that "the more religious a person becomes the more violent he/she is likely to become" (Hamid, 2021, p. 64).

Thus, when Shamima Begum, a British citizen, appeared in UK media in 2019 wearing a hijab and abaya during a television interview from a Syrian refugee camp for women who'd escaped the collapse of towns held by Daesh, Begum's garments of religious dress were construed by some as markers of her radicalism. The then Home Secretary, Sajid Javid, revoked her British citizenship on security grounds, leaving her stateless.

Begum's story is, in fact, far more complex. At the age of 15 (in 2015), she ran away from her London home to Syria, with two school friends, to join Daesh. Days later, she married a fighter, and she bore and lost three children, as well as losing her husband, by the time she was nineteen. When interviewed in 2019, she said that she didn't regret leaving but wanted to return home.

Any other 15-year-old victim of grooming, trafficking and rape (she was under 16 at the time and in British law was incapable of giving consent) would have been offered support. *The Daily Mail*, a right-wing British newspaper, gives many column inches over to sympathetic coverage of victims of grooming in the United Kingdom,[1] yet the coverage of Begum was unrelentingly hostile[2]. Her identification as an extremist was not only fixed by what she said during that initial interview but also by how she looked and what she wore.

Indeed, her clothes came to symbolise everything about her. When Begum appeared in a subsequent television interview (ITV's Good Morning Britain) in 2021, wearing jeans and a vest top, her appearance prompted further debate. The *Daily Mail* quoted Eilish O'Gara, from the right-wing Henry Jackson Society, who suggested that her outfit was a tactic of her lawyers designed to, "win back the hearts and minds of the British public" (Pleasance, 2021). Her altered dress now became a symbol of her seemingly unreliable nature; of her "otherness."

The subsequent debate over Begum's clothing and what it represented, over-shadowed discussion of her youth and her right to return to England, the country where she was born and grew up, demonstrating how ideas of belonging are embodied and how conceptions of nationhood, and who does and doesn't belong, are rooted in histories of certain groups, brown[3] Muslims in Begum's case, being *othered*.

Key theory on representation and othering

There are a number of different ways of theorising otherness (or "difference"). These range from theories of language to psychoanalytic accounts. The postcolonial scholar and feminist critic, Gayatri Spivak, coined the term *othering* to describe the way dominant groups socially and psychologically marginalise other groups (see Ashcroft, Griffiths and Tiffin, 2013). Spivak was interested in the way colonial and imperial powers constructed their "others" discursively, through text, talk and other forms of communication. But every society has dominant and subordinate groups, so forms of othering exist in multiple contexts. The way groups are othered also intersects so that, as critical race theorist, Kimberlé Crenshaw (1989) demonstrates via her influential concept of *intersectionality*, people may be marginalised due to multiple aspects of their identity such as gender, race, class and religion. In Begum's case, for example, each of these markers of identity intersects to contribute to her social position and the way she may be represented.

"Difference"

For Saussure, a Swiss linguist, meaning is only possible by identifying "*difference.*" Without "difference," or opposites, objects and symbols are rendered meaningless because meaning is *relational*. So, in crude binary terms, *male* only acquires meaning in relation to *female*, *rich* to *poor* and so on. In this line of thinking, things don't carry meaning because they have an inherent, fixed essence, but because we impose meaning on them by contrasting them with *other* things. This binary view of "difference" is handy because, for instance, we need to be able to teach children about the difference between hot and cold. However, as Hall, Evans and Nixon observe (2013), binarised thinking is also problematic because conceiving of "difference" via rigid opposites doesn't leave room for nuance. Children also need to learn that there is a range of hot and cold temperatures, extremes at either end are dangerous, and some of the variations in the middle are pleasant.

Furthermore, Saussure's theorisation of "difference" does not account for the fact that binaries tend to be informed by power relations:

> As the philosopher Jacques Derrida has argued, there are very few neutral binary oppositions. One pole of the binary, he argues, is usually the dominant one, the one which includes the other in its field of operations. […]. We should really write, **white**/black, **men**/women, **masculine**/feminine, **upper class**/lower class, **British**/alien to capture this power dimension in discourse.
> *(Hall, Evans and Nixon, 2013, p. 225)*

Acknowledging this power dimension, particularly in relation to representing the "other," is crucial for reasons we address shortly.

Dialogue

Rather than identifying "difference" via binary oppositions, the Russian linguist Mikhail Bakhtin believed it was essential to engage in dialogue with the "other" to find meaning. As Hall, Evans and Nixon highlight (2013), this way of understanding how we make sense of "difference" is more fluid because it requires communication with others to make sense of things, and it is through dialogue that meaning is made. Thus, for Bakhtin, meaning can never belong to one speaker more than another, it's never fixed and is, therefore, constantly up for negotiation:

> The word in language is half someone else's. It becomes 'one's own' only when…the speaker appropriates the word, adapting it to his own semantic expressive intention. Prior to this…the word does not exist in a neutral or impersonal language…rather it exists in other people's mouths, serving other people's intentions: it is from there that one must take the word and make it one's own.
> *(Bakhtin, 1981 [1935], pp. 293–4 in Hall, Evans and Nixon, 2013, p. 225)*

Bakhtin's conception of how meaning is made, the idea that we take words via dialogue and make them our own, creates space for recognising the power dimension that informs the struggle to define the world via our lens of understanding. In this view, no *single* interpretation is complete and correct. Instead, "meaning arises through the 'difference' between the participants in any dialogue', so the 'Other' is essential to meaning" (Hall, Evans and Nixon, 2013, p. 225).

Be and being

This flux and the requirement to find meaning via the existence of the "other" may foster understanding or division. If that requirement is acknowledged, particularly by those who occupy the dominant pole in the binary[4] (e.g. **man**/woman, **straight**/gay), and they engage in dialogue with the "other" in ways that recognise their humanity, then greater understanding of self and other may be cultivated. To understand how this works, it's instructive to take heed of the assertion by the feminist writer and activist, Audre Lorde, that denial of "difference," where we are only allowed to *be*, rather than actively *being*, results in "a total denial of the creative function of difference in our lives" (Lorde, 1984, p. 111). In other words, if you simply project your assumptions onto other people so they remain fixed (they are only allowed to *be*), as you see them, rather than engaging in dialogue through which both you and they come into *being*, you are not creating space to acknowledge that you are both equally different (Lorde, 1984, p. 111), and that meaning making belongs to them as much as it does to you.

Lorde's contention that "difference" must be equalled so that there is no dominant "norm," but rather infinite differences which we can only understand through dialogue and by acknowledging our own difference, alongside Bakhtin's point that "the word in language is half someone else's" (Bakhtin, 1981 [1935], pp. 293–4 in Hall, Evans and Nixon, 2013, p. 225), is useful for journalists. Such awareness should help foster the level of professional respect that should be the foundation of any interview, or dialogue between a journalist and their subject, as it calls for enabling the other (the subject of the interview) to speak, and for the journalist to actively listen. Active listening entails being open to shifting ones view (and story angle), rather than entering into communication with preconceived ideas.

One-way speech, where the "other" can only *be*, occurred when Piers Morgan, former host of Good Morning Britain, tweeted in response to Begum's interview in September 2021:

> **Just as well I'm not interviewing this lying, snivelling, cold-hearted, self-serving ISIS bride monster or I'd have seriously lost my temper by now. Begum should never be allowed back to Britain. Let her rot in the terror bed she made for herself.**
>
> *(Morgan, 2021)*

Whatever audiences made of Begum's words,[5] they were clearly intended to convey remorse and seek forgiveness. But *her intention*, once uttered, was taken by Morgan who adapted it "to *his own* semantic expressive *intention*" (Bakhtin, 1981 [1935], pp. 293–4 in Hall, Evans and Nixon, 2013, p. 225) via his tweet. This was picked up by a number of British newspapers, including *The Mirror*, which ran the headline: "Piers Morgan slams 'ISIS monster bride' Shamima Begum during 'lying' GMB interview" (Newman, 2021).

This demonstrates how meaning can never be controlled. As someone who occupies the subordinate pole in the relation of power vis-à-vis the mainstream British press (**white**/brown, **non-Muslim**/Muslim, **middle-class**/working-class), Begum had significantly less control over meaning than Morgan or the journalists writing about her, most of whom have never entered into *dialogue* with her.

However, some news outlets did demonstrate the role journalists can play in addressing "difference" in less binarised ways. For example, *The Guardian's* coverage of the ITV interview was headlined: "Shamima Begum says she wants to prove innocence in UK courts: appearing in live TV interview from Syria detention camp, Begum says she 'did nothing in Islamic State but be a mother and wife'" (Sabbagh, 2021). The prominent use of Begum's words lends her some agency and enables the reader to enter into a form of dialogue with her, thus humanising, rather than instantly othering her. An article in *The Times* (Knight, 2021) pointed out that:

> **Begum was 15 and an apparently ordinary schoolgirl from Bethnal Green, east London, when she ran away to join Isis more than six years ago. She was a child who had undoubtedly been groomed online, perhaps even brainwashed. This kind of grooming happens all the time, as we know from recent atrocities.**

The dominant "other"

Another notion of the "other" is rooted in psychoanalytic theory. Spivak draws on a psychoanalytic conception of the "other," developed by the psychoanalyst Jacques Lacan, to argue that the colonised "**o**ther" is constructed in relation to the colonising "**O**ther."

The distinction between the lower and upper-case o/O is important for Lacan, whose theorising is rooted in the Freudian conception (see Hall, Evans and Nixon, 2013) of how subjectivity is formed, because the o/O binary represents the dominant "**O**ther" and the dominated "**o**ther." As Ashcroft, Griffiths and Tiffin explain (2013, pp. 187–190), for Lacan, the lower case "other" refers to a child's self-awareness when they first learn to recognise themselves in the mirror as an individual separate from their parent. It is via the gaze of the parent (the dominant "**O**ther") that they acquire identity. At this stage, the child wants to become like the dominant "**O**ther" rather than the "**o**ther" lacking mastery, and this desire forms the foundation of their identity which, for Lacan, is never complete.

The dominant "Other" is symbolic and Spivak uses Lacan's split between "Other" and "other" to describe how the concept can be used elsewhere. She argues that the "Other" signifies power and Empire, which discursively produces *and* excludes the dominated "other."[6] In doing so, the dominant "Other" constructs itself in relation to the "other," meaning one cannot exist without the other.

> The Other can be compared to the imperial centre [...]: first, it provides the terms in which the colonized subject gains a sense of [...] identity

as somehow 'other', dependent; second, it becomes [...] the ideological framework in which the colonized subject may come to understand the world. In colonial discourse, the subjectivity of the colonized is continually located in the gaze of the imperial Other [...]. The ambivalence of colonial discourse lies in the fact that both these processes of 'othering' occur at the same time, the colonial subject being both a 'child' of empire and a primitive and degraded subject of imperial discourse. The construction of the dominant imperial Other occurs in the same process by which colonial others come into being.

(Ashcroft, Griffiths and Tiffin, 2013, pp. 187–188)

We will consider how this ambivalence, being positioned as in need of nurturing and protection, like a child, and simultaneously degraded, continues to play out via some journalistic representations of "others."

The importance of accounting for history

Underpinning these theories on the "other" is the proposition that "difference," or opposites, whether in the form of objects, symbols, people or places, is essential to meaning (see Hall, Evans and Nixon, 2013), and our ability to make sense of the world and ourselves within it. Via this process of sense making, we invest objects, symbols (words and pictures), people and places, which have no inherent meaning, with meaning that we absorb through culture. Culture is formed over time, so meaning is derived from histories, which, in turn, enable understanding of words and pictures.

When a mural appeared on a wall in London's East End in 2012, depicting capitalists counting money on the backs of slaves, many people walked on by. However, lots of Jewish observers, and others conscious of the history, were appalled because the mural picked up the anti-Semitic imagery of the Nazi era (Segalov, 2018). Anti-Semitism stems from the first century AD when the Roman Empire became Christian and those who refused to convert were driven out. Over the years, Jews were forced to live separately, deprived of civil rights, banned from jobs and blamed for everything from famine to plague. These stories built up into stereotypes that persist and reappear during times of crisis, often summarised by an image of a man with a hooked nose, rubbing his hands.

Many who walked past the East London mural probably didn't understand its resonance, but to those who are "othered," such lack of consciousness is not an excuse. Another example: when images of Justin Trudeau, the Canadian Prime Minister, in blackface, were published in 2019 by *Time* magazine (Kambhampaty Purna and Carlisle, 2019), they caused public outcry in countries where people have some knowledge of the history of Black and brown people being mocked racially through the use of blackface, which reinforces historically *constructed* ideas of inferiority. Such sick ideas were deployed to offer perverse justification for the enslavement and colonisation of the west's Black and brown "others."

Sometimes, history builds symbolic imagery in positive ways. For instance, in 2017, when Taiwan's highest court ruled that the ban on same-sex marriage was unconstitutional, global news audiences were able to derive meaning from images of people celebrating on the streets of Taiwan holding rainbow-coloured placards which read "Love is Love" because the rainbow flag symbolises the LGBTQ+ community worldwide and the words, "Love is Love," speak to the *history* of LGBTQ+ people fighting for the same rights as those in opposite-sex relationships.

The above examples remind us that sexuality, religion and race are just a few of the many categories via which groups have long been othered in an attempt to justify unequal power relations. Crucially, they also demonstrate how history, and old ways of seeing and doing, informs contemporary modes of othering. The Taiwanese example is one demonstration of how marginalised groups whose "difference" from dominant "norms" has been used to oppress them, use symbols and words (e.g. the rainbow flag, "love is love") to subvert discriminatory ideas and construct oppositional meanings that celebrate, rather than denigrate, "difference." Meanwhile, the examples of Trudeau, and the East End mural, are stark reminders of how oppressive histories continue to inform the production of narrow representations which circulate in society, including via journalism.

Orientalism

In his seminal book, *Orientalism* (1978), Edward Said, a leading cultural critic of the late twentieth century and one of the founders of postcolonial studies, draws on his experiences as an Arab-Palestinian living in the west to explore the history of how western colonial powers, particularly Britain and France, categorised the east (North Africa, the Middle East and Asia) through the use of degrading stereotypes. Crucially, Said argued that these ideas which constructed the east, or the "Orient," as "other," persist, especially via the west's relationship with Islam.

Said's *Orientalism* (1978) provides a vital means of understanding how histories and ideas intersect to produce conditions whereby certain people and places are perceived to "fit in" (Ahmed, 2012) to narrative frames, which reflect and contribute to reinforcing unequal social relations. *Orientalism* is a critical text[7] within postcolonial studies because it helped enable enquiry into how the west constructed its "others" as *knowable* categories, not just in the "Orient" but across its colonies, and the effect these constructions had and continue to have. Said (1978) asserts that the histories, thinking and power relations that constructed the region can be exhumed to explain why the "Orient," and it's people, is thought about and represented in particular ways.

Said's (1978) focus in *Orientalism* dates back to the imperial era and the way the distinction between "east" and "west" is persistently taken up by western producers of knowledge to construct texts which span a range of fields – from poetry to politics – but pivot around the theme of the west's relationship with its Oriental "other." Said calls this body of knowledge Orientalism and identifies it as a discourse which operates within societies' culture and institutions and is "brought to bear on (and therefore always involved in) any occasion when that peculiar entity 'the Orient' is in question" (Said, 1978, p. 3).

To establish how this happens, Said (1978) uses Foucault's notion of discourse, which we'll outline shortly, as a method to understand the network of ideas which arose to construct "truths" about the Orient. Like all the west's "others", the Orient is less reflective of an actual region and people and more revealing of what the west thinks about itself (see also Douglas, 2019). This idea echoes Spivak's Lacanian conception of othering, where the dominated "other" is essential to the construction of the dominant "Other": neither would be realised without the other. As Said argues, the "Orient" is integral to European culture and its centrality to Europe, as opposed to any "real" place called the "Orient," is expressed through "supporting institutions, vocabulary, scholarship, imagery, doctrines" (Said, 1978, p. 2) which serve the relationship of power and domination which the "Occident" acquired over the "Orient." Real, *felt* ramifications of western constructions of the "other" can be traced in the work of other postcolonial scholars such as Frantz Fanon (see below).

Said explored the way ideas become ingrained within society to such an extent that they appear "true." The more they circulate, the more stereotypical these "truths" become. The media, Said asserts, is one of the main purveyors of these "truths" – constructing ever narrower frames for certain "truths" to fit in to. He shows how texts refer to each other, building webs of knowledge. Through this inter-referencing, texts become increasingly removed from the place or people they claim to refer to, whilst simultaneously reinforcing "truths" about them.

For example, in the aforementioned case of Shamima Begum, some journalists uncritically referenced Piers Morgan's tweet in their coverage of Begum's Good Morning Britain interview and, via that inter-referencing, reinforced the idea that Begum is a "lying" "ISIS monster." When journalists inter-reference like this, particularly in relation to events concerning groups who are othered, rather than talking to the person, or going to the place, that their story is about, they contribute to narrowing ways of seeing and, thus, contribute to othering.

The media, for Said, reinforce stereotypes by forcing information into "more and more standardised moulds" (Said, 1978, p. 26) so that nineteenth-century colonial ideas about "others" maintain their hold. Said uses Gramsci's theorising of hegemony (see **Chapter 4**) to argue that the *idea* of European superiority is so embedded in dominant styles of thought that it occupies a normative, common sense position which overrides differing views and in doing so it *produces* the effects that it names – the notion that Europe is superior to its "others."

> **Exercise: Orientalism**
>
> Consider occasions when you've come across journalistic representations that reinforce the idea that the west, or a western country, is superior to a non-western country or region. How is this sense of superiority evidenced in the text? Is it due to who is and is not spoken to in the text (we address the importance of voice further down)? Is it through the use of certain words and/or images that rely on past understandings in order to try and convey certain meaning about the subject of the story to the audience? If it's via words, note them down. If it's via the choice of images, list what ideas these images generate for you. Once noted, consider what comes to mind when you read those words and ideas. What past understandings (personal or learned) are your word associations informed by? Do your understandings correlate with the meaning the text/image is trying to convey? If not, how does your understanding subvert the meaning? What alternative "truths" might you include?

Foucauldian inspired discourse analysis as a method for revealing hidden meaning

One of the useful aspects of Said's work is the way he turned Foucault's theorising on discourse into a *method* for excavating histories hidden beneath words and images. This is important for unravelling subtle forms of othering that are woven so tightly into certain discourses that they become invisible,[8] normative (hegemonic) ways of thinking about certain people and places. Racism, for instance, is often silenced, materialising in covert ways via text and talk (discourse). Some scholars have referred to covert racism as the "new racism" (Gilroy, 1987; van Dijk, 2000).

Foucault's model of discourse analysis shows us that "new racism" is not disconnected from "old" forms of racism and can similarly be used to justify hatred. But problematically, such "narrative constructions of 'race' […] can […] place it 'beyond investigation'" (Gunaratnam, 2003, p. 115) because it's less obvious to the unsensitised ear or eye. Unless, that is, we can historically contextualise modes of othering in representations, as we discuss below under **fear/hate, pity and desire**.

Foucauldian discourse analysis is a valuable method as it enables inquiry into fields of knowledge and practice within and across texts (Tonkiss, 2004). This includes media texts, which serve as sites for the production and reproduction of social meanings. Although discourse is a slippery concept in Foucault's work, he used the term broadly to refer to the historical[9] legacies of statements and terms, which enable them to have meaning. He takes a socio-historical approach to "how social categories, knowledges and relations are shaped by discourse"

(Tonkiss, 2004, p. 373). In Foucault's understanding, discourse reflects *and* shapes society (Foucault, 2002 [1972]; 2007 [1970]).

The way statements come together to form a *discursive system* was Foucault's concern. Discursive systems describe the way statements and terms link together and carry meaning due to rules for organising and producing knowledge within specific contexts. For example, Foucault was interested in *socially constructed* ideas of "madness," and the way these ideas, and the statements and terms that express them, shift over time and govern the perception and treatment of people during different periods. Seen this way, "madness" is not a fixed, natural state, but is socially dependent. For instance, the United Kingdom's 1913 Mental Deficiency Act enabled women who had children out of wedlock, to be categorised as "moral imbeciles" and locked up in mental asylums. The Act was repealed in 1959, but the logic of the *discursive system* that facilitated the repressive governance of unmarried pregnant women remained so that, in 1968, over 10,000 babies were given up for adoption by women due to social pressure (Feigel, 2015), and illegitimacy as a legal status continued until 1987.

It's Foucault's theorisation of discourse as, "a group of statements which provide a language for talking about – i.e. [...] representing – a particular kind of knowledge about a topic" (Hall, 1992, p. 290 in Tonkiss, 2004, p. 373), that enables researchers to investigate how discourses set parameters for discussing and understanding certain topics. Importantly, Foucault also conceived of discourse not just as setting parameters, but helping to produce "the very categories, facts, and objects they claim to describe" (Foucault, 1972, p. 49 in Tonkiss, 2004, p. 373). In other words, categorisations like "moral imbeciles" are both productive and reflective of social context and position individuals within it so that "facts" produced about those situated within constructed categories affect their lived experience.

Revealing silences

Said's (1978) work on Orientalism turned Foucault's model into a method for attending to discourse as a tool that mediates power; producing people and places as *objects* of knowledge (as *"others"*) within the context of imperialism. In this way, discourses are theorised as producing "truths" about "others," which involve competition between different institutions and actors to establish dominant representations.

In the case of journalism, this approach to discourse as a methodological tool helps us identify historically rooted terms woven into content and shows how histories enable meaning making today. This allows us to show that it is the discourses, *not* the things-in-themselves, which produce knowledge (Hall, 2001). This relates to the point that categories (e.g. man/woman, straight/gay and so on) are *socially produced* and do not have inherent, fixed meaning.

A number of theorists (e.g. Hall, 1973; Webb, 2009) highlight that representations in news are not neutral facts but, as Hall (Hall, 1973) contends, part of ideological discourse that produce familiar recognitions within audiences who bring to their reading of news their backstories (lived experiences), which are informed by discourses that underpin society. Foucault's limited but useful thinking on racism in his 1976 lectures[10] ("*Ill faut defender la societe*") emphasises how these backstories function through time and place (Stoler, 2002a). Racial discourses, for instance, are, thus, repeatedly reinscribed beneath different themes. In Foucault's 1976 lectures on the centrality of race to "biopower,"[11] we can see how ideologies are *reused* (1976 in Stoler, 2002b). So, even though the terms change, racial discourses maintain a coherency and permanence by virtue of the fact that they are layered (Stoler, 2002b) through time. This means they could not meaningfully exist without the images and opinions (Foucault, 2002[1972]; Tonkiss, 2004) that preceded them.

Whilst the notion of layering and the power of discourse to re-attach itself to new ideas are useful for understanding how racism is sustained, it is also problematic as it suggests it is impossible to escape racialised discourse. Foucault helps us understand that meaning is not fixed because discourse is marked by: "different possibilities that it opens of reanimating already existing themes [...] of making it possible, with a particular set of concepts, to play different games" (Foucault, 1972 in (Stoler, 2002b). This suggests that systems of statements which sustain modes of othering, like racism, also provide the opportunity for disrupting them. This is critical for journalism because it suggests that alternative discourses have the power to change perceptions. It underlines the need for journalists to ground their work in an understanding of how discursive power contributes to the construction of a just [or un-just] society. We now consider this via discussion of some of the different forms othering may take within journalism.

Fear and hate of the "other"

In January 2020, just before Covid-19 hit pandemic proportions, the French newspaper, *Le Courrier Picard*, ran a story with the headline "Coronavirus Chinois: Alerte Jaune" ("Chinese Coronavirus: Yellow Alert") and "Le Péril Jaune?" ("Yellow Peril") next to an image of a woman of east Asian heritage (Boyle, 2020). An online version of the story was headlined: "Nouveau Peril Jaune?" ("New yellow peril?") (Courrier picard, 2020). Both illustrate the discursive nature of "new racism" and a form of othering which incites fear and hate.

We recognise this headline as racist because the terms "yellow alert" and "yellow peril" are racist metaphors with a history rooted in the 1904–1905 Russo-Japanese war. It is used to imply that people of east Asian decent are an existential threat to the western world. There was a huge response to the headline on social media platforms, like Twitter, with one man posting: "Je suis Chinois, mais je ne suis pas un virus!!"

Le Courrier Picard issued an apology, but the damage had already been done. Such terms formed part of a surge in anti-east Asian discourse during the pandemic, which political commentary also contributed to. For example, after

Donald Trump posted tweets describing Covid-19 as the "Chinese virus" in March 2020, Williams (2021) found that in the two days following Trump's first use of the phrase on social media, the number of anti-Asian hate tweets grew by 656 percent. The tweets came from accounts all over the world, but they were particularly high in the United States followed by the United Kingdom, where in spring 2020, police recorded a 21 percent increase in south and east Asian hate crime. There was a similar increase across Australasia, Europe, the Americas and Africa, leading researchers to conclude that there is a direct link between online hate speech and offline attacks, including physical assault, which, in the case of Covid-19, was also aimed at other marginalised groups including Muslims, Jews and LGBTQ+ people (Sciences, Lab and HateLab, 2021).

Discourse that incites fear and hate of others, such that it has a real effect on people's lived experiences, is part of a *discursive system*. An incredibly powerful account of the real effects of discursive othering was written by psychiatrist and philosopher Frantz Fanon (1991[1952]). His seminal text, *Black Skin, White Masks*, remains foundational for thinking through the ways "others," in this case Black people, are fixed in dominant discourse. In one chapter, "*The Fact of Blackness*," Fanon draws powerfully on his experience as a Black person whose sense of himself is stunted by white people's perceptions of him. Perceptions attained not by knowing *him*, but by knowing the *constructed* racialised stories which are part of the cultural fabric of western societies.

Whilst Said (1978) uses texts as his archive to explore how they, and the institutions which produced them, constructed racialised narratives that contain the "Orient," Fanon (ibid) uses psychoanalysis and the archive of his own experience to show, on a visceral level, the effects of colonial discourse on his being. These different approaches allow us to understand how two ends of a spectrum connect – how the *othering* done at the level of discourse is felt and becomes real. So that, although Fanon writes about his experiences as a Black man in the west, and the experiences of other global majority people in white dominated worlds, and Said writes about the construction of the "Orient" in texts and the institutions which produce them, the sense of containment Said (1978) evokes when he refers to a network of interests being brought to bear on any occasion the "Orient" is in question (Said, 1978, p. 3), is comparable to the sense of containment Fanon feels. Fanon describes this containment drawing in around his being through the gaze of white people who have come to "know" him via colonial discourse; a discourse which constructed "facts" about his Blackness. These "facts," as Fanon puts it, objectively cut away slices of his reality (Fanon, 1991[1952], p. 116) so that it becomes simplified and fixed (Bhabha, 1983). This sense of already being "known", and therefore pre-determined and contained, is powerfully conveyed when Fanon writes:

> The white man had woven me out of a thousand details, anecdotes and stories […]. I discovered my blackness […] and I was battered down by

tom-toms, cannibalism, intellectual deficiency, fetishism, racial defects, slave-ships, and above all: "Sho' good eatin'."

(Fanon, 1991 [1952], p. 111–112)

This "thematisation" (Fanon, ibid, p. 113) of who and what Fanon is leads to a sense of imprisonment, limiting his perceived ability to function as an equal (remember Lorde's point about *equaling* differences) in the west. Said's (1978) use of the term "grid" is another useful way of thinking about how this sense of imprisonment works. "Grid" is used by Said to describe how knowledge of others is sieved through a structured frame of reference that enables "them" to be "known" in specific ways in the west, thus dominated.

The idea of fitting into an imagined structure links with Foucault's (1977) use of Bentham's Panopticon to illustrate how power operates. Within the imagined structure of the Panopticon, a subject is visible and controlled through surveillance by an anonymous observer at the centre. Foucault theorises how those subjected to the power of discourse are also controlled: "the object of information, never a subject in communication" (Foucault, 1977, p. 200). The conception of the Panopticon highlights how knowledge and power operate as mechanisms to control others. As such, stereotypical representations can be viewed as Panoptic instruments – apparatuses which frame people not as subjects to be heard, but as objects to be observed and categorised, so they fit within certain discourses.

Exercise: Subjects or Objects

When individuals are silenced within discourse, or there is no meaningful *dialogue*, representations become the central means by which they are known within that framework of power. Hence, Fanon's (1991[1952]) sense of being imprisoned by stories about his Blackness. Think of a group of people who are marginalised in your country, or elsewhere. Search for representations of that group. Note any recurring themes and consider whether they are largely "subjects in communication" or silenced, thus "objects of information."

Pitying the "other"

The colonising "Other" constructed a paternalistic relationship with their colonial "others," who were frequently depicted as "childlike" and "helpless" (Goldberg, 1993) in order to justify the disempowering mechanisms colonisers used to oppress them. In a scathing takedown of these paternalistic power dynamics, the writer Teju Cole (Cole, 2012) coined the term: "white-savior industrial complex." He was responding to the controversial documentary Kony 2012, which was produced by the American NGO Invisible Children. The aim of the documentary was to focus global attention on Joseph Kony's Lord Resistance Army, which is said to have abducted children in Uganda, forcing them to become child soldiers and sex slaves.

However, there was a huge backlash to the documentary, including Cole's. Essentially, Kony 2012 was critiqued for contributing to age-old reductive representations of Black African "others," by centring whiteness (in this case, the documentary director, Jason Russell, who is depicted as helping to end the conflict), misrepresenting facts and reinforcing the notion that white westerners must "save" Africa, particularly children and women, from "evil black men" – another racist trope. Cole's response to the documentary, via seven tweets, went viral and were reproduced by media organisations in different countries, including the United States, Spain and Germany. In an article addressing his tweets for The Atlantic (Cole, 2012), Cole wrote:

> I disagree with the approach taken by Invisible Children in particular, and by the White Savior Industrial Complex in general, because there is much more to doing good work than "making a difference." There is the principle of "First do no harm." There is the idea that those who are being helped ought to be consulted over the matters that concern them.

Cole's point about others not being consulted speaks to stripping people of agency and voice – central to *othering*. Scholars like Spivak (1988) and American academic and activist bell hooks (1990) argue that the exclusion of the "other" from the production of discourse about him/her/them contributes to processes of othering and fuels silencing racial hierarchies of power and knowledge. These hierarchies are constructed and maintained when the "other" is spoken for and of, rather than *to* in an equal exchange of *dialogue*, so becomes "the object of information, never a subject in communication" (Foucault, 1977, p. 200). Alternatively, when we do hear the voice of the "other," it may be mediated in ways that lack context and fit the agenda and framing of the mediator (a news outlet and/or journalist, for example), rather than adequately reflecting the reality experienced by the subject of their story.

Standardised molds

Dominant western news narratives about brown and Black "others" who live in the Global South often fit what Said describes as "standardised molds" (Said, 1978, p. 26). These narratives are frequently filtered through a humanitarian and development[12] lens, which can contribute to *pitying* modes of othering. Indeed, western charities and international non-governmental organisations (INGOs), whose work is focused on humanitarian and development issues in the Global South, have found increasing space to work *within* mainstream news (Cottle and Nolan, 2007; Fenton, 2010), by supplying newsrooms with stories on the region (Kalcsics, 2011). This is at least partly because of reduced budgets in newsrooms (Hannerz, 2004; Sambrook, 2010a, b; Douglas, 2019).

Because INGOs must fundraise to do their work, they need to produce narratives that will encourage publics to donate. Fundraising imagery often features children to appeal to audiences emotions and this type of imagery, Batty argues (2000, p. 18), engages western audiences in a colonially rooted paternalistic relationship with suffering "others." Such imagery reproduces the problematic, inaccurate narrative of Southern "failure and helplessness that, through both decontextualization and desensitization, grossly misrepresents suffering and the possibilities for its alleviation" (Batty, 2000, p. 18).

Fundraising imagery isn't traditionally considered part of journalism, so it's important not to confuse such representation with journalistic imagery. However, in practice, audiences take meaning from all narratives they're exposed to. In addition, the rise of wealthy charities running press offices, often staffed by former journalists who know how to pitch stories, alongside reduced budgets in mainstream media, has seen boundaries between different genres of communication blur (Hunter and Van Wassenhove, 2010).

An example of this blurring, and problematic imagery of suffering "others," occurred during the 2014 Ebola outbreak in west Africa. Dominant global news media were initially reluctant to send journalists to cover the outbreak due to health and safety fears. This created a unique opportunity for resource-rich INGOs, that already had staff on the ground, to construct narratives and supply content.

Ebola Frontline, which the BBC aired in November 2014 on the current affairs program, Panorama (*BBC One,* 2014), was one such piece of content. It centred on following a British doctor, Javid Abdelmoneim, as he left England to work in an Ebola treatment centre in Sierra Leone, run by the charity Medicines Sans Frontiers (MSF). A camera was attached to him to give the audience a "doctor's eye view" of helping Ebola patients. We see him arriving in Sierra Leone and being transported to an unnamed area where he sets to work, voicing his thoughts to camera.

On arrival at the Ebola treatment centre, Abdelmoneim is dressed in protective clothing before entering and gives a running commentary. We see patients sprawled on beds, and on the floor, we also watch them arrive in ambulances. New patients sit on one side of a waist height fence while medical staff stand on the other side with clipboards, assigning each incoming patient a number and running through their symptoms as they sit alongside one another, before admitting them. It's worth noting that the majority of staff at the centre are Black Africans (unsurprising given the centre is in Sierra Leone), yet we barely hear from them.

The representation of this admission process has an instantly de-humanising effect. The Black African patients are presented to the audience as bodies to be treated: given no names, no opportunity to speak. The Sierra Leoneans in the programme who we do come to know by name are mostly children. This highlights Batty's (2000) argument that representations of seemingly abandoned children fuel perceptions of the helplessness of the Global South, and its need to be "parented" by the west.

Meanings attached to race are always, as Garner (2007) notes, time and place specific, "part of each national racial regime" (Garner, 2007, p. 1). In the context of the United Kingdom, where the programme was aired, Abdelmoneim's brown skin marks him as "other". Nonetheless, the fact that he's British, and only there temporarily, rather than a local doctor, who would have been there longer and arguably had more insight, speaks to wider issues at play in media-NGO storytelling on the Global South. Specifically, who's centred, who's othered, and how race and nationality play into this in, sometimes, problematic ways. Seen through this lens, Abdelmoneim, despite his brownness, is marked as "Other," rather than "other." This is made clear from the beginning of the programme when we see him in a well-appointed London apartment, having breakfast, listening to a radio broadcast about the latest news on Ebola and then packing to head out into the *other* world the radio is referencing. As the programme unfolds, Abdelmoneim's body is set apart (literally through his clothing and metaphorically because of who gets to speak) from the Black African bodies he has gone to help treat. His positioning, as a westerner in an African country, enables him to occupy a dominant location, with access to a system of privilege outside those he is treating.

Necropolitics

We can think further about westerners, as opposed to Africans or any other groups othered in the west, being centred in such narratives by drawing on philosopher Achille Mbembe's concept of *necropolitics* (2003) (death politics), which explores how constructed racial categories are used as a technique for distributing power and demarcate who is more worthy of life so that "race is ultimately linked to the politics of death" (Mbembe, 2003, p. 17).

Indeed, when Abdelmoneim says, during the programme, that it was only when white western lives were at risk that the "world" (i.e. the western world) took notice of Ebola, his observation speaks to a point Mbembe notes as being characteristic of modernity:

> The perception of the existence of the Other as an attempt on my life, as a mortal threat or absolute danger whose biophysical elimination would strengthen my potential to life and security.
>
> *(Mbembe, 2003, p. 18)*

Mbembe's (2003) argument extends Abdelmoneim's point in as much as it was only when Black African "others" with the disease were deemed to be a "threat" to "*our*" "life and security" that mainstream western media started to take an interest in "them," using fear of the thing which had turned "them" into supposed biohazards for the rest of "us" as a rationale for engaging with "them."

Mbembe developed his concept using Foucault's work on biopolitics, to address how race is used as a technique for distributing life and death. Foucault's conception of biopower shows how nineteenth-century western sciences used biological markers to justify systems like Nazism, which made the death of certain bodies more acceptable than others. Mbembe's *necropolitics* builds on this by exploring, "unique forms of social existence in which [...] populations are subjected to conditions of life conferring upon them the status of living dead" (Mbembe, 2003, p. 40). He references people living under colonialism, slavery, or siege in which discourses of power render their bodies less human, thus expendable. We can apply this to the way in which death is represented in the Panorama Ebola programme.

That the Sierra Leoneans affected by Ebola are voiceless in the programme means that, first and foremost, it is Abdelmoneim's mortality, vulnerability and agency which is implied, rather than those he's seeking to help. This speaks to Judith Butler's assertion that:

> The body implies mortality, vulnerability, agency: the *skin* and the *flesh* expose us to the gaze of others, but also to touch, and to violence, and bodies put us at risk of becoming the agency and instrument of all these as well.
> *(Butler, 2004, p. 26, emphasis added)*

The Black *skin* and African *flesh* of those bodies Abdelmoneim attempts to help are exposed to the "gaze of others," to borrow Butler's (ibid) words. Others these bodies can't see (as we watch on our televisions) and, due to their ill health may not even be aware of, as they are gazed at by "Others," with an uppercase O, through a camera.

Around halfway through the programme these patient's bodies are, we contend, exposed to an act of violence separate from the disease they are fighting. As Butler might have it, they are exposed to "the violence of derealization" (2004, p. 33) which she argues applies to lives already negated, lives which "cannot be mourned because they are always already lost or, rather, never 'were'" (Butler, 2004, p. 33). This violence is enacted thus: we see Abdelmoneim doing another round. He discovers a number of patients, some of whom we saw admitted as numbers (they never "were") at the beginning of the programme, have died. We learn this not just through his telling, which would have been enough to convey the horror of the disease and the speed at which it can work, but thanks to close up, lingering shots of their dead, and dying, bodies – faces uncovered and identifiable.

The one Sierra Leonean whose name features prominently in the programme is a child called Warrah. This highlights Batty's (2000) argument that the use of images of children in international relief efforts creates a narrative which perpetuates a colonialist mentality by depicting the absence of parents. Warrah is a baby who Abdelmoneim cradles towards the end of the programme. She was cleared of Ebola and discharged. Her father died during filming. We are shown his dead body on the floor of a make-shift shower cubicle. Here, African "others" are not afforded agency, or even status through pity. It is only a child whose vulnerability is considered sufficiently universally recognised to allow them to be named.

It's important to consider this footage within the framework of the BBC's editorial guidelines on reporting death, suffering and distress which state:

> We must consider the editorial justification for portraying graphic or intrusive material of human suffering and distress. When crews arriving at the scene of a disaster or emergency are under pressures that make it difficult to judge whether recording is an unjustified infringement of privacy, they will often record as much material as possible. However [...] care must be taken to assess any privacy implications prior to broadcast. The demands of live output and speed in the use of pictures, including those from social media, should not override consideration of the privacy of those suffering or in distress[...].
>
> *(BBC, 2021)*

Although the Panorama programme was billed as a doctor's eyeview, and clearly doctors encounter dying and dead people, this was not a live broadcast in which speed may have made it difficult to judge privacy issues. Thus, it's important to consider whether this footage was considered permissible because Black African lives are still constituted by some as lesser lives (Butler, 2004), as "other?" Content like this arguably demonstrates how "cultural imaginaries" (Mbembe, 2003, p. 26) give "meaning to the enactment of differential rights to differing categories of people for different purposes within the same space."

Life-in-death

We propose extending Mbembe's concept of "death-worlds" to thinking of humanitarian work as an administrator of "*life*-in-death." This administration of life in death-worlds (typically represented in mainstream western news as residing in the Global South) represents a shift away from the "*death*-in-life" of slavery or the "savage life" of colonialism (Mbembe, ibid). By offering *life*-in-death, humanitarian discourse positions itself as seeking to nurture Black and brown southern lives. In this way, humanitarianism may be perceived to be entirely disconnected from *necropolitics* (which Mbembe suggests is intrinsic to racism) because humanitarian discourse can be seen to be about *living*. But arguably, in playing a powerful role in who lives, it's part of a politics of death.

In his discussion of slave life as a form of death-in-life, Mbembe points to the contradiction within slavery, highlighted by Susan Buck-Morss (2000, pp. 821–866, in Mbembe, 2003), between freedom of property and the freedom of people.

> An unequal relationship is established along with the inequality of the power over life. This power over life of another takes the form of *commerce*: *a person's humanity is dissolved* to the point where it becomes possible to say that the slave's life is possessed by the master.
>
> *(Mbembe, 2003, p. 22, our emphasis)*

We are in no way suggesting that humanitarian work (or, indeed, the Panorama programme about MSF's work) is an inhumane practice. Nor are we suggesting that there isn't vital work to be done by important humanitarian organisations like MSF and others to close the gargantuan gaps between the world's haves and have-nots, and an important part of that work involves telling stories about those inequalities. But, we have highlighted this quote because humanitarian work is a form of commerce which represents power over certain lives. It is also a power which can, if those lives are othered in representational practices, dissolve humanity in certain respects. And in the world of development and humanitarianism, this giving and receiving is frequently woven along racial lines; with the givers cast predominantly as white/Westerners, and the receivers as Black and brown southern "others."

In the context of the Panorama programme, humanitarian work as a form of life-in-death becomes about giving life where only death, or the possibility of death, existed before the arrival of the humanitarian worker. This presupposition of death, which prompts the act of giving (or attempt at giving) life, sets up a power relation where those lives-in-waiting can be represented violently (disrespectfully), as "derealised" (Butler, 2004). Arguably, this is because (as Mbembe might suggest) in the eyes of some in segments of current affairs and news media, they were in a death-state before the humanitarian workers attempted to give them life. They never "were," as Butler (2004) may have it, so they were not granted the kind of respectful treatment we would normally confer on those considered equal to "us," *living* like "us."

Exercise: Grievable Lives

In Judith Butler's essay, "*Violence, Mourning, Politics*" (2004) she builds on the concept of necropolitics to ask, "what makes for a grievable life?" She argues that where our bodies are positioned in hierarchies of power, dictates the degree to which we will be perceived as vulnerable and the extent to which our loss will be felt. With this in mind, consider whose lives are considered grievable, and how they are presented, in television coverage of a humanitarian tragedy in your home country and elsewhere.

Desiring the "other"

As well as being a figure of fear and pity, the "other" is also situated by those in dominant positions at the opposite end of the spectrum – as bodies that are desired. As bell hooks writes:

> Mass culture is the contemporary location that both publicly declares and perpetuates the idea that there is pleasure to be found in the

acknowledgement and enjoyment of racial difference. The commodification of Otherness has been so successful because it is offered as a new delight, more intense, more satisfying than normal ways of doing and feeling. Within commodity culture, ethnicity becomes spice, seasoning that can liven up the dull dish that is mainstream white culture.

(hooks, 1999, p. 21)

Although hooks is writing about racial "difference," the idea of "difference" being a "spice" for mainstream culture applies, in different contexts and to differing degrees, to all groups who are positioned outside dominant culture. "Soft news," which covers topics like travel and entertainment as well as fashion stories in consumer magazines, are often sites where desire for the other finds expression. Former colonies in the Caribbean and Asia, for example, become "exotic" backdrops for western fashion shoots, where "colourful," "smiling" locals are useful accessories, contrasting in "interesting" ways with, and centring, western (often white) models in designer clothes. In this type of imagery, difference between the "**O**ther" and "**o**ther" is demarcated and power relations that underpin the binary are reinforced. Here, the "other," which "must assume recognisable forms" (hooks, 1999, p. 26), is desired to (re)assert constructed notions of western "superiority," "beauty" and power to reclaim former colonies as playgrounds.

For example, when former US President, Barack Obama, re-opened direct flights from the United States to Cuba, Vanessa Friedman (2015), fashion critic for the *New York Times*, predicted that the fashion industry would take advantage of improving relations between the countries. Friedman was right. The US edition[13] of *Marie Claire* organised a shoot in Cuba for their September 2015 issue, which involved Lithuanian model, Giedre Dukauskaite, posing in expensive designer outfits next to Cuban men selling plantain and pineapples off the back of a wooden cart, and pouting next to an elderly Cuban woman holding a Cuban cigar (Enke, 2015). Erased of any context or voice, the "others" "difference" is commodified for the purpose of making clothes appear desirable to western audiences. As a result, to paraphrase hooks (1999, p. 31), not only is the other displaced, but their history is denied via a process of decontextualisation where they are not heard, but only seen in ways that serve the dominant "Other."

Journalists as mediators

Foucault's conception of discursive systems and the institutions which maintain them and organise society highlights space for resistance. It is in this space that journalists can disrupt and re-make perceptions.[14] *Othering* largely comes about when people do not know those they "other," and perceive them as a "threat," somehow "less than" themselves, or as novelties that can "spice up" their lives. As mediators of events and other people's lives, journalists can bridge gaps between "us" and "them" and create spaces where "we" can get to know "others," and they "us," by telling stories in which people are allowed to express themselves and are represented as *equals*. But bridges are easily burned if the lives of "others" are not adequately fleshed out, so those represented recognise themselves in narratives constructed about them, and those narratives are frequent and varied enough to represent other lives in full, rather than in singular, fixed ways.

Those from marginalised groups have of course always found means of contesting and subverting hegemonic ways of seeing and reappropriating existing meanings so that new representations come to the fore. This "trans-coding" (Hall, Evans and Nixon, 2013, p. 259) is arguably easier in the social media era when problematic representations can be quickly challenged, like Teju Cole's Twitter thread about Kony2012, or reinterpreted, like responses to *Le Courrier Picard's* "Alerte Jaune" headline. This allows journalists to remediate counter narratives, amplifying them for audiences. During the process of remediation, it is useful to take heed of Audre Lorde's insistence on *equalling*:

> Difference must be not merely tolerated, but seen as a fund of necessary polarities between which our creativity can spark like a dialectic. Only then does the necessity for *interdependency* become unthreatening. Only within that interdependency of different strengths, acknowledged and *equalled*, can the power to seek new ways of being in the world generate, as well as the courage [...] to act where there are no charters. Within the interdependence of mutual (nondominant difference) lies that security which enables us to descend into the chaos of knowledge and return with true visions of our future, along with the concomitant power to effect those changes which can bring that future into being. Difference is that raw and powerful connection from which our personal power is forged.
> *(Lorde, 1984, p. 111. Our emphasis)*

Key here is the notion of "interdependence" and "mutual nondominant difference." This requires ongoing acknowledgement that both "us" and "them" are "*different*" so that neither occupies a dominant position, but rather through dialogue, which journalists are in a position to mediate, we must strive to reach a place where *all* (meaning everyone's) differences are seen and *equalled*.

Summary

- Every representation is an act of power. Journalists engage in this act whenever they construct stories.
- The "other" describes those positioned outside dominant discourse because of socially constructed markers of "difference," such as class, gender, race and religion.

- Edward Said's *Orientalism* (1978) helped enable research into how the west constructed its "others." Gayatri Spivak coined the term *othering* to describe the way dominant groups marginalise others. Frantz Fanon demonstrates how *othering* that occurs at the level of discourse has real effects on people's lived experiences.
- History, and old ways of seeing and doing, informs *othering*, so it's important to account for history when considering how "others" are represented. Foucauldian-inspired discourse analysis can help reveal historically rooted ideas in contemporary representations.
- *Othering* takes different forms, including fear/hate, pity and desire, but they all have one thing in common: representing people and/or places in distorted ways that say plenty about relations of power, and little to nothing about the people and/or places being depicted.

Notes

1. A Google search of "Daily Mail" and "Grooming Gangs" throws up 12,500 results.
2. Another way to view Begum's treatment is via the lens of "adultification". This term describes the way Black and brown children are viewed as older than they are in white majority countries, and thus treated more harshly than their white peers.
3. Begum's parents are from Bangladesh, a country which Begum has never visited, and her brownness intersects with her religion so that she may be doubly othered in white majority countries.
4. Always remembering, of course, that we all occupy multiple positions so may have power in some contexts, but not others.
5. Amongst other things, Begum said she would 'rather die' than return to ISIS and she apologised to the British public.
6. Many scholars do not recognise Lacan's distinction between "Other" and "other", instead using the spellings interchangeably.
7. Whilst no discussion of "others" can bypass Said's ground-breaking work, it's also important to acknowledge that Said's *Orientalism* has not been without critique, largely for being too generalising (Achcar, 2008).
8. In thinking about invisibility and its relation to racism and othering, it's also important to consider the invisibility of whiteness, and the way such invisibility, subsequent lack of scrutiny, as if whiteness is the universal "norm", imbues whiteness, and those identified as such, with power (see Dyer, 2017).
9. For Foucault, paying attention to history means attending to the "archaeology" or "genealogy" of knowledge production and the breaks and continuities in systems of knowledge (or "epistemes"), which inform what is considered normal and acceptable during different periods.
10. It's worth emphasising, as theorists like Foucault and Jacques Ranciere (2010) do, that the history of racism is of course rooted in the history of state policy, so comes from "above", rather than from the "masses" "below", as Begum's case exemplifies.
11. Foucault's concept of biopower (1976 in Stoler, 2002) refers to how he conceives of bodies caught in webs of power. Their position within those webs is determined by constructed categories such as race. Achille Mbembe builds on this to develop his conception of necropolitics (2003).

12 We link development and humanitarian work because, although in practice the former usually means long-term work, and the latter is about short-term relief, the two often fuse and share similar representational practices to draw attention to their work.
13 The popular women's magazine is published in different countries.
14 It must be noted, as we do elsewhere, that journalists ability to disrupt reductive representations depends on their *capital* and the *doxa* of the institution they work for. Their desire to do so also, of course, depends on their personal politics.

References

Achcar, G. (2008) 'Orientalism in Reverse', *Radical Philosophy* [Preprint], (151). Available at: https://www.radicalphilosophy.com/article/orientalism-in-reverse (Accessed: 24 March 2022).

Ahmed, S. (2012) *On Being Included: Racism and Diversity in Institutional Life*. Durham, NC: Duke University Press.

Ashcroft, B., Griffiths, G. and Tiffin, H. (2013) *Post-Colonial Studies: the Key Concepts*. London: Taylor & Francis Group. Available at: http://ebookcentral.proquest.com/lib/nyulibrary-ebooks/detail.action?docID=1244807 (Accessed: 4 September 2021).

Batty, N. (2000) '"We Are the World, We Are the Children: The Semiotics of Seduction in International Relief Efforts"', in Roderick, M. (ed.) *Voices of the Other: Children's Literature in Postcolonial Contexts*. New York: Routledge. pp. 17–38.

BBC, E.G. (2021) *Section 7: Privacy - Guidelines*. Available at: https://www.bbc.com/editorialguidelines/guidelines/privacy/bbc.com/editorialguidelines/guidelines/privacy/guidelines/ (Accessed: 1 December 2021).

BBC One - Panorama, Ebola Frontline (no date) *BBC*. Available at: https://www.bbc.co.uk/programmes/b04plw27 (Accessed: 2 October 2021).

Bhabha, H. (1983) 'The Other Question: the Stereotype and Colonial Discourse', *Screen*, 24(6), pp. 18–36. https://academic-oup-com.gold.idm.oclc.org/screen/article/24/6/18/1653403

Boyle, D. (2020) *French Asians Hit Back at Racism with 'I Am Not a virus' Hashtag*, *Mail Online*. Available at: https://www.dailymail.co.uk/news/article-7947865/French-Asians-hit-racism-not-virus-hashtag.html (Accessed: 2 October 2021).

Butler, J. (2004) *Precarious Life: The Powers of Mourning and Violence*. London: Verso Books, p. 168.

Chouliaraki, L. (2006) *The Spectatorship of Suffering*. London: SAGE.

Cole, T. (2012) 'The White-Savior Industrial Complex', *The Atlantic*. Available at: https://www.theatlantic.com/international/archive/2012/03/the-white-savior-industrial-complex/254843/ (Accessed: 3 October 2021).

Cottle, S. and Nolan, D. (2007) 'Global Humanitarianism and the Changing Aid-Media Field: "Everyone Was Dying for Footage"', *Journalism Studies*, 8(6), pp. 862–878. doi:10.1080/14616700701556104.

Cottle, S. and Nolan, D. (2009) 'Simon Cottle and David Nolan: How the Media's Codes and Rules Influence the Ways NGOs Work', *Nieman Lab*. Available at: https://www.niemanlab.org/2009/11/simon-cottle-and-david-nolan-how-the-medias-codes-and-rules-influence-the-ways-ngos-work/ (Accessed: 17 October 2021).

Courrier picard (2020) *À propos de notre une du 26 janvier, Courrier picard*. Available at: https://www.courrier-picard.fr/id64729/article/2020-01-26/propos-de-notre-une-du-26-janvier (Accessed: 18 February 2022).

Crenshaw, K. (1989) 'Demarginalizing the Intersection of Race and Sex: A Black Feminist Critique of Antidiscrimination Doctrine, Feminist Theory and Antiracist Politics', *The University of Chicago Legal Forum*, 140, pp. 139–167.

van Dijk, T.A. (2000) 'New(s) Racism: A Discourse Analytical Approach', in Cottle, S. (ed.) *Ethnic Minorities and the Media*. Buckingham; Philadelphia: Open University Press, pp. 33–49.

Douglas, O. (2019) *Backstories / Black Stories: Black Journalists, INGOs and the Racial Politics of Representing Sub-Saharan Africa in Mainstream UK News Media*. doctoral. Goldsmiths, University of London. Available at: http://research.gold.ac.uk/26352/ (Accessed: 29 June 2020).

Dyer, R. (2017) *White: Twentieth Anniversary Edition, Routledge & CRC Press*. Available at: https://www.routledge.com/White-Twentieth-Anniversary-Edition/Dyer/p/book/9781138683044 (Accessed: 24 March 2022).

Enke, A. (2015) *Giedre Dukauskaite Hangs With the People in 'Havana Days' For Marie Claire US September 2015, Anne of Carversville*. Available at: https://anneofcarversville.com/style-photos/2015/8/19/giedre-dukauskaite-hangs-with-the-people-in-havana-days-for.html (Accessed: 9 October 2021).

Fanon, F. (1991) *Black Skin, White Masks*. New Ed edition. London: Pluto Press.

Feigel, L. (2015) 'In the Family Way: Illegitimacy between the Great War and the Swinging Sixties Review – A Shameful History', *The Observer*, 25 January. Available at: https://www.theguardian.com/books/2015/jan/25/in-the-family-way-jane-robinson-shameful-history-illegitimacy (Accessed: 30 November 2021).

Fenton, N. (2010) 'NGOS, New Media and the Mainstream News: News from Everywhere', in *New Media, Old News: Journalism & Democracy in the Digital Age*. London: SAGE Publications Ltd, pp. 153–168. doi:10.4135/9781446280010.

Foucault, M. (1977) *Discipline and Punish: The Birth of the Prison*. 1st American ed. New York: Pantheon Books.

Foucault, M. (2002) *Archaeology of Knowledge*. London; New York: Routledge (Routledge classics).

Foucault, M. (2007) *The Order of Things: An Archaeology of the Human Sciences*. Repr. London: Routledge (Routledge classics).

Friedman, V. (2015) 'As Cuba Opens Up, Fashion Reacts', *The New York Times*, 15 April. Available at: https://www.nytimes.com/2015/04/16/fashion/as-cuba-opens-up-fashion-reacts.html (Accessed: 9 October 2021).

Garner, S. (2007) *Whiteness: An Introduction, Routledge & CRC Press*. Available at: https://www.routledge.com/Whiteness-An-Introduction/Garner/p/book/9780415403641 (Accessed: 2 December 2021).

Gilroy, P. (1987) *There Ain't No Black in the Union Jack: The Cultural Politics of Race and Nation*. London: Hutchinson.

Goldberg, D.T. (1993) *Racist Culture: Philosophy and the Politics of Meaning*. Oxford; Cambridge, MA: Blackwell.

Gunaratnam, Y. (2003) *Researching Race and Ethnicity*. 6 Bonhill Street, London EC2A 4PU: SAGE Publications Ltd. doi:10.4135/9780857024626.

Hall, S. (1973) 'The Determinations of News Photographs (1973)', in Greer, C. (ed.) *Crime and Media*. 1st edition. Routledge, pp. 123–134. doi:10.4324/9780367809195-13.

Hall, S. (1997) 'The Work of Representation', in Stuart, H. (ed.) *Representation: Cultural Representation and Signifying Practices*, (The Open University). Milton Keynes: Sage; The Open University. pp. 13–75. http://www.sholetteseminars.com/wp-content/uploads/2020/09/hall-representation.pdf

Hall, S., Evans, J. and Nixon, S. (eds) (2013) *Representation*. Second edition. Los Angeles: Milton Keynes: Sage; The Open University.

Hamid, R. (2021) *Defining Islamophobia: A Contemporary Understanding of How Expressions of Muslimness Are Targeted*. London: Muslim Council of Britain.

Hannerz, U. (2004) *Foreign News: Exploring the World of Foreign Correspondents*. Chicago, IL: University of Chicago Press (The Lewis Henry Morgan lectures).

hooks, b. (1999) *Black Looks: Race and Representation*. 1st Edition. Boston, MA: South End Press.

Hunter, M.L. and Van Wassenhove, L.N. (2010) 'Disruptive News Technologies: Stakeholder Media and the Future of Watchdog Journalism Business Models', *SSRN Electronic Journal* [Preprint]. doi:10.2139/ssrn.1582324.

Kalcsics, M. (2011) *A Reporting Disaster? The Interdependence of Media and Aid Agencies in a Competitive Compassion Market*, Reuters Institute for the Study of Journalism. Available at: https://reutersinstitute.politics.ox.ac.uk/our-research/reporting-disaster-interdependence-media-and-aid-agencies-competitive-compassion (Accessed: 17 October 2021).

Kambhampaty Purna, A. and Carlisle, M. (2019) *Justin Trudeau Admits to Also Wearing Blackface 'Makeup' Following TIME Report, Time*. Available at: https://time.com/5680868/justin-trudeau-brownface-photo-apology/ (Accessed: 16 October 2021).

Kapuściński, R. (2018) *The Other*. Translated by A. Lloyd-Jones. Verso Books, p. 112.

Knight, I. (2021) *Shamima Begum Has Nowhere to Go But Here | Comment | The Sunday Times*. Available at: https://www.thetimes.co.uk/article/shamima-begum-has-nowhere-to-go-but-here-xswzlqzs9 (Accessed: 1 December 2021).

Lorde, A. (1984) *Sister Outsider: Essays and Speeches*. Berkeley, CA: Crossing Press, c2007.

Mbembe, A. (2003) 'Necropolitics', *Public Culture*, 15(1), pp. 11–40. doi:10.1215/08992363-15-1-11.

Moeller, S.D. (1999) *Compassion Fatigue: How the Media Sells Disease, Famine, War and Death*. New York; Florence: Routledge; Taylor & Francis Group Distributor.

Newman, V. (2021) *Piers Morgan Brands Shamima Begum 'ISIS Monster Bride' Who Should Be Left to Rot, Mirror*. Available at: https://www.mirror.co.uk/3am/celebrity-news/piers-morgan-brands-shamima-begum-24987363 (Accessed: 25 September 2021).

Orientalism and Orientalism in Reverse - Sadik Jalal al-'Azm | libcom.org (no date). Available at: https://libcom.org/library/orientalism-orientalism-reverse-sadik-jalal-al-%E2%80%99azm (Accessed: 24 March 2022).

Piers Morgan (2021) 'Just as Well I'm Not Interviewing This Lying, Snivelling, Cold-Hearted, Self-Serving ISIS Bride Monster or I'd Have Seriously Lost My Temper by Now. Begum Should Never Be Allowed Back to Britain. Let Her Rot in the Terror Bed She Made for Herself. https://t.co/ao5BRTVFA2', *@piersmorgan*, 15 September. Available at: https://twitter.com/piersmorgan/status/1438033078832832513 (Accessed: 25 September 2021).

Pleasance, C. (2021) *French ISIS Bride Undergoes Makeover Similar to Shamima Begum, Mail Online*. Available at: https://www.dailymail.co.uk/news/article-9444067/French-ISIS-bride-undergoes-makeover-similar-Shamima-Begum.html (Accessed: 21 October 2021).

Ranciere, J. (2010) *Racism: A Passion from Above | MR Online*. Available at: https://mronline.org/2010/09/23/racism-a-passion-from-above/ (Accessed: 24 March 2022).

Sabbagh, D., Defence, D.S. and editor, security (2021) 'Shamima Begum Says She Wants to Prove Innocence in UK Courts', *The Guardian*, 15 September. Available at: https://www.theguardian.com/uk-news/2021/sep/15/shamima-begum-says-she-wants-to-prove-innocence-in-uk-courts (Accessed: 16 October 2021).

Said, E.W. (1978) *Orientalism*. London: Routledge & Kegan (Wolfgang Laade Music of Man Archive).

Sambrook, R. (2010a) *Are Foreign Correspondents Redundant? The Changing Face of International News*. Oxford: Reuters Institute for the Study of Journalism.

Sambrook, R. (2010b) 'The Changing Business of Journalism and Its Implications for Democracy', *Journalism Studies*, 13(3), pp. 477–478. doi:10.1080/1461670X.2012.662412.

Sciences, P.M.W.C. in C.-S. of S., Lab, D.-E.S.D.S. and HateLab, D.-E. (2021) *COVID-19 Political Commentary Linked to Online Hate Crime, Cardiff University*. Available at: https://www.cardiff.ac.uk/news/view/2510296-covid-19-political-commentary-linked-to-online-hate-crime (Accessed: 2 October 2021).

Segalov, M. (2018) 'If You Can't See Antisemitism, It's Time to Open Your Eyes', *The Guardian*, 28 March. Available at: https://www.theguardian.com/commentisfree/2018/mar/28/antisemitism-open-your-eyes-jeremy-corbyn-labour (Accessed: 2 November 2021).

Spivak, G. (1988) 'Can the Subaltern Speak?', in Nelson, C. and Grossberg, L. (eds) *Marxism and the Interpretation of Culture*. Basingstoke: Macmillan Education. pp. 271–317.

Stoler, A.L. (2002a) *Carnal Knowledge and Imperial Power: Race and the Intimate in Colonial Rule: With a New Preface*. Berkeley; Los Angeles; London: University of California Press.

Stoler, A.L. (2002b) 'Racial Histories and their Regimes of Truth', in Goldberg, D. and Essed, P. (eds) *Race Critical Theories*. Malden, MA: Blackwell Publishing. pp. 369–392.

Tonkiss, F. (2004) 'Analysing Discourse', in Seale, C. (ed.). London: Sage, pp. 245–260. Available at: http://www.sagepub.co.uk (Accessed: 16 October 2021).

Vigdor, N. (2021) 'Broadcaster Apologizes for "Inappropriate" Images Aired During Olympic Parade', *The New York Times*, 25 July. Available at: https://www.nytimes.com/2021/07/25/sports/olympics/mbc-broadcaster-apology-olympics-opening-ceremony.html (Accessed: 20 September 2021).

Webb, J. (2009) *Understanding Representation*. London: Sage.

Williams, M. (2021) *The Science of Hate*. Available at: https://www.waterstones.com/book/the-science-of-hate/matthew-williams/9780571357062 (Accessed: 2 October 2021).

6
SOURCES MATTER

Journalists and editors have the power to shape the perception of events by choosing who will be invited to speak, who will be left out and how those voices will be organised using methods such as ordering (who speaks first, who gets the last word), contextualising (negatively or positively) and simplifying. Such choices are driven by *ideology*, shaped by preconceptions and limited by structural factors both economic and political. Foucault describes these as procedures of "rarefaction," by which he means the simplification of issues and events, which emerges from the mass of possible interpretations. For journalists, as we have explained elsewhere, operating via procedures of "rarefaction" involves doing their jobs according to a set of rules (*doxa*) which allow them to create order and develop a coherent narrative which audiences can easily grasp (Tomlinson, 1991, p. 9). Doxa are not neutral, they are shaped by power relationships. Theorists have different views as to the relative power of journalists, sources or power elites in shaping these narratives.

Whether writing about a natural disaster, an uprising, a new vaccine or a political scandal, journalists are trained to collect information from sources who are close enough to events to be able to provide evidence and then to verify and evaluate that evidence. So, for example, if a mass of people appears in the street, shouting and running, it is not enough to look at the events as they unfold and Tweet about it. The journalist, unlike the bystander, needs to work out *who* is running; whether they are being chased or are doing the chasing; *where* and *when* they started running and *where* they are going; *what* they hope to achieve by running and *why* they feel the need to run. Then, they need to find out (if possible) *how* the event unfolded.

Very little of this can be discerned just by looking. The journalist needs to ask questions to glean information and those people questioned are usually considered within a hierarchy of importance. *Authoritative* sources (politicians,

DOI: 10.4324/9781003037651-7

government officials, police, fire-brigade officers, medical personnel) usually provide the frame for the story, to which the journalist may add their own observation, voices from people on the ground and from those they have previously accessed and feel they can trust. From all of this, a narrative will emerge. For journalists who are not at the scene, much of this will occur online, using a combination of press releases, web information sources, including other journalists' coverage, known individuals who may contact them (or be contacted) via DM or e-mail and social media.

For *liberal pluralist* thinkers, it is the journalist who is in the driving seat. While there is a recognition that journalists are limited by the media system in which they function, the assumption here is that, at least in a liberal democracy, they choose between differing versions of events and, therefore, have a powerful role in deciding which voices will be given priority. For these commentators (Kovach and Rosenstiel, 2007; Davies, 2008; Gans, 2011), journalists just need to do their jobs better and the people's stories will be told.

Critical theorists argue that journalists operate within a system of dominance (Schlesinger, 1990, p. 63) in which they are not completely free to make decisions. For Herman and Chomsky, there is a direct line between the ownership and control of the media and content produced (Herman and Chomsky, 1988). Others, while acknowledging the importance of unequal power relationships, see a more complex relationship between power, media ownership and sources. They acknowledge that, in a democracy, the media do not always side with the dominate power and that such a rigid analysis cannot account for the media's role in social change (Manning, 2001). Below, we consider some of the main strands of *critical source theory*.

Primary definers

In The Social Production of News, Stuart Hall and his colleagues argue that the power to shape the news agenda is not, in fact, in the hands of journalists themselves but in the hands of their sources (Hall, 1978). Central to this *Gramscian* approach is the recognition that certain voices have greater power and, having that power, tend to establish the *rules of the game* when a story is told.

> The media, then, do not simply 'create' the news nor do they simply transmit the ideology of the ruling class in a conspiratorial fashion. Indeed, we have suggested that, in a critical sense, the media are frequently not the 'primary definers' of news events at all; but their structured relationship to power has the effect of making them play a crucial but secondary role in *reproducing* the definitions of those who have privileged access, as of right, to the media as 'accredited sources'. From this point of view, in the moment of news production, the media stand in a position of structured subordination to the primary definers.
>
> *(Hall, 1978, p. 62)*

Sources deemed to be *primary definers* are those with power and position (politicians and industrialists), with representative status (trade or consumer organisations) or acknowledged experts (such as academics or lawyers). They make use of their position within the existing social hierarchy (their social capital) but also their capacity for being available when needed (or in advance). This accessibility is a particular property of organisations that have prior, or privileged, access to information and the means to make that information available on cue and according to the deadlines set by media organisations. All other sources are consigned secondary status which means they will usually appear further down the story, if at all, and may well be subtly de-legitimised using such words as "alleged," "suggested" or "claimed" rather than, for example, "said" when quotes are introduced.

It is, of course, the job of journalists to explain what is happening in Government, to warn of impending danger and to hold the powerful to account. If the powerful were invisible that would signal, above all, that journalists were allowing them to work without scrutiny. What Hall is alluding to here is not the everyday requirement for journalists to report what the Government is doing and what is happening in the courts, it is the way in which their structural advantage gives privileged elites the ability to define the *terms of the debate*.

Hall and his co-authors were writing in Britain in the 1970s when people got their news from television and newspapers. The authors trace the way the term "mugging" (formally only used in America) was used by the police in the 1970s and 1980s, to entirely falsely frame certain forms of crime as essentially perpetrated by Black people. The term, now racialized, was taken up and amplified by the news media leading, in turn, to an unwarranted rise in fear of violent crime and to public demands for the Government, then keen to promote a repressive law and order ideology, to crack-down on criminality. The strategy disproportionately affected young Black men who were unjustly subjected to high levels of punitive policing and were not given space within the public sphere to air their legitimate grievances, let alone be afforded the opportunity to occupy the role of *primary definer* in news narratives concerning them. This arc of referencing by authoritative sources, repetition by the press, alarm from the public, followed by Government action became known as a "Moral Panic" (Cohen, 1990).

Speed and authority signalling

Nearly half a century later, the media landscape has changed, and anyone with a mobile phone and access to the internet can, theoretically, get in touch with a journalist and set the agenda. Yet, in practice, as one British journalist on a major national daily put it: "Being a [….] journalist is rather like standing in the middle of a hurricane trying to pick out twigs. You're [….] constantly looking around to see what's significant" (Phillips, 2010, p. 94).

The pressure of speed and proliferating information has introduced new structural constraints which in many ways reinforce the prominence of *primary definers*. Journalists must be particularly careful not to reproduce information that is false, or deliberately mis-leading, because to do so would undermine not only their reliability in the eyes of their employers, but also the legitimacy of journalism. In these circumstances, they are particularly anxious to find ways of establishing their authority because, as Carlson explains:

> Authority cannot be taken for granted; it must be actively constructed and is best seen, not as an intrinsic property that inheres in individuals and organizations but 'relationally … as an understanding formed through the interactions among all the actors necessary for journalism to exist.
>
> *(Carlson, 2017, p. 7)*

Individual journalists, faced with the need to fact check at speed while at the same time putting together an account of events, are likely to cling to known sources, or at least sources whose credentials can be easily verified:

> I can't think of a decent story that I've got from somebody that I'd never met or heard of before. [….] maybe unsolicited in the respect in that I'd not actually heard of them before but it was a part of a relationship I built up with people in the area generally.
>
> *(Phillips, 2010, p. 92)*

However, knowing a source is not sufficient they must also signal this authority to their audiences. Andrew Chadwick calls this, "authority signalling" (Chadwick *et al.*, 2020, p. 912). It involves, for example, referring to sources as "independent," "respected," "impartial," "important," "official," as a means of underlining their credibility and giving them the power to shape the story. The simple repetition of these terms then establishes them as arbiters rather than participants in the discursive struggle. In the context of the Covid pandemic, labels such as "fake" or "unofficial" were also used to de-legitimise sources of information that were considered harmful.

Exercise: Primary Definers

Read stories in local and/or national newspapers. Who are the *primary definers*? Can news be legitimated without the use of *primary definers*?

Look at two international stories on the same news event, how is it covered by the press in your country, and the press elsewhere? Who are the *primary definers*? Are they the same or different? How do the included *primary definers* in the different articles alter your understanding of the event? Which sources, if any, are de-legitimised in the story?

Challenging authority

While it is clear from these examples that elites have advantages in establishing the frame of reference, critics of Hall point out that the definition of *primary definers* tends to neglect the fact that they are not unchallenged, that, "political elites are characterised by external competition and internal conflict" (Manning, 2001, p. 108), and that news media can, and do, participate in struggles for symbolic dominance rather than merely reflecting them. As Davis suggests: "Reporters have become one key component of the social and cultural construction of the political centre and the business of politics itself" (Davis, 2009, p. 208).

One way journalists take control of the agenda is in exploiting mistakes made by prominent people, either for their news value, or in order to pursue their own (or their editor's) political agenda (Manning, 2001, p. 115). For example, in 2019, the British Prime Minister, Theresa May, called an election to try and increase her majority, and her negotiating hand, in taking the United Kingdom out of the European Union. She had not bargained on the key Conservative-backing newspaper attacking her just before the poll, with headlines such as:

The Dementia tax backlash: Tories' lead slips by 5% after manifesto pledge to make more elderly pay for care

- **Proposals could mean that tens of thousands of people will face costly bills**
- **For the first time, the value of a person's home will be included in their assets**
- **Survation poll indicates 47 percent oppose Mrs May's social care funding plans**

(Walters, 2017)

The story made use of an opinion poll and the voices of two Conservative MPs, whose quotes were organised so that they appeared to be unhappy about the proposals (although a careful reading suggests that the quotes were taken out of context). May quickly amended her policy and, while it would be an exaggeration to suggest that the Brexit supporting *Daily Mail* was solely responsible for the loss of her majority, her collapse gave far more power to the most uncompromising pro-Brexiteers among her MPs. An outcome that fitted the agenda of the newspaper rather than the Government of the time.

While the power to pressurise Governments undermines the assumption that news organisations have a secondary relationship to primary definers, other studies demonstrate that source power is not always determined by proximity to the established elite or access to wealth either. Nohrstedt researched the reporting of the 1986 Chernobyl disaster in Sweden and found that official sources had difficulty maintaining their authority in the face of alternative sources from anti-nuclear campaign groups (Corner and Schlesinger, 1991). Schesinger looked at the impact of the anti-war movement in the United States, the anti-nuclear movement and the green movements and said: "if such groups were of no consequence, the political elites would not actively try to delegitimize them and co-opt their ideas. Nor would so much effort be expended in trying to manage the overall ecology of ideas" (Corner and Schlesinger, 1991). Similar arguments are made by Davis (2000) and by Manning (2001). They argue that the concept of *primary definers* remains useful as a way of describing relations of power and the way the media support the political status quo, but it is insufficient to describe variations between media or what happens when organised groups establish alternative narratives.

Spheres of controversy

Daniel Hallin (1989) finds, in his research into the reporting of the Vietnam War, that the North American news media are enmeshed in the political establishment and that their apparent independence is, in fact, a reflection of the shifts of power as elites fall out. The coverage of Vietnam is often used as an example of the independence of the American news media and evidence of the health of its public sphere, but tracing coverage of the war over several years, Hallin concludes that the news media only deviated from the official line when that line started to lose its clarity. In the early part of the war, there was a high degree of consensus and support for the Government. As time went on, and opposition within the establishment grew, the news media picked up on that unease and began to report it. He concludes that, far from generating debate about Government policy, the media waited until the elite began to disagree and then reported that disagreement.

From this insight, Hallin produces a more flexible theory of elite power suggesting that there are three spheres of media debate: *consensus, legitimate controversy* and *deviancy*. Some subjects are so much taken for granted in the mainstream news media that they are un-challenged. Political parties and their leaders may quibble over detail but rarely over substance and journalists rarely challenge this consensus. So, for example, before the global banking crisis of 2008, few politicians, or journalists, challenged the assumption that the banks could not fail, just as, afterwards, few challenged the policy of quantitative easing, which poured money into the banking system, while average wages stagnated and jobs were lost (Manning, 2013).

Then, there are spheres of *legitimate controversy*, for example, the debate over the wearing of facemasks during the Covid epidemic. Both experts and politicians around the world changed their minds in response either to evidence or political expediency and journalists tended to interview experts from both sides of the debate. Finally, there is the sphere of *deviancy*. These voices are regarded as illegitimate and are often ignored in favour of demonising description and details of their disruptive effect (Dardis, 2006). People occupying this sphere may be temporarily brought into the sphere of legitimate debate when their preoccupations are legitimised by other, more authoritative, voices. So, for example, climate change is more likely to be discussed when it is the subject of an inter-Governmental conference, but afterwards, activists may again be relegated to the *sphere of deviancy*, as a report on the *BBC* website in December 2021 demonstrates.

> *Insulate Britain: Arrests as protesters glue themselves to roads*
> Twenty people have been arrested after Insulate Britain protesters disrupted traffic around an M25 junction with some gluing themselves to a road.
> Hertfordshire Police said protesters have been at junction 23 for the A1(M) at Bignells Corner, and also on the A1081 St Albans Road.
> Officers were initially called to the area at 07:45 GMT.
> The group said on Twitter that 60 of its members were disrupting traffic in London, Birmingham and Manchester.
> Four court injunctions are in place banning Insulate Britain from obstructing major roads.
> *(BBC News, 2021)*

Although this demonstration came at a time of growing interest in the issue of global warming (shortly after the COP26 climate talks), and huge energy price hikes across the world, in 11 paragraphs, the BBC report did not link the demonstrations to the climate crisis or to world energy prices, nor did it report the voice of a protestor, the reporter did not even explain what the protest was about. The article reflects an assumed sphere of *consensus* in which demonstrators are disruptive and the police frame the debate.

While the voices of climate protestors are often delegitimised by being ignored, the voices of those considered a direct threat to society are likely to be actively demonised. Larsen (2021) in an examination of the Norwegian news media found that in the reporting of terror attacks:

> Voices deemed extremist were included in a de-contextualized, segregated, and controlled fashion that arguably were more suited to demonizing the actors, dramatizing the topic, and generating fear and anger rather than providing an understanding and discussion of the motives and thinking of these individuals and groups.
> *(Larsen, 2021, p. 118)*

The author also noted that the categories used by the media tended to be defined by the security services (*primary definers*) and those assigned the label of terrorist, extremist or jihadist were thus judged in advance as beyond the legitimate sphere of controversy (Larsen, 2021).

Polarisation and media power

While Hallin provides a useful means of analysing the debate in the news media, his analysis arguably fails to capture the full complexity of differing national media systems or shifts within them. In the politically polarised media systems of southern Europe and the printed media of the United Kingdom, for example, the situation was (and remains) different. News organisations are still heavily dependent on press releases from the Government, political parties and other powerful organisations as *primary definers* and as the starting point (and often the totality) of articles, but the interpretation and framing of events diverge between news organisations as events become politicised.

At the time Hall and Hallin were writing, the public sphere was boundaried (see **Chapter 1**). The consolidation and commodification of the news media over the twentieth century (see **Chapter 8**) meant that only those with significant money to spend, or public, or Government, backing, had opportunities for joining, and, therefore, influencing, public debate. Even in a polarised system, debate coalesced around a narrowly drawn political elite. This changed when the consensus media of the mid-twentieth century gave way to the highly polarised media of the twenty-first century, particularly in the United States (Fletcher, 2017).

In countries where the national media is highly polarised, almost any issue can become politicised, and a sphere of *consensus* is hard to find. Indeed, Taylor (2014) suggests that the sphere of consensus has disappeared and that it is only worthwhile to consider: the sphere of *full legitimacy*, the sphere of *partial legitimacy*, the sphere of *implicit deviance* and the sphere of *explicit deviance* (Taylor, 2014, p. 40). The coverage of the Corona Virus pandemic is a case in point.

In general, reports from medical journals are accepted as occupying the sphere of consensus (or full legitimacy). So, for example, when a new variant of the Corona Virus was discovered by South African researchers early in 2021, the key sources identified were the National Institute for Communicable Diseases (NICD) and the KwaZulu-Natal Research Innovation and Sequencing Platform. Publication of their findings, in the journal *Nature*, provided additional authority for news organisations around the world. Initial stories did not go far beyond reporting details from the article. Quite often that is just the news media doing its job: telling us about important things that we need to know about without the need for comment, speculation or contestation. Indeed, this sort of news can go into a bucket known as "vanilla news" (Lee-Wright, Phillips and Witschge, 2011, pp. 83–84).

Additional comments, if they were used at all, linked these new findings to current national events. Here, journalists make choices about who to contact. In some countries, such as South Africa, these tended to fall well within Hallin's single sphere of *consensus* (or Taylor's *sphere of legitimacy*): politicians or local public health officials commented and were duly reported, but their observations would, in most cases, be speculation, or reassurance:

> **For now there is nothing to worry about. If the new variant becomes a problem, the health minister will announce how best we will deal with it. For now, we are tracking it. There is no reason to worry.**
> *(Daily Sun, September 2, 2021)*

However, elsewhere the virus became highly politicised. In the United States, news organisations didn't just take quotes from one side or the other to demonstrate controversy. At times, they relegated the President to the sphere of *deviance*, using expert evidence to de-legitimise him (see also **Chapter 4** for discussion of how a similar sequence of events played out in Brazil). On the other hand, media supportive of the President attacked experts and politicians who called for caution.

The *New York Times* regularly criticised President Trump for publicising Covid cures that had no scientific backing:

> **Ignoring Expert Opinion, Trump Again Promotes Use of Hydroxychloroquine**
> **The president's advocacy of the anti-malarial drug has created tensions in his administration, and fears among doctors that it could unnecessarily expose patients to risks.**
> *(Crowley, Thomas and Haberman, 2020)*

While at *Fox News* and the *Daily Caller*, it was the experts themselves, particularly Anthony Fauci, chief Medical Advisor to the President, who were regularly attacked and vilified (Hart, Chinn and Soroka, 2020). It is hard to see this simply as a case of journalists operating within the sphere of *legitimate controversy* and it disrupts the notion that the news media, in these two countries, on this issue, took a neutral stance as merely secondary definers, dependent on the elite to frame events.

Indeed, the level of polarisation in the United States was so deep by the time of the 2016 elections, that politicians, polling organisations and the mainstream media, were unaware of what information voters were accessing. Online, no two people see the same material, and in that election year, voters received more *misinformation* and *junk news* via social media, than professionally produced news, or news from political parties. The percentage of junk news was even higher in swing states than elsewhere (Howard *et al.*, 2018). According to a report by Gabriel Gatehouse in a 2022 podcast for the *BBC*, much of the junk was generated on anonymous chat-boards such as 4chan where anti-Clinton memes were created and circulated alongside porn and jokes then re-posted on more accessible sites like Facebook (Gatehouse, 2021) where they circulated more widely. In 2017, the figure of Q emerged as a major source of conspiracy theories. Q has never been identified and Q's messages disappeared shortly before the abortive attack on the Capitol in Washington in January 2021.

Hall and Hallin's conceptions of the media as subordinate to the power of elite sources seem hard to reconcile with the activities of politically polarised media and have little purchase on the activities of 4 or 8Chan. However, in the Nordic countries, where a Reuters Digital News Report found far lower levels of polarisation (Fletcher, 2017), the media continue to use its position to maintain consensus. A study looking at the way mainstream online newspapers in Norway, Sweden and Denmark report sources from the right-wing alternative press, found that, in general, the news organisations are attempting to maintain a sphere of *liberal consensus* by banishing "populist actors to the sphere of deviance" (Nygaard, 2020, p. 779). According to the report: "journalists seem to depart from professional norms of neutrality and balance when confronted with right-wing alternative media and feel authorised to treat them as marginal and deviant" (Nygaard, 2020, p. 778).

The authors also note that right-wing alternative news attracted more attention in Norway and Denmark, "where populist actors are considered within the sphere of legitimate controversy in terms of their political cooperation with populist parties and a broader mass media corridor of opinion on immigration" (Nygaard, 2020, p. 779). However, even here the coverage was mostly negative.

By seeking to maintain a sphere of *consensus* and marginalising sources that threaten it, journalists in the Nordic countries appear to be trying to hold back the flow of populist, anti-immigrant rhetoric that has split apart the US media. In so doing, they could be regarded as protecting the legitimacy of journalism and attempting to maintain the political status-quo. In a wider study of ten European countries (Wettstein *et al.*, 2018), the mainstream news media were found to actively restrict populist sources (of the Right and the Left) and to underrepresent them even in discussion of issues in which they take a particular interest. The exceptions were the United Kingdom, Italy and the Netherlands where right-wing populist parties were significantly overrepresented in stories about immigration.

In considering whether to include particular voices, journalists and their editors are defining and legitimising the boundaries of permissible political discourse. However, as Wettstein concludes:

> One question to be pursued in future studies is whether this synchronized behavior [to close down populist views] may foster conspiracy ideas among certain groups in society that an alleged "system press" colludes with the political establishment to keep down undesirable viewpoints and actors.
> *(Wettstein et al., 2018, p. 492)*

Arguably, if the arena of legitimate debate is insufficiently flexible that debate will take place elsewhere and there is now a far lower cost of entry for those seeking to re-draw the limits of what is considered acceptable.

Source power, public relations and social media

Without reference to differing media systems or the creative power of individuals and organisations who wish to challenge the consensus, both Hall and Hallin tend to under-estimate the power of individual editors, the agency of individual journalists, the ability of "deviant" sources to manipulate the media agenda to their advantage and the power of public opinion. In this section, we will look at how sources that are not of the establishment, work to change the news agenda for a day, a year, or in some cases, for ever. It is the infiltration of these new voices, with different agendas, that offer opportunities for change. Manning refers to them as "insiders" and "outsiders."

Outsiders are grouped into three: those who are trying to find a way inside, those who lack the skills to be insiders and those who are "*ideological outsiders*" (Manning, 2001, p. 141). *Insiders* are organisations and their representatives, who move in the corridors of power and are legitimised by their inclusion in government activities in their field of expertise. They include the major resource-rich charities in, for example, the field of medicine and the care of children. They tend to cover subjects that are within the *sphere of consensus* (everybody cares about children and health) and will be circumspect in any criticism of Government to ensure that they don't lose their seat at the centre and access to funding. These, non-governmental organisations (NGOs), once delegitimised as "non-official sources" (Deacon, 2003) in mainstream western news, use their considerable resources to promote their agenda and foster relationships with journalists.

Aid organisations provide a useful study of how insiders can use their influence to set the news agenda. In recent years, cuts in news media income have meant that fewer western news organisations fund overseas trips for journalists, particularly to countries in the Global South. So, Aid organisations have stepped into the breach with public relations departments, often staffed by former journalists, writing press-releases in order to fulfil the required narrative structure that a news organisation might be seeking (Davis, 2000). This has increased the power of western aid organisations to shape news discourse in relation to events in the Global South (Franks, 2010; Douglas, 2019).

Given that their key role is to raise money for humanitarian work, the stories they supply tend to focus on human suffering. They often avoid highlighting political causes or solutions because they don't want to compromise their position by angering their hosts. The "sources" for their stories are often western aid workers, with local people who are affected by the issue at hand, or working to alleviate it, marginalised or erased from coverage (Douglas, 2019). This media–source relationship problematically facilitates dominant western news coverage of Southern regions through a narrow aid/development lens (for more on this, see **Chapter 5**).

However, while it has been possible for some organisations to establish themselves as *primary definers* by becoming useful sources of "information subsidy," the speeding up of the news cycle has had negative effects for others. Where once press officers would have had direct relationships with journalists, they may now find that the only way in which they can influence stories about public policy is to ensure that their in-put, very carefully headlined, is already in a journalist's in-box, and on Twitter, as a story breaks so that it can be easily incorporated (Fenton, 2010; Phillips, 2010). While strategic press releases might result in a mention in an article, the *primary sources* are even more likely to provide the story frame if secondary sources are relegated to input that can easily be cut and pasted into a pre-structured argument.

The position of *insider* organisations is also contingent on the patronage of the powerful. Trade Unions, for example, will be seen as *insiders* in some places, and at times when governments acknowledge them as partners in the establishment and maintenance of trade relations. In the United Kingdom, in the 1970s, when key parts of British industry were still nationalised, the General Secretaries of Trade Unions would be sought out as authoritative sources on issues of trade relations. In the 1980s, the Thatcher Government firmly relegated the trade unions to the *sphere of deviance*, and the news coverage of strikes and interest in the unions rapidly declined. Even the job of industrial (or labour) correspondent disappeared as newspapers focussed on their business pages (Manning, 2001). Fifty years later trade unionists and their leaders are routinely demonised, their activities are rarely reported outside the context of their inconvenience to the public.

Celebrities: insiders or outsiders?

Celebrities have a special power to grab media attention because of their following and ability to attract audiences, but that attention is as likely to be negative as positive, particularly for women who will have attention drawn to their bodies, their weight gain (or loss), and their relationships. Celebrities can also leverage their popularity to draw attention to other causes, but they rarely have the power to set the agenda, and, if they do so for a time, their position is often temporary. Media power, far from being subordinate to the power of these sources, is capable of both making and unmaking them.

When athletes John Carlos and Tommie Smith made Black power salutes from the winner's podium of the 1968 Olympic Games, there is no doubt that the protest drew public attention to the cause of Black civil rights. However, the athletes were largely attacked in the domestic news media and suspended from the US Olympic team. *The New York Times* prominently featured a statement from the US Olympic Committee:

> **In a statement issued early this morning, the United States committee expressed its "profound regrets" to the International Olympic Committee, the Mexican Organizing Committee and the people of Mexico for the "discourtesy displayed" by Smith and Carlos. "The untypical exhibitionism of these athletes violates the basic standards of good manners and sportsmanship, which are so highly valued in the United States," the statement said. "Such immature behaviour is an isolated incident" and "a repetition of such incidents by other members of the United States team can only be considered a wilful disregard of Olympic principles."**
> *New York Times October 16, 1968 (Sheehan, 1968)*

The two athletes were not quoted at all. They were banished to the *sphere of deviance* as representatives not of US sporting prowess, but of forces that were disrupting the political consensus of white America. They were objectified (see **Chapter 5** for a discussion of *othering*), and the clear implication of the final paragraph was that they apparently had no agency or lived experience of American racism that would provoke such a stand, but had instead been politically groomed by an older man:

> The 24-year-old Smith, a rangy, long-legged athlete who stands 6 feet 3 inches, is from Lemoore, Calif., and is a student at San Jose State University, where Harry Edwards, who initiated the black power manifestations in athletics, was a teacher last year. Carlos, 23, who is 6 feet 4 inches tall, was born and raised in New York, but now lives in San Jose and also attends San Jose State.
>
> *(Sheehan ibid.)*

When Black footballer, Marcus Rashford, called on the British Government to extend free school meals for children over the summer of the 2020 Covid pandemic, he got an overwhelmingly supportive response across the British media. He made his appeal to the Government on his own social media feed (he has 12.5 million followers on Instagram) and was, initially, hailed as a hero. Under pressure from the combined force of the mainstream media, the Government buckled and agreed to provide free meals for children during the pandemic. When Rashford then went on to be racially abused on social media for missing a penalty at a crucial football game, the press, including some right-wing newspapers, long critiqued for perpetuating racist discourse, continued to defend him:

> Everyone knew they would be racially abused on social media. It is not an exception anymore. It has not been an exception for some time. It is the norm. When anger and disillusion and impotence want to raise their voice in football now, their default mechanism is racist abuse.
>
> *(Oliver Holt, Daily Mail 17 July 2021)*

Rashford really had changed the agenda, but it soon became clear where the discursive power lies as articles started to appear suggesting that Rashford was profiting financially from his advocacy, spending money on luxury homes (Daily Mail articles on July 20 and November 14, 2020) and that his form was letting down his club[1]. Rashford's concerns had, briefly, grabbed the media agenda (no popular newspaper would want to be seen to oppose feeding children), but even his massive personal social media following could not protect him from the clear signalling by the Daily Mail (the most visited news site in the United Kingdom and one of the most popular in the English-speaking world) that he should stay in his lane.

> **Exercise: Celebrity Power**
>
> Symbolic gestures of protest by celebrities have sparked much debate in the media and have been represented in different ways around the world. Search online for examples of, for example, "taking the knee," which was started in 2016 by the American footballer Colin Kaepernick, or #MeToo and consider whose voices are heard, and the degree to which they have changed the way the issues are framed in the media.

Ideological outsiders

Many of the other organisations and groupings who count as *outsiders* could be seen as part of the "peripheral" or *subaltern public sphere* (see **Chapter 1**) which can, from time to time, exert enough pressure to change the terms of the debate, rather than just operating within it. The debate in the Indian mainstream media tends to prioritise the main parties and their spokespeople as primary definers, but in the 2015 Delhi elections, the media swung behind an insurgent party (the AAP), backed by local social movements. This appears to demonstrate that even an apparently solid coalition between news media and the political elite can shift when: "a third, external, force, in the shape of massive popular opposition to the business-politics alliance, renders complete subservience to the latter impossible to reconcile with the continued credibility of the journalistic field as a whole" (Maheshwari and Sparks, 2021, p. 244).

The force of the social movements and groups applying pressure to the centre is designed to move the *sphere of consensus*. They are particularly vocal in periods of rapid social change as new ideas bubble to the surface and disrupt old assumptions. While the very nature of their interests (on class, gender, race, equality, poverty, etc.) means that they are generally outside the centre of power, their relationship with journalism is often far more fluid than source theory acknowledges.

The environmental movement is a case in point. Climate change is a slow, remorseless and largely invisible process. For long periods, organisations such as Greenpeace and more recently Extinction Rebellion, are completely ignored because their concerns do not fit within what journalists learn to understand as the daily news agenda. The on-going problem for *outsider* organisations is to stay relevant. Journalism prefers events that are novel and have a beginning, middle and foreseeable conclusion (see **Chapter 3** for discussion of news values). Environmental organisations have learned to create news events that will grab attention, briefly, to put across some stark and simple messages. Campaigners combine small activities, aimed at engaging members and perhaps attracting local coverage, as a way of building towards spectacular events, for which large numbers of people can be mobilised to attract the maximum attention. The news media provide the stage on which these activities play-out.

While the way these events are covered often seems to push them into the *sphere of deviance*, in a sense that is the intention. Activists are prepared to use their *outsider* status to both enrage and engage. Blocking traffic, getting arrested, super-gluing themselves to buildings are not gestures aimed at ingratiating themselves with power. Their outrage is the point. Their behaviour is performative. They are saying to the public: "I am prepared to go to prison for this. It is that important. What are you going to do?" Just by getting people to *notice*, journalism plays an important role (Kilgo and Harlow, 2019). See also the discussion on *agonism* in **Chapter 1**.

Journalism, sources and social media

International events are usually framed according to national interests (see **Chapter 4**) and, in the Global North, if there are no conflicting national political narratives, a pro-democracy or human rights frame is usually utilised which often creates *insiders* of those who would normally be framed as *outsiders*. So, for example, when the BBC filmed the events in Tiananmen Square, China, in 1989, the journalists' sympathy was clearly on the side of the student demonstrators. The ideological framing of the events ensured that the student leaders, rather than the leaders of the country, were given primacy in the international media. In the Chinese media, on the other hand, the students were defined as deviant and the Chinese political leaders were the *primary definers*.

The same pro-democracy frames were used by the western media in the coverage of the Arab Spring. The key difference lay, not in the framing, nor the ability of social media to publicise events, but the fact that news organisations that were not on the ground, were able to see events as they unfolded, get access to key individuals via their mobile phones and social media feeds and use their greater authority to publicise events far beyond the initial circles of activists. This allowed the protestors to counter attempts by their governments to cover-up or dismiss the uprisings.

While the internet and social media were decisive in allowing evidence of the uprisings to be captured, it was the television channel, Al Jazeera, which broadcast into homes all over the Arab world, spreading the message. In an interview, sociologist Manuel Castells, said:

> Al Jazeera has collected the information disseminated on the Internet by the people, using them as sources, and organized groups on Facebook, then retransmitting free news on mobile phones. Thus was born a new system of mass communication built like a mix between an interactive television, internet, radio and mobile communication systems. The communication of the future is already used by the revolutions of the present.
>
> *(Khondker, 2011, p. 678)*

Journalists in the western media were initially suspicious of material being uploaded onto social media because they were unable to verify where it came from, or who had uploaded it (see **Chapter 12**). There ensued a period of negotiation in which the protestors began to learn the necessary standards imposed by the broadcasters and to operate accordingly, by tagging their videos and incorporating material that would allow broadcasters to verify it more easily. At the same time, broadcasters established ways of searching social media posts automatically and bringing to the surface tweets that were being widely shared, or which provided original images (Hänska Ahy, 2016).

Over time, journalists and technologists have developed systems that can search for people posting information directly from an event and sort them out from the far larger number of people who are re-tweeting or commenting. Many are also trained in techniques which allow them to search social media, using minimal information, and track down individuals, or friends and family who may have been involved in an incident. While the technological shift may have changed the nature of the job, it is not these sources who typically control these interactions. What we are seeing here is the way in which new technologies are absorbed and re-purposed to increase the reach of journalists.

The capacity of journalists to access, and verify, evidence direct from the scene, has without doubt increased the power of those sources who might previously have been side-lined in favour of more powerful *primary definers*. It is, today, far harder, for example, for the police, or other arms of the state, to dictate the framing of a story when verifiable information from the scene can be collected and disseminated nationally and internationally.

The events of Ferguson, Missouri, in 2014, provide a useful and well-documented example of this shift in power. Protests were initiated by the police shooting of an un-armed Black teenager, Michael Brown, which was then met by a violent police response. Local journalist, Grant Bissell, from the local TV station, KSDK, tweeted a photograph of the protest which was picked up by Antonio French, a local politician, journalist and the publisher of a blog called *The Public Defender* (Freelon, McIlwain and Clark, 2016, p. 42). The events were in mainstream national news within a few hours, initially using the police as the *primary definers* and suggesting that they were being threatened by angry crowds. As reported by the Associated Press:

> **A law enforcement spokesman says a large crowd has confronted officers, yelling such things as "kill the police" after a police officer fatally shot a male in a St. Louis-area neighborhood.**
> *(AP and NewsOne, 2014)*

The framing of the events changed, however, as journalists started to make use of social media feeds coming directly from the scene and tweet about them:

> Make no mistake: if not for Twitter, Vine, Livestream etc, we'd have NO IDEA what was happening to protesters in #Ferguson. Police would lie.
> *(Barnard, 2018, p. 2261)*

> Were it not for Twitter, #Ferguson would have remained just another town no one outside of St. Louis ever heard of.
>
> *(ibid.)*

It is clear from the analysis of social media activity that many of the tweets of police activity came directly from journalists who were at the scene at the height of the protests and were themselves targeted by the police. The volume of tweets rose in direct response to the growing media coverage and was driven by:

- Police attacks on and/or detention of several prominent information sources, including Wesley Lowery of the Washington Post, Ryan Reilly of the Huffington Post, Antonio French and an *Al-Jazeera* television crew;
- Dramatic photos of tear gas diffusing through the crowd that were widely shared;
- The gradual increase in global interest in the story, driven by the first two factors;
- A marked uptick in the number of highly visible accounts (specifically those with over 100,000 followers) sharing information about the protests (Freelon, McIlwain and Clark, 2016, p. 45).

While activists on Twitter provided key information for people who were interested in following or joining the protests and made use of their mobile phones to record events, it was journalists and high-profile individuals who spread the word beyond the local community. The events of Ferguson provide useful lessons because they demonstrate how social media, rather than supplanting journalism, can provide the eyes and ears for journalists and enable them to hold power to account more effectively.

This power is, of course, contingent. The Egyptian state used social media networks to target and arrest activists. The Russian state uses social media to spread misinformation and undermine its enemies (see **Chapter 12**). The state in a democracy still maintains a range of means with which it can maintain its position as *primary definer*, not least of which is the simple expedient of distracting attention by making a major policy announcement or burying unwelcome news on a day when the media are distracted by other events.

While any consideration of media and its place in society must still be viewed, as Hall and Hallin demonstrated, from "within a theory of dominance" (Schlesinger, 1990, p. 63), nevertheless, there are strategies that sources and journalists can use to shift the frame. For journalists concerned about climate change, gender, racial or other forms of inequality, the answer is unlikely to be writing more, longer, serious articles or trawling social media for good quotes. It is about being aware of how small issues link to one another, how they can be brought into the *sphere of legitimate debate* and who can provide the quote which will make that link. For an astute journalist that may well mean cultivating contacts with campaigners and getting a relevant, expert quote whenever a story arises that links to that cause. Small changes: making sure that those perceived as experts come from under-represented groups whenever possible, including people with non-mainstream views without marginalising or minimalising them, and finding stories that illustrate issues rather than writing *about* issues. All these are ways in which journalists can change the pattern of source representation and open the *sphere of legitimate controversy* to marginalised voices.

Summary

- *Liberal pluralists* see journalists in a democracy as, ideally, independent agents who operate within a set of rules of ethical and professional behaviour, subject only to the instructions of their editors and the law.
- The theory of *primary definers* suggests that authoritative sources have the power to define events and that journalists are subordinate to them and tend to operate according to scripts established by them.
- Empirical research suggests that the theory of primary definers, although useful, is too simplistic and doesn't take into account the times when, for example, news organisations oppose Government policy and Government sources are unable to define the narrative. Or, indeed, when social movements use the media, successfully, to pressurise government.
- Hallin concludes that the media appear to be independent but are only reflecting power struggles within a narrow *sphere* of *legitimate debate*, established by the ruling elite. Those people and organisations who are considered *deviant* are not given the same level of respect and may be marginalised or demonised.
- *Critics of these approaches* do not accept that journalism is entirely dominated by the power elite and, while recognising that media systems are not fully autonomous from existing power structures, nevertheless, see journalists as participants in power struggles, not merely as bystanders passively reproducing power.

Note

1 This kind of racialised reporting has been critiqued by Black players, like Raheem Sterling, who has also been subjected to attack by the British press regarding his spending, whilst white players have not. (Sterling, 2018)

References

AP and NewsOne (2014) 'Ferguson, Missouri Crowd after Fatal Shooting Of Unarmed Teen: "Kill The Police"', *NewsOne*, 9 August. Available at: https://newsone.com/3042999/missouri-crowd-after-shooting-kill-the-police/ (Accessed: 3 March 2022).

Barnard, S.R. (2018) 'Tweeting #Ferguson: Mediatized Fields and the New Activist Journalist', *New Media & Society*, 20(7), pp. 2252–2271. doi:10.1177/1461444817712723.

BBC News (2021) 'Insulate Britain: Arrests as Protesters Glue Themselves to Roads', *BBC News*. Available at: https://www.bbc.com/news/uk-england-beds-bucks-herts-59131225 (Accessed: 15 February 2022).

Carlson, M. (2017) *Journalistic Authority: Legitimating News in the Digital Era*, *Journalistic Authority*. Columbia University Press. doi:10.7312/carl17444.

Chadwick, A. et al. (2020) 'Authority Signaling: How Relational Interactions between Journalists and Politicians Create Primary Definers in UK Broadcast News', *Journalism*, 21(7), pp. 896–914. doi:10.1177/1464884918762848.

Cohen, S. (1990) *Folk Devils and Moral Panics: Creation of Mods and Rockers*. 2nd edition. London: Wiley Blackwell.

Corner, J. and Schlesinger, P. (1991) 'Editorial', *Media, Culture & Society*, 13(4), pp. 435–441. doi:10.1177/016344391013004001.

Crowley, M., Thomas, K. and Haberman, M. (2020) 'Ignoring Expert Opinion, Trump Again Promotes Use of Hydroxychloroquine', *The New York Times*, 6 April. Available at: https://www.nytimes.com/2020/04/05/us/politics/trump-hydroxychloroquine-coronavirus.html (Accessed: 16 February 2022).

Dardis, F.E. (2006) 'Marginalization Devices in U.S. Press Coverage of Iraq War Protest: A Content Analysis', *Mass Communication and Society*, 9(2), pp. 117–135. doi:10.1207/s15327825mcs0902_1.

Davies, N. (2008) *Flat Earth News: An Award-Winning Reporter Exposes Falsehood, Distortion and Propaganda in the Global Media*. Paperback – 1 Jan 2009 edition. London: Vintage.

Davis, A. (2000) 'Public Relations, News Production and Changing Patterns of Source Access in the British National Media', *Media, Culture & Society*, 22(1), pp. 39–59. doi:10.1177/016344300022001003.

Davis, A. (2009) 'Journalist–Source Relations, Mediated Reflexivity and the Politics of Politics', *Journalism Studies*, 10(2), pp. 204–219. doi:10.1080/14616700802580540.

Deacon, D. (2003) 'Non-Governmental Organisations and the Media', in *News, Public Relations and Power*. London: SAGE Publications Ltd, pp. 99–116. doi:10.4135/9781446221594.

Douglas, O. (2019) *Backstories / Black Stories: Black Journalists, INGOs and the Racial Politics of Representing Sub-Saharan Africa in Mainstream UK News Media*. doctoral. Goldsmiths, University of London. Available at: http://research.gold.ac.uk/id/eprint/26352/ (Accessed: 4 March 2021).

Fenton, N. (2010) 'NGOS, New Media and the Mainstream News: News from Everywhere', in *New Media, Old News: Journalism & Democracy in the Digital Age*. London: SAGE Publications Ltd, pp. 153–168. doi:10.4135/9781446280010.

Fletcher, R. (2017) *Polarisation in the News Media*, *Reuters Institute Digital News Report*. Available at: https://www.digitalnewsreport.org/survey/2017/polarisation-in-the-news-media-2017/ (Accessed: 17 June 2021).

Franks, S. (2010) 'The Neglect of Africa and the Power of Aid', *International Communication Gazette*, 72(1), pp. 71–84. doi:10.1177/1748048509350339.

Freelon, D., McIlwain, C.D. and Clark, M.D. (2016) *Beyond the Hashtags: #Ferguson, #Blacklivesmatter, and the Online Struggle for Offline Justice*. Centre for Social Media Impact. Availableat:https://cmsimpact.org/resource/beyond-hashtags-ferguson-blacklivesmatter-online-struggle-offline-justice/ (Accessed: 2 February 2022).

Gans, H.J. (2011) 'Multiperspectival News Revisited: Journalism and Representative Democracy', *Journalism*, 12(1), pp. 3–13. doi:10.1177/1464884910385289.

Gatehouse, G. (no date) 'Q Drops'. (The Coming Storm). Available at: https://www.bbc.co.uk/programmes/m001324r (Accessed: 2 February 2022).

Hall, S. (1978) *Policing the Crisis: Mugging, The State, and Law and Order*. London: Macmillan.

Hallin, D.C. (1989) *The Uncensored War: The Media and Vietnam*. Oakland, CA: University of California Press.

Hänska Ahy, M. (2016) 'Networked Communication and the Arab Spring: Linking Broadcast and Social Media', *New Media & Society*, 18(1), pp. 99–116. doi:10.1177/1461444814538634.

Hart, P.S., Chinn, S. and Soroka, S. (2020) 'Politicization and Polarization in COVID-19 News Coverage', *Science Communication*, 42(5), pp. 679–697. doi:10.1177/1075547020950735.

Herman, E.S. and Chomsky, N. (1988) *Manufacturing Consent: The Political Economy of the Mass Media*. New York: Pantheon Books.

Howard, P.N. et al. (2018) 'Social Media, News and Political Information during the US Election: Was Polarizing Content Concentrated in Swing States?', *arXiv:1802.03573 [cs]* [Preprint]. Available at: http://arxiv.org/abs/1802.03573 (Accessed: 2 February 2022).

Khondker, H.H. (2011) 'Role of the New Media in the Arab Spring', *Globalizations*, 8(5), pp. 675–679. doi:10.1080/14747731.2011.621287.

Kilgo, D.K. and Harlow, S. (2019) 'Protests, Media Coverage, and a Hierarchy of Social Struggle', *The International Journal of Press/Politics*, 24(4), pp. 508–530. doi:10.1177/1940161219853517.

Kovach, B. and Rosenstiel, T. (2007) *The Elements of Journalism: What Newspeople Should Know and the Public Should Expect*. New York: Three Rivers Press.

Larsen, A.G. (2021) 'Newsworthy Actors, Illegitimate Voices: Journalistic Strategies in Dealing with Voices Deemed Anti-democratic and Violent', *Journalism*, 22(1), pp. 104–121. doi:10.1177/1464884918760865.

Lee-Wright, P., Phillips, A. and Witschge, T. (2011) *Changing Journalism*. 1st edition. Routledge.

Maheshwari, S. and Sparks, C. (2021) 'Political Elites and Journalistic Practices in India: A Case of Institutionalized Heteronomy', *Journalism*, 22(1), pp. 231–247. doi:10.1177/1464884918761630.

Manning, P. (2001) *News and News Sources: A Critical Introduction*. London. doi:10.4135/9781446218082.

Manning, P. (2013) 'Financial Journalism, News Sources and the Banking Crisis', *Journalism*, 14(2), pp. 173–189. doi:10.1177/1464884912448915.

Nygaard, S. (2020) 'Boundary Work: Intermedia Agenda-Setting Between Right-Wing Alternative Media and Professional Journalism', *Journalism Studies*, 21(6), pp. 766–782. doi:10.1080/1461670X.2020.1722731.

Phillips, A. (2010) 'Old Sources, New Bottles', in Fenton, N. (ed.) *New Media, Old News*. London: SAGE, pp. 87–101.

Schlesinger, P. (1990) 'Rethinking the Sociology of Journalism: Source Strategies and the Limits of Media-Centrism', in Ferguson, M. (ed.). Public Communication: The New Imperatives. London: SAGE Publications, pp. 61–83.

Sheehan, J., M. (1968) 'Olympics Ouster, This Day in Sports', *New York Times*. Available at: http://archive.nytimes.com/www.nytimes.com/packages/html/sports/year_in_sports/10.16a.html?module=inline (Accessed: 9 February 2022).

Sterling, R. (2018) *Raheem Sterling x ☐ (@sterling7) posted on Instagram • Dec 9, 2018 at 9:54am UTC*, *Instagram*. Available at: https://www.instagram.com/p/BrKYvF3gH9e/ (Accessed: 18 August 2022).

Taylor, I. (2014) 'Local Press Reporting of Opposition to the 2003 Iraq War in the UK and the Case for Reconceptualizing Notions of Legitimacy and Deviance', *Journal of War & Culture Studies*, 7(1), pp. 36–53. doi:10.1179/1752628013Y.0000000006.

Tomlinson, J. (1991) *Cultural Imperialism: A Critical Introduction*. London; New York: Continuum. Available at: http://hdl.handle.net/2027/heb.02149 (Accessed: 4 November 2021).

Walters, S. (2017) *Tories' Lead Slips by 5% after Care Funding Manifesto Pledge*, *Mail Online*. Available at: http://www.dailymail.co.uk/~/article-4525918/index.html (Accessed: 16 February 2022).

Wettstein, M. *et al.* (2018) 'News Media as Gatekeepers, Critics, and Initiators of Populist Communication: How Journalists in Ten Countries Deal with the Populist Challenge', *The International Journal of Press/Politics*, 23(4), pp. 476–495. doi:10.1177/1940161218785979.

7
AUDIENCES, ALGORITHMS AND OPTIMISATION

An understanding of audiences is important for journalists, who must find ways to relate, sometimes entertaining, but often complex or alarming, real-world events to time starved, distracted people. In doing so, they have to understand that they are competing for the attention of people who may not be engaged citizens, will often have more urgent or more compelling priorities and will certainly have agendas of their own which shape the way they receive information. To reach specific audiences, media companies target groups with roughly similar requirements and pitch their products accordingly. Mass media may offer different time slots, channels, editions or pages for sports, politics, fashion or music. More niche media focus their wares only on the people they think will be interested in their products. In pre-digital days, this was based on audience research. In the digital era, audience selection is achieved via personalisation using algorithms.

In the commercial marketplace, the relationship with audiences is conditioned via the advertising which subsidises it. Commercial journalism needs to be the most popular in its market and attract the largest audiences if it is to bring in the highest advertising subsidy. The broader the reach and the higher the subsidy, the greater the profit to the company (see **Chapter 8**). Thus, popular products undercut less popular ones, while still making larger profits, and niche products can attract an advertising premium for their exclusivity as well as charging more to consumers.

News of the kind that is important to citizenship (see **Chapter 1**) has always ridden, to some extent, on the coattails of more popular entertainment that is attractive to a wider audience. This relationship is disrupted by a click economy which allows users to select only the subjects they enjoy and disregard the more serious information. This change has implications for news producers as well as

DOI: 10.4324/9781003037651-8

audiences because journalists are torn between offering the stories that they think are important for citizenship and attracting attention from people who prefer lighter items.

In the commercial world, understanding how to reach people is a skill that can often overwhelm any consideration of why we are trying to reach them and what effects our work may have on them as individuals and on the society in which we all live. We will now look beyond the superficial commercial understanding of audiences and try to grasp what, if any, effects mass media can have on audiences, both positive and negative. To do so, we use *functionalist* theories, which consider how media help (or hinder) the integration of people into society and *ideological* theories, which consider the media mainly in the context of power relationships. We will then look beyond these divisions at *cultural* theories which consider the audiences as part of a cycle of information in which power always plays a part but is never fixed.

Mass media effects

Fears about the power of mass media, in particular its effect on children and young people, come and go in cycles. In the 1920s, *functionalist* theorists worried that too much cinema attendance was associated with declining morals and delinquent behaviour. Today there is a similar concern about addiction to games and fear that Instagram is fuelling an epidemic of low self-esteem and that these *effects* may harm the smooth functioning of society.

Marxist scholars of the *Frankfurt School* were concerned about the *ideological* influence of the media and concerned that its structures and ownership determine not only what information is conveyed but, in large part, the way in which audiences receive it. Adorno saw the mass media, of which journalism was a part, as a means of selling the attention of audiences to the highest bidder for cash, or for political influence. "The concoctions of the culture industry" are, he writes, "exhortations to toe the line, behind which stand the most powerful interests. The consensus, which it propagates, strengthens blind, opaque authority" (Adorno, 1963/1999, p. 36).

The two-step flow and minimal effects theory

Paul Larzarsfeld[1] was also concerned about media effects, but he was interested in empirical findings rather than theoretical concepts. In the run-up to the 1940 American presidential elections, large numbers of people were interviewed at intervals. Excluding the 20 percent of the original sample who did not vote at all as "psychologically outside the campaign" (Lazarsfeld, 1944, p. 327), researchers found that, by the time the candidates were selected, nearly 80 percent had already made up their mind, leaving only about 20 percent who were genuinely undecided but still went on to vote.

These undecided voters were more likely to be influenced by someone with whom they had a personal connection than directly by the media. These *opinion leaders* were not necessarily people who had any special position; they were just more likely to consume media themselves and more likely to talk about it. Based on these findings, Lazarsfeld concluded that media had *minimal* direct effect on voting intentions: "formal media reach mainly opinion leaders, who in turn pass it on to the rest of the people by word of mouth" (Lazarsfeld, 1944, p. 327). This he called the *two-step flow*.

Lazarsfeld was criticised by Adorno and the Frankfurt School adherents for what they saw as an "administrative approach" to media research, in which the researchers focus on answering questions posed by media companies, about how best to attract and then service an audience, rather than considering broader questions about the way in which people are influenced and channelled by more powerful social forces. This, they felt, let the media off the hook and distracted people from analysing the effect of media power. While Lazarsfeld's research did suggest that media effects were being over-interpreted, he also found that the media have powerful *indirect effects* such as the conferral of status on people, issues and social movements, and the enforcement of social norms (Lazarsfeld and Merton, 1999). Indirect effects are not less important than direct effects.

The 1996 launch of the pro-Republican, Fox News channel, in a handful of States, offered the opportunity for a natural experiment in understanding news influence. Comparing the shift towards the Republicans, in Fox and Fox-free states, between 1996 and 2000, researchers found that, although the station paid little attention to local elections, or senate races, the move towards the Republican Party by Fox viewers happened in all elections. Fox appeared to be changing the mood music in the areas in which it was viewed so that when other variables were taken into account: "exposure to Fox News induced a substantial percentage of the non-Republican viewers to vote for the Republican party" (DellaVigna and Kaplan, 2007, p. 1228). By focussing on certain ideas that are associated with Republicans in general (such as the right to bear arms) and problematising ideas that are associated with Democrats (such as racial equality) Fox was changing the political discourse. These ideas are explored further in **Chapter 4** where we address agenda-setting.

Two-step flow theory emerged at a time in which television had yet to make an appearance as a mass medium and the internet did not exist, but these findings are by no means confined to a specific medium. Indeed, social media provide the perfect means for the dissemination of material by opinion leaders. In a sense, Facebook, TikTok, Telegraph, YouTube and other social media platforms offer a two-step flow as the default setting for the majority of users because, although in surveys people tend to say they don't trust news on social media, when asked directly we find that: "news shared by a friend on Facebook is perceived as more trustworthy than stories received directly from the media outlet" (Turcotte *et al.*, 2015, p. 531).

According to Facebook, close to 80 percent of posts in the average news feed come from friends or groups that people choose to follow[2] and:

> people's trust in the news they see on social media is strongly related to who shares it, and even if it comes from an unknown outlet, they are willing to pass it along to others if it comes from a person they trust. They are also more likely with a trusted public figure sharing news to say they would engage with the article in ways like sharing it or recommending the source to friends or family.
>
> (Sterrett et al., 2019, p. 795).

This magnifies the impact of those *opinion leaders* who consume news from primary sources and then pass on titbits with commentary. This is also what Katz and Lazarsfeld ([1955] 2017) had found in the 1940s. In those days, it required some level of real-life contact with the opinion leader, in the social media era, *influencers* use *para-social* relationships to leverage their impact as intermediaries. Through this, they gain *social capital* (through their numbers of followers), *economic capital* (through promoting brands) and *cultural capital* (through self-promotion) (for an explanation of "capital," see **Chapter 2**).

Leveraging the power of intermediaries has allowed news organisations to circulate stories far beyond the reach of print and to far wider audiences. It allows individuals to set up small businesses selling products by word of mouth, it allows groups of people to gather around political projects or community activities, but it can also have negative, real-world effects one of which we discuss below.

Exercise: Your Influences

Consider one issue in which you differ in opinion from your parents or friends. At what point did your attitude shift? What were your major influences? What role did the media play in your change of heart? Interview two other people about their own strongly held beliefs and ask them to try and remember what influences led them to make up their minds.

Audience power

While Lazarsfeld was measuring political engagement, other researchers working with him were considering why people make media choices. They concluded that people used media to satisfy certain psychological needs. This led to a line of *functionalist* research, revived later in the 1970s and 1980s, known as the *uses and gratifications* approach (Katz, Blumler and Gurevitch, 1973) which considered that the way people make use of media for their own ends which might not be the way in which the publishers expected or intended. The *Uses and Gratifications* approaches opened a new vein of qualitative research which moved into people's homes and dug into the reasons for the enjoyment of different genres and brands. Researchers started to see media as interactive and that helped move the research agenda forward towards a more nuanced view of audiences as active partners in the communication process.

Encoding decoding

A new, critical, cultural studies, using these engaged, qualitative research methods, emerged in the 1970s around the Centre for Cultural Studies in Birmingham, UK, where Stuart Hall and his students and colleagues combined these empirical approaches to audiences with ideas derived from more ideological approaches. Recognising that the impact of mass media was not something direct, which injected ideology into a passive mass audience, but concerned not to lose the critique of media power, they turned to Gramsci and Foucault for a more flexible way in which to understand how power circulates through language and media but also how it is resisted.

Gramsci was interested in the way dominant ideas in a society become part of what we understand as *common sense* (also see **Chapter 4**). Ideas which may be alien to audiences are received and absorbed only if they can be made to appear familiar, or at least inescapable. For example, while it is true that 90 percent of murders worldwide are carried out by men, they mostly kill other men, women are far less likely to be victims of murder (81:19 percent) and the majority of femicides are perpetrated by intimate partners or family members.[3] However, fairy tales and religious mythology portray women as being constantly in need of male protection. This myth of feminine vulnerability is so pervasive that many don't question it. The media magnify and reinforce the idea that women are at greater risk than men so, therefore, have to police their behaviour and be more cautious than men. Hegemony (as Gramsci called it) is a self-reinforcing system. Except that it is never total. There are always gaps and slippages in which people glimpse another possibility.

Stuart Hall's paper, *Encoding Decoding* (Hall, 1991 [1973]), considered those moments when the media's message fails to fit, or is simply rejected. "In the study of popular culture we should always start here: with the double stake in popular culture, the double movement of containment and resistance, which is always inevitably inside it" (Hall, 1981, p. 443).

Hall argues that the author of a text produces material which incorporates a *dominant*, or *preferred* reading. That meaning may be inferred by the way terminology is used, headlines are produced, images are chosen and so on. However, he argued, messages are not unreflectively absorbed. The process of communication is not linear; it is circular. It is as dependent on the receiver as it is on the author.

Same content, different audience interpretations

Stuart Hall suggests that there are three possible ways in which the circuit of communication can be completed or broken by readers.

1. *Dominant or hegemonic reading.* A portion of the audience will simply accept this version of events. This would include many people in the Lazarsfeld experiment who had already decided who they would vote for before the election. They were using the media to confirm prior decisions which had, of course, already been conditioned by their previous assumptions and consumption of media.
2. *Negotiated reading.* Others may have a certain experience of the subject under discussion and will bring their own knowledge to bear. Probably, those people who had not made up their mind would fit into this group. They would try to work out what each of the candidates would offer them in the light of their own life experience, looking to advice from a trusted intermediary to help them make up their mind.
3. *Oppositional reading.* Finally, there will be people who simply reject the message. They are very unlikely to be persuaded to take on board the preferred interpretation because their lived experience collides with what they are hearing. For some, this collision of understanding results in a refusal to take part, but they might also have been found among those who had very definitely made up their minds in advance. They are likely to be people whose prior assumptions and the firmness of their views would put them into the group of influencers.

David Morley (1983) set out to consider how prior life experiences and social positioning conditions the way media artefacts are "read." He interviewed groups of people in England about their response to watching an episode of Nationwide, an early evening news programme. He found that a group of young Black students had a clearly *oppositional* reading to what they were shown. The students felt that it did not engage with their lives in any way. Factory floor trades union representatives were also *oppositional* in their response to the programme, while trades union officials *negotiated* their understanding, accepting or rejecting information on the basis of their life experience. On the other hand, male apprentices expressed a cynical view of the programme but, in fact, accepted the dominant (*hegemonic*) meaning of the message offered.

One thing missing from the analysis is that the mass media are rarely monolithic, few people get all their information from a single source and, "The news that people want, make and circulate among themselves may differ widely from that which the power block wants them to have" (Fiske, 1992, p. 46). So, for example, in the 1980s, the front pages of the British tabloid newspapers ran what appeared to be a war against gay people, but the messages were not uniform. The advice columns of the same newspapers often provided a very different and far more sympathetic view of homosexuality (Phillips, 2008) while public service provider, Channel 4, produced a weekly programme (Out on Tuesday), by and for lesbian and gay people.

Gay people, or those who had gay friends or children, would no doubt take an *oppositional* stance to these homophobic news stories while accepting the more inclusive messages from the back pages. Through these gaps, slippages, reflexive reinterpretations of information and related campaigning, public opinion changed so dramatically that, in 2014, a Conservative Government legalised gay marriage.

Exercise: How Do You Read?

We all "read" texts in the light of our own experience, or lack of experience. Surveying stories in the news today, select one that you accept completely (hegemonic reading), one that you accept with some reservations and a third that you reject. What factors help you to decide on your attitude to what you consume?

Harnessing Opposition

Oppositional readings are no longer the object only of angry chat over a coffee or a drink, it is possible to use forums, message boards, comment columns and social media to speak back directly to the source of media power. Journalists who might have ignored critical letters, or even emails, are called out in public on Twitter and comment spaces below articles. A study of the comments on Al Jazeera.net and Al Arabiya.ne found that they provided a space, outside these outlets heavily policed and censored national media, where there was a wide-ranging discussion in which opinions were divided and often took a very different line from that of the hosts (Douai and Nofal, 2012).

For *cultural theorists*, the internet opened up vistas of genuinely democratic exchange and exploration in which audiences were no longer passive receivers of information but had become its creators:

> we have seen an expansion of the communicative and organization resources available to everyday people (and grassroots organizations) as we become more and more accustomed to using networked communications towards our collective interests ... with grass roots media being deployed as a tool by which to challenge the failed mechanisms of institutional politics.
>
> *(Jenkins et al., 2016, p. 3)*

The internet and social media were hailed as the means by which, for example, young, educated people living under authoritarian regimes could bypass state censorship and force democratisation (Vargas, 2012) or even provide an alternative means of holding the authorities to account. Critical theorists, on the other hand, have been pessimistic about the democratising potential of the internet from early on. They point out that, although everyone apparently has an equal right to speak and be heard online, since the advent of search engines, it has been the hierarchical design of search that largely determines what we are most likely to see or read (Hindman, 2008, 2018; Fenton, 2010). Those who build the algorithms are not part of the technology, they are members of society and they impose their own values and biases (or the values and biases of their employers) on the way they design systems. The possibilities of lateral communication have been harnessed in ways that were not fully understood in the early days of the internet.

Affinity groups and audience atomisation

Elizabeth Noelle-Neumann (1974) found that, when confronted with a group of people with opposing views, most people will moderate their own view to conform with the majority or remain silent. Over time, the majority view is strengthened. She referred to this as the *Spiral of Silence*. A meta-analysis of behaviour online found that the majority of people are even less likely to express dissent online than they are around a dinner table and this is particularly so when the issue is personally important to them (Matthes, Knoll and von Sikorski, 2018). Noelle-Neumann saw this propensity to favour harmony over discord as a necessary *function* of a harmonious society.

There are, however, always people who stand against the tide. Noelle Neumann (1974, pp. 48–49) found them to be a minority among those she studied in the early 1970s. Later research (Matthes, Rios Morrison and Schemer, 2010) found less evidence of the silencing effect of group behaviour. The key difference they found between those who speak their mind and those who do not is their certainty. When people are sure that they are right, they are more likely to speak up. This effect is particularly strong in countries where individualism is prized. In a comparison of the United States and Singapore, the *spiral of silence* was found to be far stronger among the Singaporean sample where interdependence is more socially valued than individualism and freedom of expression is constrained (Lee et al., 2004).

Social media have offered opportunities for loud voices to be heard, and to gather like-minded followers, because these are the voices that are magnified by social media platforms. Where the spiral of silence was thought to lead to consensus, "reinforcing spirals" appear to lead to atomisation, as people who are uncertain of their beliefs, or unsure about their identities, gravitate towards those with more certainty (opinion leaders) and cluster together in small, but self-reinforcing, groups (Slater, 2007).

Groups of like-minded people can then more easily cluster together to establish their own safe space where dissent will, in turn, be silenced. The more people are exposed to information that reinforces their beliefs (however, unlikely they seem to outsiders), the more confident they become that they are right (Del Vicario et al., 2016; Karlsen et al., 2017).

> Users tend to aggregate in communities of interest, which causes reinforcement and fosters confirmation bias, segregation, and polarization. This comes at the expense of the quality of the information and leads to proliferation of biased narratives fomented by unsubstantiated rumours, mistrust, and paranoia.
> *(Del Vicario et al., 2016, p. 558).*

News organisations that do not necessarily intend to make use of this higher level of polarisation find that their material is now being circulated, out of context, by people who stridently disagree with its content (Karlsen et al., 2017). Others wade in and take advantage of polarisation and segregation to increase audience engagement. In the United Kingdom, the tabloid media made use of the group bonding effect of social media during the campaign on leaving the European Union. Existing newspapers already have a large following, on and offline, so that, when they post emotional or polarising material it is seen, and potentially shared, by a large number of people. The posts that were most often circulated on social media came from the pro-Leave tabloid, the *Daily Express* (Phillips, 2019).

Politically polarised journalism is not new. In the context of social media, however, it has become easier to build an audience around a single issue or a cluster of concerns. In Poland, this is referred to as "identity journalism." Jacek Karnowski, chief editor of the news portal *Sieci,* uses the term "watchtowers" to describe this media:

> Newsrooms are watchtowers of community. In our case, of the Catholic, Christian, and conservative community. Without such towers we fall. Protesting won't change much. We need to have our towers. Without centres that consciously analyse reality, are able to react, the community is toothless. (…) Strong newsrooms are centres of interpretation, power, community defence and work against reactions of adversaries.[4]
> *(Klimkiewicz, 2021).*

Journalism that is organised around building an in-group may have a strong bonding function, which can be helpful for minority groups, looking for solidarity in resisting oppression and a means of engaging in the public sphere from a position of strength. When similar media are established as a means of circulating misinformation and intimidating, or silencing others, they start to feel menacing.

> **Exercise: "In-group" Belonging**
>
> We strengthen our feeling of "in-group" belonging by increasing our distance from and tension with the "out-group"—us versus them. Our cognitive universe isn't an echo chamber, but our social one is. This is why the various projects for fact-checking claims in the news, while valuable, don't convince people. Belonging is stronger than facts.
>
> (Tufekci, 2018)
>
> Consider the above statement from Tufekci in the light of media coverage of inter-communal violence, "culture wars" or "wokeness." How would you apply the *spiral of silence* concept to these discussions?

Money flows

Platform technology is designed to constrain the ways in which it can be used and, in some cases, to hide its true use (Shaw, 2017). When we sign up to use a search engine, an app, or a platform, we are given the illusion that we are in charge, but we are guided to use it in particular ways and served information that is chosen for us. Reader engagement is the commercial lubricant, it allows data about us to be extracted: (a) to help us find what we want but (b) to help others find us. It is the second function that dominates. Roger McNamee, a former advisor to Mark Zuckerberg, CEO of Facebook, describes how algorithms are designed to take advantage of the way human beings trust and the way we react: "Getting a user outraged, anxious or afraid is a powerful way to increase engagement" (McNamee, 2019, p. 88).

If we try to tailor our social media feeds to our own requirements, we will find it is very difficult. For example, if we search for, or click on, particular terms, just once out of curiosity, that will be interpreted as an interest and more similar material will follow on the grounds that if you "like" this then you will "like" that. Facebook then uses your reactions and preferences, as well as information about your age, gender and location, to add you to a group of people like you (a *lookalike* audience) which it can then pass on to advertisers who think you are likely to be attracted to their products.

An article in the *Financial Times* (Murgia, 2021) described the experience of a young pregnant woman, with a history of anxiety issues around health, who found she was being served disturbing ads about terminally ill children. She tried using Facebooks ad selection tools, even switching off the parenting topic, but even after a month, there had been no significant change in the number of these items she was served. The problem she faced was that companies use algorithms to predict future behaviour based on past behaviour, and as a woman with health anxiety issues her preferences were fixed around those topics. This information is then used to keep people engaged, while the companies gather data from them and sell that data to third-party advertisers (McNamee, 2019; Zuboff, 2019).

This *personalisation* is offered to us as a feature. We use Google because it knows what interests us and saves us time in searching. But in allowing the algorithms to direct our attention, we are also giving technology companies the opportunity to record and store everything about our likes, dislikes and preferences because of the way we interact with what we see. This allows us to be served an increasingly *personalised* diet. For those with already formulated opinions, this means getting more and more of the material that we are most likely to engage with. For people whose opinions are unformed, if might mean that any tentative interest we show is reinforced with a barrage of similar information.

> Findings show that participants exposed to political information on Facebook exhibit increased levels of issue salience consistent with the issues shared compared with participants who were not shown political information; these effects are strongest among those with low political interest.
> *(Feezell, 2018, p. 482)*

For the platform, it doesn't much matter what the messages are, it is the income that they generate that is important. The greater the engagement, the more money is earned through the advertising that flashes up alongside it. For each view of an advertisement, a tiny fraction of the ad sale price is returned to the publisher – the rest goes to the platform. The more the attention, the higher the rates that can be extracted for it. Some forms of information are more attractive than others and publishers do their best to provide headlines, tweets and posts that will attract clicks and, therefore, rise higher up the search lists, or the news feed, where they are more likely to be shared and reach even more people increasing the potential income for the news organisation.

> The editor decides what's sexy by looking at who is searching for what on Google. [...] Twice a day, there's an email that goes through to the foreign desk on the most searched terms on Google news… they get this thing in the morning. And a lot of editors would definitely respond to that.
> *(Bunce, 2015, p. 18)*

Emotional and contentious material travels particularly well. One group of researchers came up with a category of stories that seemed to garner the most shares. They termed them "teaming" stories. They are the ones that elicit group bonding either around urging on one's own side or, ganging up on others (Crawford, Filipovic and Hunter, 2017).

Finding attractive headlines is easier for those who invent stories. They work out that certain themes and trigger words are more likely to capture attention and write their posts to fit. This may be why researchers found that misinformation travels faster than verified information "in all categories of information, and the effects were more pronounced for false political news than for false news about terrorism, natural disasters, science, urban legends, or financial information" (Vosoughi, Roy and Aral, 2018, p. 1146). They also found that anger drives sharing (Hasell and Weeks, 2016; Leikes, Sood and Iyengar 2016). A fact which Facebook made use of when it invented an Emoji to signify anger and then bumped any post with an angry emoji response higher up in news feeds to make sure people would see it (Merrill and Oremus, 2021).

Since advertising online is sold via automated marketplaces, the advertiser usually has only a general idea of where their product is being placed (Ali et al., 2019). When journalists find and expose the fact that respectable brands are being sold on far-right websites, advertisers are not happy (Elvestad and Phillips, 2018). Facebook's reaction to such criticism has been to try and avoid criticism by tweaking it's algorithms, downplaying the role of news organisations of all kinds and increasing the importance of friends, family and groups (Facebook, 2018). The effect of this has been to decrease the amount of news in feeds circulated by media organisations and increase the impact of trusted opinion leaders who share news with people in their affinity group.

Selling politics

This understanding of how people use trusted intermediaries for news is manipulated not only by people creating fake news sites or advertising products but also by politicians and political organisations who use the same *lookalike* capabilities to bombard people with propaganda. Some populist politicians have learned that one way to create trust and followers amongst people who feel disenfranchised is to denounce the mass media as corrupt and elitist (Selva, 2020). This also allows them to by-pass the critical mediation of journalists by appointing themselves as the trusted intermediaries of the dispossessed. The use of anti-elite messaging allows populist political parties to appeal directly to those people who Lazarsfeld considered to be "psychologically outside the campaign" (Lazarsfeld, 1944, p. 327), or *oppositional* readers (Morley, 1980) of mass media. Appealing to them through an understanding of their life experience and producing messages that appear to be individually tailored to their prejudices and needs.

In the 2016 American Presidential elections, lookalike Facebook groups searched out those small town home-owners who are susceptable to messaging about corrupt liberals in the city. At the same time, other messages were seeking out Black voters, not to persuade them to vote for Trump but to dissuade them from voting at all (Brym et al., 2018). According to Frances Haugen, a Facebook whistle-blower, Facebook allowed the same functions to be used to turn religious majority populations against minorities in Myanmar and fan the flames of inter-group tension in Ethiopia (Kang, 2021).

While the political use of Facebook and YouTube has been widely reported, in some countries, the political messaging has been via WhatsApp (also owned by Facebook). WhatsApp doesn't use micro-targeting in the same way as Facebook, but research suggests that it has also been manipulated (Evangelista and Bruno, 2019). In Brazil, detailed research on WhatsApp groups found that misinformation tended to arise from within closed groups, usually posted by a definable group of people, moving out from WhatsApp into wider circulation (Evangelista and Bruno, 2019). This suggests to the researchers that the information was being manipulated centrally and was not arising spontaneously. Similar reports have emerged from India where the BJP party used sympathisers to establish WhatsApp groups and to stir up communal violence (Farooq, 2018). It is notable that, in Brazil and India WhatsApp appears to be more trusted as a news medium than it is in the United Kingdom or the United States (Toff et al., 2021).

Calls for reform

The use of technology built for persuasion, as a tool for manipulating audiences during elections, engendering civic unrest between elections and bewildering people during a pandemic, raised the temperature on campaigns for regulation, but it was the explosive effect of an internal Facebook research paper, finding that teenage girls blamed Instagram for their low self-esteem and suicidal thoughts, which united law-makers in the Global North, in efforts at regulation (Wells, Horwitz and Seetharaman, 2021). In response, a Facebook spokesperson pointed out that:

> among those same girls who said they were struggling with body image issues, 22 percent said that using Instagram made them feel better about their body image issues and 45.5 percent said that Instagram didn't make it either better or worse.
>
> *(Raychoudhury, 2021)*

Concerns about the impact of media on body image are not new. A 2006 study, before the advent of Instagram, found that: "as early as school entry, girls appear to already live in a culture in which peers and the media transmit the thin ideal in a way that negatively influences the development of body image and self-esteem" (Dohnt and Tiggemann, 2006). A more recent study in Ghana, where the idealised female body has traditionally been larger, found that western body ideals are being adopted by Ghanaian adolescents who were also beginning to be concerned that they are not thin enough (Michels and Amenyah, 2017). This would suggest that westernised images, travelling through search and social media, are making inroads into something as apparently culturally rooted as the idealisation of the female body.

The internet was designed and built in the public sector as a public service, but the platforms, Apps and publishers that have organised its information are private companies making use of audience data to create profits.

> Facebook therefore has a strong economic incentive to maximize the amount of time users spend on the site and to collect and commodify as

much user data as possible. By and large, addictive user behaviour is good for business. Divisive and inflammatory content is good for business. Deterioration of privacy and confidentiality norms is good for business.

(Pozen and Khan, 2019, p. 505)

Some suggested approaches to reform suggest that Governments need to change the way in which these companies do business by regulating their behaviour. One result has been the increasing restrictions on cookies (pieces of code that are dropped onto our computers to track our movement across the web). The platforms have developed workarounds using Artificial Intelligence (AI) which separates the tracking activity from individual identifiers, but still sweeps individuals into groups, according to their behaviour and characteristics, to find ever more accurate ways of providing advertisers with people who are most likely to be sensitised to their products or projects.

More critical approaches suggest that the very function of the internet as a space for democratic engagement has been damaged by the way advertising has been deeply embedded into its systems. This suggests that it is the ownership and structure of the platform businesses that need to be attended to, using such approaches as the nationalisation of search engines, the banning of data targeting for third-party advertising and breaking up monopolies (Couldry and Hepp, 2016; Phillips and Mazzoli, 2021).

Towards deep mediatisation?

In a hundred years, we have moved full circle from alarm about mass media effects, through a period of revision, in which the direct effects were considered minimal, to a period of utopianism in which the internet was thought to have removed the concerns because of its inherently democratising effects, and back again, to a new era of strong effects, with concerns about the impact of *datafication*. Far from offering greater control to individuals, data seem to trap us in a world constructed from and through the media, ordered by the institutional power of (as yet) unregulated global companies. Couldry and Hepp describe this as *deep mediatisation* (Couldry and Hepp, 2016). They suggest that media of various forms are now intimately involved in the construction of our reality and that:

> A problem for any social order that hopes to carry some measure of legitimacy over the longer term comes when our spaces and processes of mutual recognition get themselves blurred with the private interests to generate profit *from* those very same spaces and processes.
>
> *(Couldry and Hepp, 2016, p. 223)*

This takes us back to Adorno and his jaundiced view that: "The customer is not king, as the culture industry would have us believe, not its subject but its object" (Adorno, 1963/1999, p. 32). And here again, it is helpful to think about the insights of Stuart Hall in his essay Encoding Decoding, which we discussed earlier. The customer may not be king, but people will continue to resist *hegemonic* messages even when they are personalised, provided to us in bite-size pieces and customised to fit in with our prejudices. The preferred codes embedded in texts do not always fit with our own perceptions of the world. Journalists are also audiences, capable of oppositional reading and very often the code embedded in information offered by elite sources (see **Chapter 6**) jibes with their own experiences. Indeed, contradictory messages often appear within the same publication.

Opinion surveys tell us that most people approach news sources *reflexively*. They might be suspicious of news, but they differentiate between the news they choose (which they tend to trust) and news in general (which they treat with more suspicion; Newman, 2019). These surveys also tell us that people are contradictory. Thus, Indian respondents to a survey on news were able to say both that they think that news should be entertaining (65 percent) and that it should "provide analysis of complex problems" (Toff et al., 2021, p. 44). But while this tells us that people are not consistent, it also tells us that most people have a sense of what they believe to be right. The relationship between medium and audience doesn't follow a straight line.

Summary

- Audience research follows *ideological* as well as *functionalist* lines of enquiry. These traditions, at times, borrow from one another and, at other times, appear distinct.
- Frankfurt school scholars were more interested in *ideology* and concerned about the influence of commercialisation on media messages and reception.
- Lazarsfeld and his colleagues and followers were interested in empirical research that would explain how media messages *function* in maintaining and changing society.
- Lazarsfeld's *two-step flow* theory found that most people were not directly impacted by media messages. They are more likely to be influenced by intermediaries who are themselves big news consumers.
- Social media provide a fertile environment for the *two-step flow* as people increasingly receive news via trusted intermediaries.
- *Uses and gratifications* theory looks more closely at the way in which people use media artefacts and concludes that they choose media that fulfils psychological needs rather than being injected with ideas from above.
- *Encoding/decoding* describes the way ideas circulate through media and are received in the context of different life experiences. Stuart Hall suggested three different modes of reception: hegemonic (when the message is received in the same terms as it is sent), *negotiated* (when the

- subject receives part of the message but questions part of it) and *oppositional* (when the subject rejects the content of the message).
- Platforms have learned to design *affordances* as closed systems so that people use the technology in pre-defined ways with the minimum choice so that everyone is streamed onto pathways that optimise advertising revenue.
- The pathways that are set out for us are described as *personalisation* and sold to us as a benefit.
- *Spirals of silence* describe the ways in which people are socialised into avoiding conflict and will say nothing rather than be attacked for having the "wrong" thoughts.
- *Reinforcing Spirals* describe the way the affordances of the internet and social media allow people with minority opinions to break away from the mainstream and establish groups in which they reinforce each other's beliefs.
- The desire to form groups and to promote the voices of influencers has been monetised by platforms which stimulate conflict and then derive data from the "interactions." The data are used to tailor-targeted messages from third parties selling products and ideas.
- *Personalisation* is a means of selling targeted ads to the people who will be most receptive to them.
- *Lookalike groups* are created by AI to bundle together people who are most likely to be influenced by messages.
- *Datafication* describes the way our data are used to drive our on-line world.
- *Reflexivity* describes the way we are able to learn from our own actions and adapt responses accordingly. Reflexive audiences learn that their data are being used to target them and this means that they are less trusting of what they see online. This to some extent protects them from the *effects* of *datafication*.

Notes

1 Paul Lazarsfeld was one of the pioneers of empirical audience research. He established panel studies in which large groups of people are asked similar questions over time, allowing researchers to investigate changes in behaviour. He also pioneered the use of focus groups. Both forms of research are still in use today.
2 Facebook Q1 Content Transparency Report VO (US) 2021. https://drive.google.com/file/d/13QTrZsIPb0TZ76s5stfWcWOUbsQqZa2p/view
3 UN statistics 2017 https://www.unodc.org/unodc/en/data-and-analysis/global-study-on-homicide.html
4 Karnowski, Jacek. 2013. "Redakcje to ośrodki, które są wieżami strażniczymi …." [Newsrooms Are Watchtowers of Communities….] wPolityce.pl. https://wpolityce.pl/polityka/166912-jacek-karnowski-redakcje-to-osrodki-ktore-sa-wiezami-strazniczymi-wspolnot-protestowaniem-niewiele-zmienimy-musimy-miec-swoje-wieze.

References

Adorno, T. (1963/1999) 'Culture Industry Reconsidered', in Paul, M. and Thornham, S. (eds) *Media Studies a Reader*. Edinburgh: Edinburgh University Press. pp. 31–38.

Ali, M. et al. (2019) 'Ad Delivery Algorithms: The Hidden Arbiters of Political Messaging', *arXiv:1912.04255 [cs]* [Preprint]. Available at: http://arxiv.org/abs/1912.04255 (Accessed: 4 October 2021).

Brym, R. et al. (2018) 'Social Movement Horizontality in the Internet Age? A Critique of Castells in Light of the Trump Victory', *Canadian Review of Sociology= Revue Canadienne de Sociologie*, 55(4), pp. 624–634.

Bunce, M. (2015) 'Africa in the Click Stream: Audience Metrics and Foreign Correspondents in Africa', *African Journalism Studies*, 36(4), pp. 12–29. doi:10.1080/23743670.2015.1119487.

Costa, E. (2018) 'Affordances-in-Practice: An Ethnographic Critique of Social Media Logic and Context Collapse', *New Media & Society*, 20(10), pp. 3641–3656. doi:10.1177/1461444818756290.

Couldry, N. and Hepp, A. (2016) *The Mediated Construction of Reality: Society, Culture, Mediatization*. 1st edition. Cambridge; Malden, MA: Polity.

Crawford, H., Filipovic, D. and Hunter, A. (2017) *All Your Friends Like This: How Social Networks Took Over News*. Sydney, Australia: HarperCollins.

Del Vicario, M. et al. (2016) 'Echo Chambers: Emotional Contagion and Group Polarization on Facebook', *Scientific Reports*, 6(1), p. 37825. doi:10.1038/srep37825.

DellaVigna, S. and Kaplan, E. (2007) 'The Fox News Effect: Media Bias and Voting*', *The Quarterly Journal of Economics*, 122(3), pp. 1187–1234. doi:10.1162/qjec.122.3.1187.

Dohnt, H. and Tiggemann, M. (2006) 'The Contribution of Peer and Media Influences to the Development of Body Satisfaction and Self-esteem in Young Girls: A Prospective Study', *Developmental Psychology*, 42(5), pp. 929–936. doi:10.1037/0012-1649.42.5.929.

Douai, A. and Nofal, H.K. (2012) 'Commenting in the Online Arab Public Sphere: Debating the Swiss Minaret Ban and the "Ground Zero Mosque" Online', *Journal of Computer-Mediated Communication*, 17(3), pp. 266–282. doi:10.1111/j.1083-6101.2012.01573.x.

Elvestad, E. and Phillips, A. (2018) *Misunderstanding News Audiences: Seven Myths of the Social Media Era*. Abingdon, Oxon: Routledge. doi:10.4324/9781315444369.

Evangelista, R. and Bruno, F. (2019) 'WhatsApp and Political Instability in Brazil: Targeted Messages and Political Radicalisation', *Internet Policy Review*, 8(4), pp. 1–23. doi:10.14763/2019.4.1434.

Facebook (2018) *News Feed FYI: Bringing People Closer Together, News Feed FYI: Bringing People Closer Together | Facebook Media*. Available at: https://www.facebook.com/formedia/blog/news-feed-fyi-bringing-people-closer-together (Accessed: 27 September 2021).

Farooq, G. (2018) 'Politics of Fake News: How WhatsApp Became a Potent Propaganda Tool in India', *Media Watch*, 9(1). doi:10.15655/mw/2018/v9i1/49279.

Feezell, J.T. (2018) 'Agenda Setting through Social Media: The Importance of Incidental News Exposure and Social Filtering in the Digital Era', *Political Research Quarterly*, 71(2), pp. 482–494. doi:10.1177/1065912917744895.

Fenton, N. (2010) *New Media, Old News: Journalism & Democracy in the Digital Age*. London: SAGE. doi:10.4135/9781446280010.

Fiske, J. (1993) 'Popularity and the Politics of Information', in Dahlgren, P. and Sparks, C. (eds) *Journalism and Popular Culture*. London: SAGE, pp. 45–64.

Hall, S. (1981) 'Notes on Deconstructing the Popular', in Storey, J. (ed.) *Cultural Theory and Popular Culture. A Reader*. 2nd edition. Athens: University of Georgia Press, pp. 442–453.

Hall, S. (1991) 'Encoding, Decoding', in During, S. (ed.) *The Cultural Studies Reader*. London: Routledge, pp. 90–103.

Hasell, A. and Weeks, B.E. (2016) 'Partisan Provocation: The Role of Partisan News Use and Emotional Responses in Political Information Sharing in Social Media', *Human Communication Research*, 42(4), pp. 641–661. doi:10.1111/hcre.12092.

Hindman, M. (2008) *The Myth of Digital Democracy*. Illustrated edition. Princeton, NJ: Princeton University Press.

Hindman, M. (2018) *The Internet Trap: How the Digital Economy Builds Monopolies and Undermines Democracy*. Princeton, NJ: Princeton University Press.

Jenkins, H. *et al.* (2016) *By Any Media Necessary: The New Youth Activism: 3*. New York: NYU Press.

Kang, C. (2021) 'Facebook Whistle-Blower Urges Lawmakers to Regulate the Company', *The New York Times*, 5 October. Available at: https://www.nytimes.com/2021/10/05/technology/facebook-whistle-blower-hearing.html (Accessed: 6 October 2021).

Karlsen, R. *et al.* (2017) 'Echo Chamber and Trench Warfare Dynamics in Online Debates', *European Journal of Communication*, 32(3), pp. 257–273. doi:10.1177/0267323117695734.

Katz, E., Blumler, J.G. and Gurevitch, M. (1973) 'Uses and Gratifications Research', *The Public Opinion Quarterly*, 37(4), pp. 509–523. Available at: https://www.jstor.org/stable/2747854 (Accessed: 14 October 2021).

Katz, E. and Lazarsfeld, P.F. (2017) *Personal Influence: The Part Played by People in the Flow of Mass Communications*. New York: Routledge. doi:10.4324/9781315126234.

Klimkiewicz, B. (2021) 'The Public Sphere and the Changing News Media Environment in Poland: Towards Structural Polarisation', *Javnost - The Public*, 28(1), pp. 53–74. doi:10.1080/13183222.2021.1861408.

Lazarsfeld, P.F. (1944) 'The Election Is Over', *The Public Opinion Quarterly*, 8(3), pp. 317–330. Available at: http://www.jstor.org/stable/2745288 (Accessed: 20 September 2021).

Lazarsfeld, P.F. and Merton, R., K. (1999) 'Mass Communication, Popular Taste and Organised Social Action', in Marris, P. and Thornham, S. (eds) *Media Studies, A Reader*. 2nd edition. Edinburgh: Edinburgh University Press, pp. 18–31.

Lee, W. *et al.* (2004) 'A Cross-cultural Test of the Spiral of Silence Theory in Singapore and the United States', *Asian Journal of Communication*, 14(2), pp. 205–226. doi:10.1080/0129298042000256758.

Matthes, J., Knoll, J. and von Sikorski, C. (2018) 'The "Spiral of Silence" Revisited: A Meta-Analysis on the Relationship Between Perceptions of Opinion Support and Political Opinion Expression', *Communication Research*, 45(1), pp. 3–33. doi:10.1177/0093650217745429.

Matthes, J., Rios Morrison, K. and Schemer, C. (2010) 'A Spiral of Silence for Some: Attitude Certainty and the Expression of Political Minority Opinions', *Communication Research*, 37(6), pp. 774–800. doi:10.1177/0093650210362685.

McNamee, R. (2019) *Zucked: Waking Up to the Facebook Catastrophe*. Washington: HarperCollins.

Merrill, J.B. and Oremus, W. (2021) 'Five Points for Anger, One for a 'Like': How Facebook's Formula Fostered Rage and Misinformation', *Washington Post*. Available at: https://www.washingtonpost.com/technology/2021/10/26/facebook-angry-emoji-algorithm/ (Accessed: 27 October 2021).

Michels, N. and Amenyah, S.D. (2017) 'Body Size Ideals and Dissatisfaction in Ghanaian Adolescents: Role of Media, Lifestyle and Well-being | Elsevier Enhanced Reader', *Public Health*, 146, pp. 65–74. doi:10.1016/j.puhe.2017.01.006.

Morley, D. (1980) *The Nationwide Audience: Structure and Decoding*. London: British Film Institute.

Morley, D. (1983) 'Cultural Transformations: The Politics of Resistance', in Marris, P. and Thornham, S. (eds) *Media Studies, A Reader*. 2nd edition. Edinburgh: Edinburgh University Press, pp. 471–481.

Morozov, E. (2011) *The Net Delusion: How Not to Liberate The World*. London: Penguin.

Murgia, M. (2021) 'Time to Turn off Facebook's Digital Fire Hose', *Financial Times*, 28 September. Available at: https://www.ft.com/content/d5dcfece-4e3c-4937-81ac-20dc736c4c27 (Accessed: 4 October 2021).

Newman, N. (2019) 'Reuters Institute Digital News Report 2019', Oxford. p. 156.

Noelle-Neumann, E. (1974) 'The Spiral of Silence A Theory of Public Opinion', *Journal of Communication*, 24(2), pp. 43–51. doi:10.1111/j.1460-2466.1974.tb00367.x.

Phillips, A. (2008) 'Advice Columnists', in Franklin, B. (ed.) *Pulling Newspapers Apart: Analysing Print Journalism*. Abingdon, Oxon: Routledge, pp. 97–105.

Phillips, A. (2019) 'The Agenda-Setting Role of Newspapers in the UK 2017 Elections', in Wring, D., Mortimore, R., and Atkinson, S. (eds) *Political Communication in Britain: Campaigning, Media and Polling in the 2017 General Election*. Cham: Springer International Publishing, pp. 83–97. doi:10.1007/978-3-030-00822-2_6.

Phillips, A. and Mazzoli, E. (2021) 'Search, Data and Targeting: Public Interest Solutions', in Tambini, D. & Moore M. (eds) *Dealing with Digital Dominance*. Oxford: Oxford University Press. pp. 110–127.

Pozen, D.E. and Khan, L.M. (2019) 'A Skeptical View of Information Fiduciaries', *Harvard Law Review*, 133, pp. 497–541. Available at: https://harvardlawreview.org/2019/12/a-skeptical-view-of-information-fiduciaries/ (Accessed: 27 October 2020).

Raychoudhury, R. (2021) 'What Our Research Really Says About Teen Well-Being and Instagram', *About Facebook*, 26 September. Available at: https://about.fb.com/news/2021/09/research-teen-well-being-and-instagram/ (Accessed: 30 September 2021).

Roelens, I., Baecke, P. and Benoit, D.F. (2016) 'Identifying Influencers in a Social Network: The Value of Real Referral Data', *Decision Support Systems*, 91, pp. 25–36. doi:10.1016/j.dss.2016.07.005.

Selva, M. (2020) *Fighting Words: Journalism Under Assault in Central and Eastern Europe*, Oxford: Reuters Institute for the Study of Journalism. Available at: https://reutersinstitute.politics.ox.ac.uk/fighting-words-journalism-under-assault-central-and-eastern-europe (Accessed: 25 November 2021).

Shaw, A. (2017) 'Encoding and Decoding Affordances: Stuart Hall and Interactive Media Technologies', *Media, Culture & Society*, 39(4), pp. 592–602. doi:10.1177/0163443717692741.

Slater, M.D. (2007) 'Reinforcing Spirals: The Mutual Influence of Media Selectivity and Media Effects and Their Impact on Individual Behavior and Social Identity', *Communication Theory*, 17(3), pp. 281–303. doi:10.1111/j.1468-2885.2007.00296.x.

Sterrett, D. et al. (2019) 'Who Shared It?: Deciding What News to Trust on Social Media', *Digital Journalism*, 7(6), pp. 783–801. doi:10.1080/21670811.2019.1623702.

Toff, B. et al. (2021) *Overcoming Indifference: What Attitudes Towards News Tell Us About Building Trust*. 3. Oxford: Reuters Institute for the Study of Journalism, p. 70.

Tufekci, Z. (2018) 'How Social Media Took Us from Tahrir Square to Donald Trump', *MIT Technology Review*. Available at: https://www.technologyreview.com/2018/08/14/240325/how-social-media-took-us-from-tahrir-square-to-donald-trump/ (Accessed: 30 September 2021).

Turcotte, J. *et al.* (2015) 'News Recommendations from Social Media Opinion Leaders: Effects on Media Trust and Information Seeking', *Journal of Computer-Mediated Communication*, 20(5), pp. 520–535. doi:10.1111/jcc4.12127.

Vargas, J.A. (2012) 'Spring Awakening', *The New York Times*, 17 February. Available at: https://www.nytimes.com/2012/02/19/books/review/how-an-egyptian-revolution-began-on-facebook.html (Accessed: 1 October 2021).

Vosoughi, S., Roy, D. and Aral, S. (2018) 'The Spread of True and False News Online', *Science*, 359(6380), pp. 1146–1151. doi:10.1126/science.aap9559.

Wells, G., Horwitz, J. and Seetharaman, D. (2021) 'Facebook Knows Instagram Is Toxic for Teen Girls, Company Documents Show', *Wall Street Journal*, 14 September. Available at: https://www.wsj.com/articles/facebook-knows-instagram-is-toxic-for-teen-girls-company-documents-show-11631620739 (Accessed: 30 September 2021).

Zuboff, P.S. (2019) *The Age of Surveillance Capitalism: The Fight for a Human Future at the New Frontier of Power,* London: Profile Books.

8
ADVERTISING, THE DEVIL'S PACT?

From sensational crime stories in early twentieth-century America to polarising political punditry on twenty-first-century Indian TV; from glossy magazines to girl-next-door celebrity influencers, advertising has always subsidised and influenced journalism. In this chapter, we examine the way it influences what is made and distributed. As Bourdieu observed (see **Chapter 2**), fields are relational; that is, they define their own boundaries in relation to the boundaries of neighbouring fields. The more closely connected they are, the greater the necessity to demarcate differences from one another. Advertising (and its connected field of Public Relations) has grown in tandem with the field of publishing, using the products of journalism to further its ends. Journalism, while benefiting from the economic benefits of this relationship, has struggled to remain the dominant partner and to establish its separation from, and power over, the field of advertising and public relations. In this chapter, we consider journalism as a commercial product (we consider other, non-commercial forms of journalism in **Chapter 9**).

Funding journalism

Commercial journalism relies on a balance between the costs of production (journalism, design, printing and distribution) the income from sales to consumers and sales of space to advertisers. The cost of origination (reporting, photography, illustration, etc.) drops as it is spread over a larger number of customers, but print products carry the additional costs of both paper and distribution, which are less elastic. Electronic and broadcast media, on the other hand, have low distribution costs, and no fixed paper costs, so extra numbers can be added at little (if any) additional cost. If all things are equal, the larger the audience, the lower the costs per unit and the higher the possible profit. But, all things are

DOI: 10.4324/9781003037651-9

not equal. There are other ways in which the cost of an individual product can be changed:

- Taxation artificially raises prices.
- Tax concessions can reduce costs.
- Subsidies from wealthy individuals, political parties or Government lower prices.
- Advertising provides an additional income stream which reduces prices.

In the countries of Northern Europe, independent news media attract a degree of state support (see **Chapter 9**), elsewhere advertising has grown to provide the lion's share of economic support, not only in democracies but also, for example, in China, where media are state controlled but funded by advertising. To understand just how critical advertising has become, it helps to look back to the earliest days, before it had such an important part to play, and then to move forward and see how it has shaped the journalism field.

A history of the advertising subsidy

Habermas (see **Chapter 1**) chose to look primarily at developments in England when developing his theories about the *public sphere*, because England provides a classic example of the way in which a growing merchant class broke free of the monarchy and established its own rules. He showed how the *bourgeoisie* gradually gained control of the public narrative, not directly, using censorship, and repressive press laws, but indirectly, through structures of ownership and the advertising subsidy. Following Habermas, this chapter will focus mainly on the development of advertising, in Britain and America, to demonstrate how the influence of commerce has grown and, in turn, influenced the development of news media across the world.

The earliest handwritten newssheets emerged in China during the T'ang dynasty (616–907). There is evidence of dissemination of various forms of written news by the fifteenth century in Europe (Conboy, 2004) and among the fourteenth to sixteenth century manuscripts in the library of Timbuktu, there is evidence that merchants recorded the market prices of salt, spices and gold (Djian, 2007, p. 8). The first printed news publications are recorded in China in the mid-seventeenth century and "newsbooks" were also circulating in England at that time. Advertisements emerged in England, along with the newsbooks (Conboy, 2004, p. 37) and the earliest recorded newspaper advertisement in North America followed around half a century later, in 1704 in the *Boston Newsletter* (Thussu, 2009a).

These publications were mainly dedicated to informing people engaged in business, of the prices of raw materials, the times of tides and the movement of shipping. They were written for merchants, and those who dealt with them, and they were profitable because these people were prepared to pay for privileged information. With the development of printing across the world, more publishers entered the business, looking for new audiences and it became increasingly common to include political commentary, which, in turn, encouraged political debate, higher readership and, therefore, a lower unit cost of origination.

State control of printing initially kept the press under tight control. When it was briefly lifted in England during the period of the civil war, the number of publications soared. By 1645, there were 722 "newsbooks" circulating (Siebert, 1965, p. 209). Most also gave space to advertisements, initially just to fill space, then as additional income (Conboy, 2004, p. 37). By the time the monarchy had been restored, in 1660, printing was under state control again. Newspapers were licensed and libel and blasphemy laws restricted the content. Then in 1712, stamp duties (taxes) were introduced, artificially inflating prices and advertising itself was taxed, holding back its development as an alternative income stream to support the press.

English journalism then, as now, was a pretty mixed bag. While political talk and news reports were an important mainstay, the press was beginning to broaden out towards a less serious audience. The launch of the *Athenian Gazette* in 1691 by John Dunton was based on letters from readers and responses to them. Queries ranged from concerns about love and health to queries about the nature of the universe. Another of his publications, the *Post Angel*, covered domestic and foreign news but otherwise focussed on grisly crimes and other sensational material, foreshadowing the preoccupations of twentieth-century tabloids (Kent, 1979). In the first half of the eighteenth century, a number of magazines aimed at women were published, one was published by Lady Mary Montague, who used her publication to champion women's rights, and others were more concerned with entertaining and educating the new members of the developing bourgeoisie (Conboy, 2004).

Taxes imposed by Government were intended to ensure that the legitimate press in Britain was affordable only to those who were relatively well-off (and, therefore, considered, by legislators, to be more "trustworthy"; Curran and Seaton, 2018, p. 20). Fear of the export of revolution from France and America ensured that the laws controlling the press were kept in place, with frequent amendments, until the early part of the nineteenth century (Conboy, 2004, p. 69). They extended also to the countries Britain colonised. In India, for example, a law passed in 1799 stipulated that all printed material should be approved by the colonial government before publication (ironically, it initially applied only to British editors, who could be deported, and did not stop the rise of an indigenous press; Sonwalkar, 2015).

However, an unstamped press (though illegal), in fact, thrived in Britain, rising as agitation for reform spread across Europe in the wake of the French Revolution of 1789 (Conboy, 2004). Without the burden of taxes, unstamped news sheets were affordable for people on low wages.

While Europe had yet to come to terms with the idea of a legal free press, the concept of press freedom was written into the constitution of the United States in 1791 as the First Amendment. Indeed, Thomas Jefferson declared that offered the choice between: "a government without newspapers or newspapers without a government, I should not hesitate a moment to prefer the latter" (Jefferson, 1787). Newspapers proliferated in the United States including, in 1828, the first African American owned and operated newspaper, *Freedom's Journal*. Press freedom was backed with Government subsidies for postage on newspapers in order to inform the public and encourage debate (McChesney and Nichols, 2011).

In Britain, by the 1830s, the fear of revolution had somewhat subsided and it became clear that repression was ineffective in stifling debate, so the state switched to a policy of repressive tolerance, cracking down on un-stamped newspapers, while at the same time reducing the stamp duty to encourage compliance. The radical press reacted by going "legitimate," and in the first half of the nineteenth century, its circulation numbers outpaced those of the "respectable" press (Curran and Seaton, 2018, p. 11). With low stamp duties and a squeeze on advertising revenue through taxation, this was a period in which there was a more level playing field for opinions, including those of working-class activists. This shifted debates that had taken place only amongst a small ruling class, to one in which a broader public was vociferously involved.

> Radical papers helped to foster the growth of progressive organisations like the National Union of the Working classes and the Chartists Movement by giving them the oxygen of publicity.
> *(Curran and Seaton, 2018 14)*

In India, also, a limited freedom of the press meant that:

> By 1835, Indians were already using print journalism to lecture to the British on how to run their empire, and writing extensively about the Irish and the revolutionary struggles in Spain and Italy as part of veiled attacks on the (East India] company's rule in India.
> *(Sonwalkar, 2015, p. 625)*

The freedom to publish was, of course, relative (as we discuss in **Chapter 1**). The press was still dominated by men from the emerging bourgeoisie who stood to gain most from political reform. It was a period that could be compared to the earliest days of the radio (Wu, 2010) and the internet, when a degree of democratisation allowed more voices to be heard (still predominantly those of white men), before the field went on to be disrupted, in each case, by commercialisation and by the introduction of advertising (Elvestad and Phillips, 2018).

Despite being taxed, advertising income in Britain was already growing. Tax receipts from the 1930s demonstrate how the advertising subsidy was differentially applied. Newspapers catering to middle-class audiences attracted fifty times more revenue per one thousand copies than competing publications aimed at working-class people (Curran and Seaton, 2003, p. 12). Nevertheless, while advertising was still taxed, the major publishers saw little value in catering to working-class readers and the radical press had the field to itself.

Curran argues that the recognition of the power of radical opinion and the failure of repressive laws to hold it back gave rise to the campaign to repeal the taxes on advertising, in the hope that the further development of an advertising subsidised, commercial press would price the radical press out of the market. Others saw it differently pointing out that advertising lowered the cost of newspapers and that this extended discussion to a far wider variety of people, who were able to purchase a daily or weekly newspaper to read for themselves (Harrison, 1982). The advertising taxes were lifted in 1853 and, in some accounts, this was the magic wand that enabled an independent press to develop in liberal democracies, freeing it from the direct control of the state and political parties (Asquith, 1975).

The argument was that a commercial press would be powerful enough to stand up to vested interests and hold power to account. By the early part of the twentieth century, the British press did achieve that level of independence:

> What made the press magnates different is that they sought to use their papers, not as levers of power within the political parties, but as instruments of power against political parties.
>
> *(Curran and Seaton, 1997, p. 49)*

However, advertising also created a major shift in the journalism field, tipping it far further in the direction of commercial interests and away from its role as a space for political debate.

The rise and rise of the advertising subsidy

The New York Sun was the first newspaper in the United States to be published expressly to attract advertising. It launched in 1833 and, selling at a loss, the first edition dramatically under-cut the price of the other more serious newspapers of the time. The proprietor, a printer, was interested in a product that would make money. His method was simple: he would attract readers by publishing sensational stories about crime, much of it relating to domestic violence, suicide and prostitution, all of it easily picked up in the local courts. When the courts didn't furnish good enough stories, the journalists made them up. On the back of high sales, it would be easy to attract advertisers. In his first editions, he gave the advertising space away to encourage future sales.

Within a year, *The Sun* was the highest circulating newspaper in New York. It had disrupted the *journalism field* (see **Chapter 2**) and was undercutting its more serious rivals and still making its proprietor a healthy profit (Wu, 2017, p. 13). Soon the other publications had set up their own advertising departments and *The Sun* was finding itself under competitive pressure from an even more sensational rival: *The Morning Herald*. The proprietors of these new publications had discovered, nearly two centuries before Twitter, that there is nothing like a good argument to attract attention and, to attract controversy, they started to bait their rivals (Wu, 2017, p. 9).

In Britain, after 1853, advertising sales also took off. The price of popular papers halved and then halved again as the unit cost of producing a newspaper began to rely more and more heavily on the subsidy of advertising. Even the radical Reynolds Press increased the percentage of advertising in its pages by over 50 percent in the four years after repeal of the taxes (Curran and Seaton, 2018, p. 35). At the same time the capital investment required in starting a newspaper was rising, as press technologies became more complex, benefitting from faster printing of multiple copies and higher distribution. The emphasis on high circulation and lower returns on individual copies led to fierce competition for audiences and the advertising they would attract. It also meant that those without capital struggled to enter the market.

Advertisers preferred readers with the means to buy their products. A handbook of the time detailed the political leanings of newspapers so that advertisers could put their money where their interests lay and advised them that, "character is more important than number, a journal that circulates a thousand among the upper or middle classes is a better medium than would be one circulating a hundred thousand among the lower classes" (Curran and Seaton, 2018, p. 35). The bias towards middle-class readers left radical news organisations with a problem. They could either sell at a higher price than the commercial press or appeal more to middle-class readers in an attempt to capture some of the advertisers' bounty.

By the end of the nineteenth century, mass-market newspapers, produced in huge numbers by industrialists, dominated the news landscape in the United Kingdom and the United States. The two most popular New York newspapers of the late nineteenth and early twentieth centuries were the *New York World*, owned by Joseph Pulitzer, and the *New York Journal*, owned by Randolf Hearst. Both majored in sensation and often published "fake news," but they also maintained journalistic legitimacy by providing serious news coverage and backing progressive causes.

British newspaper proprietors backed the political status-quo. There was not a single mass market daily newspaper that supported the Labour party. *The Daily Mail's* view in 1906 was that support for the Labour Party, "must of necessity conflict with the organizations of industrial enterprise" (Thomas, 2007, p, 8) and it pretty much summed up the editorial direction of the British daily press. Even when the Labour Party garnered 22 percent of the vote in the UK 1918 elections, the position didn't change.

The commercial mass market newspapers in the United Kingdom and the United States reflected the political position of their proprietors, who were often directly involved in mainstream politics, but they were not dependent on the parties as their pay-masters. This independence gave them increased political power at the same time as diminishing the power of other voices. In the United Kingdom, Labour supporters launched the *Daily Herald* to try and get a voice in the mainstream. For the first few years, it lurched from one funding crisis to another. Its circulation rose steadily but, in the market of the United Kingdom, it was unable to attract advertising and was having to sell newspapers below cost

(Curran and Seaton, 2018, p. 60). Every rise in circulation meant a greater loss to the company and the paper was taken over by the Trade Union Congress and the Labour Party in 1922. They supported it until the 1930s when better readership data and audience surveys woke British advertisers to the value of advertising to working-class readers (Curran, 2011, p. 156), and the *Daily Herald* attracted a commercial buyer. The more commercially minded new owners turned it into the largest circulation newspaper in the country.

Advertising, competition and homogenisation

The impact of competition for audience is described by Bourdieu as a force for homogenisation in which all the different organisations in the field move towards the centre to try and monopolise the largest audience (Bourdieu, 1998). The arrival of the advertising subsidy had this effect, and as Curran notes: "all national newspapers launched [in Britain] between 1855 and 1910, and the overwhelming majority of new daily local papers, encouraged positive identification with the social system, in contrast to their radical predecessors" (Curran and Seaton, 2018, p. 39).

As publications started to compete for larger audiences, they also started to reduce the ratio of serious coverage and political commentary and increase sensational content and entertainment. Where, in the eighteenth century, women had contributed to political debate, in the mid-nineteenth century, journals for women were produced largely to provide advice on the behaviour and comportment expected of middle-class families – alongside relevant advertising of all the trappings of a respectable middle-class life (Conboy, 2004, p. 136). A situation which some might argue has, to varying degrees, continued in the intervening years.

Success breeds competition and soon a rival entered the scene. In 1934, a headline in the *Daily Mirror* had called on readers to: "Give the Blackshirts [*fascists*] a helping hand" (Rothermere, 1934), but by the following year, the company had made a strategic decision to eschew fascism in order to capture politically engaged, younger working-class readers. Its re-brand into an American-style tabloid with large pictures and headlines was the result of advice from US advertising agency: J. Walter Thompson (Curran and Seaton, 2018).

The Mirror's rise was meteoric, and in 1960, it overtook the more serious *Daily Herald* becoming the single pro-Labour voice in the highly competitive marketplace of the British daily press. Then, in 1969, Australian media magnate, Rupert Murdoch, bought the ailing *Daily Herald* (by then re-named *The Sun*). An editorial in the second week set the tone: "The Sun is on the side of youth. It will never think what is prim, must be proper" (Engel, 1996, p. 255). Anything that had a sexy angle, from naughty vicars to a problem page dealing with sexual problems, were IN; serious articles on foreign policy were OUT. Where *The Daily Herald* had used sport and entertainment to sweeten the news, *The Sun* just piled on the sugar and the readers and advertisers loved it.

Advertising and the crisis of legitimacy

When a field is disrupted, attempts will be made "to change or preserve its boundaries and form" (Bourdieu and Wacquant, 1992, p. 17). Some journalists and news organisations recognised that advertising was in danger of damaging journalism. If advertisers were unregulated and their products were indistinguishable from editorial, they feared (and still fear) a loss of trust in the news media in general.[1] This tension between commercial requirements and journalistic autonomy leads to regular *crises of legitimacy* for journalism. If journalism is to retain its autonomy, as a field separate from advertising, it needs continually to re-state the distinction between journalism and advertising or public relations (Benson, 1999). This tension led to campaigns, starting in early twentieth-century America, to regulate advertising and ensure that any material paid for by advertisers is clearly labelled and separated from editorial. This is discussed in more detail in **Chapters 2 and 10**.

Exporting the commercial model of news

The idea that a market in news, supported by advertising, was the best way to free news from the dead hand of political intervention was rapidly exported throughout the world to post-colonial and post-Soviet markets with similar effects. In South Africa, during the period of Apartheid, the biggest selling newspaper for the Black population had been *The Sowetan*, a political paper, supporting the African National Congress (ANC), with a highly engaged readership. In post-Apartheid South Africa, when the ANC became the party of Government, the popularity of the newspaper, and its income, declined. A company that had previously catered entirely to the white Afrikaner market saw a commercial opportunity, to extend its business by targeting the Black population in South Africa's major urban centres and, in 2002, launched the *Daily Sun*. Majoring on crime and violence it amassed a large audience and, therefore, the lion's share of the advertising revenue available. Within five years, it was the largest selling newspaper in South Africa (Wasserman, 2008).

A similar pattern emerged in India where media had been advertising supported since its inception. It was:

> the first fully formed print culture to appear outside Europe and North America ... distinguished by its size, productivity, and multilingual and multinational constitution, as well as its large array of Asian languages and its inclusion of numerous non-Western investors and producers among its participants.
>
> *(Dharwadker, 1997, p. 112)*

In the period after independence, India developed public service broadcasting and banned foreign-owned media. This held hyper-commercialisation at bay until the early 1990s when liberalisation of the media opened the door to foreign broadcasters, sharply increasing competition and commercialisation. Criticism of the commercialisation of Indian media since then has been loud, both from academics and journalists (Thussu, 2009b).

> Some media organizations totally surrender to market forces by sensationalizing news and falling to the lowest common denominator of reporting. Big advertising and circulation revenues have increasingly interfered with good investigative journalism and at times have prevented news media from reporting negative news to protect commercial interests.
> *(Rao and Wasserman, 2015, p. 652).*

Advertising drives print consolidation

In the beginning, the rise of the advertising subsidy allows a thousand voices to be heard but, in every niche, in every country, the medium- and long-term effects of the advertising subsidy encouraged consolidation and conservatism as newspapers moved to the political middle-ground (or towards accommodation with political elites) in order to attract the largest readership. In some countries, notably Hungary, the Government uses its own advertising investment to benefit news organisations that support its programme, thus rigging the advertising subsidy in its own support. The unbalanced subsidy allows less favoured outlets to die, thus producing consolidation which, in turn, ensures that the Government has fewer outlets to subsidise (Bátorfy and Urbán, 2020).

From an advertiser's point of view, the only point of a newspaper, magazine or website is to provide the means by which a product can be put in front of an audience that is likely to buy it. Advertisers want to find the best medium to get to as many relevant people as possible, at the lowest possible price, and with the least chance of attracting legal sanctions. The result of this process of selection is that advertisers seek out the highest circulation publication catering for broadly the group they hope to sell to. Once a newspaper is the biggest in the field, then advertising is likely to attach itself. The second best at reaching that particular audience will have to undercut the price of advertising space in order to compete for advertising and will be less profitable. The winner, in the end, takes all:

> even where the number of choices in metropolitan newspapers is reduced from three to two, or even from four to two, the circulation of the remaining papers rises to meet all but a small proportion of the original readership.
> *(Bogart, 1963, p. 119)*

In the United Kingdom and the United States, the mainstay of the local press was advertising for house sales, second-hand goods and local services. It was an extremely lucrative market and, bit by bit, the largest titles in the market bought up the smaller ones. In the United States, in 1910, there were on average 16 daily papers in every large city. By 1930, the number of newspapers had halved (McChesney and Nichols, 2010). Those that survived were hugely successful financially, making profits far higher than most other comparable services, but the shrinking number of titles meant little possibility of competing voices.

Thus, advertising freed the press from overt political control, to become a thriving and highly competitive industry, but competition and the inevitable homogenisation constrained the number of voices able to compete for a hearing. In the United States, the rhetoric of a free press in service to democracy, no longer made any sense in a marketplace of one or two titles and this gave rise to the need for a new way of presenting news. If there was to be only one voice in every market, then how would liberal democracy be sustained? (Schudson, 2001).

As American news organisations attempted to rationalise monopoly news provision, the notion of "objective news" gradually became the mainstay of the liberal press. This led to a form of mainstream news that refuses to take sides politically but tends always to follow the status quo (Hallin, 2005). Gaye Tuchman referred to this as "a strategic ritual of objectivity" (Tuchman, 1972). The idea that neutrality could replace diversity in news was then exported across the world to provide a means of justifying media oligopolies, supported by advertising funding.

While monopoly newspapers were making enormous profits from advertising, the ability to keep a division between news content supportive of the status quo, and advertising, was sustainable. Both advertisers and journalists were able to operate in their separate sphere. The separation works less well, however, when news organisations either fall under the control of the state (we discuss this further in the chapter on regulation) or come under financial pressure. The power of the advertiser starts to grow as competition increases for scarce resources, tipping coverage away from serious subjects and increasing the level of sports and celebrity coverage (Rao and Wasserman, 2015).

Broadcasting: a license to print money?

In the early days, radio was largely an amateur medium. Chrystal sets were relatively cheap to buy and could be used for both broadcasting and receiving. The anarchic nature of the medium was similar to that of the early days of the World Wide Web: anyone could speak, but much of what was being said was really not worth listening to and, without a way of funding it, there was little hope that the quality would improve enough to make it worth the effort involved in dredging for the good bits.

Licensing brought some order to the anarchy by sharing out available radio waves. In 1921, the Argentinian city of Buenos Aires introduced licensing, followed by the United Kingdom, in 1922, where a single consortium of radio manufacturers was given a license to establish the BBC (British Broadcasting Company). It was funded by sponsorship and the sale of radio sets. A year later, a Parliamentary committee recommended that advertising should not be allowed as a funding mechanism and, in 1927, the British Broadcasting Corporation was set up as an independent, publicly owned body (see **Chapter 9**).

A similar direction might have been taken in the United States. Indeed, future president Herbert Hoover said in 1922: "In is inconceivable that we should allow so great a possibility for service, for news, for entertainment, for education and for vital commercial purposes to be drowned in advertising chatter" (Rothafel and Yates, 1925, p. 156). However, by the time Hoover became president, radio had been tied up, signed, sealed and delivered to a single commercial organisation.

In the United States, licenses were initially local (radio didn't travel very far) but by the early 1920s, a very big player, indeed, came into the game: A.T &T was the monopoly owner of the US telephone network and, therefore, the only organisation capable of allowing for nation-wide networked radio. The Radio Corporation of America owned and represented the radio stations. After a vicious anti-trust battle, the companies agreed to work together and the National Broadcasting Company was born, providing monopoly network access across the United States (Wu, 2010). With the help of the Federal Radio Commission (established in 1927), smaller radio stations were gradually deprived of licenses, opening up the channels to the biggest commercial stations, all of which were supported by advertising.

Argentina established networked radio in 1920. It was exuberantly commercial and dominated by music. In France, there was a mix of commercial and public, but news was tightly controlled by the state. In Germany, radio was launched in 1923 on similar lines to the BBC, with a listening fee that paid for the costs of programming. Content was tightly controlled by the Government and, in 1933, after the election of Hitler, radio was taken under full Government control. These differences in regulation, ownership and funding would have a profound effect not only on the development of radio but also on television broadcasting which arrived a few years later (see **Chapter 9**).

Television had been a very expensive niche product until the 1950s when TV sets gradually started to spread into the homes of ordinary people, offering advertisers an ideal way to speak to whole families, across large swathes of the country, all at the same time. In the wake of a war in which hate-speech, propaganda, fake news and polarisation had accompanied mass killing on every side, governments were understandably nervous of a means of communication which could reach into the private realm with such efficiency.

In Europe, the instinct was to control this new medium by keeping it, initially, in public hands (see **Chapter 9**). In the United States, licenses to broadcast were handed out to favoured companies and, the Government enacted a *fairness directive* to ensure that no single voice could dominate (Schudson, 2001). This was a perfect arrangement for the TV companies because it ensured that audiences had no more than one or two local channels to watch, alongside the national networks, and lack of competition kept advertising rates high.

The post-war media boom

The 1950s were a period of booming consumerism in western democracies. The total amount of money invested in advertising rose. An increasing share of that money went to television advertising. The popular press, and general illustrated magazines aimed at national, mass working-class audiences, suffered because they competed directly with television, producing entertainment alongside short news items, with very little extra information. Circulations started to drop and the least successful newspaper in every niche was swallowed up, producing even greater press concentration in most markets (Curran, 1981).

The serious newspapers, with smaller circulations, aimed at well-off educated readers, were less impacted by television, partly because better-educated audiences were more likely to read newspapers as well as watching TV news but also because advertisers with luxury products to sell, wanted to put them in front of buyers who could afford them and were prepared to pay a premium to do so. In the 1960s, *The Times* newspaper, for example, earned nearly ten times as much per 1000 readers, as the mass market *Sun* (Curran and Seaton, 2018, p. 91).

The regional and local press were far less damaged by the changes because that was where local businesses and local people bought and sold. A job that could not easily be done by television. In the United States, most news is local and the revenue from local advertising continued to be buoyant. Some companies used the money to build up their newsrooms; others paid it out in dividends to shareholders (Meyer, 1995). The amount spent on television advertising globally did not pass that spent on print until the year 2000 and the amount going into newspapers and magazines continued to grow as newspaper sales boomed in the Global South, where a thirst for information was satisfied by an increasingly popular local print media. Print advertising peaked as the financial crisis hit in 2008 (Wood, 2020).

But there was an unconsidered side effect of the growing dependence of the *field* on advertising. News organisations, particularly in those countries wedded to what Hallin and Mancini (2004) refers to as the western, liberal model of media, had stopped thinking of news as a product to be paid for by users. The news had become a "non-revenue generating overhead" (Phillips, 2014, p. 112) for a media business concerned mainly with generating advertising income for shareholders. In 2007, 90 percent of US newspaper revenue was generated via advertising (Benson, 2013, p. 43). This meant that, when the crunch came, and advertisers took their business elsewhere, it was those newspapers with the highest advertising to cover-price ratio that suffered the steepest drop in revenue and local news, in particular, began to shrink as advertising revenue dropped off a cliff (Phillips, 2014).

> **Exercise: Comparing News Organisations**
>
> Looking at all the news sources available to you in the place where you live, group them according to their source of income: advertising, public subsidy, subscription, philanthropy or a mix of elements. Compare the quality of their coverage of news events and consider the impact of source of income on the types of story covered; the depths of coverage and the ability to do original investigations.

Advertising deserts the news media

The 2008 financial crisis at first seemed like every other recession. Newspapers cut staff expecting a rebound – but it never came. For the first time in the life of commercial news, advertising did not rush back to fill the depleted coffers. The recession had coincided with another revolutionary change. At the turn of the century, Google moved into advertising, using its growing trove of personal data, to match advertisers with potential clients. In 2007, the social media company Facebook also entered the digital advertising market. The platforms amassed data on everything that their customers were doing and offered advertisements that were designed to fulfil their needs before they even expressed them.

The advertisers had only ever used the news as a host which would carry their messages in front of the eyes of the audience. They had always paid what publishers demanded. If they wanted to show rich people advertisements for expensive cars that would cost a great deal more than the cost of showing second-hand cars to poorer people. Now, online market-places were offering space for ordinary people to sell their wares for free, and Google, Facebook and Amazon were offering advertisers a very much cheaper means of getting their wares in front of a very much larger number of people at a fraction of the price charged by magazines and newspapers. The platforms held online advertising auctions so that advertisers could bid against each other to put their advertisements in front of exactly the right customers irrespective of what they happened to be reading at the time.

For the first time, advertisers were told that they would be able to measure the success of their advertising in clicks and not depend on some magical connection between publishers and audience to sell their products (Auletta, 2010, p. 9). They quickly learned to love it. News organisations had already gone online. Initially, they assumed that they too could take a share of the advertising cake and provide services to their audiences just like TV and radio had done before. Early disruptors, such as *OhmyNews* in South Korea and the *Huffington Post* in America, did, indeed, make money by making use of free labour from their contributors. Legacy news organisations also embraced the idea that news could be provided for free, but, at the same time, lost control of the direct income from sales that they needed to pay for their newsrooms (Phillips, 2014).

Google and Facebook were happy to cut deals with publishers in order to encourage them to come on board the internet train to the future, but they wouldn't share their data nor would they give the publishers any control over the way algorithms determined which story would be shown to which audience member. Instead, they offered the publishers tiny amounts of money per click for advertisements placed alongside their stories. This opened up a channel for organisations on the fringes to earn money. As long as they kept over-heads very low and learned how to encourage their audiences to share their stories, it was possible to make an income from advertising as it followed users across the web (see **Chapter 7**).

The levels of advertising going directly to print and internet news organisations collapsed (Wood, 2020). Publishers panicked. Some followed the logic of the platforms and put everything into extending their audience reach. If advertising was now their only form of income, then they would have to amass a vast audience in order to make enough money per click to fund their basic production costs. Others took a different route. They set up paywalls and offered subscriptions, hoping that audiences would return to the old days of paying directly for the journalism they consumed.

On the whole, the print news organisations that already had audiences prepared to pay more for well-researched journalism have moved towards a subscription model in which audiences pay for content. These are almost always organisations with a national, international or highly specialist audience. Those who decided to remain free have had more difficulty staying afloat. The most successful have organised their output to maximise audience, often competing directly with companies that set out to gather audiences via sensationalised "click-bait." Those who took the advertising-funded route found that they were now at the mercy of the platforms and that the size of their audience (and income) could be dramatically impacted by a mere tweak of the platform algorithms (Elvestad and Phillips, 2018).

Local news organisations have suffered particularly as they have small audiences and are, therefore, unable to gather sufficient income through the pitifully small payments per click for online advertising. They have been forced to consolidate and centralise operations, reduce staff numbers (which affects the quality of material) or push further towards popular entertainment in an effort to maintain high audience numbers. Some have managed to keep their heads above water by appealing to philanthropy. Large numbers have simply disappeared leaving news deserts in their wake (Nygren, Leckner and Tenor, 2018), many of them have sacrificed quality of output in an attempt simply to keep publishing (Nielsen, 2015).

In the United States,

> two-thirds [of counties]—2,000—no longer have a daily newspaper, which means residents in those counties typically turn to social media or regional television stations in distant cities for daily news … Residents of counties

with no newspaper—or only one newspaper—tend to be much poorer, older and less educated than the average American. Eighteen percent are living in poverty, compared with a national average of 12 percent.

(Abernathy, 2020, p. 19)

Paid content

The precipitate drop in advertising funding led to a change in the power relationship between the advertising and journalism fields. As the money started to dwindle, companies such as *BuzzFeed, Mashable, Vice, Forbes* and, increasingly, cash-strapped daily papers, invited the advertisers inside the editorial tent and started producing promotional material (*native* or *sponsored* content) written to look like editorial (Sonderman and Tran, 2013) thus blurring the distinction between editorial and advertising. While this has always happened in a small way, now publishers were making a virtue out of producing advertising with the same look and feel as the editorial (Patel, 2017).

In countries with less established regulation, and less embedded professional practices, covert payments to journalists for favourable coverage became endemic (Ristow, 2010). In China, despite heavy state regulation of content, publications have depended on advertising for income since the 1970s. As publications went online, and advertising income dropped, journalists have been drawn into directly soliciting sponsored content from public officials, eroding even the limited possibility of independence afforded to them (Wang and Guo, 2021). Advertising had finally jumped back over the walls that had been erected a century earlier to protect editorial from advertising.

A new breed of *influencers* has also emerged. These are people who have worked out how to manipulate the sharing potential of the social media platforms to their advantage. They identify a niche audience, work hard to build up a following of fans and then start to monetise their operation by taking money from brands and dropping mentions into their video or Instagram feeds. Some influencers have started their own brands so that they can sell direct to the public, cutting out the traditional media and retail industries altogether (Grigoriadis, 2021). As single-person operators (albeit with sometimes large teams of personal staff), they had very low overheads compared to magazine companies who were paying for staff salaries, offices, printing and paper costs, but they quickly started to attract audiences and advertisers away from the more established publications.

As the money from brands moved to the influencers, magazines covering similar topics (gossip, fashion, health and hobbies) moved online, often closing altogether as they struggled, and failed, to compete with much nimbler and cheaper alternatives (Ponsford, 2019, Tobitt, 2020). Recognising the value of this new form of relatively unregulated communication, the advertising agents started to move into the *field* too, building up "social influencer agencies" which allowed them to cut out the relationship with publishers altogether and provide branded material direct to audiences in the guise of personal testimony (Stewart, 2018).

Television news has so far been less impacted by this change, as most people across the world still watch TV news (Newman *et al.*, 2020), but we are also seeing large numbers of people switching to on-demand television, avoiding news altogether (Blekesaune, Elvestad and Aalberg, 2010; Aalberg, Blekesaune and Elvestad, 2013). The business model for commercial television allows popular programming to cross-subsidise news. To encourage this, in many countries, broadcasting licenses are only given where networks agree to provide a minimum level of news coverage (see **Chapter 10**), but as younger audiences move away from programmed to on-demand viewing, the pressure to drop news programming will grow.

Thorough, investigative journalism is expensive to produce, as advertising rates decrease, there has been a move towards cheaper programming, based on opinionated commentary. Opinionated broadcasting plays well in social media and gathers large numbers of followers and shares which are catnip to advertisers, but it relies heavily on other organisations to do the newsgathering and has little to offer the majority of people who prefer news to be relatively non-partisan (Newman *et al.*, 2020). This leaves the publicly funded news operations as sometimes the only mass market organisations with enough independent financial backing to pay for reporters.

For those who have no independently funded public news operations, high-quality news is increasingly available only to the elite, who can afford to carry the bulk of the cost of production. For those who don't, or cannot subscribe, news stories are paid for individually by the advertising that comes alongside it, and the stories that raise the highest emotions are the ones that are most likely to be shared and will draw most clicks (Crawford, Hunter and Filipovic, 2015). Advertising is, finally, in the driving seat. It now creates the news it most enjoys. The developers of Google, Sergey Brin and Lawrence Page, had a pretty good idea what the use of data to drive advertising would do in the long run:

> We expect that advertising funded search engines will be inherently biased towards advertisers and away from the needs of consumers. Since it is very difficult, even for experts to evaluate search engines, search engine bias is particularly insidious.
>
> *(Brin and Page, 1998, p. 18)*

Taking back control

The *journalism field* has been slow to respond to the new circumstances. Used to an accommodation with its funders, business leaders spent most of the first two decades of digital advertising trying to find a way of monetising its products by collaborating with the platforms (Tofel, 2012). Gradually, as it has become clear that there is no direct means of winning back its funding partner, the field has turned to strategies of control (Bourdieu and Wacquant, 1992, p. 17), using its relationship with the *field of power* to undermine the legitimacy of the platforms and engaging the state and law-makers in an effort to re-establish the importance of journalism and its place in the public sphere (Cairncross, 2019; Napoli, 2019; Helberger, 2020).

Sponsored editorial and online influencers are now increasingly regulated, and required to label material clearly as advertising, to separate it from editorial. Governments, across the world, are engaged in discussions about platform regulation as journalism tries to regain its damaged autonomy and re-establish its role within the *public sphere* (Helberger, 2020). The dilemma is to find neutral ways of regulating platforms that reduce the harms of commercialisation without diminishing speech rights (see **Chapter 10**).

Exercise: How the Journalism Field Fights Back

Choose two mainstream news websites and track the way the subject of Google and Facebook have been covered over time. Consider how the narrative has changed and analyse the way in which editorial has shifted as the journalism field seeks to engage law makers and Government in the protection of journalism.

Summary

- Advertising and journalism function in separate but related fields.
- Advertising allows news to be provided cheaply, or even free, to large numbers of people; however, it extracts a price in terms of autonomy.
- The impact of competition for audience and advertising both popularises and homogenises content in the push to attract large audiences.
- Journalism was able to push back against commercialisation while it had a monopoly of "eyeballs," particularly among those groups with higher incomes and a greater interest in independently verified news.
- The disruption of the relationship between news publishers and their audiences has increased the power of advertisers vis-à-vis publishers.
- Increasingly, we see attempts by news media, to make use of their relationship with the *field of power*, in order to seek political assistance in regulating digital advertising.
- As advertising finds other channels for reaching audiences, journalism has been forced to find alternative funding models.

Note

1 See for example: The Trust in News Project from the Reuters Institute for the Study of Journalism, based in the United Kingdom; The Trust Project, based in the United States and The Trusted News Initiative, from the BBC.

References

Aalberg, T., Blekesaune, A. and Elvestad, E. (2013) 'Media Choice and Informed Democracy: Toward Increasing News Consumption Gaps in Europe?', *The International Journal of Press/Politics*, p. 1940161213485990. doi:10.1177/1940161213485990.

Abernathy, P.M. (2020) 'News Deserts and Ghost Newspapers: Will Local News Survive?', *Center for Innovation and Sustainability in Local Media, School of Media and Journalism, University of North Carolina at Chapel Hill*. Available at: https://www.usnewsdeserts.com/wp-content/uploads/2020/06/2020_News_Deserts_and_Ghost_Newspapers.pdf [Preprint].

Asquith, I. (1975) 'Advertising and the Press in the Late Eighteenth and Early Nineteenth Centuries: James Perry and the Morning Chronicle 1790–1821', *The Historical Journal*, 18(4), pp. 703–724. doi:10.1017/S0018246X00008864.

Auletta, K. (2010) *Googled: the End of the World as We Know It*. New York: Penguin Books.

Bátorfy, A. and Urbán, Á. (2020) 'State Advertising as an Instrument of Transformation of the Media Market in Hungary', *East European Politics*, 36(1), pp. 44–65. doi:10.1080/21599165.2019.1662398.

Benson, R. (1999) 'Field Theory in Comparative Context: A New Paradigm for Media Studies', *Theory and Society*, 28(3), pp. 463–498.

Benson, R. (2013) *Shaping Immigration News: A French-American Comparison*. Cambridge: Cambridge University Press. doi:10.1017/CBO9781139034326.

Blekesaune, A., Elvestad, E. and Aalberg, T. (2010) 'Tuning out the World of News and Current Affairs—An Empirical Study of Europe's Disconnected Citizens', *European Sociological Review*, p. jcq051. doi:10.1093/esr/jcq051.

Bogart, L. (1963) 'Newspapers in the Age of Television', *Daedalus*, 92(1), pp. 116–127. Available at: https://www.jstor.org/stable/20026760 (Accessed: 15 December 2020).

Bourdieu, P. (1998) *On Television*. New York: New Press.

Bourdieu, P. and Wacquant, L. (1992) *An Invitation to Reflexive Sociology*. Chicago: Polity Press.

Brin, S. and Page, L. (1998) 'The Anatomy of a Large-Scale Hypertextual Web Search Engine', *Computer Networks and ISDN Systems*, 30(1), pp. 107–117. doi:10.1016/S0169-7552(98)00110-X.

Cairncross, F. (2019) *The Cairncross Review: A Sustainable Future for Journalism*, GOV.UK. Available at: https://www.gov.uk/government/publications/the-cairncross-review-a-sustainable-future-for-journalism (Accessed: 28 January 2021).

Conboy, M. (2004) *Journalism: A Critical History*. London: SAGE.

Crawford, H., Hunter, A. and Filipovic, D. (2015) *All Your Friends Like This: How Social Networks Took Over News*. Sydney: HarperCollins.

Curran, J. (1981) 'The Impact of Advertising on the British Mass Media', *Media, Culture & Society*, 3(1), pp. 43–69. doi:10.1177/016344378100300105.

Curran, J. (2011) *Media and Democracy*. 1st edition. Oxford; New York: Routledge.

Curran, J. and Seaton, J. (1997) *Power Without Responsibility: Press, Broadcasting and the Internet in Britain: Press and Broadcasting in Britain*. London; New York: Routledge.

Curran, J. and Seaton, J. (2003) *Power Without Responsibility: The Press, Broadcasting, and New Media in Britain*. London /New York: Routledge.

Curran, J. and Seaton, J. (2018) *Power Without Responsibility: Press, Broadcasting and the Internet in Britain*. Abingdon, Oxon: Routledge.

Dharwadker, V. (1997) 'Print Culture and Literary Markets in Colonial India', in Masten, J., Stallybrass, P., and Vickers, N., J. (eds) *Language Machines: Technologies of Literary and Cultural Production*. London: Routledge, pp. 108–133.

Djian, J.M. (2007) *Timbuktu Manuscripts: Africa's Written History Unveiled - UNESCO Digital Library*. Available at: https://unesdoc.unesco.org/ark:/48223/pf0000189636 (Accessed: 2 March 2022).

Elvestad, E. and Phillips, A. (2018) *Misunderstanding News Audiences : Seven Myths of the Social Media Era*. Abingdon, Oxon: Routledge. doi:10.4324/9781315444369.

Engel, M. (1996) *Tickle The Public: One Hundred Years of the Popular Press*. First Edition. London: Orion.

Grigoriadis, V. (2021) 'The Beauty of 78.5 Million Followers', *The New York Times*, 23 March. Available at: https://www.nytimes.com/2021/03/23/magazine/addison-rae-beauty-industry.html (Accessed: 2 April 2021).

Hallin, D. (2005) *We Keep America on Top of the World : Television Journalism and the Public Sphere*. New York: Routledge. doi:10.4324/9780203977477.

Hallin, D.C. and Mancini, P. (2004) *Comparing Media Systems: Three Models of Media and Politics*. Cambridge; New York: Cambridge University Press.

Harrison, B. (1982) 'Press and Pressure Group in Modern Britain', in Shattock, J. and Wolff, M. (eds) *The Victorian Periodical Press: Samplings and Soundings*. Leicester: Leicester University Press, pp. 261–295.

Helberger, N. (2020) 'The Political Power of Platforms: How Current Attempts to Regulate Misinformation Amplify Opinion Power', *Digital Journalism*, 8(6), pp. 842–854. doi:10.1080/21670811.2020.1773888.

Jefferson, T. (1787) *Extract from Thomas Jefferson to Edward Carrington, 16 Jan. 1787 [Quote] | Jefferson Quotes & Family Letters, Jefferson Quotes and Family Letters*. Available at: https://tjrs.monticello.org/letter/1289 (Accessed: 28 January 2021).

Kent, R. (1979) *Aunt Agony Advises: Problem Pages Through the Ages*. London: W.H. Allen / Virgin Books.

McChesney, R.W. and Nichols, J. (2010) *The Death and Life of American Journalism: The Media Revolution That Will Begin the World Again*. Philadelphia, PA: Nation Books.

Meyer, P. (1995) 'Learning to Love Lower Profits', *American Journalism Review*, 17(10), pp. 40–45. Available at: https://go.gale.com/ps/i.do?p=AONE&sw=w&issn=10678654&v=2.1&it=r&id=GALE%7CA17829094&sid=googleScholar&linkaccess=abs (Accessed: 4 December 2020).

Napoli, P.M. (2019) *Social Media and the Public Interest: Media Regulation in the Disinformation Age*, Columbia University Press. doi:10.7312/napo18454.

Newman, N. et al. (2020) *Reuters Institute Digital News Report 2020*. Oxford: Reuters Institute for the Study of Journalism. Available at: https://www.digitalnewsreport.org/survey/2020/overview-key-findings-2020/ (Accessed: 20 January 2021).

Nielsen, R.K. (ed.) (2015) *Local Journalism: The Decline of Newspapers and the Rise of Digital Media*. London; New York: I.B.Tauris.

Nygren, G., Leckner, S. and Tenor, C. (2018) 'Hyperlocals and Legacy Media: Media Ecologies in Transition', *Nordicom Review*, 39(1), pp. 33–49. doi: 10.1515/nor-2017-0419.

Patel, S. (2017) 'How Vice Plans to Prove to Advertisers Its Branded Content Works', *Digiday*, 9 May. Available at: https://digiday.com/media/how-vice-plans-to-show-advertisers-its-branded-content-is-valuable/ (Accessed: 23 April 2021).

Phillips, A. (2014) *Journalism in Context: Practice and Theory for the Digital Age*. 1st edition. London; New York: Routledge.

Phillips, A. (2018) 'The Technology of Journalism', in Vos, T.P. (ed.) *Journalism*. Berlin: Walter de Gruyter GmbH & Co KG, pp. 321–340.

Rao, S. and Wasserman, H. (2015) 'A Media Not for All', *Journalism Studies*, 16(5), pp. 651–662.

Ristow, B. (2010) 'Cash for Coverage: Bribery of Journalists Around the World.' Center for International Media Assistance. Available at: https://www.centerforinternationalmediaassistance.org/wp-content/uploads/2015/02/CIMA-Bribery_of_Journalists-Report.pdf.

Rothafel, S.L. and Yates, R.F. (1925) *Broadcasting: Its New Day*. New York, London: Century.

Rothermere, V. (1934) 'Give the Blackshirts a Helping Hand', *Daily Mirror*, p. 12.

Schudson, M. (2001) 'The Objectivity Norm in American Journalism*', *Journalism: Theory, Practice & Criticism*, 2(2), pp. 149–170. doi:10.1177/146488490100200201.

Siebert, F.S. (1965) *Freedom of the Press in England, 1476–1776: The Rise and Decline of Government Control*. Champaign, IL: University of Illinois Press.

Sonderman, J. and Tran, M. (2013) 'The Rise of Sponsored Content and Native Advertising in News', *American Press Institute*, 14 November. Available at: https://www.americanpressinstitute.org/publications/reports/white-papers/understanding-rise-sponsored-content/ (Accessed: 28 January 2021).

Sonwalkar, P. (2015) 'Indian Journalism in the Colonial Crucible', *Journalism Studies*, 16(5), pp. 624–636. doi:10.1080/1461670X.2015.1054159.

Stewart, R. (2018) 'M&C Saatchi Acquires Two Influencer Agencies and Unveils New Talent Business', *The Drum*. Available at: https://www.thedrum.com/news/2018/06/27/mc-saatchi-acquires-two-influencer-agencies-and-unveils-new-talent-business (Accessed: 9 February 2021).

Thussu, D.K. (ed.) (2009a) *International Communication: A Reader*. London; New York: Routledge.

Thussu, D.K. (2009b) *News as Entertainment: The Rise of Global Infotainment*. Thousand Oaks, CA: SAGE Publications Ltd.

Tobitt, C. (2020) *Immediate Media to Close 12 Magazines and Cut Up to 113 Jobs in Post-Covid Savings*, Press Gazette. Available at: https://www.pressgazette.co.uk/immediate-media-closing-12-magazines-cutting-113-jobs-covid/ (Accessed: 9 February 2021).

Tofel, R.J. (2012) *Why American Newspapers Gave Away the Future*. Venice, CA: Now and Then Reader, LLC.

Tuchman, G. (1972) 'Objectivity as Strategic Ritual: An Examination of Newsmen's Notions of Objectivity', *American Journal of Sociology*, 77(4), pp. 660–679. Available at: https://www.jstor.org/stable/2776752 (Accessed: 30 July 2020).

Wang, D. and Guo, S.Z. (2021) 'Native Advertising in the Chinese Press: Implications of State Subsidies for Journalist Professional Self-Identification', *Digital Journalism*, 9(7), pp. 974–990. doi:10.1080/21670811.2021.1968919.

Wasserman, H. (2008) 'Attack of the Killer Newspapers!', *Journalism Studies*, 9(5), pp. 786–797. doi:10.1080/14616700802207797.

Wood, T. (2020) 'Visualizing the Evolution of Global Advertising Spend (1980–2020)', *Visual Capitalist*, 10 November. Available at: https://www.visualcapitalist.com/evolution-global-advertising-spend-1980-2020/ (Accessed: 15 December 2020).

Wu, T. (2010) *The Master Switch: The Rise and Fall of Information Empires*. New York: Knopf.

9
THE ROLE OF PUBLIC SERVICE MEDIA

In the first chapter of this book, we discussed the concept of the *public sphere* which should ideally provide the critical space in which the deliberation necessary for a fully functioning democracy can be achieved. *Liberal theories* of the press assume that diversity of attitudes and opinions will best be catered for via free media which depend on the operation of the market to cater for varied interests and facilitate an exchange of views. *Critical theorists*, on the other hand, doubt that the market alone can deliver a recognisable public sphere in which all voices can be heard. In this chapter, we will consider the role of public service media (PSM) and how it might contribute to the provision of such a public space. By this, we mean a form of media (on or offline) that operates alongside commercial media but is independent of both the state and commerce. We start with a look at what PSM should, ideally, provide, outlining how, and why this sector of the media emerged and developed. We will then look at the academic literature which has evaluated the social benefits of public service provision and discuss the main arguments against the provision of non-market solutions to media diversity, and how disadvantages can best be mitigated. Finally, we will consider the future for this form of news delivery.

What is public service media?

In the chapter on advertising (**Chapter 8**), we outline the way in which the operation of the market tends to move away from diversity towards popularity and homogeneity or, to create atomised groups of like-minded people talking only to themselves and re-enforcing difference (see **Chapter 7**). One of the key arguments for PSM is that, without the need to cater to commercial requirements, it can build a service based on citizenship and provide something approaching a communicative space where people can: "confer in an unrestricted fashion-that is, with the guarantee of freedom of assembly and association and the freedom to express and publish their opinions-about matters of general interest" (Habermas, Lennox and Lennox, 1974, p. 49). To achieve this, PSM should be:

1   Universal (freely available to all).
2   Independent of both the state and the market.
3   Aware of its audiences as citizens with communicative rights and representative of citizens from all walks of life.
4   As far as possible, impartial in its content.
5   Give a voice to people at all levels of society, across all regions and ensure that minority voices are represented both in the production of news and in its content.

Universality

Georgina Born and Tony Prosser argue that PSM are more than a contributor to the public sphere; they have a very particular role in fostering: "social unity through the creation of a 'common culture'" (Born and Prosser, 2001, p. 676). This is achieved not only via news and current affairs programming but also through fostering local cultural enterprise and providing universal access to national and international culture. The fact that PSM are free and provided to everyone regardless of political and personal preference offers an opportunity for open public debate across social divisions. This breaks down artificial barriers that are often encouraged by commercial media's use of personalisation to target their products to specific people. Evidence from surveys suggests that, in practice, nations with well-funded and independent PSM do, indeed, have lower levels of polarisation (Fletcher, Cornia and Nielsen, 2020).

Independence

In order to function as a universal space in which everyone can both contribute and be heard, it is critical that PSM are established with structures that ensure, "distance from all vested interests, and in particular from those of the government of the day" (Broadcasting Research Unit, 1985, p. 9). This distance requires that PSM are independently, and adequately, financed and organised in such a way that they cannot become the mouthpiece of the Government nor be intimidated by threats to their funding.

Pluralism

If PSM are to encourage civic participation, they must also foster a sense of safety, identity and belonging to all members of society (Hall, 1981; Shomron and Schejter, 2020); this lies in the assurance that media will be *hospitable* (Silverstone, 2006) and avoid engendering social conflict. Building on the work of philosopher Amartya Sen (2005), scholars also conclude that access to media, as an audience, is not sufficient to fulfil the rights of citizens. They need also to be seen and heard *fairly* if they are truly to exercise their *communicative capabilities*. The authors suggest a list of seven "attributes" that people should expect of a representative media: (1) to be informed, (2) to have their security respected and protected,[1] (3) to be offered pleasurable entertainment, (4) to have the opportunity for identification and imitation, (5) to allow civic participation, (6) to foster identity and belonging and (7) to be heard (Shomron and Schejter, 2020).

In practice, if women, and those from minorities, are to be able to identify with what they see and hear on the news, they need to be engaged in selecting what is deemed important (Knobloch-Westerwick, Appiah and Alter, 2008). If people from elite, social groups are over-represented, as journalists and producers, that will affect the kind of stories considered (see **Chapters 6 and 3**). Diversity for audiences can only be achieved if diversity is built into production and governing structures, regularly monitored and the findings are effectively acted upon so that meaningful change occurs.

Impartiality

Journalism provided by PSM should, "provide comprehensive, varied, accurate and balanced news and current affairs programming of high quality for reception by the entire public" (Mendel, 2011, p. 86). The inclusion of the requirement for impartiality, in law or regulation, lays out an *intention* of fairness in the coverage of competing ideas and provides the means by which public service broadcasting (PSB) can maintain its independence from government and from other political or corporate elites. While the intention to be fair does not always end in fairness per se, where there is a legal requirement for impartiality, a public service provider can be held to account. This provides an important form of leverage for civil society organisations campaigning for changes in editorial and employment policies.

Exercise: Evaluate your PSM

Consider your own national media. Is there a media provider which aspires to provide a service which would fulfil the requirements of PSM? If, in your opinion, it fails to meet the standards expressed here, is there a means by which it can be held to account for impartiality and representativeness? Consider whether your PSM allow citizens to exercise their *communicative capabilities*?

The emergence of public service media

Public service media emerged in the early twentieth-century, as a solution to the technical problem of limited bandwidth for radio signals. In an unregulated market, broadcasts would compete for the same space, creating interference making it very hard for anyone to hear anything and interfering with ship to shore radio used by the navy. To separate the civilian use of the air waves from the predominant military use, and to make radio commercially viable, Governments intervened to regulate the market using licenses.

In the United States (as we discussed in **Chapter 8** on advertising), the solution to the problem was to create a private radio monopoly, funded by advertising, leading to: "the incorporation of the entire broadcasting industry into the marketing, sales and advertising sector of American business" (Burns, 1977, p. 6). In 1927, the British Government launched the first public service broadcaster. It was also a monopoly, funded, not by advertising, but by a licence fee levied, by the Post Office, on the sale of every radio set.

The initial goal was the same: to produce a reliable stream of broadcast material which could be received without undue interference. However, the British solution was to establish a media organisation owned collectively by the public and held, in trust, outside the control of either the Government or private business. Given its monopoly position, the fact that the license fee was to be a legal obligation, and non-payment punishable by the courts, it was necessary to establish a moral case for its existence. Lord Reith, the first director General of the BBC, adopted the mission to "inform, educate and entertain."

So, at the very point at which, according to Habermas (see **Chapter 1**), rampant commercialisation of the media was "refeudalizing" the public sphere and robbing it of its role as a space for reasoned debate, public broadcasting emerged, providing an opportunity for re-balancing. Scannell argues that the BBC effectively created a public sphere for the first time: "In the sum of its parts broadcasting has brought into being a culture in common to whole populations and a shared public life of a quite new kind" (Scannell, 1989, p. 138).

It was clear from the start that, if everyone was obliged to pay for broadcast services, then those services must represent the broadest possible range of interests and that included entertainment as well as the more "improving" material that Lord Reith felt it his duty to include. It was then a natural step to expand the same public service system to manage the arrival of television. It would be nearly 20 years after the establishment of BBC TV before the first commercial TV stations were licensed in the United Kingdom and they were also obliged to follow public service obligations of impartiality as well as to cover a broad range of cultural, informational and educational material.

A similar PSB model spread across Europe, Canada, Australia, Japan and beyond becoming, in the second half of the twentieth century, the default arrangement for broadcasting for many millions of people. In Nordic countries and France, direct public subsidy has also been provided to newspapers; typically, the subsidies have been paid to the second most popular newspaper in any market as a means of countering the tendency for newspapers to become local monopolies, thereby ensuring greater political diversity (Kammer, 2016). In some countries, PSM have also moved into the digital space, producing both text and video, but this arena has been heavily contested as we discuss below.

This approach did not prevail in the United States where questions of diversity and fairness have been left to the market. The per-capita subsidy to public media in the United States is correspondingly the lowest amongst the western democracies (Benson, Powers and Neff, 2017) and a similar approach to the media prevails in much of South and Central America.

The social value of public service media

If we are to make useful judgements about the value of PSM, it is not sufficient to consider it simply in terms of its own success or failure, we must consider it in a comparative context. It may often fail to represent the whole nation, or to fully reflect diversity, it may tend to reproduce the status quo rather than challenging it, but when measured against commercial media, does it come closer to delivering the kind of journalism society needs? And does its existence, within the ecosystem of news, mean that the media system functions better than it would do without it?

One of the key arguments against the need for maintaining public service media is that information needs will be automatically met in a media environment that delivers a high degree of choice. The advent of cable television, and then the internet, appeared to provide the ideal environment in which people could be informed, heard, and in which civic participation would be encouraged. However, research in both the United States and Europe suggests that, in a high-choice environment, a large number of people don't access information or news at all (Markus Prior, 2007). *News refusers* do not emerge equally across social groups. They are more likely to be young, from the least educated groups and they are more likely to be women. At the other end of the spectrum, we find *news junkies* who tune into many different news sources every day. These are people who are usually well informed and tend to be from groups with higher levels of education (Knobloch-Westerwick and Alter, 2007; Poindexter, Meraz and Weiss, 2008; Curran *et al.*, 2009).

The separation between news junkies and news refusers is not limited to purely commercial media environments. As the choice of media has increased, the gap has also grown across Europe, where PSM are institutionalised (Blekesaune, Elvestad and Aalberg, 2010). Several studies have, however, demonstrated that, "inequalities in media use and knowledge gaps are greater in more commercially oriented media systems" (Van Aelst *et al.*, 2017). In addition to this, Baek (2009) found that, in a study of 74 countries, those with access only to commercial news products had the lowest turn-out at election times. This suggests that commercial news media do not turn audiences into citizens keen to exercise their political rights. A 2020 study found that this discrepancy has been maintained into the social media era (Desilver, 2020).

Research into news knowledge (Curran *et al.*, 2009) found a profound difference between a sample of countries with high and low levels of education in the commercialised, *liberal* system of the United States and no significant difference in news knowledge based on education in the *democratic corporatist* systems (Hallin and Mancini, 2004) of Finland and Denmark. The difference was also stark if ethnicity was considered. In the United States, ethnic minority audiences were considerably less likely to be well informed about news events than were members of the white majority. There was no difference in relation to ethnicity in the British sample where everyone has access to PSM (data on ethnicity was only collected for Britain and the United States).

These differences were attributed by the researchers to the fact that, in Europe, television was still the major source of news and the most watched news broadcasts came from public service broadcasters. They found that non-commercial, PSB provides a broader and deeper diet of serious news, public affairs and international news, as well as a greater diversity of speakers and viewpoints, and is more critical of elites than commercial broadcasters (Benson, Powers and Neff, 2017, p. 11). This, it is suggested, could be because PSBs are "under enormous pressure to connect to all sections of society in order to justify their continued public funding" (Curran *et al.*, 2009, p. 19).

In addition, in regulated news environments, television news programmes are provided more regularly and during the peak viewing times which, in a commercial environment, are typically kept for light entertainment (Aalberg, van Aelst and Curran, 2010; Esser *et al.*, 2012). This means that those watching television for other purposes are more likely to stumble across a serious news broadcast, with a high percentage of national and international news. This incidental exposure has the effect of providing good quality news information even to people who are not seeking it out, thus filling in the news gap that is found in more commercially oriented media systems.

News knowledge and social media

Later investigations looking at the impact of social media on news knowledge also found that, in the commercialised news environment of the United States, people getting their news as a by-product of social media use, believe themselves to be well-informed, but they are, in fact, less knowledgeable about news and current affairs than those who actively seek out news from mainstream sources (Gil de Zúñiga, Weeks and Ardèvol-Abreu, 2017, p. 118). Conversely, a survey of social media use and political engagement in the European context (Britain, Germany and Italy) found that social media use tended to increase news knowledge and political engagement (Valeriani and Vaccari, 2015).

This difference could also be explained by the greater use of PSB in the European sample and the fact that much of the news shared online in Europe comes from legacy news providers (which includes public service providers). Research into students' news use found that trust in mainstream news was linked with an increased interest in exploring online news sources in addition to mainstream consumption (Elvestad, Phillips and Feuerstein, 2018). In other words, a broad diet of mainstream news (on or offline), with the addition of more polarised or niche news sources, provides a better basis for a deeper understanding of news and current affairs than either does in isolation.

In a world of choice, in which people's news information arrives via social media (or not at all), the existence of mainstream, public service news may provide the only space in which citizens, across partisan political divides, hear news and opinions from opposing factions. Knowing what counts as "mainstream," within a particular society, has an important role in anchoring our sense of ourselves and our society, even if our own political perspective is at variance with views expressed. Indeed, research finds far higher levels of polarisation in media consumption in the United States than is typical of countries with public service media, where the same news bulletins are consumed by audiences across the political spectrum (Fletcher, 2017; Boxell, Gentzkow and Shapiro, 2020).

Healthy public spheres require public service media

There seems to be clear evidence that independent, public service media are better able to engage a broad spectrum of citizens and more likely to provide news and current affairs information that will help them to become informed and orient themselves in terms of public knowledge and understanding. The regulatory requirement to be aware of diversity and sensitive to differing requirements means that PSM should take note of civil society campaigns for improvement. This suggests national media systems, that include PSM, come closer to providing the normative conditions for a functioning public sphere, than do purely market-based systems. These advantages are, however, contingent on the independence of their governance and the willingness of those governing bodies to review questions of identity and belonging among marginalised groups and to act on these reviews.

Independence and the problem of state capture

Public Service Media reflect the political systems from which they emerge. Where a single party has overwhelming control, the need to please can undermine the independence of PSM without the need for direct censorship. For example, the South African public service broadcaster (SABC) is theoretically independent, but the board is appointed by the President, and without independent oversight, editorial autonomy can be undermined:

> people are not going to do things due to their fear of upsetting someone higher up. And they are very well aware that there is a political element to that. The majority of them are very scared of doing things that are going to rock the boat.
>
> *(Ciaglia, 2017, p. 825).*

Similar structures are found in Poland where the majority of board members of the public broadcaster are members of the ruling party (Krewel, 2015). In Spain, appointments of chair and board members of the public broadcaster are ratified by a simple majority of the Parliament which ensures that control is always in the hands of the ruling coalition. In Hungary, public service television is effectively controlled by the state (Griffen, 2020).

Where Governments know that they are likely to spend periods out of power, they are much less likely to rig appointment committees in ways that favour the incumbent because to do so would disadvantage their own party in periods of opposition. Where such changes have been made, they may, in any case, be reversed when the Government is replaced (Dragomir and Aslama Horowitz, 2021). In France, for example, the conservative Sarkozy government changed the law to allow the President to appoint the director of the Public Broadcaster. This caused a public outcry and the Socialist Party Government then reversed the change when it was returned to power (Benson, Powers and Neff, 2017, p. 11).

In Spain, the Government, in 2012, introduced a law allowing the Government to appoint the CEO of the main public broadcaster. According to newsroom staff, the result was that controversial stories were either played down or ignored (Minder, 2015). This arrangement means that, when power changes hands, those appointed by one government are vulnerable and this is likely to have an impact on the editorial decision-making, particularly in areas of controversy and in the run-up to elections.

In each case, the possibility for successful state capture depends critically on the health of civil society and the degree to which state power has either nurtured a critical polity or done its best to strangle it. When a single party is in power for an extended period, it is more likely to start treating the public service media as part of the state apparatus, unless there are strict safeguards for independence. Where there is a significant, independent commercial media, that is not closely aligned with the Government, attempts to control public service outlets will be harder to achieve.

Thus, in the case of Spain, journalists have themselves been actively critical of Government interference, as has the commercial media (Dragomir and Aslama Horowitz, 2021). In South Africa, numerous attempts have been made by powerful interests in Government to undermine the independence of the SABC. These have been vigorously opposed by journalists (BBC, 2016) and independent media, much of which is not supportive of the Government (Bronstein and Katzew, 2018). In Hungary, on the other hand, the commercial media have largely been taken over by supporters of the Government, and the public service media are essentially an arm of the state and criticism of government media policy is muted (Griffen, 2020).

When considering the independence of PSM, it is also important to bear in mind that, in the commercial media, there is far less scrutiny and public control is limited to the ability to influence via the decision to purchase: "the mechanism by which proprietors can exert control is through their power to appoint key personnel...who become the proprietor's 'voice' within the newsroom, ensuring that journalistic independence conforms to the preferred editorial line" (McNair, 2003, p. 57).

In a study of commercial media in Kenya, for example, researchers found that:

> Most of the interviewed journalists admitted, 'it is always at the back of their minds when they are handling a story about an affiliate company or a shareholder.' This means that they have to be cautious how they approach such stories and sometimes it might mean 'forgetting the story altogether' even if it is in the public interest.
>
> *(Wasserman and Maweu, 2014, p. 628)*

Funding and independence

Public media typically rely on a mix of funding, the majority from some form of license fee, and the rest from a mixture of state grants and advertising. The most successful PSM have independence written into their funding structures. In Germany, for example, a special committee, with representation from every Lander (region), sets the level of a license fee paid per household. These members must also represent key areas of expertise from media to accounting.

Funding paid out of general taxation, on a short-term basis, is less satisfactory than license fees because it is vulnerable to cost-cutting in periods of austerity. In the Netherlands, for example, the license fee was replaced with money allocated from taxation in 2000 and since then the amount of money spent has gradually declined (Benson, Powers and Neff, 2017).

Without long-term funding, or financial independence, audiences are also likely to decline. In Canada and New Zealand, where funding is also allocated by the Government, funding and audiences are far smaller than is typical for public service media. Benson, Powers and Neff found that: "the worst funded public media systems in our sample, such as those of Canada ($31), New Zealand ($25), and the United States ($3), have had the most difficulties ensuring wide diffusion of independent, civically oriented programming" (2017, p. 4–5).

In low or middle-income countries, such as South Africa, where there is greater competition for scarce public resources, funding for public service media is harder to justify and license fees are hard to collect. This has meant that, for example, although the South African Broadcasting Corporation (SABC) is a public service provider in name, 80 percent of its funding comes from advertising, much of the rest has come from Government bailouts to cover deficits. In Poland where license fees are not only very low but also very often unpaid, there is a similarly high percentage of advertising funding (Mendel, 2011).

The need to raise advertising cash means that these PSM are in direct competition with commercial rivals, in publishing as well as television. However, if the public sector is also competing for the same shrinking pot, it is subject to the same logics and the same need to prioritise popular mainstream programming, rather than catering to small audiences and will struggle to fulfil a public service remit or provide for the *communicative capabilities* of its citizens (Mendel, 2011, Klimkiewicz, 2015, p. 114, Ciaglia, 2015).

Where media are funded directly, by license fee, they are not only better protected from Government influence and from the impact of budget cuts (Klimkiewicz, 2015, p. 114), they are also more likely to be trusted, "by contributing to their national public broadcaster, citizens felt that it was more accountable to them than to the politicians" (Papathanassopoulos, 2007, p. 156).

Where PSM have been successful and enjoy a healthy market share of the audience, private media companies may oppose attempts to move them towards advertising funding. The Peacock Committee, set up by the British Government in 1986 to consider the future of the BBC, decided against advertising funding out of concern that advertisers would move much of their money to the BBC were they offered the chance. This would decrease incomes to commercial media and arguably reduce plurality and the amount of funding available to support a vibrant media sector.

Unfair competition and the theory of "crowding out"

While PSM are widely supported across the world, their provision is increasingly being challenged on the grounds that, what might have been a solution to spectrum scarcity, when there was a limit to the number of broadcasting channels that could be accommodated, is no longer required in a multi-channel digital world with a wide range of possible options for all audiences.

> [A] more commercial (and American) model of electronic publishing in which the emphasis is placed on private ownership and 'free' entrepreneurial activity and on consumer sovereignty and choice. [....] broadcasting has become analogous to the press and deserves the same 'freedom'.
>
> *(Dyson, Humphries, and Negrine, 1988, p. 96)*

This argument starts from the assumption that it is the commercial marketplace that guarantees a democratic public sphere and that public broadcasting, paid for by citizens, and controlled by bodies set up to safeguard its integrity, should merely be condoned as a means of making up for deficiencies in supply by the private sector. This deficit model of PSM underlies even largely positive attitudes:

> The market and other private sector forces do not lead to the satisfaction of all public informational interests and, as a result, there is a need to supplement them with public service broadcasting. In part this is a result of economic forces, as certain types of programming are either too costly or attract too small an audience to generate cost-recovery revenues.
>
> *(Mendel, 2011, p. 86)*

The argument that PSM are only allowable as a response to market failure permeates discussion of the future of the sector. The assumption that the internet and cable can now cater for the needs of even the smallest of minority audiences has influenced much of the recent discussion about PSM and its place in the media system. Deregulation and marketisation have become the mantra. In the 1990s, across the anglophone world, PSM started to be seen as an impediment to globalisation and an unnecessary interference in markets. As a result, TV licenses in many countries were targeted as a source of Government revenue and sold off to private companies. (Ibarra, Nowak and Kuhn, 2015)

Soon local stations, in smaller states, were swamped under the flow of foreign-made material. The English-speaking Caribbean had little protection from the neighbouring American super-power, nor did English-speaking Canada. Indeed, a report in 2004 found that, in Canada, only 32 percent of peak time production is produced at home, on English services, despite a quota system for home-made production. In French-speaking Canada, without competition from the United States, 76 percent of production is domestic.

While most journalism is locally produced and is not, therefore, competing directly with foreign products, commercial news and current affairs on television is typically dependent on cross-subsidy from popular entertainment, or on competing directly for audiences and the advertisements that they attract. So, the health of the whole media market has a bearing on the capacity to produce in-depth, high-quality journalism. In India, for example, most broadcasting companies are local but increased commercial competition has had a knock-on effect on the quality of news which has become increasingly sensational (Thussu, 2009). An effect which has been noted elsewhere and which tends to be exacerbated by audience fragmentation as commercial services compete for audience share (Arbaoui, De Swert and van der Brug, 2020).

In the Caribbean, attempts have been made to revitalise the concept of public service using radio and digital services (Storr, 2011). However, without steady funding, via a license fee, services struggle to maintain their position in a highly competitive market. In the European Union, PSB has special protection under competition regulation. A 1999 resolution of the Council of European Union states: "public service broadcasting, in view of its cultural, social and democratic functions which it discharges for the common good, has a vital significance for ensuring democracy, pluralism, social cohesion, cultural and linguistic diversity" (Council of Europe, 1999, p. 0001).

However, the movement of European broadcasters into the digital world has been patchy. Commercial publishers have complained that the production of text products online is unfair because it competes with their products. In 2017, for example, the Finnish Media Federation, which represents publishers, complained to the EU Commission that Yle, the Finnish public broadcaster, was in breach of state aid rules because it published textual online content in competition with publishers (Dragomir and Aslama Horowitz, 2021). These attacks have made it more difficult for public service organisations to innovate and held back development of genuine PSM in some countries (Klimkiewicz, 2015, p. 115).

Crowding out

The main argument used by commercial media against PSM is that its existence damages the public sphere by "crowding out" the private sector. Commercial media often use their position to campaign against the public media sector on these grounds. James Murdoch, while CEO of Sky News in the United Kingdom, put the case thus:

> Dumping free, state-sponsored news on the market makes it incredibly difficult for journalism to flourish on the internet. Yet it is essential for the future of independent digital journalism that a fair price can be charged for news to people who value it. We seem to have decided as a society to let independence and plurality wither. To let the BBC throttle the news market and then get bigger to compensate.
>
> *(Murdoch, 2009)*

At the time of this speech, BSkyB was a part of News Corporation, the third largest media organisation in the world (Fitzgerald, 2011).

But research does not find any correlation between the availability of PSM and willingness to pay for news content (Fletcher and Nielsen, 2017). Norwegians, who benefit from one of the highest PSM subsidies, top the league for those most willing to pay for news online (Newman, 2020). The problem for newspapers lies elsewhere. As the habit of buying a daily print newspaper had declined in many western nations, the national newspapers (particularly the popular press) have been affected not only by loss of sales but also by the loss of advertising revenue which they cannot make up via online readers (see **Chapter 8**). Indeed, in the 2020 Annual Report of News Corporation, Executive Chairman, Rupert Murdoch, suggested that the fate of a free and unfettered press was once again in the balance, but this time, he blamed, not PSM, but the monopolistic tendencies of the technology companies and called for more regulation (News Corporation, 2020).

The key factor favouring Norwegian publishers appears to be the quality and depth of reporting in local, publicly subsidised, newspapers (Benson and Powers, 2011), which maintained the loyalty of subscribers when they moved online. In the United States, on the other hand, many local newspapers have closed. Relying more heavily on advertising than their Norwegian counterparts, the loss of advertising revenue has meant that they are unable to maintain their depth of news coverage and struggle to attract subscribers online to make up for the deficit in funding.

A study of 28 European Union countries found that the crowding-out theory is flawed even in terms of its own logic.

> Across countries we find no significant negative correlation between PSM revenues and commercial broadcaster revenues or pay TV revenues. In fact, we find the opposite. EU countries with large per capita PSM revenues also have large commercial broadcaster revenues and large pay TV revenues even while controlling for differences in per capita gross domestic product (GDP).
> *(Sehl, Fletcher and Picard, 2020, p. 391)*

This, the researchers suggest, might be because commercial media actually benefit from what the researchers describe as "a race to the top," in which public funding supports media infrastructure, services and high-quality content.

Indeed, the higher the proportion of money coming from license fees, controlled by the broadcasters, the better the health of the commercial media sector as well as the public broadcasters. Conversely, in the new democracies of Central and Eastern Europe, where a strong public broadcasting tradition has yet to emerge from the state-controlled institutions of the past, and most subsidy comes directly from the government, the researchers found that media markets were weaker (Sehl, Fletcher and Picard, 2020).

Exercise: Funding and Quality of News

Thinking about your own local and national newspapers, consider which of them have the greatest depth of what you consider to be high-quality news content? How are they funded? Do they require a subscription or are they free to access online?

Strategic rituals and the creation of consensus

While commercial organisations attack PSM for undermining the commercial sector, critical theorists attack PSM as a means of maintaining ideological *hegemony* (Pickard, 2010). This is a concept, developed by Marxist, Antonio Gramsci, to explain how, even in a democracy, the elite maintains power by establishing a common sense worldview to which ordinary people are encouraged to adhere. According to this account, media, particularly if they are ostensibly run for the enlightenment of the public, play a role in interpreting the world and establishing what is considered normal, or at the very least, sayable (see **Chapter 4**).

Bourdieu argues something similar when he suggests that elites compete for the power to "construct reality" (Bourdieu, 1979, p. 79) by helping to shape an apparently common purpose, which draws people to accept a shared view of the world. This, in turn, entrenches that view as the normative assumption of that society (also see **Chapter 4**). When a common purpose is embodied within an organisation paid for and maintained in the public interest, the sense of shared values engendered can be powerful. Bailey (2007, p. 97) uses Foucault's theories to suggest that PSBs are on: "a civilizing mission whose political rationality [is] to render the listening public more amenable to techniques of cultural governance and particular regimes of citizenship."

Tom Mills, in his research on the BBC, found evidence that appears to confirm the *hegemonic* nature of its governance and editorial policy which, he finds: "has been routinely constructed in a manner skewed towards the interests of powerful groups" (Mills, 2016, 3). Indeed, journalists working for the major PSM tend to see themselves, and be seen as, elite actors. They often went to school or university with people in Government (and, indeed, there is a certain amount of exchange between those working in politics and those working in the media). The PSM are staffed by people who share a similar *habitus* and pass on a particular *doxa* (see **Chapter 2** for an explanation of these terms) working alongside powerful people who are a lot like them.

In order to guard against capture by powerful interests, and to avoid accusations of bias, editors and journalists working in PSM may find themselves adopting strategies of *professionalism* and a *"ritual of impartiality"* (Tuchman, 1972), in much the same way as those working for the major mainstream American newspapers. In both cases, the reflexive position taken by those in charge is almost always to cleave to the centre of politics (wherever that is thought to be) or to bow to accepted social norms until urged by public pressure to change course.

Impartiality, fairness and the maintenance of representative rights are particularly hard to maintain in periods of political turbulence when apparently settled positions are upended and long-held assumptions are challenged (Pickard, 2010). For example, a decision by South African Broadcasting Corporation (SABC) to avoid filming scenes of property destruction during riots, in 2016, has been defended by some as an example of *Ubuntu*, a Zulu expression that relates to reconciliation and harmony. In this context, the suggestion is that the maintenance of harmony is a legitimate alternative to the more combative norms of a public sphere, which is seen as a construction of the west (Phakathi, 2020). Other South Africans saw it as an act of censorship and an attempt to keep unrest out of the headlines in order to support the Government (BBC, 2016).

The debates that surround PSM are part and parcel of their strength. If they are to maintain independence from Government and reflect the society that they are there to serve, contestation and complaint is a critical part of their constitution. When there is no debate about independence, then it is a reasonable bet that complaint has been stifled and autonomy is under threat.

Exercise: Evaluate Your National PSM

Evaluate your PSM in terms of the audiences it serves and the views that it validates. How well does it perform the task of balancing competing views?

Securing independence and representativeness

The best protection against state capture of PSM lies in the way it is established and regulated. Legal autonomy is critical and needs to be safeguarded. So, for example, the Swedish public broadcaster, SVT, is owned by an independent foundation with multiyear funding. The BBC was set up by a Royal Charter to ensure that it is independent of Government. In a 13 country study, researchers found that: "oversight agencies and/or administrative boards of one type or another exist in all countries to serve as a buffer between the public broadcasters and the government in power" (Benson and Powers, 2011, p. 13).

Efforts can be made to improve independence by giving the power of key appointments to an independent committee which is itself non-partisan. A non-partisan committee is hard to achieve so; in some cases (such as Sweden), the governing board is appointed to reflect the balance in Parliament. In Denmark, the board is balanced between Government appointments, parliamentary appointments and two members who are selected by employees. It must contain a mix of backgrounds, from media and the arts to politics and business experience. In Germany, board members are appointed to represent the regions and different sectors of society. Staggering appointments and ensuring that the tenure of such appointments does not coincide with parliamentary elections also helps insulate appointees from political influence.

Given the tendency for a large, centralised public service organisation to reproduce itself and to maintain the status quo both in terms of its recruitment policy and its output (see **Chapter 2**), it is important that systems and rules are put in place to counteract these tendencies. When the BBC was established, there was no mention at all of representation. Recent BBC Charters have been amended to include the words: "the BBC should accurately and authentically represent and portray the lives of the people of the United Kingdom today, and raise awareness of the different cultures and alternative viewpoints that make up its society" (*Equality, Diversity and Inclusion Statement*, 2020). The post-Apartheid South African Broadcasting Act of 1999, established, in its original preamble, that the system must "reflect the identity and diverse nature of South Africa" (Government of South Africa, 1999). This applies both to the licensing of commercial services and to the public service broadcaster (SABC).

However, rules and regulations are only as good as the effort that goes into ensuring that they are implemented. This requires a civic society willing and able to engage with broadcasters and improve representation. A good example of a campaign of this kind is the Expert Woman Project, run from City University in London, which monitored the number of female experts used on flagship news and current affairs programmes encouraging producers to compete with one another for the accolade of greatest improvement in representation. In 2014, when the campaign began, the ratio of male to female experts on air was 4.4 to 1. Four years later, it had improved to 2.2:1 (City University, 2018).

Even in a mature democracy, with a commitment to public funding and independence, it is never possible to rule out political influence in PSM. Regulations may be long standing and have worked well over the years, but there will always be moments when they need to be updated. This is when the risk of politicisation is highest, and the need for vigilance is greatest.

Where political parties fully recognise the importance of media impartiality, there are several safeguards that can be put in place to ensure that PSMs cannot easily be highjacked in periods of political turbulence. In their study of 12 democracies, Benson, Powers and Neff conclude that the factors which best ensure that PSM are able to meet: "democratic normative ideals for professional autonomy and civic accountability" (Benson, Powers and Neff, 2017, p. 14) are:

- Generous funding, established for multiyear periods, paid via a license fee rather than tax revenues, reduces the risk of linking funding to approval or disapproval of editorial decision-making.
- Legally installed charters that underpin independence and require the provision of high-quality programming that caters to diverse audiences.
- Arm's length oversight by an organisation that is also diverse and independent with appointments made for staggered terms.
- Councils which represent the audience and commission research to ensure that diverse publics are being catered for.

Comparing the independence of commercial and mixed systems, Benson and Powers found the PSMs fair well:

> Inside corporate-owned newsrooms, as profit pressures have increased, informal "walls" protecting the editorial side from business interference have crumbled. In contrast, the walls protecting public media are often made of firmer stuff such as independent oversight boards and multiyear advance funding to assure that no publicly funded media outlet will suffer from political pressure or funding loss because of critical news coverage.
>
> *(Benson and Powers, 2011, p. 9)*

Where civil society organisations and academics monitor the health of their PSMs based on these criteria there is a far better chance that the services themselves will implement improvements to their recruitment policy and monitor their output. As public institutions, they are vulnerable to pressure. However, those pressures come from across the political spectrum. In the end, representative PSM seek to represent society as it is, rather than as some people might wish it was.

The future of public service media

Public service media occupy a very particular space. They are funded by the public of a nation, to represent that nation to itself. They establish the boundaries of national debate and set standards of what is considered "sayable" in public. The very nature of the balancing act which they are obliged to maintain, between competing political tendencies, ensures that changing attitudes are relatively slow to be absorbed and reflected. For example, the BBC introduced a female news presenter in 1960 but ended the "experiment" after a few weeks because of audience objections and did not re-introduce them until the mid-Seventies after concerted pressure from civil society organisations.

The tendency to hold onto existing norms, rather than rushing to embrace seemingly radical ideas, may, paradoxically, be the reason why they, nevertheless, maintain substantial public support.

> Indeed, despite the massive proliferation of options for broadcasting consumers, public service broadcasters still command a surprisingly large market share, particularly where they are independent and receive a reasonable amount of public funding. It may even be that these broadcasters have become more important in a world in which broadcasting markets are so fractured, and in which a central source of trusted news is indispensable.
>
> *(Mendel, 2011, p. 86).*

The future of PSM is not clear in a digital environment. As things stand, television is still a major platform for news, alongside online media, in much of the world (Newman *et al.*, 2020) and, where it is available and well-funded, PSB tends to dominate as the preferred provider. However, younger people are increasingly turning away from broadcast programmes of any sort, preferring on-demand viewing which rarely includes news programming.

In a more fragmented media system, Governments across the world are grappling with the questions of how to collect revenue for PSM. Licenses for the use of television sets are outdated as users increasingly access material via their computers or smartphones. In Italy, and Germany for example, the license fee is now paid for via utility bills and other countries are exploring adding a charge to broadband bills or local taxes.

Another concern is how to ensure that people have access to impartial news programming wherever they view, for example, by ensuring that PSM feature high up in channel selection. Online, however, PSM have no special place or priority. Indeed, as we have seen above, in some countries, commercial providers have fought to keep PSM off the internet altogether for fear that their own commercial position might be eroded. There are technical ways of ensuring that the algorithms which personalise content for users (see **Chapters 7 and 10**) could be required to prioritise public service news, but this would require a degree of public support and political will as it would almost certainly be opposed by the platforms, the publishers and the advertisers that pay the bills.

One other way forward would be through the creation of public service search engines (Phillips and Mazzoli, 2021) which would ensure that search terms are

The Role of Public Service Media **197**

aligned to public service requirements rather than being optimised for advertisers in ways which reward sensationalism. This would require collaboration on a global scale which, although difficult to achieve, should not be ruled out. The evidence provided here suggests that PSM are a vital part of the public sphere which should be modernised for the digital age rather than being allowed to die out with the analogue broadcasting that gave birth to it.

Summary

- PSM provide news and information based on citizenship rather than commerce.
- PSM should allow matters to be publicised and debated outside the control of the state or the market.
- To achieve their aims, PSM must provide the means by which citizens can feel included, represented and able to fulfil their communicative capabilities.
- PSM must provide news and information which is impartial and allows a diversity of voices to be heard.
- Research suggests that well-funded PSM, in the context of a thriving commercial media sector, provide a broad diet of in-depth news and current affairs which crosses ideological barriers as well as barriers of education and ethnicity. Audiences with access to PSM are better informed and more likely to be politically engaged than those who have a purely commercial media diet.
- Commercial arguments against PSM have been found to be largely unfounded. They do not "crowd out" commercial media. They do, however, provide an additional injection of cash into the media sector.
- The way PSM are funded impacts on its success and its independence. License fee funding engenders independence and provides impetus to a thriving media sector. Direct, state funding undermines independence and stifles creativity and long-term planning. Advertising funding of PSM also undermines independence and may provide unwelcome competition for commercial providers.
- Independence from the Government is crucial for PSM to function and statutory underpinning for independence is a necessary pre-condition for healthy PSM.
- The size and status of PSM and the need to maintain impartiality tend to encourage PSM to cleave to the centre of politics in order to avoid accusations of bias.
- Some scholars interpret this tendency as *hegemonic*.

Note

1 This would require a responsible media that does not use 'hate speech' to set citizens against one another.

References

Aalberg, T., van Aelst, P. and Curran, J. (2010) 'Media Systems and the Political Information Environment: A Cross-National Comparison', *The International Journal of Press/Politics*, 15(3), pp. 255–271. doi:10.1177/1940161210367422.

Arbaoui, B., De Swert, K. and van der Brug, W. (2020) 'Sensationalism in News Coverage: A Comparative Study in 14 Television Systems', *Communication Research*, 47(2), pp. 299–320. doi:10.1177/0093650216663364.

Baek, M. (2009) 'A Comparative Analysis of Political Communication Systems and Voter Turnout', *American Journal of Political Science*, 53(2), pp. 376–393. doi:10.1111/j.1540-5907.2009.00376.x.

Bailey, M. (2007) 'Rethinking Public Service Broadcasting: The Historical Limits to Publicness', in Butsch, R. (ed.) *Media and Public Spheres*. Basingstoke: Palgrave Macmillan, pp. 96–108.

BBC (2016) 'South Africa Sacked Reporters win SABC Censorship Case', *BBC News*. Available at: https://www.bbc.com/news/world-africa-36867985 (Accessed: 18 June 2021).

Benson, R. and Powers, M. (2011) 'Public Media and Political Independence': Free Press. Available at: http://rodneybenson.org/wp-content/uploads/Benson-Powers-2011-public-media-and-political-independence-1-1.pdf.

Benson, R., Powers, M. and Neff, T. (2017) 'Public Media Autonomy and Accountability: Best and Worst Policy Practices in 12 Leading Democracies', *International Journal of Communication*, 11(0), p. 22. Available at: https://ijoc.org/index.php/ijoc/article/view/4779 (Accessed: 26 May 2021).

Blekesaune, A., Elvestad, E. and Aalberg, T. (2010) 'Tuning out the World of News and Current Affairs—An Empirical Study of Europe's Disconnected Citizens', *European Sociological Review*, p. jcq051. doi:10.1093/esr/jcq051.

Born, G. and Prosser, T. (2001) 'Culture and Consumerism: Citizenship, Public Service Broadcasting and the BBC's Fair Trading Obligations', *The Modern Law Review*, 64(5), pp. 657–687.

Bourdieu, P. (1979) 'Symbolic Power', *Critique of Anthropology*, 4(13–14), pp. 77–85. doi:10.1177/0308275X7900401307.

Boxell, L., Gentzkow, M. and Shapiro, J.M. (2020) *Cross-Country Trends in Affective Polarization*. Working Paper 26669. National Bureau of Economic Research. doi:10.3386/w26669.

Broadcasting Research Unit (1985) *The Public Service Idea in British Broadcasting: Main Principles*. London: Broadcasting Research Unit.

Bronstein, V. and Katzew, J. (2018) 'Safeguarding the South African Public Broadcaster: Governance, Civil Society and the SABC', *Journal of Media Law*, 10(2), pp. 244–272. doi:10.1080/17577632.2018.1592284.

Burns, T. (1977) *The BBC: Public Institution and Private World*. Palgrave Macmillan UK. doi:10.1007/978-1-349-63672-3.

Ciaglia, A. (2017) 'Explaining Public Service Broadcasting Entrenched Politicization: The Case of South Africa's SABC', *Journalism*, 18(7), pp. 817–834. doi:10.1177/1464884915614245.

City University (2018) 'Top TV Editors and MPs Praise Impact of City Research into Gender Imbalance | City, University of London'. City, University of London. Available at: https://www.city.ac.uk/news-and-events/news/2018/06/top-tv-editors-and-mps-praise-impact-of-city-research-into-gender-imbalance (Accessed: 3 March 2022).

Council of Europe (1999) *EUR-Lex -41999X0205- EN, Official Journal C 030, 05/02/1999 P. 0001-0001;* OPOCE. Available at: https://eur-lex.europa.eu/LexUriServ/LexUriServ.do?uri=CELEX:41999X0205:EN:HTML (Accessed: 3 March 2022).

Curran, J. *et al.* (2009) 'Media System, Public Knowledge and Democracy: A Comparative Study', *European Journal of Communication*, 24(1), pp. 5–26. doi:10.1177/0267323108098943.

Desilver, D. (2020) 'In Past Elections, U.S. Trailed Most Developed Countries in Voter Turnout', *Pew Research Center*. Available at: https://www.pewresearch.org/fact-tank/2020/11/03/in-past-elections-u-s-trailed-most-developed-countries-in-voter-turnout/ (Accessed: 7 February 2022).

Dragomir, M. and Aslama Horowitz, M. (2021) 'Media Capture and Its Contexts: Developing a Comparative Framework for Public Service Media', in , Túñez-López, M. Campos-Friere, F. Rodriguez-Castro, M. (eds) *The Values of Public Service Media in the Internet Society*. Cham: Palgrave, Macmillan. pp. 217–246. doi:10.1007/978-3-030-56466-7_12.

Dyson, K., Humphries, P. and Negrine, R. (1988) *Broadcasting and New Media Policies in Western Europe*. London: Routledge. doi:10.4324/9780203194676.

Elvestad, E., Phillips, A. and Feuerstein, M. (2018) 'Can Trust in Traditional News Media Explain Cross-National Differences in News Exposure of Young People Online?', *Digital Journalism*, 6(2), pp. 216–235. doi:10.1080/21670811.2017.1332484.

Equality, Diversity and Inclusion Statement (2020) *Connected Histories of the BBC*. Available at: https://connectedhistoriesofthebbc.org/equality-diversity-and-inclusion-statement/ (Accessed: 3 March 2022).

Esser, F. *et al.* (2012) 'Political Information Opportunities in Europe A Longitudinal and Comparative Study of Thirteen Television Systems', *The International Journal of Press/Politics*, 17(3), pp. 247–274. doi:10.1177/1940161212442956.

Fitzgerald, S.W. (2011) *Corporations and Cultural Industries: Time Warner, Bertelsmann, and News Corporation*. Lanham, MD: Lexington Books.

Fletcher, R. (2017) *Polarisation in the News Media, Reuters Institute Digital News Report*. Oxford: Reuters Institute for the Study of Journalism, Available at: https://www.digitalnewsreport.org/survey/2017/polarisation-in-the-news-media-2017/ (Accessed: 17 June 2021).

Fletcher, R., Cornia, A. and Nielsen, R.K. (2020) 'How Polarized Are Online and Offline News Audiences? A Comparative Analysis of Twelve Countries', *The International Journal of Press/Politics*, 25(2), pp. 169–195. doi:10.1177/1940161219892768.

Fletcher, R. and Nielsen, R.K. (2017) 'Paying for Online News', *Digital Journalism*, 5(9), pp. 1173–1191. doi:10.1080/21670811.2016.1246373.

Gil de Zúñiga, H., Weeks, B. and Ardèvol-Abreu, A. (2017) 'Effects of the News-Finds-Me Perception in Communication: Social Media Use Implications for News Seeking and Learning About Politics', *Journal of Computer-Mediated Communication*, 22(3), pp. 105–123. doi:10.1111/jcc4.12185.

Government of South Africa (1999) 'Act No. 4 of 1999: Broadcasting Act, 1999'. Government Gazette. Government of South Africa. https://www.gov.za/documents/broadcasting-act

Griffen, S. (2020) 'Hungary: A Lesson in Media Control', *British Journalism Review*, 31(1), pp. 57–62. doi:10.1177/0956474820910071.

Habermas, J., Lennox, S. and Lennox, F. (1974) 'The Public Sphere: An Encyclopedia Article (1964)', *New German Critique*, 3, pp. 49–55. doi:10.2307/487737.

Hall, S. (1981) 'The Whites of Their Eyes: Racist Ideologies and the Media', *Silver Linings: Some Strategies for the Eighties*, London: Lawrence and Wishart. pp. 28–52.

Hallin, D.C. and Mancini, P. (2004) *Comparing Media Systems: Three Models of Media and Politics*. Cambridge; New York: Cambridge University Press.

Ibarra, K.A., Nowak, E. and Kuhn, R. (2015) *Public Service Media in Europe: A Comparative Approach*. London: Routledge.

Kammer, A. (2016) 'A Welfare Perspective on Nordic Media Subsidies', *Journal of Media Business Studies*, 13(3), pp. 140–152. doi:10.1080/16522354.2016.1238272.

Klimkiewicz, B. (2015) 'Between Autonomy and Dependency: Funding Mechanisms of Public Service Media in Selected European Countries', in Ibarra, K., Arriaza, Nowak, E., and Kuhn, R. (eds) *Public Service Media in Europe, A Comparative Approach*. London: Routledge, pp. 27–41.

Knobloch-Westerwick, S. and Alter, S. (2007) 'The Gender News Use Divide: Americans' Sex-Typed Selective Exposure to Online News Topics', *Journal of Communication*, 57(4), pp. 739–758. doi:10.1111/j.1460-2466.2007.00366.x.

Knobloch-Westerwick, S., Appiah, O. and Alter, S. (2008) 'News Selection Patterns as a Function of Race: The Discerning Minority and the Indiscriminating Majority', *Media Psychology*, 11(3), pp. 400–417. doi:10.1080/15213260802178542.

Krewel, M. (2015) 'Autonomy and Regulatory Frameworks of PSM', in Ibarra, K.A., Nowak, E., and Kuhn, R. (eds) *Public Service Media in Europe*. London: Routledge.

Markus Prior (2007) *Post-Broadcast Democracy, How Media Choice Increases Inequality in Political Involvement and Polarizes Elections*. Princeton: Cambridge University Press. Available at: https://www.cambridge.org/core/books/postbroadcast-democracy/A0D17A3CD156A0D1BB4318EE5DBCC60B

McNair, B. (2003) *News and Journalism in the UK*. London: Routledge.

Mendel, T. (2011) 'Public Service Broadcasting: A Comparative Legal Survey - UNESCO Digital Library', UNESCO. Available at: https://unesdoc.unesco.org/ark:/48223/pf0000192459 (Accessed: 30 April 2021).

Minder, R. (2015) 'Spain's News Media Are Squeezed by Government and Debt', *The New York Times*, 6 November. Available at: https://www.nytimes.com/2015/11/06/world/europe/as-spains-media-industry-changes-rapidly-some-worry-about-objectivity.html (Accessed: 1 July 2021).

Newman, N. (2020) Overview and Key Findings of the 2020 Digital News Report, *Reuters Institute Digital News Report*. Oxford, Reuters Institute for the Study of Journalism Available at: https://www.digitalnewsreport.org/survey/2020/overview-key-findings-2020/ (Accessed: 14 June 2021).

Newman, N. et al. (2020) *Reuters Institute Digital News Report 2020*. Oxford: Reuters Institute for the Study of Journalism, p. 112. Available at: https://reutersinstitute.politics.ox.ac.uk/sites/default/files/2020-06/DNR_2020_FINAL.pdf.

News Corporation (2020) 'News Corporation Annual Report'. News Corporation. Available at: https://newscorp.com/wp-content/uploads/2020/10/news-corp-2020-annual-report.pdf.

Phakathi, M. (2020) 'An Ubuntu Critique of the Decision of the South African Broadcasting Corporation to Stop Showing the Destruction of Public Property during Protests', *African Journal of Gender, Society and Development*, 9(2). Available at: https://journals.co.za/doi/abs/10.31920/2634-3622/2020/9n2a9 (Accessed: 14 June 2021).

Phillips, A. and Mazzoli, E. (2021) 'Search, Data and Targeting: Public Interest Solutions', in Tambini, D. and Moore, M. (eds) *Dealing with Digital Dominance*. Oxford: Oxford University Press. pp. 110–127.

Pickard, V. (2010) '"Whether the Giants Should Be Slain or Persuaded to Be Good": Revisiting the Hutchins Commission and the Role of Media in a Democratic Society', *Critical Studies in Media Communication*, 27(4), pp. 391–411. doi:10.1080/15295030903583523.

Poindexter, P.M., Meraz, S., and Weiss, A.S. (2008) Women, men, and news: divided and disconnected in the news media landscape. New York, London: Routledge.

Scannell, P. (1989) 'Public Service Broadcasting and Modern Public Life', *Media, Culture & Society*, 11(2), pp. 135–166. doi:10.1177/016344389011002002.

Sehl, A., Fletcher, R. and Picard, R.G. (2020) 'Crowding Out: Is There Evidence That Public Service Media Harm Markets? A Cross-national Comparative Analysis of Commercial Television and Online News Providers', *European Journal of Communication*, p. 0267323120903688. doi:10.1177/0267323120903688.

Sen, A. (2005) 'Human Rights and Capabilities', *Journal of Human Development*, 6(2), pp. 151–166. doi:10.1080/14649880500120491.

Shomron, B. and Schejter, A.M. (2020) 'The Communication Rights of Palestinian Israelis Understood Through the Capabilities Approach', *International Journal of Communication*, 14, p. 19.

Silverstone, P.R. (2006) *Media and Morality: On the Rise of the Mediapolis*. Cambridge; Malden: Polity.

Storr, J. (2011) 'The Disintegration of the State Model in the English Speaking Caribbean: Restructuring and Redefining Public Service Broadcasting', *International Communication Gazette*, 73(7), pp. 553–572. doi:10.1177/1748048511417155.

Thussu, D.K. (2009) *News as Entertainment: The Rise of Global Infotainment*. Thousand Oaks, CA: SAGE

Tuchman, G. (1972) 'Objectivity as Strategic Ritual: An Examination of Newsmen's Notions of Objectivity', *American Journal of Sociology*, 77(4), pp. 660–679. Available at: https://www.jstor.org/stable/2776752 (Accessed: 30 July 2020).

Valeriani, A. and Vaccari, C. (2015) 'Accidental Exposure to Politics on Social Media as Online Participation Equalizer in Germany, Italy, and the United Kingdom', *New Media & Society*, p. 1461444815616223. doi:10.1177/1461444815616223.

Van Aelst, P. et al. (2017) 'Political Communication in a High-Choice Media Environment: A Challenge for Democracy?', *Annals of the International Communication Association*, 41(1), pp. 3–27. doi:10.1080/23808985.2017.1288551.

Wasserman, H. and Maweu, J.M. (2014) 'The Freedom to Be Silent? Market Pressures on Journalistic Normative Ideals at the Nation Media Group in Kenya', *Review of African Political Economy*, 41(142), pp. 623–633. doi:10.1080/03056244.2014.928277.

10
PRESS FREEDOM, REGULATION AND THE LAW

Ideally, media regulation is used to balance rights to freedom of expression and press freedom, with the need to improve diversity and protect people from hate speech and unfair personal attack, but it can also be used by institutions to protect their own interests and by governments to control exposures that threaten their power. Regulation changes frequently to cope with changing social and technical requirements, so this chapter will give only a brief overview of (1) the protection of democracy and of individuals from harm, (2) the regulation of the journalistic field in the interests of incumbent institutions (which will also have an impact on democracy) and (3) regulation as a means of protecting the state.

The protection of the right to free expression is enshrined in article 19 of the UN International Covenant on Civil and Political Rights (ICCPR):

> Everyone shall have the right to freedom of expression; this right shall include freedom to seek, receive and impart information and ideas of all kinds, regardless of frontiers, either orally, in writing or in print, in the form of art, or through any other media of his choice.

However, even among those countries that are signatories to the convention, there is a great deal of ideological and cultural variation over the meaning of free expression and the media freedom that is implied by Article 19. Western liberal democracies tend to take a *monitorial* approach in which the media's role is to watch over, and critique, the working of governments. Media freedom is seen here as an extension of individual rights and debate, however, conflictual, and a means of arriving at resolution.

In east Asian countries, Confucian philosophy prioritises the creation of harmony and stability. This can be interpreted as bringing wrongs to the attention of the community so that they can be corrected, but it often means that the role

DOI: 10.4324/9781003037651-11

of the journalist is to support the state and defuse conflict (Elstein, 2020). In sub-Saharan Africa, the good of the community has traditionally been valued as much as, or more highly than, individual rights, a concept that is referred to in South Africa as *Ubuntu*. A sense of mutual obligation may at times come into conflict with a liberal attitude to individual speech rights (Metz, 2015).

These differences can sometimes be used as reasons to reject media freedom. Amongst those countries that have not signed up to the ICCPR, some (notably Singapore) look to Confucius to justify controlling the media in the interests of "socio-political stability" (Feng, 2022); religious autocracies may use divine authority to justify their control of the media, some refer to the requirements of *development journalism* which emphasises the need for the media to protect the newly emerging state; while authoritarian governments do not necessarily need to find a philosophical reason to protect themselves and their system. In all these cases, regulation may be used to close-down opposition by limiting debate and opportunity for democratic organisation.

Nation states establish norms according to their own political and philosophical priorities. At one end of the spectrum lie countries where these freedoms are protected and upheld by the courts, at the other end sit authoritarian regimes where journalists can be imprisoned for speaking out. In practice, most democracies fall somewhere in between.

The protection of democracy

Democracy, as discussed in **Chapter 1**, rests on the normative assumption that governance works best when the voices of all people are heard, and decisions are made through reasoned debate between representatives freely chosen by the people. Habermas, who we discuss in more detail in **Chapter 1**, argues that, ideally, an independent media should provide the opportunity for the contestation of free and unfettered debate in which facts are sifted and truths emerge. It should also allow for the voices of the unheard to emerge and be listened to with respect.

However, people and ideas do not have equal access to publicity and equal weight in the public sphere. As we discussed in **Chapter 1**, and elsewhere, inequality is built into the circulation of ideas, and inequality of power ensures that those closest to the *field of power* will always get privileged access, more of a hearing and be able to establish the official view of events. Indeed, Foucault, as we discussed in **Chapter 4**, sees power as inseparable from the establishment of what comes to be known as truth (Foucault, 1980). So, for example, the understanding of where a boundary lies is bound up in multiple discourses, built up through history and ultimately decided, not through the individual stories of those who live on the border, but the power that can be exercised to maintain belief in that border, and to uphold the belief that the border exists.

Knowing that information can be manipulated does not, however, diminish the need to listen to evidence, consider alternative points of view and endeavour to establish an independent understanding. Indeed, it makes it even more important because it is only through the circulation of independently sourced information that societies are able to confront what Arendt refers to as, "organized lying" (Arendt, 1968, p. 232). There are numerous examples, from Nazi Germany to Rwanda, Myanmar and modern Brazil, in which people with greater power misuse their position to rouse communities against one another, to belittle and bully minority groups or to spread misinformation in the hopes of protecting their own power.

Arendt argues, in the face of organised lying that,

> Truth, though powerless and always defeated in a head on clash with the powers that be, possesses a strength of its own: whatever those in power may contrive, they are unable to discover or invent a viable substitute for it. Persuasion and violence can destroy truth, but cannot replace it.
> *(Arendt, 1968, p. 258)*

So, we return to the normative assumptions of democracy, that only through the freedom to listen to a diversity of voices, search for information, publish what we believe to be true and debate, without coercion, are we able to come close to understanding, however imperfectly, the state of the world. We now consider how these rights can be protected.

Regulating the delivery of information

If any single organisation has a monopoly in the media field, they have a disproportionate degree of power over the information and views that are circulated. The assumption of a market economy is that competition is self-regulating, will respond to need and that this will provide diversity. When this fails, democratic nations, faced with diminishing media diversity, and concerned about the threat to democracy, use regulation to try and correct the imbalances of the market. One of the chief instruments for regulating the media field has been competition or anti-trust legislation.

Competition laws can have a role to play, but they have not been effective, for example, in preventing the consolidation of local newspaper chains which have cut staff, centralised news gathering and generally depleted the news landscape in the Global North over the last 40 years. This is partly because regulators tend to back-off in the face of media power. Media professor Rod Tiffin explains how, in the mid-1980s, media mogul, Rupert Murdoch, managed to manipulate competition concerns in his favour:

> Murdoch's takeover [of The Herald and Weekly Times] gave him control of papers constituting more than 75 per cent of Australian metropolitan daily circulation, including new monopolies in several cities. To stave off official moves, he announced the sale of several titles, especially afternoon papers. The regulator, the Trade Practices Commission, was in an

all-but-impossible position. Any rejection would have been akin to trying to unscramble eggs. Nevertheless, the TPC justified its approval on the grounds that in each city there would still be local competition, with a different owner having the morning and afternoon newspaper. This proved a false expectation, as all afternoon papers closed in the next few years.

(Tiffen, 2020)

The fear of angering a powerful media owner, or of forcing a closure, means that decisions by competition regulators tend to hinge on political considerations rather than on the need for democratic accountability. But even when brave decisions are taken, breaking up monopolies won't magically create diversity of views because, while competition works for driving down prices, it doesn't necessarily provide diversity of content. Indeed, as Bourdieu observes, competition in the mass media pushes institutions towards the centre ground and increases homogeneity rather than encouraging differentiation (Bourdieu, 2005). This is because, the subsidy produced by advertising, goes mainly to the most popular publication creating a pressure towards popular themes and similarity of content (see **Chapter 8**).

Regulating platforms

The early days of the internet provide a useful demonstration of how diversity is quickly subsumed in a highly competitive field. It was initially assumed that virtually equal access to the means of distribution would transform journalism, creating the perfect market conditions within which a public sphere could flourish (Negroponte, 1995). In a study in 2008, Hindman was able to demonstrate that, already, the biggest news organisations were attracting the majority of views (Hindman, 2008) and, in the intervening years, competition for views has encouraged greater convergence and more reliance on fewer news sources (Hindman, 2018), while the numbers of journalists and publications have decreased (Pickard, 2020).

Once again it is the role of advertising that has intervened to homogenise the market. The fortunes of the platform giants, Meta (Facebook and Instagram) and Alphabet (Google and YouTube), are built on selling advertising space alongside content provided by users (including news organisations). As we have explained, advertising revenue is tied to popularity. Popular items come up higher on search engines and social media feeds and make more money. Not content with volume sales, the platforms have used their access to personal data to target advertising to individual users, based on their past preferences (see **Chapter 7**). This has given them an additional advantage in selling advertising, damaging all the smaller online companies, which cannot compete with the sheer scale of the platforms and their data troves (Moore, 2018; Zuboff, 2019).

As the number of people accessing news via social media and search has increased, the power, reach and income of the platform giants have increased with them, and the income of the news publishers has diminished along with their ability to access audiences directly. The sheer size of the platforms and the degree to which they have become a vital part of all our lives has given them unprecedented power not only over news organisations but also over governments. When the Spanish government tried, in 2014, to help news organisations by requiring Google to pay them for snippets used in their search engine, Google responded by closing its Spanish news service. When Facebook was threatened with similar action in Australia in 2021, it simply cut Australia off from news on Facebook.

The recognition that platform power now challenges nation states, as well as disadvantaging smaller online companies, has forced US regulators to consider how anti-Trust laws can be used to break up the platforms and dilute their power. But, even if the law requires that the different social media platforms have different owners, as long as they are all targeting consumers in the same way, the problems that are inherent in data-targeting won't be addressed.

Regulating data targeting

As we have discussed in **Chapter 7**, platforms allow publishers and advertisers to directly target individuals or groups, on the basis of the data collected about their past preferences. This allows unscrupulous organisations to push emotionally triggering material to people, either as a means of maximising clicks and advertising revenue or to recruit them to particular causes. These abuses have drawn the attention of regulators across the world and attempts are being made to increase the transparency of algorithms and make platforms take more responsibility for content.

There is, in fact, no intrinsic reason why platforms should use data to target individuals with advertising or other material they have not requested. Surveys demonstrate that people would rather not be subject to data-driven invasions of their privacy (Mager, 2017) and yet, so far, governments seem reluctant to use regulation against targeted advertising, for fear of disrupting the growth of digital businesses, on which we have all learned to depend. Interventions (such as the European General Data Protection Regulation) put the onus on individuals to adjust their privacy settings, rather than starting from the simple premise that nobody should be targeted with material they have not specifically asked for (Zuboff, 2019; Phillips and Mazzoli, 2021).

Enabling access to information

Journalism is only as good as the information it has access to. A democratic, free press must be able to find out what is being done behind closed doors if it is to be able to hold power to account. This means that journalists need protection and information rights.

Fairness mandates

There are other ways in which media structures and technologies can be regulated to improve access to socially useful content and promote diversity and fairness (see also **Chapter 9**).

1. *Regulation for fairness* requires broadcasters to ensure that major parties in an election get equal representation. This form of regulation is written into broadcast licenses in many countries. For example, South Africa and the United Kingdom. It has the value of being easy to monitor and can dilute the dominance of the governing Party (Phillips, 2019).
2. *Regulation of scheduling* is useful to ensure that news broadcasts are available at peak times. In countries where scheduling is unregulated, such as the United States, broadcasters tend to reserve peak viewing hours for popular programming to maximise advertising revenue. When news scheduling is regulated and news appears regularly at times when audiences are most likely to be watching or listening, it ensures that the broadest possible audience will encounter news programming during their evening viewing. It has been demonstrated that this narrows the gap between the least and best-educated groups (Aalberg, van Aelst and Curran, 2010; Esser *et al.*, 2012).
3. *Must-carry mandates.* There is concern, particularly in Europe, that the inexorable move towards on-demand services will undermine the democratic gains made in regulating public service broadcasting. Some of the ideas under discussion include requiring television channel selectors and interfaces to give precedence to public service media (PSM) and regulated channels and must-carry mandates which would require streaming services and platforms to ensure that public service news broadcasts are readily available irrespective of platforms (Brevini, 2013). Research demonstrates that polarisation is lower in countries that have independent PSM (see **Chapter 9**).
4. *Net Neutrality* which gives everyone the same rights to publish online, irrespective of size and importance, could be undermined as the streaming giants clamour for higher speeds and more space, elbowing out the smaller, independent producers. So far, the *idea* of the internet as a space that is equally available to all has been maintained in most countries, but it will require vigilance to ensure that equality of access remains and that internet providers cannot give priority to dominant providers or establish a "fast lane" that prioritises entertainment channels over access to public interest material such as news.

Freedom of information

Laws which improve access to the workings of government have had an increasingly important role to play in establishing the conditions for democracy (Vadlamannati and Cooray, 2017, p. 135). The first Freedom of Information Act was passed in 1766, in Sweden, as part of a law guaranteeing the freedom of the press. The United States didn't implement such a law until 1966 and the United Kingdom as late as 2000. By 2019, 125 countries from Albania to Zimbabwe had FOI laws (UNESCO, 2019). Unfortunately, the adoption of such laws does not always mean that they are useful. In order to be effective, they need to be accompanied by: "a free press, greater political competition and an increased role for NGOs which are important precursors to the access of information as they enhance transparency and make governments more accountable to their citizens" (Vadlamannati and Cooray, 2017, p. 135). If the only media outlets are owned and controlled by the government or its close allies, and journalists or independent bloggers are intimidated, then the existence of a freedom of information law is meaningless. Such laws enhance democracy, they cannot create democracy where none exists.

Protection of sources

Journalism also needs legal protection to be extended to sources of information, because without legal protection, it can be very difficult to get people to reveal information for fear of reprisals. Journalists are theoretically protected from revealing sources under Article 10 of the European Convention on Human Rights, and UNESCO encourages member states to:

> Recognise the value to the public interest of source protection, with its legal foundation in the right to freedom of expression (including press freedom), and to privacy. These protections should also be embedded within a country's constitution and/or national law.
>
> *(Posetti, 2017, pp. 132–133)*

The framework covers the need to protect data as well as conventional contacts and, in particular, to protect journalists from surveillance of any kind.

However, this has not stopped the courts from intervening, and journalists in many countries, even those that have explicit laws protecting journalists from revealing their sources, have come under pressure when national security, or business interests, are at stake. In 2022, police in the United Kingdom used terrorism laws to try and extract information about the sources of a book written in 1986 by journalist Chris Mullin (Ponsford, 2022). A case taken to the European Court of Human Rights in 2016, regarding the Turkish Government and the Nokta weekly magazine, demonstrates how little protection journalists receive there:

> The interference had consisted in the seizure, retrieval and storage by the authorities of all of the magazine's computer data, even data that was unrelated to the article, with a view to identifying the public-sector whistle-blowers. Lastly, the Court considered that this measure was such as to deter potential sources from assisting the press in informing the public on matters of general interest, including when they concerned the armed forces.
>
> *(Council of Europe, 2018, p. 7)*

Without adequate protections for journalists and their sources, there can be no real media freedom and yet the list of countries taken to the European Court of Human Rights over breaches of source protection includes the Netherlands, the United Kingdom, Norway, Belgium and France, all of them democracies that are signatories to international agreements on press freedom.

Protecting the public

We have so far considered only the freedom of the news media to report, but we need also to consider the need to protect people from unfair publicity. Using speech deliberately to bully the powerless, or circulate disinformation, can have a real world, negative impact. Rumours spread about an individual can do immense harm reputationally and psychologically. We see this in social media pile-ons as well as in newspapers when individuals are held up to ridicule or have personal information exposed that they had not wished to share.

The need to be proportionate in reporting, and avoid harm, is unexceptional considered from a Confucian perspective, where the principle of *harmony* requires that, even if conflict is reported, the reporting should not exacerbate the conflict but should move towards conflict resolution and forgiveness (Feng, 2022). European-free speech principles allow a more combative approach, but even John Stuart Mill (see **Chapter 1**) recognised that speech acts can be harmful: "Acts, of whatever kind, which, without justifiable cause, do harm to others, may be, and in the more important cases absolutely require to be, controlled by the unfavourable sentiments, and, when needful, by the active interference of mankind" (Mill, 1859, p. 52).

Article 20 of the International Covenant on Civil and Political Rights (ICCPR) makes explicit that: "Any advocacy of national, racial or religious hatred that constitutes incitement to discrimination, hostility or violence shall be prohibited by law."

Laws vary across the world with some states adding a broader category of protected characteristics so that sexual orientation and gender are included and many also adding a lower threshold of offense such as speech that is threatening, likely to stir up hatred or provoke. Recognising that some curbs on media freedom are necessary, it helps to think of media regulation as a balance between absolute freedom to publish and protection of the interests of the powerless. The question we address next is where that balance lies.

Defamation, libel and reputational damage

The right to defence of *reputation,* and to some extent the right to *privacy,* is understood in most countries in the world. It is generally illegal to steal information, to tap telephones or to bribe officials to obtain private information. Those who hold public positions, or who deliberately court publicity, may, in some countries, have fewer privacy rights than those who try to stay out of the limelight, but if the media reveals intimate information, that has no bearing on their public role, or they are unjustifiably accused of something they have not done, anyone should have some right to redress via the courts. These cases will hinge on the question of *justification*. Media lawyer Hugh Tomlinson explains of the European courts:

> The right to reputation concerns the protection of a public reputation against *unjustified* (our emphasis) damage. If reputation is damaged by a publication then the issue has traditionally been understood to be whether that damage can be justified: either because the reputation was undeserved (because the allegation was true) or because the damage was justified (because, for example, it was a responsible statement on a matter of public interest).
>
> *(Tomlinson, 2014 p. 18)*

Laws are drafted by national Governments and the emphasis varies. Sometimes, the law comes down on the side of individual rights and, sometimes, on the side of press freedom. A case that revealed that difference of emphasis came to the European Court of Justice in 1986. It concerned the right of a journalist to insult an elected premier. In an article in *Profil* magazine, an Austrian journalist, Peter Lingen, described Kreisky, the recently elected Chancellor of Austria, as "immoral," "undignified" and his conduct as "basest opportunism."

The issue at stake was Kreisky's public support of a former Nazi and member of the SS. Kreisky sued for defamation on the grounds that, even though the facts of the case were not disputed, Lingen's use of language was defamatory. The case then went to the European Court of Justice which decided that, if the facts were not in dispute, then in contesting the journalist's right to comment on those facts, the Austrian court: "infringes freedom of opinion itself."[1]

In this case, the political prominence of the complainant meant that, in the eyes of the court, there was a genuine public interest in the case and Kreisky should have been prepared to cope with criticism of his motives and behaviour. In other words, they took the strictly *liberal* position that politicians should not be protected from criticism if they are to be held to account.

In most democracies, defamation and privacy complaints are broadly considered private matters and are dealt with in civil courts, but in some, defamation, particularly if it involves public officials, may also be a criminal offence. Indeed, Alberto Spampinato, President of Ossigeno per L'Informazione, an Italian organisation monitoring freedom of expression, noted that criminal libel was so often used against journalists in Italy that it had become the means by which the Italian press was regulated (Botsford, 2016). In Poland among a number of European countries, simply insulting the head of state can result in a prison sentence (Zimmerman, 2021). The same *illiberal* approach is taken in most authoritarian states as well as in religious autocracies.

Where laws specifically outlaw criticism of the head of state, it is not the protection of the individual which is at stake, so much as protection of the system as it is embodied by the head of state. A democracy which cannot tolerate criticism is fragile, indeed. However, there is also a limit to the values of an un-civil press. When news organisations, or influencers, engage in bullying an individual politician with whom they have political differences, that can also threaten democracy. Online abuse, in particular, has become a concern and governments are yet to find an adequate response, capable of balancing free speech rights and the rights of individuals to protection from emotional harm (Bigio and Vogelstein, 2020).

While politicians and celebrities are most likely to find themselves maligned by the media, they are also most able to defend themselves using available legal remedies. Indeed, wealthy individuals can use their access to the courts as a means of intimidating publishers, who cannot afford the legal cost of defending themselves against accusations of libel, even when information is clearly both verified and in the public interest. In one case, a hugely wealthy Russian oligarch tried (and failed) to suppress a book (*Kleptopia*) about his activities. The publisher, Harper Collins, defended the case which they described as, "*lawfare* - legal action that poses such massive financial risks to a defendant it has the effect of silencing them or making them withdraw" (Casciani, 2022).

Ordinary people are less likely to be caught in the media spotlight, but they have fewer options for defending themselves when they are. Suing a media organisation for libel can be prohibitively expensive and outcomes are uncertain. In cases of racism, the serious psychological harms done to individuals may be hard to pursue under laws outlawing racial hatred, or to fit into the legal frame of defamation. In many countries, this inequality is bridged somewhat by the establishment of Press Councils or Ethics Councils which provide a cheaper avenue for redress or public apology and to some extent regulate deliberately harmful language. We discuss ethical self-regulation in **Chapter 11**.

Protecting justice

The right to fair trial is guaranteed under Article 14 of the International Covenant on Civil and Political Right (ICCPR) and in Article 7 of the African

Charter on Human and People's Rights as well as in most national constitutions. This right is largely interpreted as providing openness and fairness, but there are fundamental differences in approach. In some jurisdictions, the protection of a fair trial is believed to require protection *from* the media, whereas in others, it is interpreted as requiring protection *for* the media.

In the United States, even though there is evidence that prior publicity can influence juries (Moran and Cutler, 1991), the right of the press to report takes precedence over the defendant's right to a fair trial. The focus of concern here is the fairness of the police and the court. The jury, as representatives of the people, are assumed to be acting in the interests of society. Judges do have some discretion. They can order juries to avoid press coverage of the case and they may agree to a change of trial venue if prejudice against a defendant appears to render a fair trial impossible.

In England, Australia and New Zealand, a media blackout is imposed and maintained, from impending arrest to trial, under strict *sub judice* rules. Under these rules, only statements made by the police, and court proceedings themselves, can be reported. The assumption is made here that media speculation will influence the jury who should be listening only to the evidence presented in court. News organisations who breach these rules can be found to be in contempt of court and fined while those found responsible can even be imprisoned.

Exercise: Finding a Balance

Taking a few well-known cases in two different countries, consider the pros and cons of each approach. Should the media be allowed to report everything they can find out or does this harm justice and prejudice the jury?

Policing the field

As we explained in **Chapter 2**, media organisations exist within a field of similar institutions, which develop in relation to one another (Powell and DiMaggio, 1991; Bourdieu, 2005). While there is a tension between organisations as they compete to dominate the field, there is also a need to protect the field as a whole and maintain its separation from neighbouring fields.

> The acquisition and maintenance of power within organizational fields requires that dominant organizations continually enact strategies of control, most notably through the socialization of newcomers into a shared world view or via the support of the state and its judicial arm.
>
> *(Powell and DiMaggio, 1991, p. 31)*

Maintaining legitimacy

To maintain *legitimacy* and through that, the trust of its audiences, journalism must be seen to fulfil certain expectations. This gives journalists themselves opportunities for self-protection when they fear that the activities of some institutions or actors are threatening the legitimacy of the field as a whole. A number of scholars have referred to the way news organisations establish shared rules and then police them as: *paradigm repair* (Carlson, 2016).

News organisations are, therefore, always alert, on the one hand, to possible incursions by the state which might curb their freedom of action. On the other hand, they are also likely to use the power at their disposal to draw the state to their aid to prevent disruption of the field by new entrants, or indeed by incumbents with differing views on how the field should operate and the standards that need to be set. Matt Carlson refers to this activity as *boundary work:* "moments of contestation when taken for granted practices come under fire, which then spurs efforts to define appropriate practices while dispelling deviant or outsider actions" (Carlson, 2016, p. 352).

Boundary work

As we discussed in **Chapter 8**, advertising has long been the paymaster of journalism and, as its importance grew, the need to clearly differentiate journalism from advertising became acute. Starting early in the twentieth century, helped by campaigns in the media, bodies were established to regulate the wilder excesses of the advertising industry. The object was to protect consumers from misleading advertisements, but the outcome protected journalism too because it helped to differentiate between editorial, which seeks to expose wrong-doing or provide an independent evaluation, and advertising which is simply there to sell a product. Clarifying the differentiation between and within fields is an important part of *boundary work*.

More recently, these consumer laws have been used to regulate the way "influencers" can do business. In over 60 countries across the world, media organisations have championed the use of advertising regulation to ensure that social media influencers must declare when they take money for mentioning products. In France, influencers can be heavily fined or even imprisoned for up to two years for failure to disclose payments (Garson, 2019). The requirement to declare that they use their posts to sell products has had the secondary effect of clarifying their difference and separation from those who occupy the journalism field and are not involved in the direct sale of goods.

This separation is not merely a means of clarifying the role of journalists and securing their position. It also enables them to create norms and produce ethical guidelines (see **Chapter 11**) which, though not necessarily backed by law, carry moral force. Some of these codes are extremely detailed and elaborate (the Indian code runs to 111 pages). While not all of them are effective in policing standards, they do offer a public description of the agreed standards that journalists feel that they ought to live up to. It is this agreement that confers legitimacy on the field of journalism and allows organisations and individuals some power in policing the field.

Paradigm repair

One notable case of *paradigm repair* concerns the role of the UK Guardian newspaper in its pursuit of what the editor took to be the excesses of the popular press. In 2009, the Guardian organised an investigation into the use of unethical and illegal phone hacking by the *News of the World* (NOW), an activity which produced scandalous and sensational headlines but also damaged the people targeted. The editor of *The Guardian* felt that such illegal activities were spilling over into public perceptions of the press as a whole and that they needed to stop (Martinson, 2015).

The popular press ignored the allegations, but the revelation, in 2011, that NOW reporters had hacked into the mobile phone of a murder victim (Milly Dowler), meant that it was no longer possible for the State to turn a blind eye (phone hacking is illegal). Rupert Murdoch, proprietor of News Corporation which owned the newspaper, apologised and closed the NOW (Plunkett, 2011). The Government responded by ordering a public inquiry (The Leveson Inquiry) into the behaviour of the press. The inquiry recommended a public complaints system that would be independent but backed by law.

The police, who had also ignored the allegations of phone hacking when they first arose, compensated for their inaction by organising dawn raids on journalists thought to have hacked phones, or made improper payments (bribes), to police officers for information. Altogether 33 journalists were arrested and 11 were convicted of crimes relating to bribery or tampering with private communications.

This example shows how media organisations can draw the state into the field (Powell and DiMaggio, 1991) to maintain ethical standards, but it also shows how the most powerful institutions in the field can close ranks to isolate those who seek to challenge their power. Once the NOW had closed, and the subsequent enquiry had run its course, the popular newspaper proprietors got together to build a solid front against any attempt to regulate their activities. The newspaper editors, many of whom had been in blatant breach of their ethical codes, and in some cases, the law, called on their right to press freedom as a means of blocking any attempt at further regulation of their activity (Thomas and Finneman, 2014).

The Daily Telegraph editorial proclaimed: "What happened at the *News of the World* was unconscionable…however, this must not be used as an excuse to impose the first statutory controls on the press since censorship laws were abolished in 1695." July 9, 2011 (Thomas and Finneman, 2014, p. 177).

The Daily Mail, insinuated that it was all a plot: "the political class would love tame and heavily regulated newspapers." July 9, 2011. (ibid)

The Daily Mirror was concerned that: "understandable revulsion over phone hacking [would be used] to shackle a free press" May 2, 2012 (Thomas and Finneman, 2014, p. 178).

The Press Gazette, which sees itself as the voice of British Journalism, summed it up thus: "I suspect that future generations will look back on this and be shocked not by the illegal interception of voicemails, but by the witch-hunt of journalists which ensued" (Ponsford, 2015).

The Guardian, which started the whole process of reform, was marginalised. The popular press used its combined muscle to defend itself from any form of external control, while still engaging in *paradigm repair*, by reforming its system of self-regulation (*The Guardian* refused to join this new *Press Complaints Commission*). During the crisis, trust in the British press plunged. According to the 2011 Edelman Trust Barometer, the UK press was the least trusted of all countries surveyed across the world.

While in the end, nothing much changed in terms of law or regulation, *The Guardian's* actions did successfully draw the state into an act of boundary control and, in doing so, halt some of the activities which were, in their opinion, contributing to the gradual delegitimisation of the press. The exercise did nothing to reduce the power of the popular press in the United Kingdom, but it reminded editors that they are not above the law and that the pressure of civil society and public displeasure cannot be ignored.

Economic threats to the journalism field

From time-to-time journalism finds itself confronting a technical change that appears to create an existential threat. When this happens, news organisations make use of their proximity to the *field of power* (see **Chapter 2**) to campaign for state aid in some form. The invention of the electric telegraph in the mid-nineteenth century was one such threat. The telegraph had collapsed the time required for news to be spread around the world from days or weeks to seconds. Organisations without access to timely news would be unable to compete, or would be forced to pay substantial fees, for the privilege of accessing information. Recognising that the telegraph monopoly presented an existential threat to news plurality, European governments, pressured by newspaper proprietors, nationalised the technology to ensure that everyone had equal rights to information.

The internet and the platforms (as we mentioned earlier) have had a similar threatening impact on news organisations, completely disrupting the business model for journalism. With direct access to audiences undermined, on the one hand, and direct access to advertising threatened, on the other hand, the news companies found themselves in existential crisis and used all the power at their disposal to bring audiences on board for what they describe as a struggle to save democracy. These headlines demonstrate how, across the world, journalism moves in concert to protect its interests:

> **Facebook Has Been a Disaster for the World: How much longer are we going to allow its platform to foment hatred and undermine democracy?**
> *The New York Times* **September 18, 2020 (Bouie, 2020)**

> **Holding Facebook to account is a test of democracy.**
> *Times of India* **August 23, 2020 (Gopalakrishnan, 2020)**

> **Facebook's threats to Australian news imperil democracy everywhere.**
> *Canadian Globe and Mail*, **September 3, 2020 (Bernhard, 2020)**

While the news organisations deplore the way in which Facebook allows misinformation to be circulated, they have been very quick to take advantage of any benefits that Facebook appeared to offer them, including targeting their material. But, although the concerns of the media companies are primarily protective, they cannot be dismissed as purely self-seeking. Journalism organisations are subject to the combined pressure of the field, the expectations of consumers and the law. This establishes norms and safeguards which, although often inadequate, provide a higher level of transparency and accountability than the flux of information online.

Exercise: Paradigm Repair and Boundary Control

Thinking about the news media in your country, look for example of *paradigm repair* and *boundary control*. To what extent do these activities protect ethical journalism and to what extent do they merely protect business practices?

Regulation for control

So far we have described the ways in which regulation can support democracy and the news media and how news organisations seek to pressure Governments for regulation as a means of maintaining ethical standards, controlling entry to the field and safeguarding their businesses. We now turn to the ways in which regulation can be used to attack democracy and undermine press freedom.

National security

The protection of a free press is written into the United National International Covenant on Civil and Political Rights, but there is a get-out clause. Article 19 of the ICCPR allows for the restriction of speech rights and press freedom if it is for: "the protection of national security or of public order." The ECHR has a similarly worded clause allowing the state to suppress information on grounds of national security.

In a plural democracy, journalists at least have theoretical protection under the law and the assurance that the media and civil society will speak out in their defence if they reveal state secrets. In regimes where civil society is controlled, the threat of loss of a license, or of imprisonment, acts as a potent weapon for silencing dissent, with the added value of allowing for public intimidation of those who might wish to dissent in the future. A count of jailed journalists in 2020 reads like a *Who's Who* of top autocracies: China (47), Turkey (37), Egypt (27), Saudi Arabia (24), Eritrea (16), Iran (15), Vietnam (15) and Russia (10) (CPJ, 2020).

In China, the National Security law, passed in 2020, during pro-democracy protests, outlaws: secession, subversion, terrorism and "collusion with foreign forces." It has since been used to arrest and imprison journalists and news executives who backed the pro-democracy movement or opposed moves to curtail freedoms previously enjoyed by Hong Kong citizens. In their annual report for 2021, the Hong Kong Journalists' Association reported: "An air of fear and anxiety has blanketed the city. Pressure on freethinking is mounting. Chilling effect and culture of censorship are growing… the room for freedom is shrinking swiftly" (Tang *et al.*, 2021, p. 7).

In Zimbabwe, journalists are also under pressure from the arbitrary use of loosely worded laws ostensibly protecting national security. In 2020, journalist Hopewell Chin'ono was twice arrested and charged with inciting unrest, obstructing justice and demeaning Zimbabwe's National Prosecution Authority. Tabani Moyo, head of the Media Institute of Southern Africa in Zimbabwe, said,

> The attacks on the industry have been aggressive and we have seen the weaponizing of the law; the introduction of the Cyber Security Bill which seeks to snoop and empower the military to crackdown on expression. The heavy handedness on the media has been highly pronounced.
>
> *(Mavhunga, 2020)*

In Russia, the Committee to Protect Journalists reported that at least 10 journalists were detained by police in the Spring of 2021 while covering rallies in support of anti-corruption campaigner, Alexei Navalny. Most were released, but some were held on a variety of charges connected with incitement to protest, organising protests, or blocking traffic. Many of those arrested were holding valid press credentials at the time (CPJ, 2021).

In Kashmir, the Indian government, having rescinded the semi-autonomous status of the region, disconnected telecommunications, arrested journalists and set up a government-controlled media centre where journalists were supposed to work. In the guise of controlling "fake news," the Indian government censors all journalistic content produced in Kashmir and decides what is "fake" and what is acceptable (RSF, 2020).

Censorship

A broad range of law and regulation is used by governments to censor the work of journalists. Criminal libel, blasphemy and hate speech laws can be re-engineered so that they no longer provide support to the powerless but instead limit the possibilities for free thinking. In Singapore, for example, material that is deemed to be harmful or immoral is not allowed and anything that might "excite disaffection against the Government" is out of bounds. Russia has laws against promoting "non-traditional" sexual relationships as well as a very wide definition of extremism which can be used to prosecute journalists. In Malaysia, speech with "a seditious tendency" is illegal. Which seems to mean everything that the censors disagree with. Venezuela outlaws anything that might "discredit legitimately constituted authorities" – which renders the role of journalists pretty much redundant. Just to reinforce the authority of the state, journalists in all four countries are also licensed by the state and can have their licenses revoked should they break these catch-all laws (Hem, 2014).

Media capture

Control of media organisations allows Governments to keep up a pretence of liberality in relation to journalists while at the same time ensuring that those who criticise the Government are unlikely to find anywhere to work. One of the first targets of state control by an authoritarian state may be capture of public service media (discussed further in **Chapter 9**). This is usually achieved by putting government-approved people into positions of power within them. For example, in the aftermath of the civic unrest of 2019–2020, the Director of Broadcasting at Radio Television, Hong Kong, was sacked and replaced by an administrative officer with the remit to get rid of "incorrect" content and "disobedient editorial staff" (Tang et al., 2021).

Capture of privately owned interests is less direct. In Hungary, for example, news organisations have gradually been absorbed by friends of the ruling party, who have then been rewarded by large injections of cash in the form of government advertising (Griffen, 2020). The same is true in the Czech Republic where oligarch Marek Dospiva was completely open about his reasons for moving into the media field: "the fact that we own media gives us the assurance that it will be more difficult for anyone to attack us" (Balčytienė et al., 2015, p. 123). These countries are members of the European Union and have signed up to European conventions that guarantee media freedom, however:

> On the surface, rhetorics of media freedom and pluralism prevail, mainly in the preambles of all media laws. But, beyond this, media law is widely conceived as a means to redistribute resources among clients of political parties and some oligarchs associated with parties. Media is captured through the capture of media policy and media law, creating new nomenclature systems

that allow parties to delegate people to key decision-making positions in control of media resources.

(Balčytienė et al., 2015, p. 126).

> **Exercise: Regulation and Democracy**
>
> Consider your own media system. To what extent does regulation help to democratise media and to what extent does it concentrate power in the hands of the most powerful groups?

How regulation and the law helps and hinders

Ideally, the job of journalism is to report what has happened and reveal what has been hidden. As this chapter has demonstrated, law and regulation can both help and hinder. It can enable journalism by setting standards, distributing resources, protecting journalists and news organisations from improper influence and intimidation, and ensuring that those reported on are given support against unreasonable reporting. But, regulation is also a means of controlling what is said and disseminated and protecting powerful people from scrutiny. The law is not neutral. It is the expression of the will of those in power and is held in check only by a healthy and engaged civil society.

Summary

- National states use regulation to balance the needs of competing groups in society.
- In authoritarian states, the balance usually comes down on the side of the ruling elite and protects the interests of the state.
- In democratic countries, regulation ideally attempts to balance press freedom, the rights of the individual and the power of the state.
- Regulation for democracy is usually intended to prevent the build-up of monopolies, improve diversity of views and protect journalists.
- Some countries go further than others in protecting and promoting diversity.
- Legal protection for individuals is widespread, but sometimes, it is abused to provide special protection for the ruling elite while providing very little protection from harm for ordinary people.
- Media organisations may use regulation, both statutory and voluntary, to maintain their status within the journalism field and prevent incursions from allied professions.
- The state may use media regulation to control free expression and prevent the dissemination of views it finds threatening.

Note

1 Judgement in the case of Lingens v Austria (1986), Application no. 9815/82, European Court of Human Rights.

References

Aalberg, T., van Aelst, P. and Curran, J. (2010) 'Media Systems and the Political Information Environment: A Cross-National Comparison', *The International Journal of Press/Politics*, 15(3), pp. 255–271. doi:10.1177/1940161210367422.

Arendt, H. (1968) *Between Past and Future*. (ed) J. Kohn. London: Penguin Classics.

Balčytienė, A. et al. (2015) 'Oligarchization, de-Westernization and vulnerability: Media between Democracy and Authoritarianism in Central and Eastern Europe', *Tidsskrift for Medier, Erkendelse Og*, 3(1), p. 23.

Bernhard, D. (2020) 'Opinion: Facebook's Threats to Australian News Imperil Democracy Everywhere', *The Globe and Mail*, 3 September. Available at: https://www.theglobeandmail.com/opinion/article-facebooks-threats-to-australian-news-imperil-democracy-everywhere/ (Accessed: 17 February 2022).

Bigio, J. and Vogelstein, R. (2020) 'Women under Attack', *Foreign Affairs*, February, pp. 131–138. Available at: https://www.proquest.com/docview/2331238316/abstract/AC89F9901B194767PQ/1 (Accessed: 14 February 2022).

Botsford, P. (2016) *Word Crimes - Defamation and Freedom of Expression*, International Bar Association. Available at: https://www.ibanet.org/article/9E40E124-20BB-4533-A919-C7B5345F34C4 (Accessed: 30 August 2021).

Bouie, J. (2020) 'Opinion | Facebook Has Been a Disaster for the World', *The New York Times*, 18 September. Available at: https://www.nytimes.com/2020/09/18/opinion/facebook-democracy.html (Accessed: 8 September 2021).

Bourdieu, P. (2005) 'The Political Field, the Social Science Field, and the Journalistic Field', in Benson, R. and Neveu, E. (eds) *Bourdieu and the Journalistic Field*. Cambridge; Malden, MA: Polity Press ; Blackwell, pp. 29–47.

Brevini, B. (2013) *Public Service Broadcasting Online: A Comparative European Policy Study of PSB 2.0*. Basingstoke: Palgrave Macmillan.

Carlson, M. (2016) 'Metajournalistic Discourse and the Meanings of Journalism: Definitional Control, Boundary Work, and Legitimation', *Communication Theory*, 26(4), pp. 349–368. doi:10.1111/comt.12088.

Casciani, D. (2022) 'Journalist Wins "Kleptocrat" Book High Court Libel Case', *BBC News*, 2 March. Available at: https://www.bbc.com/news/uk-60595266 (Accessed: 3 March 2022).

Council of Europe (2018) *The Protection of Journalistic Sources, A Cornerstone of the Freedom of the Press*, Platform to Promote the Protection of Journalism and Safety of Journalists. Strasbourg: Council of Europe.

CPJ (2020) 'Record Number of Journalists Jailed Worldwide', *Committee to Protect Journalists*, December 2020. Available at: https://cpj.org/reports/2020/12/record-number-journalists-jailed-imprisoned/ (Accessed: 3 March 2022).

CPJ (2021) 'At Least 10 Journalists Detained While Covering pro-Navalny Rallies in Russia', *Committee to Protect Journalists*, 22 April. Available at: https://cpj.org/2021/04/at-least-10-journalists-detained-while-covering-pro-navalny-rallies-in-russia/ (Accessed: 9 September 2021).

Elstein, D. (2020) 'Confucian Reflective Commitment and Free Expression', *European Journal of Political Theory*, 19(3), pp. 314–333. doi:10.1177/1474885116681175.

Esser, F. et al. (2012) 'Political Information Opportunities in Europe A Longitudinal and Comparative Study of Thirteen Television Systems', *The International Journal of Press/Politics*, 17(3), pp. 247–274. doi:10.1177/1940161212442956.

Feng, Y. (2022) 'A Confucian Approach to Journalism Ethics', in Price, L., Trifonova, Saunders, K., and Wyatt, W. (eds) *The Routledge Companion To Journalism Ethics*. Abingdon, Oxon: Routledge, pp. 36–45.

Foucault, M. (1980) *Power/Knowledge*. Brighton: Harvester Press.

Garson, J. (2019) 'How To Be an Influencer and Not Get Sued', *Forbes*. Available at: https://www.forbes.com/sites/jackgarson/2019/05/07/how-to-be-an-influencer-and-not-get-sued/ (Accessed: 8 September 2021).

Gopalakrishnan, A. (2020) 'Holding Facebook to Account Is a Test of Democracy', *The Times of India*, 23 August. Available at: https://timesofindia.indiatimes.com/blogs/to-name-and-address/holding-fb-to-account-is-a-test-of-democracy/ (Accessed: 17 February 2022).

Griffen, S. (2020) 'Hungary: A Lesson in Media Control', *British Journalism Review*, 31(1), pp. 57–62. doi:10.1177/0956474820910071.

Hem, M. (2014) 'Evading the Censors: Critical Journalism in Authoritarian States', *Reuters Institute for the Study of Journalism*. Available at: https://reutersinstitute.politics.ox.ac.uk/sites/default/files/2017-10/Evading_the_Censors_Critical_journalism_in_authoritarian_states_0.pdf.

Hindman, M. (2008) *The Myth of Digital Democracy*. Princeton, NJ: Princeton University Press.

Hindman, M. (2018) *The Internet Trap: How the Digital Economy Builds Monopolies and Undermines Democracy*. Princeton, NJ: Princeton University Press.

Mager, A. (2017) 'Search Engine Imaginary: Visions and Values in the Co-production of Search Technology and Europe', *Social Studies of Science*, 47(2), pp. 240–262. doi:10.1177/0306312716671433.

Martinson, J. (2015) 'Alan Rusbridger Takes Aim at Press Over Phone Hacking and Snowden', *The Guardian*, 18 October. Available at: https://www.theguardian.com/media/2015/oct/18/alan-rusbridger-press-phone-hacking-edward-snowden-surveillance-society-of-editors (Accessed: 14 February 2022).

Mavhunga, C. (2020) *Critics Decry Zimbabwe's Press Freedom Failures | Voice of America - English*, *VOANews*. Available at: https://www.voanews.com/press-freedom/critics-decry-zimbabwes-press-freedom-failures (Accessed: 9 September 2021).

Metz, T. (2015) 'African Ethics and Journalism Ethics: News and Opinion in Light of Ubuntu', *Journal of Media Ethics*, 30(2), pp. 74–90. doi:10.1080/23736992.2015.1020377.

Mill, J.S. (1859) *On Liberty*. Available at: https://courses.lumenlearning.com/sanjacinto-philosophy/chapter/john-stuart-mill-on-liberty-chapter-2-of-the-liberty-of-thought-and-discussion/ (Accessed: 19 February 2021).

Moore, M. (ed.) (2018) *Digital Dominance: The Power of Google, Amazon, Facebook, and Apple*. New York: Oxford University Press.

Moran, G. and Cutler, B.L. (1991) 'The Prejudicial Impact of Pretrial Publicity1', *Journal of Applied Social Psychology*, 21(5), pp. 345–367. doi:10.1111/j.1559–1816.1991.tb00524.x.

Negroponte, N. (1995) *Being Digital*. London: Hodder & Stoughton.

Phillips, A. (2019) 'The Agenda-Setting Role of Newspapers in the UK 2017 Elections', in Wring, D., Mortimore, R., and Atkinson, S. (eds) *Political Communication in Britain: Campaigning, Media and Polling in the 2017 General Election*. Cham: Springer International Publishing, pp. 83–97. doi:10.1007/978-3-030–00822-2_6.

Phillips, A. and Mazzoli, E. (2021) 'Search, Data and Targeting: Public Interest Solutions', in Tambini, D. and Moore, M. (eds) *Dealing with Digital Dominance*. Oxford: Oxford University Press. pp. 110–127.

Pickard, V. (2020) 'Restructuring Democratic Infrastructures: A Policy Approach to the Journalism Crisis', *Digital Journalism*, 8(6), pp. 704–719. doi:10.1080/21670811.2020.1733433.

Plunkett, J. (2011) 'Rupert Murdoch Says "Sorry" in Ad Campaign', *The Guardian*, 15 July. Available at: https://www.theguardian.com/media/2011/jul/15/rupert-murdoch-sorry-ad-campaign (Accessed: 14 February 2022).

Ponsford, D. (2015) 'The 67 UK Journalists Arrested and/or Charged in the Course of Their Jobs since 2011', *Press Gazette*. Available at: https://www.pressgazette.co.uk/the-67-uk-journalists-arrested-andor-charged-in-the-course-of-their-jobs-since-2011/ (Accessed: 10 September 2021).

Ponsford, D. (2022) 'Chris Mullin versus West Midlands Police Legal Fight to Protect Sources', *Press Gazette*. Available at: https://pressgazette.co.uk/chris-mullin-west-midlands-police-sources/ (Accessed: 17 February 2022).

Posetti, J. (2017) 'Protecting Journalism Sources in the Digital Age - UNESCO Digital Library', *WWW.UNESCO.ORG*. Available at: https://unesdoc.unesco.org/ark:/48223/pf0000248054 (Accessed: 30 August 2021).

Powell, W.W. and DiMaggio, P.J. (1991) *The New Institutionalism in Organizational Analysis*. Chicago: University of Chicago Press.

RSF (2020) *India: A Year of Throttling Journalism in Kashmir | Reporters without Borders, RSF: Reporters without Borders*. Available at: https://rsf.org/en/news/india-year-throttling-journalism-kashmir-0 (Accessed: 10 September 2021).

Tang, C. *et al.* (2021) '2021 Annual Report: Freedom in Tatters'. Edited by C. Yeung. Hong Kong: Hong Kong Journalists Association. Available at: https://www.hkja.org.hk/wp-content/uploads/2021/07/HKJA_AR2021_eng_outline_single-1.pdf.

Thomas, R.J. and Finneman, T. (2014) 'Who Watches the Watchdogs?', *Journalism Studies*, 15(2), pp. 172–186. doi:10.1080/1461670X.2013.806068.

Tiffen, R. (2020) 'Submission 9 to Inquiry into the State of Media Diversity Independence and Reliability in Australia', Senate Environment and Communications References Committee. Available at: https://www.aph.gov.au/Parliamentary_Business/Committees/Senate/Environment_and_Communications/Mediadiversity/Submissions.

Tomlinson, H. (2014) *Privacy and Defamation, Strasbourg Blurs the Boundaries – Hugh Tomlinson QC, Inforrm's Blog*. Available at: https://inforrm.org/2014/01/23/privacy-and-defamation-strasbourg-blurs-the-boundaries-hugh-tomlinson-qc/ (Accessed: 23 August 2021).

UNESCO (2019) *Powering Sustainable Development with Access to Information: Highlights from the 2019 UNESCO Monitoring and Reporting of SDG Indicator 16.10.2- UNESCO Digital Library*. Available at: https://unesdoc.unesco.org/ark:/48223/pf0000369160 (Accessed: 30 August 2021).

Vadlamannati, K.C. and Cooray, A. (2017) 'Transparency Pays? Evaluating the Effects of the Freedom of Information Laws on Perceived Government Corruption', *The Journal of Development Studies*, 53(1), pp. 116–137. doi:10.1080/00220388.2016.1178385.

Zimmerman, A. (2021) 'European Countries Where Insulting the Head of State Can Land You in Prison', *POLITICO*. Available at: https://www.politico.eu/article/european-countries-where-insulting-head-of-state-can-land-prison-belgium-denmark-france-germany/ (Accessed: 3 March 2022).

Zuboff, P.S. (2019) *The Age of Surveillance Capitalism: The Fight for a Human Future at the New Frontier of Power: Barack Obama's Books of 2019*. London: Profile Books.

11
ETHICS IN PRACTICE

In this chapter, we discuss the ethical possibilities and responsibilities of individual journalists, taking into consideration the structural constraints upon them and the means at their disposal for ethical action. In doing this, we consider what we mean by ethics and ethical responsibility; how journalists generate collective responsibility for ethical behaviour; and how they view their role, and the commercial, political and physical constraints that they face in behaving ethically. We recognise that, for many journalists, the pursuit of a story is not the straightforward decision of an individual agent, but a series of compromises often made at speed and, in some cases, in the face of considerable pressure.

What do we mean by ethics?

Christians and Nordenstreng (2004, p. 20) see *truth-telling*, *respect* and *non-violence* as the three basic universal ethical requirements. They say: "Living with others is inconceivable if we cannot tacitly assume that people are speaking truthfully." For journalists, the necessity to tell the truth is even greater than it is for most people because journalism travels further, faster and carries more authority. With that power should come responsibility (2004, p. 22).

Finding the *truth* is not straightforward. Journalists can listen to evidence but don't always know which version is correct. They are often forced to make fast judgements, but their view may be clouded, or even obscured, by personal experience (habitus – see **Chapters 2 and 3**). They may give more credence to people with power and dismiss those on the fringes. They may lean towards members of their own class, cultural background or political persuasion and ignore, or downplay, conflicting perspectives. Finding the truth requires making the effort to look beyond the obvious and set aside our own prejudices.

DOI: 10.4324/9781003037651-12

An ethic of *respect* requires that journalists listen to others as equals, have regard for difference (see Chapter 5), but also the courage to expose abusive behaviour hateful or violent acts. In embracing the ethic of *non-violence* journalists must balance the primary job of truth-telling with the injunction to avoid doing harm. At times, these requirements feel contradictory. Truth-telling can lead to anger and even violence. Balancing these universal, basic ethical requirements is not always easy.

Virtue ethics

Aristotle's *virtue ethics* can help us find our way. Aristotle looks, not to inflexible rules, but to the development of personal "virtues" of courage, compassion, self-love, friendship and forgiveness, to guide us. If we consider the contradictions mentioned above, these five virtues help us to balance our responsibilities to ourselves and others. He then asks us to consider fundamental questions: "How should I live?" and "how should each of us conduct our lives so that it is a life any of us should live?" This is an injunction to think, not only about how to live our best life but also to consider the impact of our behaviour on others. The way journalists act is not just about career, company or awards, it has an impact on the world that is bigger than our own lives (Phillips, Couldry and Freedman, 2010, p. 51).

A sense of responsibility for others is not always liberating, it can be paralyzing to fear at every turn that we may be making the wrong choices. If people interviewed have very different explanations for something they have witnessed, how does a journalist decide which version is correct? The disclosure of wrongdoing may be necessary, but what if innocent family members are caught in the subsequent fallout? Bernard Williams (Williams, 2010, p. 44) argues for the additional virtues of *accuracy* and *sincerity* as guidance. Journalists can do no more than record what they *sincerely* believe to be true. They must balance the likely harm that a disclosure will cause, with the requirement to tell the truth and they must be prepared to issue a correction, and if necessary, an apology, if subsequent events demonstrate that they have been mistaken.

Hospitality and proper distance

Roger Silverstone (Silverstone, 2006, p. 136) argues for the importance of *hospitality* and *proper distance* as particular journalistic virtues, making use of the injunction to welcome the stranger (*hospitality*), that is more deeply embedded in the philosophies of the East and the Global South, and recognising the need for journalists to stand back from their own entanglements in order to see the point of view of the "other" (*proper distance*) (also see **Chapter 5**).

> This is not to suggest that journalists should be better than the rest of us as human beings (though why should they not be?), only that they

should recognize that what they do...has consequences for the rest of us as human beings.

(Silverstone, 2006, p. 184)

Silverstone speaks to Christians and Nordenstreng's third universal ethical requirement of non-violence in its recognition of the harm that journalism can do in inciting violence if it fails to offer hospitality. A striking example of the failure to offer *hospitality* was demonstrated by what came to be known as the Muhammed Cartoons Affair when, in 2005, a Danish newspaper organised a competition for images of the Prophet Muhammed. They did this, knowing that, for most Muslims, picturing the Prophet is considered blasphemous.

The editor at the centre of the cartoon affair was defended, in most mainstream news outlets in the Global North, on the grounds of press freedom and freedom of expression. Few asked the simple question: why would an editor, with considerable power at his disposal, make a choice to publish material knowing that it would make the Muslim minority in his country feel marginalised and unwelcome? (Eide, Kunelius and Phillips, 2008). This requires us to take into consideration the question of power. While the provocation of the powerful has an important role in truth-telling, the provocation by the powerful, of those without power, looks a lot like bullying.

If we consider journalism in the context of the universal basic ethics of truth-telling, respect for human dignity, non-violence, hospitality, proper distance and power, rather than simply in the context of press freedom, we may get closer to finding an ethical core we can rely upon. If we then consider Aristotle's five personal virtues of: courage, compassion, self-love, friendship and forgiveness, we can start to consider how we, as individuals, can manage the tricky balancing act of ethical practice, which requires that we have care for ourselves, concern for others and the courage to take risks when the greater good demands it. None of this comes automatically, it is achieved through experience.

Exercise: Journalistic Judgement

In what circumstances would it be ethical to publish information about a well-known person, who has been seen in an embrace with someone other than their established partner?
   Consider:

- The evidence – can you trust it?
- The people – do they have a public responsibility and does the embrace impact on that in anyway?
- The circumstances – could this be a long-lost brother?
- The fall-out – who will be damaged by this revelation?
- Is the revelation more important than the damage it will do to others?
- Provide examples of real cases to back up your case.

Ethical rule making

While virtue ethics provide us with a bedrock from which to consider ambiguities in the work we do, knowing how to be good doesn't mean we will all behave well. In practice, laws and codes of conduct are also necessary; to ensure individuals don't misuse the power at their disposal; to provide journalists with protection from unethical proprietors, politicians and editors, and to provide the public with protection and redress from journalists who fail to act ethically in dealing with them and writing about them.

Laws (as we explain in **Chapter 10**) deal with the most egregious breaches of behaviour. However, concern about the impact of state regulation on the freedom of the press has meant that self-regulation is the dominant mode of ethical regulation of content in democracies and an important means by which the journalism field is both constructed and protected. Codes of conduct are drawn up by journalists in most countries, to shore up their legitimacy in the face of public criticism; to provide themselves with protection against unreasonable editorial demands and as a means of drawing international support to their aid in the event of dispute with state authorities. In an era in which misleading information is regularly circulated by non-journalists, online and on social media, the existence of a code of conduct, and a body which enforces it, is also a means by which journalism seeks to differentiate itself, police its own behaviour, build trust with audiences and sustain its legitimacy.

International codes of ethics and standards

Internationally agreed ethical norms and the bodies that support them, such as the International Federation of Journalists (IFJ – see Box 1 for a list of ethical norms they outline), Journalism Without Borders (JRF) and the Committee to Protect Journalists, have an important role in maintaining the legitimacy of journalism worldwide and protecting journalists working under pressure. Indeed, international solidarity may be the only means of keeping a semblance of critical journalism alive in countries that are hostile to press criticism (Musa and Domatob, 2007, p. 219). In a press release in May 2020, from the Federation of African Journalists[1] (an affiliate of the International Federation of Journalists), FAJ President, Sadiq Ibrahim Ahmed, gives some sense of the reality experienced by many journalists:

> African Governments must respect and accept the role of the independent media and not use their powers to control and stifle press freedom and the right to access information. Journalists must not be forced, cajoled or intimidated to either work in a situation of fear or favour the government of the day.

Ethics bodies and agreed ethical standards provide some means by which individual journalists can protect themselves and the integrity of their work, as well as providing members of the public with an understanding of what is considered acceptable. For those working in authoritarian countries or for unscrupulous employers, they provide a guide to what ought to be done, even if they are unable to regulate what is actually done.

IFJ Global Charter of Ethics for Journalists

1. Respect for the facts and for the right of the public to truth is the first duty of the journalist.
2. In pursuance of this duty, the journalist shall at all times defend the principles of freedom in the honest collection and publication of news, and of the right of fair comment and criticism. He/she will make sure to clearly distinguish factual information from commentary and criticism.
   The journalist shall report only in accordance with facts of which he/she knows the origin. The journalist shall not suppress essential information or falsify any document. He/she will be careful to reproduce faithfully statements and other material that non-public persons publish in social media.
3. The journalist shall use only fair methods to obtain information, images, documents and data and he/she will always report his/her status as a journalist and will refrain from using hidden recordings of images and sounds, except where it is impossible for him/her to collect information that is overwhelmingly in the public interest. He/she will demand free access to all sources of information and the right to freely investigate all facts of public interest.
4. The notion of urgency or immediacy in the dissemination of information shall not take precedence over the verification of facts, sources and/or the offer of a reply.
5. The journalist shall do the utmost to rectify any errors or published information which is found to be inaccurate in a timely, explicit, complete and transparent manner.
6. The journalist shall observe professional secrecy regarding the source of information obtained in confidence.
7. The journalist will respect privacy. He/she shall respect the dignity of the persons named and/or represented and inform the interviewee whether the conversation and other material is intended for publication. He/she shall show particular consideration to inexperienced and vulnerable interviewees.
8. Journalists shall ensure that the dissemination of information or opinion does not contribute to hatred or prejudice and shall do their utmost to avoid facilitating the spread of discrimination on grounds such as geographical, social or ethnic origin, race, gender, sexual orientation, language, religion, disability, political and other opinions.

9 The journalist will consider serious professional misconduct to be
   - plagiarism
   - distortion of facts
   - slander, libel, defamation, unfounded accusations
10 The journalist shall refrain from acting as an auxiliary of the police or other security services. He/she will only be required to provide information already published in a media outlet.
11 The journalist will show solidarity with his/her colleagues, without renouncing his/her freedom of investigation, duty to inform and right to engage in criticism, commentary, satire and editorial choice.
12 The journalist shall not use the freedom of the press to serve any other interest and shall refrain from receiving any unfair advantage or personal gain because of the dissemination or non-dissemination of information. He/she will avoid – or put an end to – any situation that could lead him/her to a conflict of interest in the exercise of his/her profession. He/she will avoid any confusion between his activity and that of advertising or propaganda. He/she will refrain from any form of insider trading and market manipulation.
13 The journalist will not undertake any activity or engagement likely to put his/her independence in danger. He/she will, however, respect the methods of collection/dissemination of information that he/she has freely accepted, such as "off the record," anonymity or embargo, provided that these commitments are clear and unquestionable.
14 Journalists worthy of the name shall deem it their duty to observe faithfully the principles stated above. They may not be compelled to perform a professional act or to express an opinion that is contrary to his/her professional conviction or conscience.
15 Within the general law of each country the journalist shall recognise in matters of professional honour, the jurisdiction of independent self-regulatory bodies open to the public, to the exclusion of every kind of interference by governments or others.

How self-regulation defines the field

Self-regulation is important for maintaining standards, but it is also a means by which journalism establishes its legitimacy as a field distinct from other forms of information provision (see **Chapter 2**). If we compare the Norwegian Press Code, drawn up by the Norwegian Press Association, with the UK code, drawn up by the Independent Press Standards Organisation (IPSO), we can see how these two different organisations also reflect their respective fields and legitimise the ways in which journalists operate in these countries.

The Norwegian media are typical of Hallin and Mancini's *democratic corporatist media system* (see **Chapter 1**). The press has assumed a public responsibility role and is partly supported by Government subsidies, which help to sustain political and cultural diversity (see **Chapter 9**). Norway has very high newspaper readership, both on and offline, and came top of the Reporters Without Borders (RSF) 2021 international rankings for press freedom (the United Kingdom is 33). The committee that draws up the code in Norway consists of two members from the journalist's trade union and two from the editor's association, along with three lay members. This composition recognises that the interests of journalists as employees are not identical to the interests of editors as employers. The code explicitly supports the autonomy of individual journalists and provides for members of the public who might be treated unfairly.

The UK press sector fits into Hallin and Mancini's *liberal media model* (see **Chapter 1**). The Editors' Code (which covers much of the print and equivalent internet media) is produced by a committee dominated by editors of the largest circulation, national newspapers. Rank and file journalists and their trade unions are not represented. The Code sets out what is not to be done within very narrow parameters. While it provides some redress to the subjects of press intrusion, or unfair reporting, its object is primarily to provide legitimacy to a particular form of highly combative and commercial journalism.

Paul Dacre, then editor of *The Daily Mail*, and a key player in the formation of the latest iteration of the UK ethics body, IPSO, said: "the red tops[2] can be vulgar, irreverent, outrageous and even malign. (…) My greatest concern (…)– is that any future reforms must take into consideration the needs and commercial realities of all newspapers" *Daily Mail* October 13, 2011 (Daily Mail Reporter, 2011).

These differences in approach are written into their respective codes of conduct. The first three sections of the Norwegian code concern issues of autonomy from commercial concerns: freedom of the press, the integrity and responsibility of journalists and relationships with sources. In the UK version, the freedom to entertain is seen as a key component of press freedom alongside the right to "inform, to be partisan, to challenge, shock, be satirical" (IPSO, 2019). Responsibility and integrity are not mentioned at all, and the protection of sources gets a scant one line compared to eight paragraphs in the Norwegian version.

In both Norway and the United Kingdom, it is made clear that journalists must seek accuracy. However, when an inaccuracy is spotted, in Norway, the code requires that: "incorrect information must be corrected and, when called for, an apology given, as soon as possible" (Pressens Faglige Utvalg, 2020). In the United Kingdom, editors are told: "A *significant* (our emphasis) inaccuracy, misleading statement or distortion must be corrected, promptly and with due prominence, and — where appropriate — an apology published." Clause 1, section 2 (IPSO, 2019)

In Norway, if someone is heavily criticised in the media, they should be given the opportunity to reply, at the same time or, "at the earliest opportunity." This is seen as a matter of fairness. It is also accepted best practice for journalists everywhere, including the United Kingdom. A ruling by IPSO in 2021 made it clear however that: "There is no obligation imposed by the Code for newspapers to approach individuals for comment prior to their inclusion in an article."[3] A right to be heard is only mentioned in the case of "significant" inaccuracies, and then only when "reasonably called for" (Clause 1 section 3) (ibid). The downplaying of the right to reply demonstrates that IPSO's concerns are not in line with established best practice, or with fairness, but with reinforcing the freedom of editors.

When Norwegian journalists intrude on grief or interview children, they are asked to show consideration and think about the implications of their actions. In effect, to consider "how we should all live together." And, since they cannot be ordered to do anything that is contrary to their convictions, the code would offer them some backing should they decline to ask intrusive questions of a grieving mother, for example. In the United Kingdom, "sensitivity" is expected, but journalists are not expected to consider the impact of their behaviour. Complaints about the press after major tragedies are common in the United Kingdom. These comments were made after a bombing at the Manchester Arena in 2017, where 22 people died:[4]

- The whole family felt 'hounded' by the press
- By far the worst thing was the press
- They ... are a disgrace, they don't take no for an answer, they have a lack of standards and ethics
- The press and media have been horrible in response to this. The press got hold of family members' mobile numbers and 'bombarded' them. (Tobitt, 2018)

The mass market daily press tends to set the agenda for the British news media. IPSO, therefore, has a major role in establishing the boundaries of the field in the United Kingdom even though it has no jurisdiction over broadcast media (which is regulated by Ofcom[5] and under an obligation to be impartial) and several of the most trusted news organisations (such as *The Guardian* and *Financial Times*) have declined to join. In Norway, the codes are drawn up to protect the autonomy of all journalists, no matter what news organisation they work for, so they have more freedom to apply and develop *virtue ethics* in their practice, and the make-up of the code committee ensures that it is relatively independent of commercial interests.

Ethics in practice

According to the Worlds of Journalism Study (Hanitzsch *et al.*, 2019), journalists see their core role as to: "report things as they are, provide analysis of current affairs, let people express their views, and be a detached observer" (2019, p. 173). The Reuters Institute Digital News Report (2021) found that 66 percent of audiences say news outlets should try to be neutral on every issue, while 74 percent of their sample, across all studied countries, felt that news outlets should try to reflect all sides in a debate.

Detachment, objectivity, neutrality

Detachment is often confused with objectivity (being uninfluenced by personal bias or opinion), neutrality (reporting each side in a dispute without drawing a conclusion) or impartiality (giving a hearing to all sides irrespective of who they represent). As we discussed elsewhere, people are rarely completely objective, they view the world through the prism of their own subjective lives and experience. Neutrality is also hard to achieve as it requires that a journalist presents all information as though it was equally important (though that is rarely the case). Impartiality (discussed in more detail below) is more useful because it is about fairness and requires that all voices should be listened to with equal attention.

The idea that journalism should be objective was in many ways a response to the increasing consolidation of the American press in the mid-twentieth century, which meant that, instead of many news outlets all arguing from different perspectives, there was now only one in each city trying to serve people from across the political spectrum (Schudson and Anderson, 2009). In many other parts of the world, such as Southern Europe, the liberal idea of a combative press, in which different publications approach news from differing perspectives, was retained (see **Chapter 1**). In these countries, objectivity or neutrality is not expected and impartiality is only required for public broadcasting.

The almost universal acceptance of normative ideals of journalistic neutrality and detachment would suggest, therefore, that this is part of the *discursive construction* of journalistic identity (Hanitzsch and Örnebring, 2019). By discursive construction, we mean an idealised understanding of journalism that is created through a particular discourse and, therefore, becomes the unexplored assumption of both journalists and their audiences. This may be why people tend to regard the news organisation that they favour as "unbiased" (Newman, 2019) and why, arguably, some journalists see the political and economic constraints of their role as an unremarkable part of the job (Hanitzsch *et al.*, 2019, p. 113).

Impartiality and proper distance

The fact that the practice of journalism is rarely one of detached neutrality, in no way exempts journalists from behaving ethically, or reporting factually. Nor does it require the abdication of responsibility for drawing conclusions. Robert Peston, previously at the BBC and now Political Editor at British commercial news programme ITN, like all British broadcasters, works under rules that require impartiality. He explains that the job of a journalist is: "Weighing the evidence and saying on the balance of probabilities … this is the truth. It is the role of a journalist to say, 'we've got these two contradictory arguments, I'm now going to advise all of you which is likely to be closer to the truth'." (Brown, 2018).

Neutral, both-sides-journalism, in which different voices are simply introduced without any attempt at contextualising them, can often obscure rather than illuminate. Peston again: "The problem with the BBC, during the [Brexit] campaign, it put people on with diametrically opposed views and didn't give their viewers and listeners any help in assessing which one was the loony and which one was the genius" (Brown, 2018).

In the same way, apparently neutral quotes from the public (vox pops), produced to give the appearance of balance, are rarely based on evidence of the distribution of opinion in a community, are regularly left unchallenged and often give inaccurate or sensational statements a salience that they do not deserve. This matters even more when there is a scientific consensus on one side. To what extent is it ethical to ask the public (who have no specialist knowledge), to decide between two positions that are presented as equal?

The both-sides strategy of giving equal airtime (or quoting) people with conflicting views, without comment, may at times be used as a means of avoiding saying anything meaningful and thereby avoiding conflict with powerful people. A Ghanaian journalist describes how such a strategy can be adopted to protect journalists from the anger of their proprietors. She explains that, when companies, or allies, of their proprietors are engaged in unethical activities, their explanations are simply presented unchallenged, even when the journalists are aware that they are not true: "In this way, we do not provide the public with reliable information and conclusive 'truths' because that would require us exposing the allies of media owners. As such, we've become unwitting participants of the collective open secret-keeping culture" (Agyemang Asante, 2020). In these circumstances, objectivity or neutrality becomes a shelter from criticism rather than an ethical norm.

For a journalist working in a country with a politically partisan news culture (such as Southern Europe or the British press), evidence will inevitably be inflected (biased). This will mean, for example, that a conservative newspaper might highlight stories about crime and violence, while a progressive newspaper will highlight stories on human rights. In each case, it is possible to tell stories based on evidence and proper distance. When lies or distortions are knowingly told to discredit opponents, attack minorities or produce sensational headlines, partisanship provides no excuse. Indeed, if partisans are to be effective, they should be particularly keen to employ *proper distance* to ensure that the parties and individuals they support live up to public expectation. Lies damage those who tell them as well as those who receive them and, in the end, they destroy trust in journalism.

Situation and context

Journalists surveyed for the Worlds of Journalism study agree that they: "should always adhere to codes of professional ethics, regardless of situation and context" (Hanitzsch et al., 2019, p. 205). Nevertheless, a large minority also found that adherence to ethical norms and codes of behaviour depends, to some extent, on circumstances which vary. For example, according to research from Rao and Lee (2005), journalists in India and the Middle East value truth-telling as a basic ethical principle but would avoid a story rather than breach the higher principles of respect for community, person or privacy. Studies in Europe found that 31 percent had toned down sensitive or critical stories to avoid conflict (Horsley, 2022).

This could be seen as lack of courage, or a desire to be cautious in the hope of revealing a greater truth in time to come. For many, the only realistic adjustment is to "play the game" (Schimpfössl and Yablokov, 2020). This can mean a degree of self-censorship to avoid potential political risks. Within the context of Chinese journalism, this takes the form of avoiding criticism of the Communist Party.

Tong describes how Chinese journalists negotiate over the tiniest details of a story that may be sensitive to the Communist Party, in the hope of getting information of events, such as public protests, out into the public domain. When, for example, in 2006, officials destroyed everything inside a local temple to turn it into a "cultural centre," local people were angry and compared it to the events of the "Cultural Revolution." The need to report the story without annoying local officials required a long negotiation over the exact words that could be used and six different headlines were tried before a final, bland, headline was formulated that would not attract attention (Tong, 2009, p. 609). In these challenging circumstances, Tong sees this apparent self-censorship as a "force that increases media freedom instead of a threat to media freedom" (Tong, 2009, p. 593).

Journalists in western democracies are more likely to claim to be *absolutist* in their attitudes to obeying ethical codes and yet, under certain circumstances, are far more prepared than those in, for example, East Asia to use "deceptive practices" such as: making use of confidential business or government documents without authorisation; taking employment in organisations they are investigating to gain inside information or using hidden microphones if it would serve what they see as the higher goal of truth seeking (Hanitzsch *et al.*, 2019).

The "deceptive practices" that are considered acceptable in western democracies are usually justified because they concern the extraction of information from people who are attempting to conceal wrongdoing. These practices are, therefore, considered to be in the *public interest*. David Leigh, investigations editor at the *Observer* newspaper, in the 1980s, explains:

> One story, which I did publish at a time, when I was running investigations for the *Observer*, partially involved subterfuge and a balancing of the public interest against a person's right to keep private business arrangements private… I considered this subterfuge justifiable in the public interest. There was no other way I could have obtained the crucial information.
>
> *(Leigh, 2011, p. 6)*

In a US survey, the need to compete (with colleagues and other news organisations) was found to be the most important predictor of a willingness to use deception in pursuing a story (Lee, 2005). When competition is considered,

234 Ethics in Practice

market rationalities often erode ethics and claims of "public interest" are not always plausible. Indeed, self-interest is often more in evidence, than compassion or courage. In evidence to the Independent Inquiry into the Leveson Inquiry into the Culture, Practice and Ethics of the British Press in 2011[6], ex-journalist Paul McMullan, said: "Circulation defines the public interest. You have to appeal to what the reader wants" (Phillips, 2013, p. 257). This included revealing that the daughter of a well-known actor was homeless and working as a prostitute. McMullan told the Inquiry: "When I heard a few years later that she'd killed herself I did think, 'yeah, that was one that I really regret'" (Robinson, O'Carroll and Halliday, 2011).

Some unethical practices are overwhelmingly rejected by journalists everywhere: "exerting pressure on unwilling informants to get a story, making use of personal documents, such as letters and pictures without permission; publishing stories with unverified content; and accepting money from sources" (Hanitzsch et al., 2019, p. 231). A journalist who takes money to flatter a source, or cover up wrong doing, knows that they are behaving unethically, but taking money, or gifts, from a brand you like, or a politician you admire, is also wrong because it means that your *proper distance,* as a journalist, is undermined. You are not able to say, with sincerity, that you will report truthfully what you know. In effect you are working for that company or person, and not for your audience. When these norms are flouted, journalists in most of the world recognise that they are threatening the legitimacy of their role (see also **Chapter 10**).

Even these norms are not, in practice, adhered to everywhere, always. Downloading a subject's phone messages without permission was found to be a regular occurrence in the British phone-hacking scandal (see Leveson Inquiry, **Chapter 10**). Accepting money from sources is also a wide-spread occurrence, particularly in countries where salaries are low. In China, there is a special word for it: red envelope cash (Xu, 2016); in some African countries, it is referred to as a brown envelope (Skjerdal, 2018) or soli (solidarity money), similar practices are also common in Central and Eastern Europe (Örnebring, 2016), India (Mudgal, 2015) and elsewhere.

When ethical behaviour is pushed too far, it is not unusual to see those at the more autonomous end of the journalism field take action to restore public trust. In India, for example, it was *The Hindu*, one of the largest circulation English language newspapers, that exposed the practice of political candidates paying newspapers for the opportunity to publish un-edited "news items" during the 2009 elections in the state of Maharashtra (Mudgal, 2015). Just as it was *The Guardian* newspaper that blew the whistle on illegal phone hacking at *The News of the World* (see **Chapter 10**).

Autonomy

The requirement to act ethically and report truthfully and with sincerity requires journalists to be able to make up their own minds. Bourdieu (see **Chapter 2**) argues that the position of the individual journalist cannot be understood outside his or her organisation, which is itself subject to its place within the organisational field: "To understand what is happening in the journalistic field, one has to understand the degree of autonomy of the field and, within the field, the degree of autonomy of the publication that a journalist writes for" (Bourdieu, 2005, p. 43).

The Worlds of Journalism survey (Hanitzsch et al., 2019) finds that most journalists (outside a handful of autocracies) perceive themselves to be autonomous practitioners. However, this flies in the face of the evidence. Helle Sjøvaag, reviewing the global research literature, found that autonomy is restricted everywhere by structures "at the political, economic, and organizational levels of news production, negotiated at the editorial level, and exercised at the level of practice" (Sjøvaag, 2013, p. 155).

Those working in independent public service media tend to have greater autonomy. Sjøvaag (2013) also noted greater autonomy for those working in what she describes as full democracies. For the *New York Times*, for example, the appearance of autonomy and the cultural capital that it engenders is a vital component of its financial success. It cannot afford to be seen to print stories that have been fabricated, and will unceremoniously fire, and make an example of those "deviant" journalists found to have acted unethically (Carlson, 2014). On the other hand, a mass market tabloid, such as Britain's *Daily Star*, is not expected to contribute a great deal more than a chuckle to the life of the nation and, while adhering to the law as an act of self-protection, will cheerfully push the ethical boundaries (Peppiatt, 2011).

This review also found that autonomy is impacted by commercial considerations (see **Chapters 7 and 8**). In Kenya, for example, researchers report a culture in which editorial interference by advertisers, and politicians, is common:

> If you expose some mischief by big advertisers, the next day they pull out their adverts. It's almost suicidal in the business sense not to check the way you cover some of these companies. Sometimes, you are told that the majority shareholder does not like this; then you don't want to touch it.
> *(Obuya and Ong'ondo, 2019, p. 12)*

Insecure work

The practice of trying journalists out via insecure short term or freelance contracts makes it easier for managements to select people who are prepared to conform to the particular *doxa* (rules) of the organisation. Junior staff will, sometimes, be handed jobs which strain the boundaries of what they consider to be journalism, as well as their consciences. Some may feel uncomfortable but keep their heads down, do what they are asked and look for an alternative job. Others will get used to such practices and regard them as the price to be paid for advancement in their particular career (Phillips, Couldry and Freedman, 2010). In each case, they will then perceive their subsequent decisions as a series of negotiations over procedural and organisational issues.

> It was very soon after I joined and looking back on it, it may have been some kind of test. It was a story to do with Asylum seekers and it was a project to see how many crimes asylum seekers had committed in a year. They started off by saying "only rapes and murders", by the end of the week we covered things like parking tickets because there weren't enough [bigger crimes]. I thought that the whole exercise was false and was very unhappy about it and considered leaving. I talked to a senior reporter and said that I wasn't very happy about it and he said to keep my head down and say nothing. He said that I would lose my job if I raised it with anybody more senior than him.
>
> *(Phillips, Couldry and Freedman, 2010, p. 56)*

The experience of working in a fast paced, mass market newsroom, provided the journalist mentioned above with the necessary skills (*cultural capital*) to move on to a job in an organisation with higher ethical standards. In a precarious labour market, it is more difficult to move on. Bourdieu finds that precarious employment creates, "a loss of liberty, through which censorship can more easily be expressed" (Benson and Neveu, 2005, p. 43). This is the situation reported in Kenya:

> There was [...] a lack of interest from media houses to invest or put resources in some key areas like employing people on a decent salary and not trying to keep everybody as a correspondent [stringer] for many years on a small retainer making them toil to make an additional fee. How do you hold that person accountable on anything, whether it is code of ethics or corruption?
>
> *(Obuya and Ong'ondo, 2019, p. 10)*

Michelle Stanistreet, General Secretary of the National Union of Journalists, (the United Kingdom and Ireland) explained to the Leveson Inquiry (2011) why competition tends to exert extreme pressure on journalists to do what they are told and to bring in stories at any cost.

> It is not possible for a journalist to burn their bridges with one newspaper and walk into a new job at another. Those with a staff job are clinging on to them as it is. Journalism is a small world - journalists move between newspaper groups - to broaden their experience, for a promotion, to pursue a specialism - and employers and editors are well aware of those journalists working at competitor titles. [...]. For freelancers and casuals, their employment is totally precarious - their services can be dispensed with on

a whim, and they are particularly anxious about the reputational damage and impact on their work of speaking out.

(Stanistreet, 2012) (paragraph 8)

One Swedish journalist told researchers:

> My tipping point was probably when I heard from a manager that, "you don't have to do it well. You only need to make it good enough". And then I left the meeting and said that, "then I'm not supposed to do this", I cannot go to work knowing that I should do "good enough". And that's when I felt that it's not possible. That's not the way it's supposed to be.
>
> *(Örnebring and Möller, 2018, p. 1055)*

Fear and intimidation

While tight economic conditions and commercialisation create constraints in newsrooms at times, the constraints may entail more than the loss of a job. Many journalists cope with daily intimidation online and via social media. Women journalists and journalists of colour are particularly likely to be targeted. The International Women's Media Foundation[7] found that 70 percent of women journalists have experienced threats and a third had considered leaving the profession as a result. Marianna Spring, the specialist disinformation reporter for the BBC, writes:

> I receive abusive messages on social media daily. Most are too offensive to share unedited. The trigger? My coverage of the impact of online conspiracies and fake news. I expect to be challenged and criticised - but misogynistic hate directed at me has become a very regular occurrence. [...] Messages are laden with slurs based on gender, and references to rape, beheading and sexual acts. Some are a mish-mash of conspiracy theories - that I'm "Zionist-controlled", that I, myself, am responsible for raping babies. The C-word and F-word are repeatedly used.
>
> *(Spring, 2021)*

Online intimidation doesn't always stay online. Every day, somewhere in the world, a journalist is going out in the morning unsure that they will make it home that night. The Committee to Protect Journalists keeps a regular update of journalists killed, injured or imprisoned in the pursuit of their work. They found, in 2020, that the journalists most at risk in Mexico are those who write about the intersection between local politics and the drug cartels. In China, journalists have been arrested and imprisoned for challenging government accounts of the Covid pandemic. In Nigeria, journalists covering a protest against police brutality were beaten, harassed and fined. One reporter, Onifade Emmanuel Pelumi, was found dead after being arrested by police (Rozen, 2021). In India, in 2018, three journalists were killed in hit-and-run accidents in 24 hours (Selva, 2020, p. 9).

Most journalists, living in countries where intimidation is the norm will, "adjust their practice to take into account the potential consequences of their actions" (Hanitzsch et al., 2022, p. 49). A Ghanaian journalist says:

> Sources in the army called to warn me of possible violent attacks against me if I broke the story. I broke the story anyway, but not [until] I received a verbal assurance from the director of Public Affairs of the Ghana Armed Forces about my safety. I was scared about making the publication due to our history with the military. [Since then], I always seek assurances from any concerned security agency about my safety before publishing a story about them.
>
> *(Agyemang Asante, 2020)*

When pressures of this kind form the backdrop to daily work, it is remarkable that so many journalists still insist on the need to maintain ethical standards and, despite the need for compromises, to get as close as they can to reporting truthfully while respecting the norms within which they function. Waisbord (2000) found that those journalists who see their role as encouraging democracy in their countries are particularly likely to hold autonomy as a professional ideal, even if they have difficulty in exercising it. These journalists may hold onto their sense of autonomy as a "defensive discursive strategy" to hold together the boundaries of the field against incursions from the state (Hanitzsch et al., 2019, p. 131).

Being ethical

Conservative journalist, Peter Oborne, walked out when an ethical line was crossed. He found that Britain's *Daily Telegraph* appeared to be suppressing unfavourable stories to please an advertiser. In his resignation statement, he said:

> *Telegraph* readers are intelligent, sensible, well-informed people. They buy the newspaper because they feel that they can trust it. If advertising priorities are allowed to determine editorial judgments, how can readers continue to feel this trust? The *Telegraph's* recent coverage of HSBC amounts to a form of fraud on its readers. It has been placing what it perceives to be the interests of a major international bank above its duty to bring the news to *Telegraph* readers.
>
> *(Oborne, 2015)*

Oborne was in a privileged position within the newspaper which gave his decision greater force. His letter was re-printed and discussed widely. Those with less status or *cultural capital* (see **Chapter 2**) find it more difficult to protect ethical norms and their own position. While Oborne has since been given many opportunities to write for other publications, Richard Peppiatt, who resigned with a similarly explosive letter to the proprietor of the Daily Star about racism and low ethical standards, was unable to find work elsewhere and no longer works as a journalist (Peppiatt, 2011).

Those people at the bottom of the chain of command often feel intimidated and may, sometimes, feel bullied by those with more power. This may also apply to journalists from marginalised or minority groups in the countries where they work. For example, many Black journalists in white majority countries report being unheard if they object to the racist assumptions of their white editors. One Black journalist working for a mass market newspaper in the United Kingdom said,

> you draw a personal, ethical line and, if something happens, you say: 'bugger it' and walk out. That's how it has always been. Everyday could be your last day. If people push you beyond that mark which you are prepared to go, you just walk out. If you talk to Black television presenters, if you talk to Black reporters in print, they will all tell you the same thing.[8]

This particular journalist did not walk out and the everyday racism that he lived with gradually eroded his sense of self-worth and any belief that he had that journalism was a worthwhile job. In failing to stand up for higher ethical standards arguably he failed himself, but he was also failed by those he worked with:

> journalists often ignore attacks on other journalists from different outlets, leaving room for more of the same. We ought to extend solidarity to every colleague who comes under attack, no matter who employs them or how we view their work.
>
> *(Agyemang Asante, 2020)*

This is particularly important for more senior colleagues who could do much by consciously extending the protection of their status to younger members of staff who may struggle to stand up for what they believe in the face of commercial or political pressure.

Finally, journalists can help each other through building protective institutions such as unions and professional associations. These organisations have an important part to play, as do international organisations established to protect journalists. But if they are to play a role in advancing and protecting journalism, they have to put an understanding of ethics at the centre of their work and make it clear, both to members and to employers, that they are not there only to protect the pay and employment of their members, but also to protect the legitimacy of journalism as an institution.

Summary

- The core values of journalism, according to Christians and Nordenstreng, are truth-telling, respect and non-violence
- Bernard Williams offers accuracy and sincerity as particular virtues for journalists who deal with ambiguity.
- Roger Silverstone adds that these virtues should extend to "proper distance" and "hospitality."
- Self-regulation of journalism turns values into rules of behaviour which demonstrate to journalists, their sources and audiences, the ethical boundaries of journalistic freedoms.
- Self-regulation is also a means of regulating the journalism field and earning legitimacy and trust. Regulatory codes are used as a means of establishing the boundaries of the field.
- Journalism in practice is limited by structural and societal boundaries and practices which impact the opportunities for "proper distance."
- Impartiality, rather than objectivity or neutrality, allows proper distance because it prioritises fairness without losing sight of the importance of making judgements based on evidence.
- Journalists with more security can take greater risks in identifying wrong-doing – but may misuse that freedom to harass people who cannot defend themselves. Those who are under threat may need to compromise if they are to be able to get information out at all.
- Autonomy is required for ethical action but may be constrained by economic or political factors: insecure work, pressure of competition, bullying, bribery or threats.
- Journalists should offer solidarity to colleagues, near and far, who may have to cope with serious constraints on their work and lives.

Notes

1 Federation of African Journalists, press release posted 3 May 2020. African journalists' body decries media repression and absolute impunity in the continent, Relief Web, https://reliefweb.int/report/world/african-journalists-body-decries-media-repression-and-absolute-impunity-continent
2 Red tops are a colloquial expression referring to the mass market popular press in the UK.
3 IPSO rulings, Decision of the Complaints Committee – 29183-20 Abassi v Daily Mirror, https://www.ipso.co.uk/rulings-and-resolution-statements/ruling/?id=29183-20
4 Kerslake Commission. An independent review into the preparedness for, and emergency response to, the Manchester Arena attack on 22nd May 2017 commissioned by the Mayor of Manchester, https://www.jesip.org.uk/uploads/media/Documents%20Products/Kerslake_Report_Manchester_Are.pdf
5 Ofcom is the UK communications regulator which covers all broadcast media.

6 The Independent Inquiry into the Culture, Practice and Ethics of the British Press, usually known as the Leveson Inquiry was instituted by Prime Minister David Cameron when it emerged that journalists had been hacking the phone of a murder victim in the days before her body was found. https://www.gov.uk/government/publications/leveson-inquiry-report-into-the-culture-practices-and-ethics-of-the-press
7 The International Women's Media Federation (IWMF is an NGO providing support and safety training for women journalists internationally). https://www.iwmf.org/about/
8 Author's interview with journalist, 2003, London England.

References

Agyemang Asante, N.A. (2020) 'How Free Is Ghana's Media?', *Reuters Institute for the Study of Journalism*. Available at: https://reutersinstitute.politics.ox.ac.uk/how-free-ghanas-media (Accessed: 18 November 2021).

Benson, R.D. and Neveu, E. (2005) *Bourdieu and the Journalistic Field*. Cambridge; Malden, MA: Polity.

Brown, M. (2018) 'Robert Peston: BBC Not Impartial during EU Referendum Campaign', *The Guardian*, 6 October. Available at: https://www.theguardian.com/media/2018/oct/06/robert-peston-bbc-not-impartial-during-eu-referendum-campaign (Accessed: 24 November 2021).

Carlson, M. (2014) 'Gone, But Not Forgotten', *Journalism Studies*, 15(1), pp. 33–47. doi:10.1080/1461670X.2013.790620.

Christians, C. and Nordenstreng, K. (2004) 'Social Responsibility Worldwide', *Journal of Mass Media Ethics*, 19(1), pp. 3–28. doi:10.1207/s15327728jmme1901_2.

Daily Mail Reporter (2011) 'This Threat to Press Freedom: Mail Editor Tells Leveson Inquiry Politicians Want to Muzzle Newspapers in Revenge for Exposing Expenses Fraud', *Mail Online*, 12 October. Available at: https://www.dailymail.co.uk/news/article-2048480/This-threat-press-freedom-Mail-Editor-tells-Leveson-inquiry-politicians-want-muzzle-newspapers-revenge-exposing-expenses-fraud.html (Accessed: 3 March 2022).

Eide, E., Kunelius, R. and Phillips, A. (2008) *Transnational Media Events: The Mohammed Cartoons and the Imagined Clash of Civilizations*. Gotenburg: Nordiskt Informationscenter. Available at: http://research.gold.ac.uk/id/eprint/14606/ (Accessed: 23 June 2021).

Hanitzsch, T. et al. (2019) *Worlds of Journalism: Journalistic Cultures Around the Globe*. New York: Columbia University Press.

Hanitzsch, T. et al. (2022) 'Journalism Culture and Ethical Ideology', in *The Routledge Companion to Journalism Ethics*. Abingden, OX: Routledge. pp. 45–53.

Hanitzsch, T. and Örnebring, H. (eds) (2019) 'Professionalism, Professional Identity, and Journalistic Roles', in *The Handbook of Journalism Studies*. 2nd edition. New York and London: Routledge.

Horsley, W. (2022) 'Media Capture in Central and Easter Europe', in Price, L., Trifonova, Sanders, K., and Wyatt, W. (eds) *The Routledge Companion to Journalism Ethics*. Abingdon, OX: Routledge, pp. 280–289.

IPSO (2019) 'Editors Code of Practice'. Independent Press Standards Organisation. Available at: https://www.ipso.co.uk/media/1817/69196-ipso-editors-code-2019.pdf.

Lee, S.T. (2005) 'Predicting Tolerance of Journalistic Deception', *Journal of Mass Media Ethics*, 20(1), pp. 22–42. doi:10.1207/s15327728jmme2001_3.

Leigh, D. (2011) *Witness Statement of David Leigh*, Leveson Enquiry into the culture, practices, and ethics of the press. London: Guardian News and Media. p. 6.

Mudgal, V. (2015) 'News for Sale: "Paid News", Media Ethics, and India's Democratic Public Sphere', in Rao, S. and Wasserman, H. (eds) *Media Ethics and Justice in the Age of Globalization*. London: Palgrave Macmillan UK, pp. 100–120. doi:10.1057/9781137498267_6.

Musa, B.A. and Domatob, J.K. (2007) 'Who Is a Development Journalist? Perspectives on Media Ethics and Professionalism in Post-Colonial Societies', *Journal of Mass Media Ethics*, 22(4), pp. 315–331. doi:10.1080/08900520701583602.

Newman, N. (2019) 'Reuters Institute Digital News Report 2019', Oxford: Reuters Institute for the Study of Journalism. p. 156.

Oborne, P. (2015) *Why I Have Resigned from the Telegraph*, London: openDemocracy. Available at: https://www.opendemocracy.net/en/opendemocracyuk/why-i-have-resigned-from-telegraph/ (Accessed: 8 September 2021).

Obuya, J. and Ong'ondo, C. (2019) '"Caught between a Rock and a Hard Place": How Kenyan Journalists are Coping with Pressure for Media Accountability', *African Journalism Studies*, 40(2), pp. 1–15. doi:10.1080/23743670.2019.1601118.

Örnebring, H. (2016) 'Journalists, PR Professionals and the Practice of Paid News in Central and Eastern Europe: An overview', *Central European Journal of Communication*, 9(16), pp. 5–19. Available at: https://www.ceeol.com/search/article-detail?id=458787 (Accessed: 17 November 2021).

Örnebring, H. and Möller, C. (2018) 'In the Margins of Journalism', *Journalism Practice*, 12(8), pp. 1051–1060. doi:10.1080/17512786.2018.1497455.

Peppiatt, R. (2011) *Leveson Inquiry, Discover Leveson*. Kingston University Available at: https://www.discoverleveson.com/witness/Richard_Peppiatt/4038/ (Accessed: 17 November 2021).

Phillips, A. (2013) 'Journalism, Ethics and the Impact of Competition', in Couldry, N., Pinchevski, A., and Madianou, M. (eds) *Ethics of Media*. Basingstoke: Palgrave Macmillan, pp. 255–271.

Phillips, A., Couldry, N. and Freedman, D. (2010) 'An Ethical Deficit? Accountability, Norms, and the Material Conditions of Contemporary Journalism', in Fenton, N. (ed.) *New Media, Old News: Journalism & Democracy in the Digital Age*. London: Sage. pp. 52–67.

Pressens Faglige Utvalg (2020) *Code of Ethics of the Norwegian Press*, Presse.no. Available at: https://presse.no/pfu/etiske-regler/vaer-varsom-plakaten/vvpl-engelsk/ (Accessed: 3 March 2022).

Rao, S. and Lee, S.T. (2005) 'Globalizing Media Ethics? An Assessment of Universal Ethics Among International Political Journalists', *Journal of Mass Media Ethics*, 20(2–3), pp. 99–120. doi:10.1080/08900523.2005.9679703.

Robinson, J., O'Carroll, L. and Halliday, J. (2011) 'Andy Coulson and Rebekah Brooks "Knew About Phone Hacking at Now"', *The Guardian*, 29 November. Available at: https://www.theguardian.com/media/2011/nov/29/andy-coulson-rebekah-brooks-phone-hacking (Accessed: 15 November 2021).

Rozen, J. (2021) 'A Nigerian Journalist Took Photos at the Scene of Killings His Government Denies. Then the Harassment Started', *Committee to Protect Journalists*, 10 November. Available at: https://cpj.org/2021/11/a-nigerian-journalist-took-photos-at-the-scene-of-killings-his-government-denies-then-the-harassment-started/ (Accessed: 25 November 2021).

Schimpfössl, E. and Yablokov, I. (2020) 'Post-socialist Self-censorship: Russia, Hungary and Latvia', *European Journal of Communication*, 35(1), pp. 29–45. doi:10.1177/0267323119897797.

Schudson, M. and Anderson, C. (2009) 'Objectivity, Professioalism, and Truth Seeking in Journalism', in Wahl-Jorgensen, K. and Hanitzsch, T. (eds) *The Handbook of Journalism Studies*. New York: Routledge. pp. 88–103.

Selva, M. (2020) *Fighting Words: Journalism under Assault in Central and Eastern Europe*. Oxford: Reuters Institute for the Study of Journalism. Available at: https://reutersinstitute.politics.ox.ac.uk/fighting-words-journalism-under-assault-central-and-eastern-europe (Accessed: 25 November 2021).

Silverstone, P.R. (2006) *Media and Morality: On the Rise of the Mediapolis*. Cambridge; Malden, MA: Polity.

Sjøvaag, H. (2013) 'Journalistic Autonomy: Between Structure, Agency and Institution', *Nordicom Review*, 34(s1), pp. 155–166. doi:10.2478/nor-2013–0111.

Skjerdal, T. (2018) 'Brown Envelope Journalism: The Contradiction Between Ethical Mindset and Unethical Practice', in Mabweazara, H.M. (ed.) *Newsmaking Cultures in Africa: Normative Trends in the Dynamics of Socio-Political & Economic Struggles*. London: Palgrave Macmillan UK, pp. 163–183. doi:10.1057/978-1-137-54109-3_8.

Spring, M. (2021) 'I Get Abuse And Threats Online - Why Can't It Be Stopped?', *BBC News*, 17 October. Available at: https://www.bbc.com/news/uk-58924168 (Accessed: 4 February 2022).

Stanistreet, M. (2012) *2nd Witness Statement*. Discover Leveson, London: Kingston University. Available at: https://www.discoverleveson.com/witness/Michelle_Stanistreet/4077/ (Accessed: 15 November 2021).

Tobitt, C. (2018) *Kerslake Report: Press Watchdog Should Create New Guidelines for Media Operating in Aftermath of Terror Attacks*, Press Gazette. Available at: https://www.pressgazette.co.uk/kerslake-report-press-watchdog-should-create-new-guidelines-for-media-operating-in-aftermath-of-terror-attacks/ (Accessed: 18 November 2021).

Tong, J. (2009) 'Press Self-censorship in China: A Case Study in the Transformation of Discourse', *Discourse & Society*, 20(5), pp. 593–612. doi:10.1177/0957926509106412.

Waisbord, S. (2000) *Watchdog Journalism in South America: News, Accountability, and Democracy*. New York: Columbia University Press, p. 288.

Williams, B. (2010) *Truth and Truthfulness: An Essay in Genealogy, Truth and Truthfulness*. New Jersey: Princeton University Press. doi:10.1515/9781400825141.

Xu, D. (2016) 'Red-Envelope Cash: Journalists on the Take in Contemporary China', *Journal of Media Ethics*, 31(4), pp. 231–244. doi:10.1080/23736992.2016.1220253.

12
GLOBAL FLOWS

In an era when media produced in different countries are available 24/7 to anyone connected to the internet, anywhere in the world, it's easy to take the term "global media," and the flows of communication it speaks to, for granted. For instance, in October 2021, Netflix's South Korean dystopian drama, Squid Game, became a social media phenomenon and the number one show in 90 countries – from Jamaica and Morocco to Oman and Vietnam –, making it the most in demand show in the world (Hicap, 2021; Tassi, 2021).

Squid Game's international success exemplifies some key issues in relation to the notion of global flows. Here is an idea conceived of by a South Korean writer and director, Hwang Dong-hyuk, produced by an American streaming service, distributed internationally and enjoyed by people in countries that may not share a common language or culture. Yet, despite the digitised era seemingly facilitating transnational connections in ways never seen before, western media organisations, particularly American, dominate global flows, just as they have done for decades.

In this chapter, we explore whether, despite ongoing US hegemony in the international mass media sphere, the internet era has opened up communication channels to enable non-western media players to influence the global communication ecology. Are we seeing a challenge to dominant western news narratives? We will consider, too, why a concern with global flows matters and whether "global events and phenomena also lead to the emergence of a transnational mediated public sphere in which collective learning and problem solving may be established" (Wozniak *et al.*, 2021, p. 689).

How western media organisations came to dominate global flows

Wherever European colonists went from the late 1400s, their languages went with them, embedding themselves in the countries colonised. From this

DOI: 10.4324/9781003037651-13

beginning, English, French and Spanish became dominant languages far beyond the geographic locations of the colonising countries. Such was the dominance of English that, for example, in India the most established newspapers, like *The Times of India* and the *Hindustan Times* (Statista Research Department, 2021), are still published in English and English is still used, as a second language to Hindi, in official and legal documents.[1] In the business world, most international trade is conducted in English, and technology was key to cementing English as the global lingua franca.

The Telegraph

When a British inventor, William Fothergill Cooke, and a British scientist, Charles Wheatstone, installed the first electric telegraph between London's Camden Town and Euston stations in 1837, their aim was to improve rail safety. They probably had no sense that they were laying the foundations for people to communicate at speed over long distances, not just within cities but across nations, with Britain going on to lay submarine telegraph lines to India in 1870 and Australia in 1872, during the imperial era (see also Winston, 1998).

Of course, people had long communicated across distances via letter writing and other ways of carrying messages, but the invention of the telegraph laid the foundation for fast global mass communication and established the dominance of north-western news agencies in the nineteenth century, such as Reuters in the United Kingdom, Agence France-Presse in France and Associated Press in the United States. These agencies reinforced the dominance of French and English as international languages and were able to transmit news around the world due to the evolution of technology. The global transmission of western perspectives also supported imperialism, enabling dominant European centres to rule not only through violent means and the physical presence of colonisers in colonies but from a distance via the transmission of their views (see Said, 1994; Ashcroft, Griffiths and Tiffin, 2013, pp. 139–140).

So, western dominance of global information flows is tied to the spread of European languages, technological shifts as well as the distribution and control of information "in the cultural sphere," including entertainment and news media (Said, 1994, p. 291). Indeed, postcolonial theorists argue that control of representation and the power of imperial discourse played a greater role than military or economic activities in establishing and sustaining an "imperial hegemony" (Ashcroft, Griffiths and Tiffin, 2013).

News agencies and broadcasters

The influence of Reuters, for instance, throughout the English-speaking Commonwealth was so great that, in 1930, it's then Chairman, Sir Roderick Jones, stated that "no other single factor has contributed so much to the maintenance of British prestige" (New Internationalist, 1981).

The power of Reuters, and other major western news agencies (see also Curran and Morley, 2005; Phillips, 2014), continued into the postcolonial era and tended to be tied to old colonial and imperial maps, and the use of news agencies as tools of empire were used to establish the hegemony of colonial and imperial powers. So, news from Agence France Presse was present throughout French-speaking Africa and United Press International and Associated Press, both US agencies, had a wide sphere of influence in Latin America.

This control over global news resources led some critics to assert that western news agencies, much later supplemented by international broadcasters such as the BBC World Service and Radio France Internationale, contributed to creating "particular perceptions of the South as being a place of 'corruption, coup and disaster' for Western audiences" (Matos, 2012) and also led to major Southern events not being reported internationally or being refracted through western eyes. For instance, when Surinam gained independence in 1975 from the Netherlands, other South American newspapers bought a report about the occasion from United Press International, which was over 5,000 kilometers away in New York (New Internationalist, 1981). That is akin to British newspapers buying coverage of the United Kingdom's Brexit referendum result from a news agency in Chile, rather than commissioning content from their own correspondents on the ground in Britain.

Media imperialism

As direct colonial power faded during the second half of the twentieth century, the disparity of information flows remained. This imbalance of who was reporting on whom and ownership of media resources led to the development of the concept of *media and cultural imperialism* (see Golding and Harris, 1996; Curran and Morley, 2005; Sparks, 2012, 2015) and debates about the New World Information and Communications Order (NWICO).

Media imperialism describes the imposition of western perspectives on the non-western world. For Herbert Schiller, one of the main exponents of the media imperialism thesis (Schiller, 1979), it contributed to the *core-periphery* global system which structurally maintained the dependence of former colonies on the west. In this view, media imperialism served modern global capitalism by enabling multinational western corporations, including media organisations, to exploit world markets, promote the "American way" and nurture consumerism (Tomlinson, 1991). In the 1990s, scholars, such as McChesney and Herman, remained concerned with the dominance of global media by western companies whose primary aim is to make money. The notion of western ideas being imposed elsewhere is today seen as too simplistic because it doesn't account for the wealth of cultural production beyond the west and the very different readings audiences have of the same texts. Nevertheless, concern regarding the marketisation of news remains live.

> The experience from Western markets is that entertainment, rather than news in the public interest, makes money for shareholders. Herman and

McChesney rightly feared that vast global media companies interested only in their return on investment might 'erode the public sphere and create a "culture of entertainment" (1997:9).

(Phillips, 2014, p. 34)

The dominance of colonial languages, the economics of global communications and the structural imbalance that money, or lack thereof, creates in the field are also highlighted by Rohan Samarajiwa (1984) as the reason western transnational news agencies dominate the global news market. This is simply because the cost of entry prohibits news agencies in poorer nations from gaining equal access.

Due to such concerns, countries in the Global South lobbied the United Nations to endorse a New World Information and Communications Order (NWICO), which was sponsored by UNESCO in 1978. As Thussu (2015, p. 293) highlights, NWICO dominated debates on global communication in the 1970s and 1980s when the argument was that:

> The international information system [...] perpetuated inequality, with serious implications for the countries of the Global South, which were heavily dependent on the West for both information software and hardware [...]. It was argued by NWICO supporters that, owing to economic, political, social and technological imbalances, there was a 'one-way flow' of information from the 'centre' to the 'periphery', which created a wide gap between the 'haves' and the 'haves nots'. This 'vertical' flow [...] was dominated by Western-based transnational corporations, which treated information as a 'commodity' and subjected it to the rules of the market.[...] Therefore, 'by transmitting to developing countries only news processed by them, [...] which they have filtered, cut, and distorted, the transnational media imposed their own way of seeing the world upon the developing countries'.
> *(Masmoudi, 1979, pp. 172–173 in Thussu, 2015, p. 243)*

As early as 1961, UNESCO, which was founded in part to work for "the unrestricted pursuit of objective truth and the free exchange of ideas and knowledge" and "increase the means of communication between peoples" (UNESCO, 1980, p.xiv), surveyed the world press and noted the control of information by western news agencies, news angles suited to western agendas and a lack of news flow between southern countries. As a result, UNESCO recommended the establishment of news agencies in Latin America, Asia and Africa. This idea gained traction, and during a meeting amongst non-aligned countries[2] in Algeria in 1973, it was recommended that a press pool be created for them. There were various other related calls for change along the way. These include a proposal by the Soviet Union, at the 17th General Assembly of UNESCO in 1972, which introduced:

> A resolution, calling for the preparation of a declaration on the fundamental principles governing the use of information and the mass media.

> Closely following the Soviet demand was the Algiers declaration emphasising indigenous control of communication in the developing world so as to preserve her cultural identity.
>
> *(Shamsuddin, 1987, p. 85)*

The proposal by the Soviet Union was discussed during the 1976 UNESCO General Assembly in Nairobi, and there was division between those in favour of a liberal democratic approach to press freedom (capitalist western countries and privately owned media organisations) and proponents of news media governed by the state (socialist and newly independent countries). For western countries, the idea of state-controlled media, which was expressed via two articles in the draft proposal,[3] posed a threat to press freedom, as well as to the economic interests of western transnational organisations and the "free flow" of information. Part of the problem was that NWICO was a critical project but only critiqued, "abuses committed by corporate and business interests while remaining blind to those of repressive states" (Sparks, 2012, p. 286).

The debates led to the establishment of The MacBride Commission in 1977, named after the Irish journalist, politician and lawyer, Sean MacBride, who led it. The commission produced a landmark report, *Many Voices, One World* (UNESCO, 1980), which was a negotiated agreement between the proponents and opponents of NWICO, and was approved by UNESCO in 1980. For the first time, the agreement "elevated information-and communication-related issues onto the global agenda" (Thussu and Nordenstreg, 2015, p. 243). However, the NWICO calls for a more balanced international communications order didn't quite come to pass. Although the NWICO demands are largely forgotten today (Thussu and Nordenstreg, 2015), the aspiration to balance global information flows, and reconfigure political and economic structures to enable this, continues to inform critiques of global news being constructed through a western gaze.

Challenge to western hegemony?

The growth of the internet shifted the direction of media dominance more firmly towards the United States in the twenty-first century. The internet platforms (Alphabet, Meta, Apple and Amazon, all owned by US companies) now dominate flows of news, information and entertainment across most of the world outside China. Even in Russia around half of searches are made on Google (Alphabet), rather than the Russian search engine Yandex (although Yandex searches increased after the Russian invasion of Ukraine), and in the Asian region, 90 percent of searches are made using Google.[4] These platforms are not news producers themselves, but they control advertising, which is the major source of news income in most parts of the world. Their stranglehold over capital has altered the basis on which it is possible for news producers to function, while at the same time, algorithmic news selection, based on metrics that are not transparent, promotes the popular at the expense of less exciting, though arguably more important, information (see **Chapters 7 and 8**). In practice, this means that people online around the world are likely to be engaging with celebrity and entertainment news, which "may transcend national borders particularly well" (Thurman, Hensmann and Fletcher, 2020, p. 17), rather than news about political decisions being made which impact their life and enable them to participate in the *public sphere*. For example, in 2021, the interview with Britain's Prince Harry and his wife Megan on US TV show, *Oprah*, was the most searched interview on Google Trends, ever.[5]

Despite the dominance of American companies in global communications, US hegemony is facing growing challenges from emerging economies such as China (Khanna, 2019), and Russia, which are keen to expand their influence. RTs[6] language choices reflect its interests. It broadcasts in English, French, Spanish and Arabic, which means it can easily be accessed across north Africa and the Middle East. Indeed, it is in the Middle East that its reach appears to be growing (Crilley *et al.*, 2022), particularly in Syria and Iraq, where Russia has been a leading player in ongoing wars. Latin America is also becoming increasingly geopolitically important. Hence, RT's "strategic choice of Spanish as one of the main broadcasting languages after English" (Morales, 2021, p. 101), along with China (which broadcasts in Spanish via CCTV-E), and Iran (whose state controlled broadcaster, IRIB, operates a Spanish channel, HispanTV). Research on audience perception of international news channels in Latin America (Morales, 2021) shows that the pre-conceived ideas Mexican and Argentinian audiences have about Iran, China and Russia undermine their acceptance of international news channels from these countries. However, Latin American audiences polled expressed less hesitancy about RT, than HispanTV and CCTV.

> RT [...] resonated better [...]. A few concerns were raised about its instrumentalization of freedom of speech, whereby it would show itself significantly more vocal in its criticisms towards western countries and relatively quiet on Russian news. Nevertheless, RT was described as culturally closer and more appealing, compared with China's CCTV [...]. Linked to the constraints of government censorship, CCTV's credibility was questioned. Furthermore, China was perceived as being hypocritical when criticizing human rights abuses in other countries but remaining silent about its own. In the case of Iran, it was the cultural distance and a preconceived idea of the country as an oppressive religious regime [...] that played a significant role in viewers' perception.
>
> *(Morales, 2021, p. 111)*

In the west, according to Ipsos Connect, RT's audiences are small and mainly older, politically engaged men who tend to watch RT alongside other channels (Crilley *et al.*, 2022). However, RT has been more successful online. A comparative study of engagement with news organisations on Twitter found that CNN had a high degree of engagement, followed by the BBC, with RT not far behind (Al-Rawi, 2017). Again though, findings show that many who consume RT are doing so alongside engaging with news from other sources, "rather than as a singular main source of news" (Crilley et al., 2022, p. 237).

Al-Jazeera English (AJE) has also shifted global news flows. Launched in 2006, 10 years after Al-Jazeera Arabic, AJE entered the broadcast field with the intention of offering global audiences a different diet of news than that produced by global heavy weights, BBC World and CNN International. AJE's aim was to emphasise southern news and perspectives, particularly Middle Eastern and African. Part-funded by the Qatari government and describing itself as the Arab world's first independent news channel, Al-Jazeera has over 70 bureaus worldwide and is said to have significantly disrupted "the hegemony of the western networks and reversed the flow of information from east to west for the first time since the middle ages" (Miles, 2017).

The channel started making waves after the 9/11 attacks and during the US-led invasion of Afghanistan when:

> It was allowed to remain in Taliban-controlled territory after Western journalists were ordered to leave [...]. It gained further notoriety by broadcasting videotapes of Osama bin Laden. News organizations that were unable to get closer than the fringes of the war turned to Al-Jazeera for help; the station's logo began appearing on newscast footage around the world.
> (Seib, 2005, p. 602)

Although the channel has been criticised for being sensationalist, subject to the influence of Qatar's emir (see Bosio, 2013), and was called a source of propaganda by former US President George Bush (Loomis, 2009), Al-Jazeera has made its mark in the international news arena. Crucially, it's viewed by many as being on a par with BBC World and CNN International in terms of producing quality journalism. In particular, it played a key role in covering the 2011–2012 Arab Spring for international audiences, winning awards for its coverage of the protests in Egypt.

Protestors across the Arab world famously made use of the internet and social media to galvanise support for their call to topple dictatorships, and when demonstrations forced the Egyptian president, Hosni Mubarak, out of office, it was seen as the beginning of the end of autocracies across the Middle East. Journalists trying to cover the protests for major news organisations were harassed and assaulted by pro-government groups, and AJE's Cairo bureau was shut down by the Egyptian authorities, as was satellite access to the channel. To get the story out, Al-Jazeera journalists capitalised on their proximity to the events, knowledge of the region and the ability of many reporting to speak Arabic, in order to interact with Egyptians on the ground and make use of the user generated content on social media. Research (Bosio, 2013, p. 340) finds AJE-integrated social media content into their reports more successfully than CNN and the BBC who "were still critical of the 'social media turn', which impacted on their role as traditional news authorities in a crisis situation."

However, despite the broadcasters increased presence in the field of international news and its respected journalism, it took AJE, sometime, to gain wide distribution in western countries, particularly the United States (Loomis, 2009). AJE did eventually launch a cable news network for the American market, positioning itself as "not infotainment" (Thielman, 2016), but it shut down in 2016, less than three years after its launch. Nonetheless, AJE continues to be a respected player on the global news scene, holding its own alongside more established English-language international news channels (Miles, 2017).

On the African continent, Radio RSA (the voice of South Africa) emerged from the Apartheid era to become SABC's Channel Africa, which is funded by the South African Ministry of International Relations and Co-operation and is available across sub-Saharan Africa via satellite, and globally via the internet. The channel produces content in Chinyanja, Kiswahili, English, French and Portuguese and describes itself as an "international radio station" with a remit to distribute content, including news and current affairs, which "promote democracy, peace and economic development" across the continent (Channel Africa). As Wasserman and Ndlovu highlight, South Africa's SABC NEWS International, as well as the state broadcasters Africa2Africa and SABC Africa channels aimed to counter "western media 'imperialism' and negative framing of the continent" (Wasserman and Ndlovu, 2021, p. 234), by supplying alternative information flows. However, all struggled due to financial constraints and are now:

> Showing signs of stagnation [...] while [...] there has been renewed and intensifying competition between Asian and Western media in Africa since 2000, which appears to be undermining the role of South African transnational media.
>
> *(Wasserman and Ndlovu, 2021, p. 223).*

Furthermore, they contend that the regional media in many African countries are becoming more focused on domestic issues, moving away from aspirations for a pan-African news journalism which "has wide implications for the representation of Africa in the global public sphere" (Wasserman and Ndlovu, 2021, p. 233).

The second most populous continent with the youngest population in the world, Africa could become one of the world's largest consumers of media (Watson, 2019). As Wasserman and Ndlovu (ibid) note, powerful western media organisations are vying for the attention of African audiences, with the once dominant CNN and BBC now competing with America's Fox News, Bloomberg Africa, MSNBC and CNBC, along with France 24, Germany's DW, Europe's Euronews and Portugal's RTP. Also in the mix is TVC News, a 24-hour pan-African news channel based in Nigeria, which boasts one of Africa's largest and most diverse media landscapes. In the competition for a share of African media markets, Britain, once a colonial power in sub-Saharan Africa, has been "successful at crafting a strategy for media presence across the continent," whilst China "has embarked on a concerted effort to penetrate the continent with its media" (Wasserman and Ndlovu, 2021, p. 233).

Due to the size of its economy, which in terms of GDP, comes second to the United States (Thussu and Nordenstreng, 2021, p. 4), China poses the biggest challenge to western hegemony in terms of the country's ability to invest in global communication, which it is doing through it's "Belt and Road Initiative" (BRI).[7] This entails "promoting China's views and vision to the wider world and countering negative portrayals of the country in the US-dominated international media" (Thussu, de Burgh and Shi, 2017, p. 2). The Chinese broadcasting network, CCTV News, has production centres in Beijing, Nairobi, Washington, DC and London, with TV channels available in over 160 countries (see Thussu and Nordenstreg, 2015). Launched as an English language service, it's now also available in Russian, Spanish, French and Arabic.

For the Global South, the direction of information flows may have shifted, but the region remains subject to domination by global powers, whose interests in southern countries tend to have more to do with a struggle for power than an attempt to enable local control of regional news flows. This speaks to an argument Sparks (2012) made a number of years ago that whilst the conception of media imperialism developed by Schiller isn't applicable today, "imperialism, cultural imperialism, and the cultural consequences of imperialism are once again an essential part of the theoretical framework for the study of international communication" (Sparks, 2012, p. 296). This is because

> the 'imperialist' dimension of cultural imperialism is determined by the presence of state action [...]. It is not the intrinsic characteristics of a television programme, or a language, that make it 'imperialist' but the use of state power to ensure it gains currency.
>
> *(Sparks, 2012, p. 293)*

Alternative flows

Inroads that China, for example, is making into African and Middle Eastern markets mean global media flows are not simply following a *contra-flow* model, when media from countries in the Global South disrupt the dominance of western media organisations by sending information north, but are also sending content south and east. For instance, in 2012, just three years after the continent became China's biggest trading partner, CCTV launched an African channel. So, underpinning the Chinese state's growing economic interests on the continent in a search for *soft power*. China's role in Africa is viewed by many critics as neo-colonial (Reuters, 2011), with the Chinese state and businesses inserting themselves more deeply across the continent. Like western imperialism, soft power, through the transmission of Chinese ideology via media platforms, goes hand in hand with economic and political power.

CCTV Africa has offices in Nairobi and broadcasts a range of content, including a news show presented by African journalists (Thussu, de Burgh and Shi, 2017, p. 2). The channel claims to present a "positive" narrative on Africa that counters western news narratives, and research (Marsh, 2018) finds that it succeeds in doing so in some respects. However, the requirement for "positive" angles on stories has "bordered on reverse Orientalism, typified by a promotional video for the channel, *The African Smile*, that showed a succession of smiling African faces and an acacia tree" (Marsh, 2018, p. 107). Despite such stereotypical tropes, which are highlighted by Binyavanga Wainaina in his satirical essay *How to Write about Africa* (Wainaina, 2019), and debate about China's interest in the African continent being far more complex than concern just with representation (Lumumba-Kasongo, 2011), Marsh finds that there is desire by African, Chinese and international staff at CCTV Africa to offer audiences a holistic representation of the continent.

To test the extent to which CCTV Africa offers an alternative narrative to the "death, disease, destruction" framing mainstream western news organisations have long been critiqued for perpetuating, Marsh (2018, p. 109) analysed the channel's news coverage of the west African Ebola epidemic in the latter half of 2015. She finds that the reporting frequently praised the response to the epidemic by African authorities, and there was an emphasis on hopeful stories. This style of "solution-focused" "constructive journalism" appeared in over 80 percent of reports (Marsh, 2018, p. 110). This is typical of the conflict avoiding style of Chinese journalism (see **Chapter 4**) which avoids criticism of Government, so we would expect praise for local officials in other regions where China has political and economic interests. We might also expect that there would be little coverage when things go wrong.

Indeed, Marsh (2018, p. 111) finds that the requirement to frame stories "positively" sometimes led to inaccurate reporting. Apart from journalistic inaccuracies that can arise when the editorial line calls for a "positive" spin on all news, the channel lacks journalistic credibility on the continent because it is funded by the Chinese state, and a lack of credibility negatively impacts "soft power" (Wasserman, 2016 in Marsh, 2018, p. 107). Furthermore, the channel also made use of Associated Press material for some of its reporting, highlighting how even when global flows move South to South, currents of information from dominant Northern news agencies still percolate through.

However, Marsh finds that overall CCTV Africa did frame the Ebola epidemic differently, including by centring African officials. This finding contrasts with research exploring mainstream western news reporting on Africa, where Douglas (2019) finds that African sources (see **Chapter 6**) are largely ignored in stories about themselves, only being quoted or paraphrased in 28 percent of mainstream British newspaper coverage on sub-Saharan Africa, with western voices dominating 72 percent of coverage across the course of a year.[8]

In CCTV Africa's coverage of Ebola, 17 percent of reports in Marsh's study mentioned China's role in fighting Ebola, and Chinese officials were featured in just three stories. The focus on African, rather than Chinese, sources conceivably reflects CCTV's *glocalisation* (see Sreberny, 2000) strategy, whereby international media organisations adapt their output for local markets. However, like western news reporting practices, elite sources (see **Chapter 6**), rather than ordinary people impacted by the event, were featured most often, and those elites included aid[9] workers. The latter finding is also reflective of some dominant western news sourcing patterns on sub-Saharan Africa (Douglas, 2019).

In their book, *Exit from Hegemony: The Unravelling of the American Global Order*, Cooley and Nexon (2020) contend that Russia and China are transforming the global order and undermining the monopoly of hegemonic western powers, specifically the United States. This process, they argue, is increasingly enabling poorer nations to source investment and forge connections with states whose support is premised on agreements that break with liberal western approaches. At a basic level, this means that China and Russia do not require countries they work with to sign agreements on democracy and human rights. This makes them a useful alternative income source for countries that do not wish to democratise. That's not to say, of course, that poorer states adhering to agreements with liberal western countries have found themselves working with nations that boast unblemished democracy and human rights records.

> There are plenty of examples of illiberal American foreign policy; the United States has supported dictators, overthrown democratic regimes, violated international law, used force unilaterally, meddled in foreign elections, and directly abused human rights.
> *(Cooley and Nexon, 2020, p. 20)*

Nonetheless, global governance agreements which the United States, the European Union and other democracies are signed up to mean that there are at least generally agreed upon international checks regarding abuses of state power and so on. This is particularly important during the current moment when populism is on the rise globally and, as Cooley and Nexon (2020, pp. 7, 81) highlight, authoritarian states like Russia and China perceive liberal norms related to issues like democracy and human rights, which are part of current global governance agreements, as threats to their regimes. Thus, they are keen to cultivate a global order of "non-interference, at least as it concerns the rights of citizens" (Cooley and Nexon, 2020, p. 81).

If global agreements regarding issues like transparency and human and political rights disintegrate, the ability of journalists to hold power to account will become even more challenging (see **Chapter 10**). Seventy three percent of countries evaluated by the World Press Freedom Index are already ranked as being "very bad," "bad" or "problematic" environments for journalists, who are finding it increasingly difficult to cover sensitive stories, particularly in the Middle East, Asia and Europe (Reporters Sans Frontier, 2021). The 2021 Nobel Peace Prize was awarded to two journalists: Maria Ressa and Dmitry Muratov. Maria

Ressa is CEO of Rappler, a Philippines[10]-based news site that has had its license suspended. She has suffered sustained state harassment for her journalism. Dmitry Muratov is editor-in-chief of Novaya Gazeta, one of Russia's last independent newspapers. While welcome, the awarding of the prize to these journalists is also a worrying sign of the times. Christophe Deloire, president of Reporters Sans Frontiers, said in an article for Britain's *Observer* newspaper that awarding the Nobel Prize to Ressa and Muratov is an alarm call to the world:

> The systems that have been established for democracy and human rights are clearly in danger. Everyone can see it. We can feel this sense of emergency. And this moment represents a crystallisation of multiple different crises.
>
> *(Cadwalladr, 2021)*

Because "communicative action" is central to power (Castells, 2009, p. 50 in Thussu and Nordenstreg, 2015, pp. 243–244), it is safe to say that continuing to make their mark on the global communication sphere is likely to remain a priority for China and Russia, alongside other rising powers.

Diversifying language and personnel

Major western global news brands increasingly employ journalists from the country or region they are reporting on, or from the diaspora. For instance, in 2017, the BBC World Service launched its biggest expansion in 70 years when it announced plans to add 12 new languages to the 28 it already broadcasts in, including Pidgin, Yoruba and Igbo in Nigeria, four new languages in India and a South Korean service. It recruited over 1,000 new staff to deliver this increase (Wang, 2017).

A shift away from producing content predominantly in English reflects an awareness by some global communication brands that they cannot take their dominance for granted. This is particularly the case in markets like India where despite the use of English by the elite, only around 10 percent of the population is fluent in English. This means a market of over a billion people, who mostly speak one of India's other twenty major languages (Shah, 2016), so it's not surprising that global communication giants are beginning to offer local language services in a bid to maintain their share of the market. India has over 560 million internet users, making it the world's second largest online market after China, around half of India's 1.37 billion population had internet access in 2020 (Keelery, 2021), and in 2013, Google launched "a Hindi handwriting tool for search, and Mozilla Firefox a Tamil version of its browser" (Thussu and Nordenstreg, 2015, p. 245). Given the importance of market demands, Thussu notes:

> It's interesting to speculate what kind of content will be circulating on the World Wide Web and in which language when 90 per cent of Chinese

and an equally high percentage of Indians get online [...]. The combined economic and cultural impact of China and India, aided by their extensive global diasporas, may create a different form of globalization – a 'Chindian' communication space.

(Thussu and Nordenstreg, 2015, p. 15)

Whilst this offers an interesting perspective for the future, it's hard to see how Mandarin or Hindi would be able to embed themselves into the national consciousness of countries whose languages are written in Latin, Arabic or any other script. Such fundamental shifts would probably require an alternative power as ruthless as colonialism and that would, we would argue, be no more helpful for the empowerment of the Global South.

Diversity

The growing racial, cultural and religious diversity of journalists working for western news outlets also contributes to disrupting traditional north-south flows, in as much as such journalists may produce more nuanced, less stereotypical coverage of the Global South due to their insider knowledge and alternative perspectives on events. For example, in her research on the involvement of journalists of colour in coverage of sub-Saharan Africa for mainstream British news organisations, Douglas (2019) finds that such journalists often enter the field hoping to produce high-quality journalism which, for them, alongside other aspects of constructing accurate, informative reports, also involves subverting racially stereotypical reporting, which western news narratives on the Global South have long been critiqued for producing.

One interviewee, who has Ghanaian heritage, but grew up in Britain, explains the hope that taking a job as a correspondent for a British news outlet in West Africa could be an opportunity to subvert stereotypical narratives by telling stories that they'd never seen in mainstream UK news. In doing so, they hoped to counter the problematic narratives that made them want to disassociate from their African heritage as a child:

> For me the correspondent job was about physically having access to Africa and a way of engaging that I felt was constructive, both intrinsically and in changing the perception. That was 100 per cent my motivation for taking the job – changing the perception. I was like [...], 'this is such an amazing opportunity for the [...] Africa correspondent to be a person who actually gets [...] Africa.
>
> (Douglas, 2019, pp. 105–106)

This journalist's account of pursuing a prestigious correspondent post with the intention of changing western perceptions of Africa speaks to some of the aspirations that informed NWICO, as well as Fanon's (2001 [1961]) assertion that post-colonial subjects wanting to engage with "passionate research," is triggered by a desire to re-narrate the stories of ex-colonies. However, this interviewee felt that their role had less financial support, and was of less interest to editors, than the roles of correspondents working in the Global North. The correspondent also often had to argue with editors to get stories through that didn't comply with standard tropes around war, famine, corruption and development:

> I won some arguments and even those stories I'd hope to avoid, I think doing them from my perspective as someone with African heritage made them more nuanced than they may otherwise have been.
>
> *(Douglas, 2019, p. 106)*

This lack of institutional support illustrates how structural imbalances in global flows may be maintained and how journalists are often forced to compromise on their ethical ideals in order to shift the narrative in small ways and remain in post (see **Chapter 11**).

Disinformation and issues of trust

The advent of the internet and social media has enabled counter-flows, but it has also opened the door to greater flows of disinformation from and within countries everywhere. In some cases, disinformation is seeded directly by autocratic governments keen to insulate their populations from flows of information that could disrupt their hold on power.

For example, just as protestors in the Middle East used sites like Twitter and Facebook to attempt to topple autocracies, those maintaining the political structures they were trying to dismantle went on to use social media to attack people calling for change by unleashing torrents of disinformation. During anti-government protests in Egypt in 2019, in what researchers say was a coordinated effort (Michaelson and Safi, 2019), establishment supporting influencers took to Twitter to galvanise support for the government by praising Egypt's military. The Arab Spring has, ironically, been highlighted by Evgeny Morosov (2011) and Marc Owen Jones (Ahmed, 2021), as being central to the growth of online disinformation in the region. This is because authoritarian regimes identified social media as a threat and thus, in a manner which illustrates Foucault's conception of the circulatory nature of power (see **Chapter 4**), turned it into a tool to maintain their power.

Those opposed to regime change in Algeria also used the protestor's online tools against them. When people took to the streets in February 2019 to oppose President Abdelaziz Bouteflika's third term in office after 20 years in power, they used Facebook to share information about demonstrations against Bouteflika's regime. The president resigned in April that year, but those who had been in his camp remained in place so the protests continued. However, activists started noticing troll-like accounts, dubbed "electronic flies," which were aimed at undermining the protester's calls for change by disseminating messages in support of the government.

As a BBC report highlights (Silva, 2019), there isn't concrete evidence that establishment figures were involved in the spread of disinformation. The nature of trolling and the use of bots make it difficult to track their origins (Michaelson and Safi, 2019). However, some state sponsored attacks against citizens are traceable. During the Hong Kong protests (see **Chapter 4**), following alerts from external sources (Stewart, 2019), Facebook and Twitter (Gleicher, 2019; Twitter Safety, 2019) took action to address attempts by the Chinese government to manipulate information on social media about the protests. Google (Huntley, 2019) also disabled 210 YouTube[11] channels which were behaving in the same coordinated manner to manipulate information.

Around the same time, researchers (Raman Sundara *et al.*, 2019) found that Kazakhstan's government was trying to intercept internet user's visiting sites like Twitter and Google. The findings prompted Mozilla and Google to take steps to protect user's data in Kazakhstan, but it was not the first time the Kazakhstan government had attempted interception of national internet traffic (Mozilla, 2019), and given the authorities regularly block websites (BBC News, 2019), it probably won't be the last. On the other hand, tech companies have also monitored and censored content at the request of the authorities in different countries (MacAskill, 2007; Dehghan, 2009; Woods, 2016). What these examples illustrate are the often-problematic relations between national governments and global tech giants vis-à-vis control of information flows. It is the internet users, engaging with platforms that are presented as open transnational spaces, who are the biggest casualties.

The flow of information, both fake and real, in multiple directions has been particularly evident during the Coronavirus pandemic when people's need for information has been acute and misinformation about the virus has spread like wildfire. Not only has this highlighted the power of global digital networks to connect people but also to divide in relation to an issue that affects us all.

In their 2021 digital news report, the Reuters Institute finds that global public concern about misinformation has increased. In Africa, 74 percent (the highest percentage of those surveyed) expressed concern. Europeans were found to have the lowest levels of concern about misinformation. For the majority of those polled, misinformation was related to Covid-19. Brazilians and Poles were particularly worried about national politicians spreading false information (Newman *et al.*, 2021, p. 22). The Reuters Institute research also highlights how false information about the virus has spread particularly fast via social media, especially in Central and Eastern Europe, Nigeria and South Africa, as well as Latin America and certain Asian countries, with people expressing the most worry in relation to information received via Facebook.

Information shared via digital platforms, like Facebook, travels as fast *within* nations as it does *between* them. In a study (Wilson and Wiysonge, 2020a) charting the link between anti-vaccine information, vaccination rates and global attitudes towards vaccine safety, a strong correlation was found between the rise in negative social media messaging about vaccination safety and increased public belief that vaccinations are unsafe. Disinformation from countries overseas, mostly Russia, significantly contributed to decreased vaccine uptake globally.

Concern about a rise in global disinformation campaigns and "fake news" has led to an increase in public levels of trust in mainstream news from recognised brands globally (Newman *et al.*, 2021). This has tended to favour the BBC and CNN. During the first wave of the pandemic, from January to March 2020, BBC News reached its biggest global audience, and those in Kenya, the United States, India and Nigeria represented the largest number of people engaging from outside the United Kingdom. The surge in global traffic, which saw 438 million people globally access BBC news weekly, up 13 percent on the previous year, prompted the BBC's then director general, Tony Hall, to say: "whatever your views on the BBC, it's a reminder that we are without question [...] synonymous with quality and accuracy worldwide" (BBC, 2020).

Fostering a global/transnational public sphere

Two issues that have highlighted the interconnectedness and interdependency of our world more than any others in the past few years are the Coronavirus pandemic, as discussed above, and climate change. Both require global cooperation – impossible without dialogue – and global news channels are key to disseminating and mediating transnational dialogue. As we highlight in **Chapter 1**, equality of access to media communication is vital if all countries are to be given the same rights to engage in determining solutions, and this requires: "an enduring structure that enables political debate and opinion formation for and with a global audience" (Wozniak et al., 2021).

Such an aspiration speaks to the notion of a democratic *global public sphere* (see **Chapter 1**), a conceptual space, where global citizens would see their views represented so that they may be responded to by those in power. But, of course, not all nations, such as China and Russia, operate under liberal democratic principles (see Thussu and Nordenstreng, 2021, p. 6), and neither, in terms of liberal democratic standards, operate a "free press." Based on analysis by Reporters Sans Frontier, China ranks 177 out of 180 countries for press freedom and Russia ranks 150 (Reporters Sans Frontier, 2021). The lack of press freedom, which extends to the jailing of journalists (Reporters Sans Frontier, 2021), means, at a fundamental level, Russia and China's *media systems* (see **Chapter 1**) are not capable of facilitating open communication between citizens and those in positions of power because they primarily work in the interests of the former.[12]

Nonetheless, given the global decision-making required in relation to major issues like climate change, it's important to consider how, indeed whether, transnational news offers a space for "collective learning and problem solving" (Wozniak et al., 2021, p. 689). It's hard to develop an informed opinion on matters concerning the globe if not all global citizens, or those who represent them, are able to participate equally in transnational conversations. In its current form, global news media is a long way off constituting a global public sphere (Sparks, 2005), where all citizens have an equal opportunity to contribute to debate and the formation of public opinion at a global level. Sparks argues that although messages concerned with public life circulate internationally, this is not enough to suggest such message circulation represents the existence of a global public sphere.

> The global dimensions of both the old and the new media are predominantly means of elite communication [...] states remain the dominant forces, and [...] inequalities of wealth and power are the central features.
> *(Sparks, 2005, p. 46)*

However, others feel that the global media can, and do, play a positive role in contributing to the possibility of a global public sphere. In their analysis of four global news providers, Cottle and Rai (2008, p. 176) find that global television news may either enable, or curtail, representation of opposing views, and this contributes to democratic deliberation. What Cottle and Rai refer to as "depth reportage" transmitted via some global TV news channels, "can [...] communicate something of the lived experiences of distant others [...]. These [...] feature differently within and across today's global news channels and give some credence to global public sphere claims" (Cottle and Rai, 2008, p. 177).

Wozniak et al. (2021, p. 688) are also interested in the conditions necessary for a global public sphere. They explore whether the annual "UN climate change conferences are conducive to an emergence of a transnational public sphere by triggering issue convergence and increased transnational interconnectedness across national media debates." To test this, they analysed coverage of climate change in German, Indian, South African and US newspapers between 2012 and 2019. However, they found that national newspaper coverage of climate change focused on domestic issues.

> During COPs,[13] we observed a reduction in the diversity of countries mentioned in climate change coverage, probably because news coverage focused even more on "big players" in international politics than usual'. [...] Our study identifies the potential for elite driven political events such as the COPs to perpetuate - rather than break - these patterns of inequality in media coverage of climate change. We can also conclude that the annual COPs do not foster transnational issue convergence.
> *(Wozniak et al., 2021, p. 688)*

Exercise: Who Speaks on Climate Change?

Country rankings by the Notre Dame Environmental Change Initiative find that the G20 countries most resilient to climate change include Germany, the United Kingdom, the United States and Canada (all also amongst the worst polluters). Poorer nations, such as Tonga, the Solomon Islands, Malawi and Nepal, are most vulnerable to climate change (Dame, 2019).

Look at news coverage of day one of the most recent COP climate talks across some of the major national news outlets in your country and one or two of the dominant transnational news outlets, like CNNI. Use the Notre Dame rankings to check whether the voices of, or information from or on, those who live in countries most vulnerable to climate change are featured, or do G20 countries with greater resilience dominate coverage?

Now consider whether coverage (a) **is dominated by elites** (Sparks, 2005), (b) **focuses on domestic angles** (Wozniak et al., 2021) or (c) **offers a vehicle for opposing interests and outlooks, which can communicate aspects of the lived experiences of distant "others" in nuanced ways that contribute to supporting global public sphere claims** (Cottle and Rai, 2008, p. 177). Do your findings indicate all countries have equality of access to global media communication, are able to equally engage in determining solutions, and national and global media facilitate: "opinion formation for and with a global audience" (Wozniak et al., 2021)?

"Post-public sphere"

Schlesinger (2020, p. 1547) writes:

> The public sphere is always structured in terms of power relations. [...] it is defined by the prevailing political order, economic relations, cultural repertoires, and the affordances of technologies.

Thus, any manifestation of a transnational or global public sphere will be marked by these relations of power and shaped by communication technologies we have at our disposal which, in the digital era, are both bringing together and fracturing publics (a *"splinternet"*). Indeed, Schlesinger highlights how Habermas (see **Chapter 1**) foresaw these circumstances, asserting that the internet has mostly fragmented the public sphere and strengthened dominant agendas, whilst also offering a tool to those who are censored by authoritarian regimes, or otherwise excluded, to find ways to express themselves.

What we seem to be seeing now is what Schlesinger describes as a: "post-public sphere" (Schlesinger, 2020, p. 1557) in which the "internet-dominated 'hybrid' media system" has converged with "the present post-democratic phase of capitalist politics" (2020, p. 1546). This has produced an unstable, transitional world order, and the unsettling of once dominant structures, which maintained the west at the top of the global hierarchy. These shifts are related to a number of factors including the lack of regulation of the internet, the increasing undermining of the western "rules-based global order" and its "claim to deliver global equity" (2020, p. 1548), and the use of communications technology by authoritarian states as a means of challenging the hegemony of the west partly via the promotion of anti-democratic populist rulers.

This means that, far from using communications technologies to create a transnational, or global public sphere, they are being used by some powerful players for establishing a new world order that appears to be by-passing, and/or threatening, the ability of citizens worldwide to participate in national public spheres, let alone global ones. In these circumstances, to borrow the words of Maria Ressa, the job of journalists globally, and not just those trying to do their work in authoritarian regimes, is, to "hold the line" and "fight back with journalism" (RSF, 2020).

Fighting back with journalism, we believe, also means *extending* the line wherever possible, in order to be more inclusive of underrepresented global voices. This could include supporting struggling independent news media, particularly those outlets operating in countries which are often marginalised in global conversations, by helping them improve their online presence via providing links to their sites and stories (see also Jacobs, 2009). This may, in turn, amplify their global media presence and ability to contribute to transnational conversations, whilst simultaneously enabling already dominant news outlets to "foster transnational issue convergence" in relation to pressing global matters (Wozniak et al., 2021, p. 688). A return to the ideas of NWICO to redress communication imbalances, and with a commitment to support local democracy through journalism so citizens feel adequately represented at a national level, may also contribute to greater inclusion of global views in global information flows.

Summary

- Western values have dominated news flows since the nineteenth century. The global transmission of western perspectives supported imperialism.
- Western news agencies were key to spreading the agenda of colonisers and constructing narratives that served colonial relations of power.
- Media imperialism describes the imposition of western perspectives on the non-western world.
- The New World Information and Communications Order (NWICO) called for more balanced global information flows.
- The United States continues to dominate global communication.

- Due to the size of its economy, China poses the biggest challenge to western hegemony.
- News circulated globally by authoritarian countries has been used to undermine democratic movements.
- Global news being presented in languages other than English, and by journalists who are more reflective of the globe, has the potential to disrupt dominant western ways of seeing.
- Disinformation is an increasingly significant feature of the global communication ecology.
- A global public sphere, which is truly inclusive of all global views, is far from being realised.

References

AFP (2021) *'Hold the Line': Maria Ressa Fights for Press Freedom under Philippines' Duterte, France 24*. Available at: https://www.france24.com/en/live-news/20211210-hold-the-line-maria-ressa-fights-for-press-freedom-under-philippines-duterte (Accessed: 10 December 2021).

Ahmed, N. (2021) 'Middle East Disinformation Wars and the Battle for Narratives in the Digital Space', *Middle East Monitor*. Available at: https://www.middleeastmonitor.com/20210922-memo-in-conversation-with-marc-owen-jones/ (Accessed: 8 December 2021).

Al-Rawi, A. (2017) 'News Organizations 2.0', *Journalism Practice*, 11(6), pp. 705–720. doi:10.1080/17512786.2016.1195239.

Ashcroft, B., Griffiths, G. and Tiffin, H. (2013) *Post-Colonial Studies: the Key Concepts*. London: Taylor & Francis Group. Available at: http://ebookcentral.proquest.com/lib/nyulibrary-ebooks/detail.action?docID=1244807 (Accessed: 4 September 2021).

BBC, N. (2020) 'BBC News Reaching Highest Ever Global Audience', *BBC News*, 23 July. Available at: https://www.bbc.com/news/world-53517025 (Accessed: 15 April 2021).

BBC News (2019) 'Kazakhstan Country Profile', *BBC News*, 9 August. Available at: https://www.bbc.com/news/world-asia-pacific-15263826 (Accessed: 8 December 2021).

Bosio, D. (2013) 'How Al Jazeera Reported the Arab Spring: A Preliminary Comparative Analysis', *Media Asia*, 40(4), pp. 333–343. doi:10.1080/01296612.2013.11689986.

Cadwalladr, C. (2021) 'Nobel Winner: "We Journalists Are the Defence Line between Dictatorship and War"', *The Observer*, 4 December. Available at: https://www.theguardian.com/world/2021/dec/04/nobel-winner-we-journalists-are-the-defence-line-between-dictatorship-and-war (Accessed: 8 December 2021).

Channel Africa (no date) *ABOUT US - CHANNEL AFRICA*. Available at: http://www.channelafrica.co.za/sabc/home/channelafrica/aboutus (Accessed: 6 December 2021).

Cooley, A. and Nexon, D. (2020) *Exit from Hegemony: The Unraveling of the American Global Order*. New York: Oxford University Press. doi:10.1093/oso/9780190916473.001.0001.

Cottle, S. and Rai, M. (2008) 'Global 24/7 News Providers: Emissaries of Global Dominance or Global Public Sphere?', *Global Media and Communication*, 4(2), pp. 157–181. doi:10.1177/1742766508091518.

Crilley, R. et al. (2022) 'Understanding RT's Audiences: Exposure Not Endorsement for Twitter Followers of Russian State-Sponsored Media', *The International Journal of Press/Politics*, 27(1), pp. 220–242. doi:10.1177/1940161220980692.

Curran, J. and Morley, D. (eds) (2005) *Media and Cultural Theory*. London: Routledge. doi:10.4324/9780203509616.

Dame, M.C.W.// U. of N. (2019) *Country Index // Notre Dame Global Adaptation Initiative // University of Notre Dame, Notre Dame Global Adaptation Initiative*. Available at: https://gain.nd.edu/our-work/country-index/ (Accessed: 10 December 2021).

Dehghan, S.K. (2009) 'Iranian Consumers Boycott Nokia for "Collaboration"', *The Guardian*, 14 July. Available at: https://www.theguardian.com/world/2009/jul/14/nokia-boycott-iran-election-protests (Accessed: 25 February 2022).

Douglas, O. (2019) *Backstories / Black Stories: Black Journalists, INGOs and the Racial Politics of Representing Sub-Saharan Africa in Mainstream UK News Media*. doctoral. Goldsmiths, University of London. Available at: http://research.gold.ac.uk/id/eprint/26352/ (Accessed: 4 March 2021).

Gilbert, G.N. and Stoneman, P. (eds) (2016) *Researching Social Life*. 4th edition. Los Angeles: Sage.

Gleicher, N. (2019) 'Removing Coordinated Inauthentic Behavior from China', *Meta*, 19 August. Available at: https://about.fb.com/news/2019/08/removing-cib-china/ (Accessed: 8 December 2021).

Global Activism, Global Media (2005). Pluto Press. doi:10.2307/j.ctt183q4qr.

Golding, P. and Harris, P. (1996) *Beyond Cultural Imperialism*. Available at: https://blackwells.co.uk/bookshop/product/Beyond-Cultural-Imperialism-by-Peter-Golding-Phil-Harris/9780761953319 (Accessed: 25 February 2022).

Grill, B. (2013) 'Chinese Investment in Africa Boosts Economies But Worries Many', *Der Spiegel*, 29 November. Available at: https://www.spiegel.de/international/world/chinese-investment-in-africa-boosts-economies-but-worries-many-a-934826.html (Accessed: 6 January 2022).

Hicap, J. (2021) *Netflix's 'Squid Game' Rises in Popularity, Hits No. 1 in 22 Countries, Manila Bulletin*. Available at: https://mb.com.ph/2021/09/22/netflixs-squid-game-rises-in-popularity-hits-no-1-in-22-countries/ (Accessed: 11 November 2021).

Huntley, S. (2019) *Maintaining the Integrity of Our Platforms, Google*. Available at: https://blog.google/outreach-initiatives/public-policy/maintaining-integrity-our-platforms/ (Accessed: 8 December 2021).

Jacobs, R.N. (2009) *Race, Media, and the Crisis of Civil Society: From Watts to Rodney King*. 1st Edition. Cambridge; New York: Cambridge University Press.

Keelery, S. (2021) *Internet Usage in India - Statistics & Facts | Statista*. Available at: https://www.statista.com/topics/2157/internet-usage-in-india/ (Accessed: 24 November 2021).

Khanna, P. (2019) *The Future Is Asian: Commerce, Conflict and Culture in the 21st Century*. New York: Simon & Schuster.

Kuo, L. and Kommenda, N. (no date) 'What Is China's Belt and Road Initiative?', *The Guardian*. Available at: http://www.theguardian.com/cities/ng-interactive/2018/jul/30/what-china-belt-road-initiative-silk-road-explainer (Accessed: 23 November 2021).

Lomoy, J. (2021) *Chinese Aid – A Blessing for Africa and a Challenge to Western Donors, CMI - Chr. Michelsen Institute*. Available at: https://www.cmi.no/publications/7750-chinese-aid-a-blessing-for-africa-and-a-challenge-to-western-donors (Accessed: 7 December 2021).

Loomis, K.D. (2009) 'A Comparison of Broadcast World News Web Pages: Al Jazeera English, BBC, CBS, and CNN', *Electronic News*, 3(3), pp. 143–160. doi:10.1080/19312430903028563.

Lumumba-Kasongo, T. (2011) 'China-Africa Relations: A Neo-Imperialism or a Neo-Colonialism? A Reflection★', *African and Asian Studies*, 10(2–3), pp. 234–266. doi:10.1163/156921011X587040.

MacAskill, E. (2007) 'Yahoo Forced to Apologise to Chinese Dissidents over Crackdown on Journalists', *The Guardian*, 14 November. Available at: https://www.theguardian.com/technology/2007/nov/14/news.yahoo (Accessed: 25 February 2022).

Matos, C. (2012) 'Mass Media', in Ritzer, G. (ed.) *The Wiley-Blackwell Encyclopedia of Globalization*. Chichester: John Wiley & Sons, Ltd, p. wbeog369. doi:10.1002/9780470670590.wbeog369.

Michaelson, R. and Safi, M. (2019) '#Disinformation: The Online Threat to Protest in the Middle East', *The Guardian*, 15 December. Available at: https://www.theguardian.com/world/2019/dec/15/disinformation-the-online-threat-to-protest-in-the-middle-east (Accessed: 8 December 2021).

Mikanowski, J. (2018) 'Behemoth, Bully, Thief: How the English Language Is Taking over the Planet', *The Guardian*, 27 July. Available at: https://www.theguardian.com/news/2018/jul/27/english-language-global-dominance (Accessed: 25 February 2022).

Miles, H. (2017) 'Al-Jazeera, Insurgent TV Station That Divides the Arab World, Faces Closure', *The Observer*, 1 July. Available at: https://www.theguardian.com/media/2017/jul/01/demand-al-jazeera-closure-shows-how-much-enemies-fear-it (Accessed: 5 December 2021).

Morales, P.S. (2021) 'International Broadcasters and Country Image Management: Comparing Audience Perceptions of China, Russia and Iran in Latin America', *Global Media and China*, 6(1), pp. 100–115. doi:10.1177/2059436420960882.

Morozov, E. (2011) *The Net Delusion: How Not to Liberate The World*. London, England: Penguin.

Mozilla (2019) *Mozilla Takes Action to Protect Users in Kazakhstan | The Mozilla Blog*. Available at: https://blog.mozilla.org/en/mozilla/mozilla-takes-action-to-protect-users-in-kazakhstan/ (Accessed: 8 December 2021).

New Internationalist (1981) *The Big Four, New Internationalist*. Available at: https://newint.org/features/1981/06/01/four (Accessed: 19 November 2021).

Newman, N. et al. (2021) *Digital News Report 2021*. 10. Oxford: Reuters Institute for the Study of Journalism. Available at: https://reutersinstitute.politics.ox.ac.uk/digital-news-report/2021 (Accessed: 22 November 2021).

Phillips, A. (2014) *Journalism in Context: Practice and Theory for the Digital Age*. 1st edition. London; New York: Routledge.

Raman Sundara, R. et al. (2019) *Kazakhstan's HTTPS Interception, Censored Planet*. Available at: https://censoredplanet.org/kazakhstan (Accessed: 8 December 2021).

Reporters Sans Frontier (2021) *2021 World Press Freedom Index: Journalism, the Vaccine against Disinformation, Blocked in More Than 130 Countries, RSF*. Available at: https://rsf.org/en/2021-world-press-freedom-index-journalism-vaccine-against-disinformation-blocked-more-130-countries (Accessed: 8 December 2021).

Reuters (2011) 'Clinton Warns Against "New Colonialism" in Africa', *Reuters*, 11 June. Available at: https://www.reuters.com/article/us-clinton-africa-idUSTRE75A0RI20110611 (Accessed: 7 December 2021).

RSF (2020) *#HoldTheLine Campaign Launched in Support of Maria Ressa and Independent Media in the Philippines | Reporters without Borders, RSF.* Available at: https://rsf.org/en/news/holdtheline-campaign-launched-support-maria-ressa-and-independent-media-philippines-0 (Accessed: 10 December 2021).

RSF (2021) *Philippines : Holding the Line against Duterte's Attacks | Reporters without Borders, RSF.* Available at: https://rsf.org/en/philippines (Accessed: 10 December 2021).

Said, E.W. (1994) *Culture and Imperialism*. New Ed edition. London: Vintage.

Samarajiwa, R. (1984) 'Third-World Entry to the World Market in News: Problems and Possible Solutions', *Media, Culture and Society*, 6, pp. 119–136.

Schiller, H.L. (1979) *National Sovereignty and International Communication*. Edited by K. Nordenstreng and H.I. Schiller. New York: Ablex Publishing Company.

Schlesinger, P. (2020) 'After the Post-public Sphere', *Media, Culture & Society*, 42(7–8), pp. 1545–1563. doi:10.1177/0163443720948003.

Seib, P. (2005) 'Hegemonic No More: Western Media, the Rise of Al-Jazeera, and the Influence of Diverse Voices', *International Studies Review*, 7(4), pp. 601–615.

Shah, H. (2016) 'India's Digital Future Isn't Just in English: BBC Launches 4 Indian Language Services', *Nieman Lab*, 16 November. Available at: https://www.niemanlab.org/2016/11/indias-digital-future-isnt-just-in-english-bbc-launches-4-indian-language-services/ (Accessed: 24 November 2021).

Shamsuddin, M. (1987) 'The New World Information Order', *Pakistan Horizon*, 40(1), pp. 80–94.

Silva, M. (2019) 'Algeria Protests: How Disinformation Spread on Social Media', *BBC News*, 16 September. Available at: https://www.bbc.com/news/blogs-trending-49679634 (Accessed: 8 December 2021).

Sparks, C. (2012) 'Media and Cultural Imperialism Reconsidered', *Chinese Journal of Communication*, 5(3), pp. 281–299. doi:10.1080/17544750.2012.701417.

Sparks, C. (2015) 'China, Soft Power and Imperialism', in Gary, D. Rawnsley and Ming-Yeh, T. Rawnsley (ed.) *Routledge Handbook of Chinese Media*. Abingdon, Oxon; New York: Routledge.

Sreberny, A. (2000) 'The Global and the Local in International Communications', in *Mass Media and Society*. London: Arnold; New York: Oxford University Press.

Statista Research Department (2021) *India - Leading English Daily Newspapers by AIR 2017, Statista.* Available at: https://www.statista.com/statistics/1053168/india-leading-english-daily-newspapers-by-average-issue-readership/ (Accessed: 4 December 2021).

Stewart, E. (2019) 'How China Used Facebook, Twitter, and YouTube to Spread Disinformation about the Hong Kong Protests', *Vox*. Available at: https://www.vox.com/recode/2019/8/20/20813660/china-facebook-twitter-hong-kong-protests-social-media (Accessed: 8 December 2021).

Tassi, P. (2021) '"Squid Game" Is Now the #1 Show in 90 Different Countries', *Forbes*. Available at: https://www.forbes.com/sites/paultassi/2021/10/03/squid-game-is-now-the-1-show-in-90-different-countries/ (Accessed: 11 November 2021).

Thielman, S. (2016) 'Al-Jazeera America to Shut Down after Less Than Three Years on Air', *The Guardian*, 13 January. Available at: https://www.theguardian.com/media/2016/jan/13/al-jazeera-america-shut-down-cable-tv-news-network (Accessed: 6 December 2021).

Thurman, N., Hensmann, T. and Fletcher, R. (2020) 'Large, Loyal, Lingering? An Analysis of Online Overseas Audiences for UK News Brands', *Journalism*, 22(8), pp. 1892–1911. doi:10.1177/1464884919892411.

Thussu, D.K., de Burgh, H. and Shi, A. (eds) (2017) *China's Media Go Global*. 1st edition. Abingdon; New York: Routledge.

Thussu, D.K., de Burgh, H. and Shi, A. (eds) (2018) 'Tiangao or Tianxia? The Ambiguities of CCTV's English-Language News for Africa', in V. Marsh (eds) *China's Media Go Global*. London; New York: Routledge. pp. 103–122.

Thussu, D.K. and Nordenstreg, K. (eds) (2015) *Mapping BRICS Media*. London; New York: Routledge.

Thussu, D.K. and Nordenstreng, K. (eds) (2021) *BRICS Media: Reshaping the Global Communication Order?* London: Routledge. doi:10.4324/9780429468759.

Tomlinson, J. (1991) *Cultural Imperialism: A Critical Introduction*. London; New York: Continuum. Available at: http://hdl.handle.net/2027/heb.02149 (Accessed: 4 November 2021).

Twitter Safety (2019) *Information Operations Directed at Hong Kong*. Available at: https://blog.twitter.com/en_us/topics/company/2019/information_operations_directed_at_Hong_Kong (Accessed: 8 December 2021).

UNESCO (1980) *Many Voices, One World: Towards a New, More Just, and More Efficient World Information and Communication Order - UNESCO Digital Library*. Available at: https://unesdoc.unesco.org/ark:/48223/pf0000040066 (Accessed: 10 December 2021).

Wainaina, B. (2019) 'How to Write About Africa', *Granta*, 2 May. Available at: https://granta.com/how-to-write-about-africa/ (Accessed: 20 November 2021).

Wang, S. (2017) 'BBC World Service Kicks Off Its Biggest Expansion in More Than 70 Years, Readying 12 New Languages', *Nieman Lab*, 21 August. Available at: https://www.niemanlab.org/2017/08/bbc-world-service-kicks-off-its-biggest-expansion-in-more-than-70-years-readying-12-new-languages/ (Accessed: 23 November 2021).

Wasserman, H. and Ndlovu, M. (2021) 'Contending Soft Powers: South African Media on the African Continent', in D.K. Thussu, and K. Nordenstreng (eds.) *BRICS Media Reshaping the Global Communication Order*. Abingdon; New York: Routledge. pp. 223–239.

Watson, A. (2019) *Topic: Media in Africa*, *Statista*. Available at: https://www.statista.com/topics/5032/media-in-africa/ (Accessed: 27 November 2021).

Wilson, S.L. and Wiysonge, C. (2020) 'Social Media and Vaccine Hesitancy', *BMJ Global Health*, 5(10), p. e004206. doi:10.1136/bmjgh-2020–004206.

Winston, B. (1998) *Media, Technology and Society: A History: From the Telegraph to the Internet*. London: Taylor & Francis Group. Available at: http://ebookcentral.proquest.com/lib/nyulibrary-ebooks/detail.action?docID=169790 (Accessed: 25 February 2022).

Woods, B. (2016) 'Facebook Deactivated Korryn Gaines' Account during Standoff, Police Say', *The Guardian*, 3 August. Available at: https://www.theguardian.com/us-news/2016/aug/03/korryn-gaines-facebook-account-baltimore-police (Accessed: 25 February 2022).

Wozniak, A. *et al.* (2021) 'The Event-Centered Nature of Global Public Spheres: The UN Climate Change Conferences, Fridays for Future, and the (Limited) Transnationalization of Media Debates', *International Journal of Communication*, 15(0), p. 27.

Notes

1 The dominance of English is of course not limited to former colonies. Nearly 400 million people speak it as their first language and "elevating English while denigrating all other languages has been a pillar of English and American nationalism for well over a hundred years" (Mikanowski, 2018). The dominance has been resisted to little avail (Mikanowski, 2018).

2 Countries that did not form an alliance with the Soviet Union or the US during the Cold War.
3 These were:

> "it was the duty of states to facilitate the application…to ensure that the mass media coming directly under their juridisction act in conformity therewith" and another article which made "states responsible for the activities in the international sphere of all mass media under their jurisdiction".
>
> *(Shamsuddin, 1987, p. 86)*

4 StatCounter, Search Engine Market Share https://gs.statcounter.com/search-engine-market-share/all
5 See https://about.google/intl/ALL_us/stories/year-in-search-2021/trends/meghan-and-harry/.
6 Formerly Russia Today
7 The billion pound initiative is set to become the biggest infrastructure project in the world creating, among other things, global communication networks (Thussu and Nordenstreng, 2021; Kuo and Kommenda, no date).
8 The year was 2012. No major sub-Saharan African "news events" (e.g. the World Cup, Nelson Mandela's death, the Ebola outbreak) occurred, meaning results were less likely to be unreflective of typical mainstream western news reporting patterns on sub-Saharan Africa.
9 China is a significant aid donor in Africa (around $6 billion a year), though not as large as the west (around $150 billion a year; Lomoy, 2021).
10 When Philippine's president, Rodrigo Duterte, was sworn into office in June 2016, he made his oppressive approach to the press clear, saying: "Just because you're a journalist, you are not exempted from assassination if you're a son of a bitch. Freedom of expression cannot help you if you have done something wrong" (RSF, 2021). Journalists who critique his regime, such as Ressa, are subjected to harassment by the authorities, including arrest and some have been killed. Independent media in the country are resisting with the rallying call to "hold the line" (AFP, 2021).
11 Google owns YouTube.
12 The 2021 World Press Freedom Index, which is not a measure of journalistic quality but an evaluation of media independence, pluralism, journalist safety and legislative framework, only lists 12 out of 180 countries as offering a good environment for journalism (Reporters Sans Frontier, 2021).
13 COP (Conference of the Parties) is the term used for global climate change talks.

INDEX

Note: Page numbers followed by "n" denote endnotes.

Aaj Tak 29–30
absolutist 233
accuracy 224, 229
Adorno, T. 141, 142
adultification 114n2
advertising 160; competition and homogenisation 166–167; and crisis of legitimacy 167; and data targeting 153, 206; deserts news media 172–174; drives print consolidation 168–169; field on 171; levels of 173; paid content 174–175; selling of 205; taxes on 162–165
advertising subsidy: advertising, competition and homogenisation 166–167; history of 161–164; rise and rise of 164–166
affinity groups 147–149
African Charter on Human and People's Rights, Article 7 of 211–212
African heritage 60, 256, 257
Aftenposten 12
Agence France Presse 245, 246
agency 97, 106; human 13, 32; of individual journalists 128; news 245–246
agenda 68–69; contesting agendas 70; debate, spheres of 124; liberal model of 171; orientating (and disorientating) audiences 69–70; media agendas, origins of 82–84
agenda-setting theory 69, 82; in factual stories 78–80; frame building 81–82; persistent frames 80–81

agonistic 11
Ahmed, Sadiq Ibrahim 226
Aid organisations 129; *see also* humanitarian organisations
Al Arabiya.ne 146
The Algerians (Bourdieu) 47
algorithms 141, 147, 149, 150, 151; audiences 54–56; digitization 52–54; news choices from 56–58; selection 4; social media 28
Al-Jazeera English (AJE) 133, 250, 251
Al Jazeera.net 146
Alphabet 205
American news network 55, 124, 169
antagonism 11; *see also* agonistic
anti-democratic organisations 14
anti-elite messaging 151
anti-publics 14–15
anti-Semitism 98
anti-Trust laws 206
Arendt, H. 1–2, 204
Argentina, networked radio 170
Aristotle 224
artificial intelligence (AI) 153; software 53
Ashcroft, B. 98
Associated Press 245, 246, 253
Athenian Gazette 162
audience atomisation 147–149
audience demographics/assumptions, about readership/audience 62n3
audiences: affinity groups and audience atomisation 147–149; assumptions

about 63n5; calls for reform 152–153; competition for 166–167; encoding decoding 144–146; funding and 188; harnessing opposition 146–147; as journalists 140–141; money flows 149–151; power of 143–154; selling politics 151–152; towards deep mediatisation 153–154
Australia: minorities in 38
authoritarianism 2, 74
authoritative sources 32, 119–121, 130
authority signalling 121–122
automated/robo journalism 53
autonomy 16, 18, 21, 27, 31, 33; advertising 167, 176; editorial 186, 193, 194, 195; ethics 229–238, 240

Baek, M. 184
Bailey, M. 193
Bakhtin, M. 95
Batty, N. 107, 109
BBC 183, 189, 193, 194, 196, 258, 259
BBC World 246, 250, 255
be and being 95–97
Bednarek, M. 53, 54
Begum, S. 93–94, 96, 97, 100, 114n2, 114n3
Belkin, A. 38
Belt and Road Initiative (BRI) 252
Benson, R. 26, 27, 29, 70, 171, 184, 188, 195
Bhabha, H. K. 48, 61; analysis of relations 62n1
biopower 103, 108, 114n11
Black journalists 39, 239
#BlackLivesMatter 11, 58
Black Skin, White Masks (Fanon) 104
blasphemy 162, 218
Boczkowski, P. J. 57
Bolsonaro, J. 69, 70, 73, 74, 86n1, 86n3
Born, G. 181
Boston Newsletter 161
both-sides-journalism 232
boundary work 213–214
Bourdieu, P. 25–27, 29, 30, 32, 33, 38, 41, 46, 47, 72, 73, 160, 166, 192, 205, 234–236; *The Algerians* 47
bourgeoisie 7, 161–163
Bouteflika, A. 257
Brazilian news organisations 70
Brazil, research on WhatsApp groups 152
Brin, S. 175
Britain *see* United Kingdom (UK)
British Broadcasting Corporation *see under* BBC

British news media, agenda for 230
British newspaper 93, 96
British phone-hacking scandal 234
broadcasters 245–246
broadcasting 169–170
broadcast media 160, 230
Brüggemann, M. 17
Buck-Morss, S. 110
Bush, G. 250
Butler, J. 109; *"Violence, Mourning, Politics"* 111
BuzzFeed, case of 28–29
Byerly, C.M. 58
Byrne, D. 38

Cameron, D. 76, 240n6
Campbell, N. 35
Canada, long-term funding/financial independence 188
Caple, H. 53, 54
captured liberal model 18, 19
Carlos, J. 130
Carlson, M. 122, 213
Castells, M. 133
CCTV 249, 252, 253; glocalisation 254
CCTV Africa 253
celebrities, insiders/outsiders 130–132
censorship 14, 147, 161, 186, 217, 218
Chadwick, A. 122
Charles, G.-U. 9
Chiminya, T. 84
China: aid donor in Africa 268n9; challenge to western hegemony 252; handwritten newssheets in 161; media role in Africa 252; National Security law 217; red envelope cash 234
Chinese Communist Party (CCP) 74, 75, 233
Chinese Exclusion Act (1882) 81
Chinese journalism 233, 253
Chinese news media 52, 74, 133
Chomsky, N. 120
Christians, C. 223, 225
civil society organisations 182, 195, 196
click bait 28, 173
click-based journalism 57
climate change 132, 260–261
CNN International 250, 259
codes of conduct 226, 229
Cohen, B. 68
Cole, T. 105, 106, 113
Collins, H. 211
colonialism 11, 47, 60, 109, 110, 256
colonial languages, dominance of 247

Index **271**

commercialisation 8, 21, 154, 163, 168, 176, 183, 237
commercial journalism 140, 160
commercial marketplace 140, 189
commercial mass market newspapers 165
commercial media: in Hungary 187; in Kenya 188; against PSM 191
commercial television, business model for 175
Committee to Protect Journalists 217, 226, 237
common sense 71, 192, 144
communication: circuit of 145; global 245 (*see also* global communications)
communicative capabilities 182
communicative rights 181
Communist Party of China 52
comparative journalism studies 15–20
competition laws 204
Conboy, M. 161, 162
Conde Nast 36
Confucian philosophy 202, 203
Conservative Government, legalised gay marriage 146
content analysis 59
context, ethics 232–234
contra-flow model 252
conviviality 13
Cooke, W. F. 245
Cook, T.E. 26, 32
Cooley, A. 254
core-periphery global system 246
cost-cutting 53, 188
Cottle, S. 260
counter-public 10; subaltern 9, 10, 14
Covid-19 pandemic 69–70, 81, 104, 258, 259
Crenshaw, Kimberlé 94
crimes against humanity 86n3
criminal libel 218
critical cultural studies 3, 144
critical political economy 8
critical race theory 94
critical scholarship 19
critical source theory 120
critical theorists 8, 120, 147, 180
Croatian newspapers 79
cross-border migration 81
crowding out 189–192
cultural capital 26, 27, 33–34, 41, 143, 239
cultural change 38
cultural imperialism 246, 252
Cultural Revolution 233
cultural theories 141

cultural theorists 146
culture 98; in news choices 46–48
culture-bound factors 49–52
culture-free factors 49–52
Curran, J. 31; advertising 162–166; PSB 184–185

Dacre, P. 229
Daily Caller 127
Daily Express 148
Daily Herald 165, 166
The Daily Mail 93, 94, 123, 165, 215, 229
The Daily Mirror 166, 215
The Daily News 83
Daily Star 235
Daily Sun 81
The Daily Telegraph 214, 238
datafication 153, 155
data targeting 153, 206
Davis, A. 123, 124
Davis, M. 14
death-worlds 110
deceptive practices 233
deep mediatisation 153–154
defamation, libel and reputational damage 210–211
DeGeneres, E. 45
Deloire, C. 255
Dementia tax 123
democracy 2, 11, 120, 211; protection of 203–204
democratic corporatist media system 185, 229; democratic corporatist model/ Northern model 16–17
democratic dissent, limits of 75–76
Democratic Republic of Congo 50
deregulation 190
Derrida, J. 95
detachment 231
deviant 128, 133, 136, 213, 235
dialogue 95–97, 106
"difference" 92–97, 99, 112
digital advertising 172–176
digital platforms, information shared via 259; *see also* social media platforms
Dijk, T.A. van 73
discourse analysis 101–103
discursive construction 231
discursive system 102, 104
disinformation 257–259, 263
disruption, political and legal 29–30
diversity 39, 256–257
dominant reading 144, 145
Dospiva, M. 218

Douglas, O. 36, 39, 46, 58, 60, 84, 100, 106, 129, 253, 256–257
doxa 32, 37, 46, 48, 61, 70, 72, 114n14, 193, 235
Dukauskaite, G. 112
Dunton, J. 162
Duterte, R. 268n10

Ebola Frontline 107
Ebola outbreak (2014) 107–108, 253–254
economic capital 41, 143
economic power 7, 8, 18
Editors' Code 229
Elliott, P.R.C. 52, 63n4
Elvestad, E. 53, 184
Encoding Decoding (Hall) 144–146, 154
England 79, 94, 107, 145, 162; developments in 161
English: dominance of 267n1; journalism 162
Enninful, E. 35–36, 41n3
Entman, R. 78, 80
equalling 113
ethical rule making 226
ethics 223–224; autonomy 234–235; detachment, objectivity, neutrality 231; fear and intimidation 237–238; hospitality and proper distance 224–225; impartiality and proper distance 231–232; insecure work 235–237; for journalists 227–228; in practice 230–238; situation and context 232–234; virtue ethics 224
European Convention on Human Rights (ECHR) 208, 216
European Court of Justice 210
European Union (EU) 76, 123, 148; global governance agreements 254; PSB in 190
Evans, J. 94, 95
exclusion 9, 10; tactics of 11
Expert Woman Project 194
Extinction Rebellion 11, 132

Facebook 127, 142–143, 149, 151, 172, 173, 206, 257–259; political use of 151
fairness 193; diversity and 184; intention of 182; mandates 207
fairness directive 170
Fairness Doctrine 29
fake news 57, 76, 151, 165, 217, 259; *see also* junk news
Fanon, F. 47–48, 61, 105, 256–257; *Black Skin, White Masks* 104
Fanonian social psychology 48

Fauci, A. 127
fear: ethics 237–238; of revolution 163
Federal Radio Commission 170
Federation of African Journalists 226
feminine vulnerability 144
field of power 27, 41, 41n1, 175–176, 203, 215
field theory 25; *see also* journalism field
financial crisis 171, 172
Financial Times (FT) 56, 57, 149
Finnish public broadcaster 190
first-level agenda-setting 78
Floyd, G. 12
Foucauldian discourse analysis 101–102; revealing silences 102–103
Foucault, M. 72, 73, 76, 78, 105, 114n9–114n11, 119, 144, 203, 257; notion of discourse 100; work on biopolitics 108
Fox News 29, 32, 127, 142
frames/framing 80; building of 81–82; national and international 84–85; persistent frames 80–81; reveal origins of media agendas 82–84
framing theory 78, 85
France: Agence France-Presse in 245, 246; influencers in 213
Frankfurt school 141, 142
Fraser, N. 8–10, 14, 15
freedom of expression 7, 71, 147, 202, 211, 225, 268n10
freedom of information (FOI) 208
Freedom of Information Act 208
Freedom's Journal 163
French Revolution (1789) 162
Friedman, V. 112
Fuentes-Rohwer, L. 9
functionalist 141, 143, 154
fundraising imagery 107

Galtung, J. 49–52
Garner, S. 107
Gatehouse, G. 127
gay 146
gender 57, 60, 92, 94, 135, 149; equality 59
Germany 188, 194, 196; radio in 170; state intervention 18
Gilroy, P. 80
global banking crisis 124
global communications 245; dominance of American companies in 249; economics of 247
global flows: alternative flows 252–255; media imperialism 246–248; news

agencies and broadcasters 245–246; the electrical telegraph 37, 215, 245; western media organisations dominate 244–245
global governance agreements 254
global media 4, 85, 244, 246, 260, 262
global news 246, 248, 250, 251, 259, 260, 262
global news flows 250
global news media 93, 107, 260
Global North 16, 55, 133, 152, 204, 225, 257
global public sphere 259–261, 263; post-public sphere 261–262
Global South 18, 61, 84, 106, 108, 129, 171, 247, 252, 256
Goffman, E. 78
Golding, P. 52, 63n4
Google 172, 173, 175, 206, 248, 255
Gramsci, A. 21n2, 71–72, 76, 100, 120, 144, 192
Greenpeace 132
Griffiths, G. 98
The Guardian 35, 53, 57, 84, 97, 214, 215, 234
Guerrero, M.A. 18

Habermas, J. 6–8, 27, 161, 183, 203; Fraser's re-formulation of 9
habitus 34, 35, 37–39, 41, 46–49, 72, 84, 193
Hallin, D.C. 16–19, 75–76, 124, 126–128, 135, 229
Hall, S. 50, 60, 94, 95, 102–103, 121, 126–128, 135; *Encoding Decoding* 144–146, 154; *The Social Production of News* 120
Hall, T. 259
Hanitzsch, T. 230–235, 238, 215
handwritten newssheets 161
Harcup, T. 63n5
hard news 45, 79
Harry, Prince 249
hate speech 197n1
hate speech laws 218
Haugen, F. 151
hegemony 9, 71, 100, 144, 192; hegemonic reading 145; hegemonic messages 154
The Herald 83
Herman, E.S. 120, 246
Herrero, L.C. 18
high-quality news 175
Hindman, M. 147, 205
The Hindu 234
Hindustan Times 245
HispanTV 249

homogenisation 166–167
Hong Kong protests 258
hooks, bell 79, 81, 106, 111–112
Hoover, H. 170
hospitality 224–225
How to Write about Africa (Wainaina) 253
Huffington Post 172
Hungary: commercial media in 187; news organisations in 218
hybridity 48, 61

identity journalism 148
ideological hegemony 19, 192
ideological outsiders 129, 132–133
ideological theories 141, 154
ideology 70–71, 119; limits of democratic dissent 75–76; power to determine meaning 78; shifting agendas 76–77; suppression of internal dissent 74–75; theory in media 71–72; truth about truth 72–74
i-D magazine 36
Il Manifesto 30
immigrants 77, 81, 82
immigration 76, 77
impartiality 240; and proper distance 231–232; PSM 182, 193
inclusion 39, 58, 129, 182, 262
independence, PSM 181; funding and 188–189; and problem of state capture 186–188; securing of 194–195
independent news media, in Northern Europe 161
Independent Press Standards Organisation (IPSO) 228–230
India: limited freedom of press 163; media commercialisation in 168; research on WhatsApp groups 152
influencers 143, 174, 213; online 176
information: enabling access to 206–207; freedom of 208; protecting justice 211–212; protecting public 209–210; protection of sources 208–209; regulating delivery of 204–205
information flows 4, 15, 245, 246, 251, 252, 258
insecure work, ethics 235–237
insiders 129, 130, 133; celebrities 130–132
Instagram 141, 152, 174
internal dissent, suppression of 74–75
international codes of ethics and standards 226–228
International Covenant on Civil and Political Rights (ICCPR) 203; Article

14 of 211; Article 19 of 202, 216; Article 20 of 209
International Federation of Journalists (IFJ) 226–228
international frames 84–85
international non-governmental organisations (INGOs) 106–107
International Women's Media Foundation (IWMF) 237, 241n7
internet 4, 17, 37, 52, 121, 133, 142, 146, 147, 173, 191, 196, 205, 244, 248, 250, 257, 258, 261; advent of 257; design 152–153; growth of 248
intersectionality 94
intimidation, ethics 237–238
investigative journalism 175
Invisible Children: American NGO Invisible Children 105
invisibility 114n8
IPSO *see* Independent Press Standards Organisation (IPSO)
Islamophobia, Islamophobic 60, 93
Italian media field 30
IWMF *see* International Women's Media Federation (IWMF)

Javid, S. 93
Jefferson, T. 7, 21n1, 163
Jenkins, C.D. 59
Johnson, B. 77
Jones, M. O. 257
Jones, Sir R. 245
journalism field 20, 25–27, 46, 164, 175, 212; boundary work 213–214; BuzzFeed case 28–29; disrupting 27–28; economic threats to 215–216; maintaining legitimacy 213; mapping of 27; paradigm repair 214–215; political and legal disruption 29–30; self-regulation defines 228–230
Journalism Without Borders (JRF) 226
journalistic identity, discursive construction of 231
journalistic subjectivity 58–60
journalists: characteristics of 84; ethics for 227–228; as mediators 112–113
junk news 127

Kaplan, R. 56
Karnowski, J. 148
Kashmir, national security in 217
Katz, E. 143
Kazakhstan, protect user's data in 258
Kenya: commercial media in 188; editorial interference by advertisers and politicians 235

Kerslake Commission 240n4
Khiabany, G. 21n1
King, Martin Luther 12
Kizilkaya, E. 40
Kony 2012 105, 106
KwaZulu-Natal Research Innovation and Sequencing Platform 126

labour market 32, 236
Labour Party 165, 166
Lacan, J. 98
land ownership, issue of 83
languages 255–257
Larsen, A.G. 125
Latin American media 18, 19, 247, 249, 258; Brazil 52, 69–70, 73–74, 152; Mexico 19, 81; South America 246
laws: anti-Trust 206; and codes of conduct 226; competition laws 204; hate speech laws 218
Lazarsfeld, P.F. 141–143, 154, 155n1
Leave campaign 76, 77
Le Courrier Picard 103
Lee, S.T. 233
legitimacy 26, 213; crisis of 167
legitimate controversy 124
legitimising strategy 32
Leong, N. 37
Leveson Inquiry 234, 236, 240n6; *see also* phone hacking
LGBTQ+ 99
libel 210–211
liberal consensus 128
liberal democracy 21n1, 120, 169
Liberal media model 229
liberal pluralist thinkers 120
liberal system, of United States 185
liberal theories 180
Libero 30
license fee for use of television sets 196
licenses 169–170
life-in-death 110–111
Lingen, P. 210
Lingens v Austria (1986) 220n1
Lippmann, W. 46
Li, W. 52
local news organisations 173
lookalike groups 151, 155
Lorde, A. 96, 113

The MacBride Commission (1977) 248
MacBride, S. 248
Malaysia, censorship in 218
Mancini, P. 16–18, 229
Mandetta, L. H. 69, 86n1
Manning, P. 124

Mare, D.A. 57
marginalised groups 9, 32, 39, 60, 99, 104, 113, 186, 239
market freedom 30
marketisation 190; of news 246
Márquez-Ramírez, M. 18
Marsh, V. 253
Martin, T. 59
Marx, K. 71, 76
mass market newspaper 165, 236, 239
mass media 140; effects of 141–143; indirect effects 142; oppositional readers of 151; two-step flow and minimal effects theory 141–143
May, T. 123
MBC *see* Munhwa Broadcasting Corporation (MBC)
Mbembe, A. 108–110, 114n11
McChesney, R. W. 246
McCombs, M.E. 77
McCreary, G. W. 86n7
McGraw, K.A. 58
McMullan, P. 234
McNamee, R. 149
MDC *see* Movement for Democratic Change (MDC)
media capture 218–219
media effects 141, 142
media freedom 30, 202, 203, 209–210, 218, 233
media imperialism 246–248, 262
media law 218
media power 125–128
media regulation 4, 202, 210, 219
media systems 259; and comparative journalism studies 15–20
Medicines Sans Frontiers (MSF) 107, 111
Mental Deficiency Act (1913) 102
Meta 205
#MeToo 58
The Michigan Journal of Race and Law 10
Mill, J. S. 7, 21n1, 209
Mills, T. 193
minimal effects theory 141–143
The Mirror 96, 166
misinformation 2, 57, 70, 127, 135, 148, 152, 204, 216, 258; *see also* fake news; junk news
Mitchelstein, E. 57
modernity, characteristic of 108
Modi, N. 30
Moeller, S.D. 93
monitorial approach 202
Montague, Lady M. 162
Moore, M. 77
Moral Panic 121

Morgan, P. 96, 100
Morley, D. 145
The Morning Herald 164
Morosov, E. 257
Mouffe, C. 11, 14
Movement for Democratic Change (MDC) 83
Moyo, D. 57
Moyo, T. 217
MSF *see* Medicines Sans Frontiers (MSF)
Mubarak, H. 250
Mugabe, R. 83
mugging 121
Muhammad cartoons affair 12, 225
Mullin, C. 208
Munhwa Broadcasting Corporation (MBC) 93
Muratov, D. 254, 255
Murdoch, J. 191
Murdoch, R. 166, 191, 204, 214
must-carry mandates 207

National Broadcasting Company (NBC) 170
national frames 84–85
National Institute for Communicable Diseases (NICD) 126
national security 216–217
National Viewers and Listeners Association 14
native/sponsored content 174
natural disasters 51, 119
Navalny, A. 217
Nazism 108
Ndlovu, M. 251
necropolitics 108–110, 114n11
Neff, T. 188, 195
negativity 50, 52, 54
negotiated reading 145
net neutrality 207
neutrality 28, 31, 71, 76, 128, 169, 231, 232
New Institutionalists 25, 27
news: events become 49–52; exporting commercial model of 167–168; funding and quality of 192; marketisation of 246
news agencies 245–246
newsbooks 161, 162
news choices 52–54, 58–60; from assumptions to algorithms 56–58; audiences 54–56; culture and subjectivity in 46–48
news junkies 184
news knowledge 184–185; and social media 185–186
news media 30; advertising deserts 172–174; ideology reproduced via 70–78

News of the World (NOW) 214
news organisations 148, 171, 213; comparision of 172; potential income for 150
newspapers 162; price of 165; proliferated in United States 163
news production 4, 28, 46, 53, 56, 68, 70, 235
news refusers 184
newsroom diversity 58–60
news selection 4, 46, 48–53, 55, 56, 61, 68, 84, 248
news values: proximity and 51; and selection 48–49
New World Information and Communications Order (NWICO) 247, 248, 262
New York Journal 165
The New York Sun 164
The New York Times 51, 75, 112, 127, 130, 216, 235
New York World 165
New Zealand: long-term funding/financial independence 188
Nexon, D. 254
NGOs *see* non-governmental organisations (NGOs)
NICD *see* National Institute for Communicable Diseases (NICD)
Nixon, S. 94, 95
Noelle-Neumann, E. 147
non-governmental organisations (NGOs) 129
non-official sources 129
non-violence 224, 225
Nordenstreng, K. 223, 225
North American news media 124
North Atlantic/liberal model 16–18
Northern Europe, independent news media 161
north-western news agencies 245
Norway: accuracy 229; media 229
Norwegian Press Association 228
Norwegian Press Code 228
Nossek, H. 85
Nothias, T. 55
Notre Dame Environmental Change Initiative 261
NWICO *see* New World Information and Communications Order (NWICO)

Obama, B. 55, 112
objective news 169
objectivity 32, 231

Oborne, P. 238, 239
Observer 233, 255
Ofcom 230, 240n5
O'Gara, E. 94
OhmyNews 172
O'Neill, D. 63n5
online abuse 211
online market-places 172
opinion leaders 142, 143
oppositional readers 151
oppositional reading 145, 146
Oprah 249
organized lying 1–2, 204
"Orient" 99–100, 104
Orientalism (Said) 99–102
"other" 92, 114n7; accounting for history 98–101; desiring 111–112; dominant 97–98; fear and hate of 103–105; life-in-death 110–111; necropolitics 108–110; pitying 105–106; representation of 92–94; standardised molds 106–108
"Other" 98, 108, 109
othered 92, 94
othering 92, 94, 106, 112, 114n8; be and being 95–97; dialogue 95; "difference" 94–95
otherness 4, 80, 94
outsiders 129, 133; celebrities 130–132; ideological 132–133

Page, L. 175
paid content 174–175
pan-African news journalism 251
Panopticon 105
Panorama Ebola programme 109–111
paradigm repair 214–215
para-social relationships 143
Patel, P. 77
path dependency 32, 33, 37, 41
People's Daily 74–75
Peppiatt, R. 239
peripheral/subaltern public sphere 132; *see also* counter-public; subaltern counter-public
personalisation 50, 52, 54, 140, 150, 154, 155, 181, 196
Peston, R. 231, 232
Phillips, A. 53, 76, 84, 171, 236
phone hacking 214, 215, 234
photography, power of 54
platforms 76, 149, 152, 153, 155, 172, 173, 175, 215; regulating platforms 176, 196, 205–206
plural democracy 217

pluralism, PSM 181–182
polarisation 17, 125–128, 148; level in United States 127; levels of 127–128
polarised pluralist 16
political disruption 29–30
political reality 69
Post Angel 162
postcolonial theory 3, 48, 245
post-public sphere 261–262
post-war media boom 171–172
power: of photography 54; source of 128–136
Powers, M. 188, 195
power to determine meaning 78
preferred reading 144
press freedom 2, 19, 70, 75, 163, 225; international agreements on 209; liberal democratic approach to 248
The Press Gazette 215
primary definers 120–121, 129, 133–135; challenging authority 123–124; speed and authority signalling 121–122
primary sources 129–130
principle of harmony 209
print news organisations 173
pro-democracy frames 133
professionalism 16, 18, 29, 193
Profil 210
proper distance 224–225, 234; impartiality and 231–232
Prophet Muhammad 12, 225
Prosser, T. 181
proximity 123; to *field of power* 215; and news values 51
PSB *see* public service broadcasting (PSB)
PSM *see* public service media (PSM)
public interest 233–234
public opinion 3, 8, 11, 27, 129, 260
public relations (PR): material 46; source of 128–136
public service broadcasting (PSB) 182, 183, 185, 190, 193, 196
public service media (PSM) 17, 180–181, 207; emergence of 182–184; funding and independence 188–189; future of 195–197; impartiality 182; independence 181; independence and problem of state capture 186–188; pluralism 181–182; public spheres require 186; securing independence and representativeness 194–195; social value of 184–186; strategic rituals and creation of consensus 192–193; unfair competition and theory of "crowding out" 189–192; universality 181

public service news 186, 196
public service search engines 196–197
public sphere 6–8, 45, 70, 161, 176, 180, 249; anti-publics 14–15; critical responses 8–11; global/transnational 259–262; radical democratic approaches 11–14; require public service media 186
Pulitzer, J. 165

race/racism 3, 4, 9, 10, 21n1, 35, 36, 39, 47, 49, 58, 59, 61, 82, 94, 101, 103, 107, 108, 114n8, 114n10, 131, 132, 192, 211, 239
racial capital 36
racial dicourses 103
radical democratic approaches 11–14
radical democratic theory 8
Radio Corporation of America 170
Radio France Internationale 246
Radio RSA 251
Rai, M. 260
Ramsay, G. 77
Ranciere, J. 114n10
Rao, S. 233
rarefaction 119
Rashford, M. 131
reader engagement 149
Record TV 73
re-feudalisation, of public sphere 8, 21
reflexivity 154, 155
regime of truth 73, 74
regulation: for fairness 207; and law helps and hinders 219; of scheduling 207
regulation for control 216; censorship 218; media capture 218–219; national security 216–217
reinforcing spirals 155
Reith, Lord 183
Reporters Without Borders (RSF) 229
representation: level of 39; theory on 94–97
reputation 210–211
Ressa, M. 254–255, 262
Reuters Institute 245–246, 258
Reynolds Press 165
right to free expression 7; protection of 202
ritual of impartiality 193
RSF *see* Reporters Without Borders (RSF)
RT, TV network 249
Ruge, M.H. 49–52
rules of the game 25, 27–31, 40, 120
Russell, J. 106
Russia 95, 135, 211, 217, 218, 248, 249, 252, 254, 255, 259; censorship in 218; Committee to Protect Journalists 217

SABC *see* South African Broadcasting Corporation (SABC)
Saha, A. 58, 84
Said, E. 104–106; *Orientalism* 99–102, 114n7
Samarajiwa, R. 247
San Francisco Chronicle 81
Saussure, F. 94, 95
Scannell, P. 183
Schiller, H. 246, 252
Schlesinger, P. 123, 261
Schoofs, M. 28
Seaton, J. 31
second-level agenda-setting 78
self-censorship 233
self-regulation 226; defines field 228–230; of journalism 240
Sen, A. 182
Serwornoo, M.Y.W. 61
sexuality 3, 14, 37–39, 58, 92, 99
Shaw, D. L. 68–70, 77, 82
Shulman, A. 35
Silverstone, R. 13, 224, 225, 240
sincerity 13, 224, 234
Singapore: censorship in 218; spiral of silence 147
situation, ethics 232–234
Sjøvaag, H. 235
Slate 12
Smith, T. 130
social capital 36, 143
social construct 46
social media 55, 147, 154; advent of 257; analysis of activity 135; group bonding effect of 148; journalism, sources and 133–136; news knowledge and 185–186; source of 128–136
social media platforms 56, 70, 103, 142, 147, 174, 206; *see also* digital platforms
social movements 11, 58, 132, 142
social value, of PSM 184–185
socio-historical approach 101–102
soft news 45, 79
soft power 252
#SomeoneTellCNN 55, 56
Sonwalkar, P. 10
sources: authoritative 32, 119–121, 130; information protection of 208–209; journalism, social media and 133–136; non-official 129; of power 128–136; primary 129–130; of public relations 128–136; of social media 128–136; source protection 208, 209
South Africa 59, 126, 187, 188, 203; cross-border migration 81; end of apartheid in 11, 167

South African Broadcasting Act (1999) 194
South African Broadcasting Corporation (SABC) 186–188, 193, 194
South Korean television network 93
Soviet Union 247, 248
Spain 106; public broadcaster 187
Spampinato, A. 211
Sparks, C. 252, 260
Sparrow, B.H. 26
sphere of consensus 124–126, 128, 129
sphere of deviance 124, 125, 127, 130, 131, 133
sphere of explicit deviance 126
sphere of full legitimacy 126
sphere of implicit deviance 126
sphere of legitimate controversy 127, 136
sphere of legitimate debate 135
sphere of partial legitimacy 126
spheres of controversy 124–125; polarisation and media power 125–128
spiral of silence 147, 149, 155
Spivak, G. 12, 94, 97, 106
Spring, M. 237
Squid Game 244
standardised molds 106–108
Stanistreet, M. 236
state capture, problem of 186–188
stereotypical reporting 55, 56, 59, 60, 256
stereotyping 4, 39, 48, 61, 93, 98–100, 105, 253, 256
Sterling, R. 136n1
strategic ritual of objectivity 31, 169
strategic rituals 192–193
subaltern counter-public 9, 10, 12, 13, 14; *see also* public sphere
subjectivity 60, 84, 98; in news choices 46–48
sub-Saharan Africa 203; British newspaper coverage on 253; coverage for mainstream British news organisations 256
The Sun 31, 79, 164, 166, 171
Swedish public broadcaster 194
symbolic capital 30
symbolic power 27, 31, 41
symbolic violence 72, 73

tabloid media 148
Tatler magazine 35
taxes, on advertising 162–165
Taylor, I. 126
television advertising 171
television news 29, 38, 75, 175
"them" 62, 63n9; frame 83; gaps between "us" and 112–113

thematisation 105
third space 48; resistance 48, 61
Thompson, J.W. 166
Thussu, D.K. 247, 255–256
Tiffin, H. 98
Tiffin, R. 204
The Times 31, 97, 171
The Times of India 51, 245
Tomlinson, H. 210
Tong, J. 233
Trade Union Congress 166
Trade Unions 130
transnational public sphere 259–261; post-public sphere 261–262
Trudeau, J. 98
Trump, D. 81, 82, 104, 127
trust, disinformation and issues of 257–259; *see also* disinformation
truth-telling 223, 225, 233
Tuchman, G. 32
Tufekci, Z. 149
Twitter 76, 135, 164, 257, 258
two-step flow theory 141–143, 154

Ubuntu 193, 203
Umbrella Movement 74
UNESCO 208, 247, 248
UNESCO New World Information Order (NWIO) 58
United Kingdom (UK): accuracy 229; advertising in 168; advertising income in 163; advertising sales in 165; commercial mass market newspapers in 165; jurisdiction over broadcast media 230; licensing 169; mass market newspaper in 239; news landscape in 165; printed media of 126; Reuters in 245–246; tabloid media 148
United States: advertising in 168–169; Associated Press in 245, 246, 253; commercial mass market newspapers in 165; global governance agreements 254; journalists in 31; liberal system of 185; minorities in 38; news landscape in 165; news organisations 127; newspaper in 164; newspapers proliferated in 163; polarisation level in 127; private radio monopoly 183
universality, PSM 181
unstamped press 162

"us" 62, 63n9; frame 83; gaps between "them" and 112–113
USA Today 57
uses and gratifications approach 143–144, 154
US–Mexico border, immigration 82

Vietnam War 75, 124
"Violence, Mourning, Politics" (Butler) 111
virtue ethics 224, 226, 230
Vogue magazine, case of 34–37

Wainaina, B. 253
Waisbord, S. 238
Wallace, M. 37–38
war of position 71, 74
Wasserman, H. 251
western hegemony, challenge to 248–252
western media organisations: dominate global flows 244–245; media imperialism 246–248; news agencies and broadcasters 245–246
western news values, in non-western contexts 60–62
Wettstein, M. 128
WhatsApp 151–152
Wheatstone, C. 245
Willems, W. 83
Williams, B. 224, 240
Williams, M. 104
Williamson, M. 21n1
Williams, R. 1
women journalists 59, 237
World Health Organisation 69
World Press Freedom Index 30, 82–83, 268n12
Worlds of Journalism study 230, 232, 235
Wozniak, A. 260

xenophobic framing 80

YouGov poll 81
Younge, G. 84
YouTube: channels 258; political use of 151

Zimbabwe: land reform issue 82; national security in 217
Zimbabwe Broadcasting Corporation (ZBC) 86n8
Zuckerberg, M. 149

For Product Safety Concerns and Information please contact our EU
representative GPSR@taylorandfrancis.com
Taylor & Francis Verlag GmbH, Kaufingerstraße 24, 80331 München, Germany

www.ingramcontent.com/pod-product-compliance
Lightning Source LLC
Chambersburg PA
CBHW051351290426
44108CB00015B/1973